단어만 알아도 영어가 된다!

2017년 9월 04일 발행
2019년 6월 17일 2쇄 발행

지은이	E & C
발행인	Chris Suh
발행처	**MENTORS**
	경기도 성남시 분당구 분당로 53번길 12 313-1
	TEL 031-604-0025 FAX 031-696-5221
	www.mentors.co.kr
	blog.naver.com/mentorsbook
등록일자	2005년 7월 27일
등록번호	제 2009-000027호
ISBN	979-11-86656-52-5
가 격	15,000원(MP3 무료다운로드)

잘못 인쇄된 책은 교환해 드립니다.
이 책에 게재된 내용의 일부 또는 전체를 무단으로 복제 및 발췌하는 것을 금합니다.

317 Useful Words for Making Speaking English Easy

"단어만 알아도 영어가 된다!"

오래전 일이다. 주위에 굴러다니는 책의 뒷부분의 부록인지 인덱스인지는 모르겠지만 단어와 단어를 이용한 표현을 깔끔하게 정리한 것을 본 적이 있었다. 그 당시 agree 다음에 사람과 사물이 오는 것에 따라 다른 전치사를 써야 된다는 것을 알고는 있었지만, 실제 사용하는 데는 어려움이 많았던 그런 때였다. 그때 agree with+사람, agree to+사물이라고 볼드로 정리되어 있고 그 아래 예문이 있는 것을 보고는 "바로 이런 책이다"라고 마음속으로 소리쳤던 적이 있었다. 그때의 기억에서 힌트를 얻어 만든 교재가 바로 이 '영어말하는데 딱 좋은 단어 317개를 활용한 영단어표현사전'인 〈단어만 알아도 영어가 된다!〉이다.

"표현 통째로 외워둬야~"

우리는 늘상 얘기를 듣는다. 단어만 외우면 필요없다고. 단어를 중심으로 함께 쓰이는 전치사나 부사 등을 함께 외워야 된다고 말이다. 아예 극단적으로 문장을 통째로 외우자는 통문장 영어도 나오지 않았는가…. 위의 예를 들자면 agree라는 동사를 쓰는데 다음에 사람인지 사물이 오게 되는데 with+사람, to+사물이 머릿속에 명확히 각인되어 있지 않으면 I agree~까지 하고 뭘 써야 될지 몰라 그만 벙어리가 되고 마는 경우가 비일비재하다. 이를 극복하기 위해서는 agree with+사람, agree to+사물을 통째로 달달 외워두어야 한다.

"단어를 기반으로 한 걸음만 더 들어가면~"

이책 〈단어만 알아도 영어가 된다!〉는 이렇게 영어회화표현들을 만들어내고 있는데 지대한 역할을 하고 있는 단어 317개를 선정한 후 이 단어들이 생산해내는 많은 영어회화표현들을 일목요연하게 정리하였다. 적게는 2개 많게는 수십 개의 실제 영어회화문장을 만들어낼 수 있는 표현들만 선택하였기 때문에 바로바로 영어회화 실전에서 무궁무진하게 사용할 수 있을 것이다. 누구의 말처럼 한 걸음만 더 들어가보면 진실이 펼쳐지듯이 이 활용도 높은 단어 317개를 기반으로 한 걸음만 더 들어가면 여러분의 영어실력이 일취월장하게 될 것임을 확신한다.

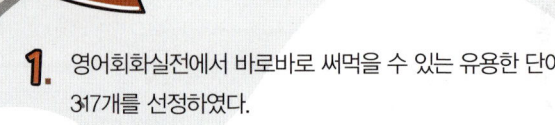

1. 영어회화실전에서 바로바로 써먹을 수 있는 유용한 단어 317개를 선정하였다.

2. 각 단어의 기본적인 품사와 의미를 명시하였다.

3. 각 단어가 생산해내는 영어회화표현을 친절하고 깔끔하게 정리하였다.

4. 지루하지 않게 가끔 실제 쓰이는 다이알로그를 넣어 확인하는 공간을 마련하였다.

5. 모든 예문은 통통 튀는 네이티브들의 원음으로 녹음되어 있다.

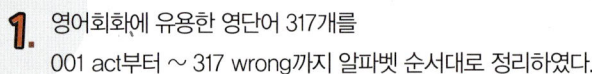

1. 영어회화에 유용한 영단어 317개를 001 act부터 ~ 317 wrong까지 알파벳 순서대로 정리하였다.

2. 각 단어 밑에는 단어를 활용한 영어회화표현을 2개 내지 수십개를 수록하였다.

3. 각 표현의 의미와 그에 해당되는 예문을 하나 혹은 필요한 때는 여러개를 넣어 이해하는데 도움이 되도록 꾸몄다.

이 책은 어떻게 봐야 할까요?

전체 317개의 영단어 넘버링

317개의 유용한 단어들

단어의 품사와 의미를 적었다.

표현의 우리말 의미를 수록하였다.

단어가 생산해내는 영어회화표현들을 왼쪽에 정리하였다.

각 엔트리에는 예문과 우리말 해석이 달려있다.

---

009 apply
ⓥ 신청하다, 지원하다, 적용하다, 바르다

apply for sth	지원하다, 신청하다 I heard that you are going to **apply for** a scholarship. 네가 장학금을 신청할 거라던데.
apply to sb [sth]	지원하다 Is it a good idea to **apply to** many colleges? 많은 대학들에 지원하는 게 좋은 생각이야?
apply to+V	…하기 위해 지원하다 My sister **applied to** study dentistry. 내 누이는 치의학을 연구하기 위해서 지원했어.
apply oneself to	열중하다 You must **apply yourself to** solving the problems. 그 문제들을 푸는데 힘을 쏟아야지.
apply sth to~	…을 …에 바르다 You'll need to **apply** some ointment **to** that wound. 넌 그 상처에는 연고를 발라야 될거야.

010 appreciate
ⓥ 감사하다

appreciate +명사	…을 감사하다 Thank you. I **appreciate** the support. 고마워. 도와줘서 고마워. I **appreciate** your help. 도와줘서 고마워.

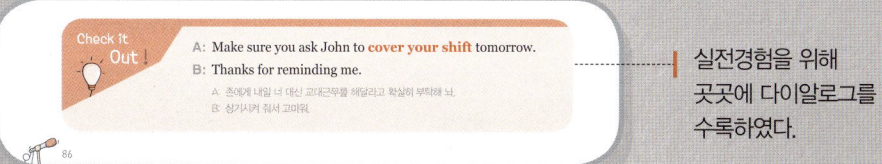

Check It Out
A: Make sure you ask John to **cover your shift** tomorrow.
B: Thanks for reminding me.
A: 존에게 내일 너 대신 교대근무를 해달라고 확실히 부탁해 놔.
B: 상기시켜 줘서 고마워.

실전경험을 위해 곳곳에 다이알로그를 수록하였다.

목차

001 ★ act 012	026 ★ bet 039	054 ★ check 069
002 ★ afraid 012	027 ★ better 040	055 ★ choose 071
003 ★ afford 013	028 ★ bid 041	056 ★ class 072
004 ★ all 014	029 ★ bill 042	057 ★ clean 073
005 ★ allow 015	030 ★ bit 042	058 ★ clear 074
006 ★ answer 016	031 ★ bite 043	059 ★ close 075
007 ★ argue 017	032 ★ black 044	060 ★ cold 076
008 ★ apologize 018	033 ★ blame 044	061 ★ come 077
009 ★ apply 019	034 ★ blow 045	062 ★ company 081
010 ★ appreciate 019	035 ★ board 046	063 ★ continue 081
011 ★ ask 020	036 ★ book 046	064 ★ cook 082
012 ★ back 023	037 ★ break 047	065 ★ cool 083
013 ★ bad 024	038 ★ breath 050	066 ★ cost 084
014 ★ ball 025	039 ★ bring 051	067 ★ count 085
015 ★ base 025	040 ★ broke 053	068 ★ cover 086
016 ★ be 026	041 ★ business 054	069 ★ credit 087
017 ★ bear 030	042 ★ busy 055	070 ★ cut 087
018 ★ beat 031	043 ★ buy 056	071 ★ damage 088
019 ★ bed 032	044 ★ call 057	072 ★ date 089
020 ★ beg 033	045 ★ care 060	073 ★ day 090
021 ★ begin 034	046 ★ carry 061	074 ★ deal 091
022 ★ behave 035	047 ★ case 062	075 ★ decide 093
023 ★ believe 035	048 ★ catch 063	076 ★ deserve 094
024 ★ belong 037	049 ★ chance 064	077 ★ die 095
025 ★ best 038	050 ★ change 065	078 ★ difference 096
	051 ★ charge 066	079 ★ discuss 097
	052 ★ chat 068	080 ★ do 097
	053 ★ cheat 068	081 ★ doubt 100

317 Useful Words for
Making Speaking English Easy

082 ★ draw	101
083 ★ dress	103
084 ★ drink	103
085 ★ drive	105
086 ★ drop	107
087 ★ due	108
088 ★ ear	109
089 ★ easy	110
090 ★ eat	111
091 ★ end	112
092 ★ enjoy	113
093 ★ envy	113
094 ★ ever	114
095 ★ every	115
096 ★ expect	116
097 ★ excuse	117
098 ★ eye	118
099 ★ face	119
100 ★ fall	120
101 ★ far	122
102 ★ feel	123
103 ★ foot	126
104 ★ fight	127
105 ★ figure	128
106 ★ fill	129
107 ★ find	130
108 ★ fine	131
109 ★ finish	132

110 ★ fire	133
111 ★ first	134
112 ★ fit	135
113 ★ fix	136
114 ★ follow	137
115 ★ forget	138
116 ★ forgive	140
117 ★ free	140
118 ★ fun	141
119 ★ get	142
120 ★ give	157
121 ★ go	162
122 ★ good	173
123 ★ grow	174
124 ★ guess	175
125 ★ hand	176
126 ★ hang	178
127 ★ happen	179
128 ★ happy	180
129 ★ hard	181
130 ★ hate	182
131 ★ have	183
132 ★ head	192
133 ★ hear	193
134 ★ heart	195
135 ★ help	196
136 ★ hell	197
137 ★ hit	198

138 ★ high	199
139 ★ hold	200
140 ★ hope	203
141 ★ hurt	205
142 ★ injure	206
143 ★ impress	207
144 ★ introduce	208
145 ★ invite	208
146 ★ job	209
147 ★ join	210
148 ★ joke	211
149 ★ keep	212
150 ★ kick	215
151 ★ kid	216
152 ★ kind	216
153 ★ know	217
154 ★ last	221
155 ★ laugh	222
156 ★ lay	223
157 ★ lead	224
158 ★ learn	224
159 ★ least	226
160 ★ leave	226
161 ★ lend	229
162 ★ let	229
163 ★ lie	232
164 ★ line	233
165 ★ like	234

Contents

166 ★ listen ... 237	194 ★ open ... 274	222 ★ run ... 308
167 ★ live ... 238	195 ★ owe ... 275	223 ★ save ... 310
168 ★ look ... 239	196 ★ part ... 276	224 ★ say ... 312
169 ★ lose ... 241	197 ★ pass ... 277	225 ★ scare ... 319
170 ★ love ... 242	198 ★ pay ... 278	226 ★ schedule ... 319
171 ★ luck ... 243	199 ★ pick ... 280	227 ★ search ... 320
172 ★ make ... 244	200 ★ place ... 281	228 ★ second ... 321
173 ★ market ... 252	201 ★ plan ... 282	229 ★ secret ... 322
174 ★ matter ... 252	202 ★ play ... 284	230 ★ see ... 323
175 ★ mean ... 253	203 ★ point ... 285	231 ★ seem ... 327
176 ★ meet ... 256	204 ★ post ... 287	232 ★ sell ... 328
177 ★ mention ... 257	205 ★ prefer ... 287	233 ★ send ... 329
178 ★ mess ... 258	206 ★ prepare ... 288	234 ★ sense ... 330
179 ★ mind ... 258	207 ★ promise ... 289	235 ★ serve ... 331
180 ★ miss ... 261	208 ★ pull ... 290	236 ★ set ... 332
181 ★ mix ... 262	209 ★ put ... 291	237 ★ settle ... 335
182 ★ money ... 263	210 ★ question ... 296	238 ★ shame ... 336
183 ★ most ... 264	211 ★ read ... 297	239 ★ shape ... 336
184 ★ mouth ... 264	212 ★ remain ... 298	240 ★ share ... 337
185 ★ move ... 265	213 ★ remember ... 298	241 ★ shock ... 338
186 ★ much ... 266	214 ★ remind ... 300	242 ★ short ... 338
187 ★ name ... 267	215 ★ ride ... 301	243 ★ show ... 339
188 ★ need ... 268	216 ★ right ... 302	244 ★ sick ... 340
189 ★ next ... 270	217 ★ raise ... 304	245 ★ side ... 341
190 ★ nose ... 270	218 ★ risk ... 305	246 ★ sight ... 342
191 ★ nothing ... 271	219 ★ rob ... 306	247 ★ skip ... 342
192 ★ nuts ... 272	220 ★ ruin ... 306	248 ★ sleep ... 343
193 ★ offer ... 273	221 ★ rule ... 307	249 ★ slip ... 344

317 Useful Words for
Making Speaking English Easy

#	Word	Page
250 ★	sneak	345
251 ★	solve	346
252 ★	sound	346
253 ★	speak	347
254 ★	spend	349
255 ★	split	350
256 ★	stand	350
257 ★	start	354
258 ★	stay	357
259 ★	step	360
260 ★	stick	361
261 ★	stock	362
262 ★	stop	362
263 ★	straight	365
264 ★	strike	366
265 ★	suck	367
266 ★	suggest	367
267 ★	suit	368
268 ★	suppose	369
269 ★	sure	370
270 ★	take	371
271 ★	talk	377
272 ★	teach	380
273 ★	tear	381
274 ★	tell	381
275 ★	thank	388
276 ★	thing	389
277 ★	think	390
278 ★	throw	395
279 ★	time	396
280 ★	tip	398
281 ★	top	398
282 ★	touch	399
283 ★	track	400
284 ★	treat	401
285 ★	trouble	402
286 ★	trust	403
287 ★	try	404
288 ★	turn	407
289 ★	understand	411
290 ★	upset	412
291 ★	use	413
292 ★	visit	415
293 ★	wait	416
294 ★	wake	418
295 ★	walk	419
296 ★	want	421
297 ★	warn	425
298 ★	wash	426
299 ★	watch	427
300 ★	way	428
301 ★	wear	429
302 ★	weigh	430
303 ★	welcome	431
304 ★	well	432
305 ★	whole	432
306 ★	win	433
307 ★	wind	434
308 ★	wish	434
309 ★	wonder	436
310 ★	word	437
311 ★	work	438
312 ★	world	442
313 ★	worry	443
314 ★	worse	444
315 ★	worth	445
316 ★	write	446
317 ★	wrong	447

317 Useful Words for
Making Speaking English Easy

영어 말하는데 딱 좋은 단어
317개를 활용한

영단어
표현사전

act부터~wrong까지

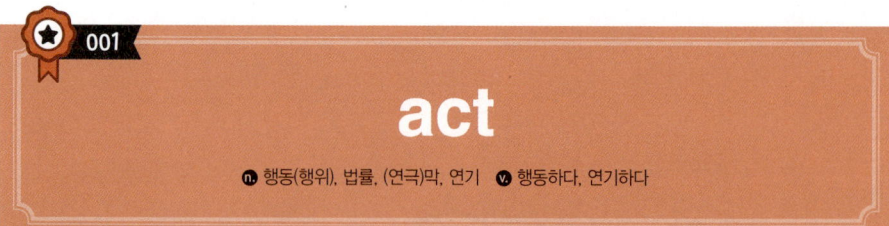

act

n. 행동(행위), 법률, (연극)막, 연기 **v.** 행동하다, 연기하다

act

법률, 연극의 막, 연극(영화) 등에서 연기하다

Leo will **act** at the theater tonight.
레오는 오늘 저녁 극장에서 연기를 할거야.

Do you think she could **act** in a movie?
걔가 영화에서 연기를 할 수 있을 것 같아?

act+형용사

…인 척하다(pretend)

We'll just **act casual.** 보통 때처럼 행동할게.

So, when you go in, **act surprised.** 안에 들어가면 놀란 척해.

act like [as though]

…인 것처럼 행동하다

We're going to **act like** nothing is happening.
아무 일도 없었던 것처럼 행동할거야.

In public, you have to **act like** a grown-up.
사람들 있는데서는 어른처럼 행동해야 돼.

act on

…에 따라 행동하다, 영향을 미치다

You need to **act on** the advice the doctor gave.
넌 의사가 준 지침에 따라 행동해야 돼.

afraid

a. 두려워하는, 걱정하는

be afraid of+ N[~ing]

걱정하다, 두려워하다

You don't need to **be afraid of** public speaking.
대중 연설을 두려워할 필요는 없어.

be afraid to+V	…하기를 두려워하다 Don't **be afraid to** speak your mind. 속내이야기를 하는데 두려워하지마.
I'm afraid that S+V	안됐지만 …야 **I'm afraid** we already have plans. 우린 이미 약속이 있어.
I'm afraid to say that S+V	말하기 미안하지만 …야 **I'm afraid to say this,** but I must do it. 말하기 미안하지만 난 그것을 해야 돼.
I was afraid that S+V	난 …을 두려워했어 **I was afraid** you'd break a hip or something. 네 엉덩뼈 같은 게 부러졌을까봐 걱정됐어.
I'm afraid so	그런 것 같아 **I'm afraid so.** This apartment building has been sold. 그런 것 같아. 이 아파트가 팔렸어.
I'm afraid not	그런 것 같지 않아 **I'm afraid not.** He's very busy right now. 죄송하지만 그럴 수 없겠네요. 지금 굉장히 바쁘세요.

003 afford
v. …할 여유가 있다

can('t) afford	여유가 있[없]다 How much **can** you **afford**? 얼마나 여유가 있어?
can('t) afford +명사	…할 여유가 있[없]다 **I can't afford** it. 난 그걸 할 여유가 없어. **I could never afford** a place like this. 이런 집을 장만할 여유가 없었어.

can('t) afford to~	…할 여유가 있[없]다
	I **can't afford to** buy you a house.
	이 집을 살 여유가 없어.

004 all
a. adv. 모든

be all alone	홀로이다
	I visited Grandma because she **was all alone.**
	할머니가 홀로이셔서 찾아가 뵈었어.

be all right with	…에 대해 괜찮다
	I see your point, I**'m all right with** it.
	네 요지를 알았고 난 그거에 괜찮아.

above all	무엇보다 *above all else 다른 무엇보다도
	You need to make money **above all else.**
	넌 무엇보다 돈을 벌어야만 해.

after all	결국
	They decided not to hire me **after all.**
	걔네들은 결국 나를 고용하지 않기로 했어.

all along	내내
	You've been lying **all along.**
	넌 처음부터 끝까지 거짓말을 하고 있어.

all-day	하루 걸리는 *all day long 하루종일
	The new guy sat on his ass **all day long.**
	새로운 친구가 온종일 앉아 있어.

all out	전력으로, 지쳐서, 전혀
	I'm gonna go **all out** for him.
	난 걔를 위해 전력을 다할거야.

afford

all over the world	전 세계에 걸쳐
	Why do you travel **all over the world**? 왜 전세계를 여행하는거야?

all the same	마찬가지인
	They're not **all the same.** You don't even know them. 걔네들은 다 똑같지 않아. 넌 걔네들 알지도 못하잖아.

all told =all together	전부 합해서
	All together we had at least four thousand dollars. 우리는 모두 합해서 4천 달러를 갖고 있었어.

at all times	언제든지
	The convenience store is open **at all times.** 편의점은 항상 열려 있어.

stay up all night	밤을 새다
	I wanted to **stay up all night,** but I was so tired that I fell asleep. 나는 밤을 새고 싶었지만 너무 피곤해서 잠이 들었어.

005

allow

v. 허락하다, 인정하다, 지급하다, 고려하다

allow sby to~	…가 …하도록 허락하다
	My laptop computer **allows** me **to** work at home and on the road. 노트북 덕분에 나는 집에서도, 여기저기 다니면서도 일을 할 수 있어.

Please allow me to~	내가 …하도록 해줘요
	Please allow me to take your coat, sir. 손님, 저에게 코트를 주시지요.

be (not) allowed to	…하는 것이 허락[금지]되어 있다
	I**'m not allowed to** drink. 나 술마시면 안돼.
	You**'re not allowed to** smoke in the office. 사무실에서 금연야.

allow oneself to+V	받아들이다, 몰두[열중]하다
	You should **allow yourself to** relax more. 넌 더 쉬어야 돼.
allow for	(계획, 판단하는데 필요한 사항 등) 고려하다
	Our vacation will **allow for** a visit to the beach. 우리 휴가는 해변에 들르는 것으로 되어 있어.
allow me in	(…에) 내가 좀 들어갈게요
	Allow me in. 들어가도 되죠, 좀 들어갈게요.
	I want you to **allow me in** your room. 방에 들어가도 되겠죠.

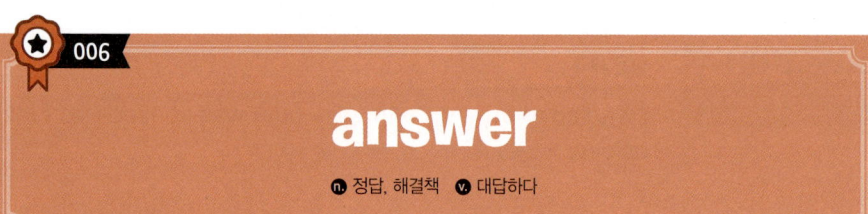

answer
n. 정답, 해결책 **v.** 대답하다

an answer	답, 해결책
	I need **an answer** now! 당장 답을 줘!
	Don't take no for **an answer**. 상대방이 거절해도 끈질기게 설득해.
the answer to~	…에 대한 답, 해결책
	I think you know **the answer to** that. 네가 알 것 같아.
	I don't have **the answer to** that question. 그 문제에 해결책이 없어.
have[know] all the answers	(실은 아니지만) 모든 것을 알고 있다
	People expect Mike to **have all the answers.** 사람들은 마이크가 모든 걸 안다고 생각해.
give sby an answer	…에게 답을 주다
	I'd like to **give you an answer** after work. 퇴근 후에 답을 줄게.
	I'll **give you a firm answer** by Friday. 금요일까지는 확답을 줄게.

allow

| answer | 대답하다 |

Go ahead and ask. He won't **answer.**
가서 물어봐. 걘 대답하지 않을거야.

You ask, I'll **answer.**
네가 물어봐, 내가 대답해줄게.

| answer one's question | …의 질문에 답을 하다 |

Don't **answer that question.**
그 질문에 답하지마.

Why didn't you **answer my e-mail?**
왜 내 이멜에 답을 안한거야?

| answer sby [sth] | …에(게) 답을 하다 |

Just **answer me** this: Why did we break up?
내게 이거 답을 해. 우리가 왜 헤어진거야?

I can't **answer that.**
난 그거에 답할 수 없어.

| answer the phone [call, door] | 전화를 받다, 문을 열어주다 |

Why didn't you **answer your cell phone?**
왜 핸드폰 받지 않았어?

He**'s not answering his cell phone.**
걘 핸드폰 받질 않아.

Could you **answer it** for me?
(전화벨 소리에) 그거 좀 받아줄래?, (초인종 소리에) 문 좀 열어줄래?

007

argue

ⓥ 말다툼하다, 주장하다

| argue | 논[언]쟁하다 |

I heard you and your father **arguing** the other day.
너와 네 아버지가 요전날 말다툼했다며.

argue sth [that~]	주장하다, (법정) 변론하다 **I can argue that** he needs money to live on. 걘 살아가는데 돈이 필요하다고 할 수 있어.
argue with sby	…와 언쟁하다 I apologize. I'm not going to **argue with you.** 사과할게. 너랑 말다툼하지 않을거야.
argue about [over]	…에 대해 언쟁하다 You really want to **argue with me about** this? 너 정말 나랑 이거갖고 말다툼할거야?

008 apologize
v. 사과하다 *apology는 사과

apologize	사과하다 I tried to **apologize** over the phone. 전화로 사과하려고 했어.
apologize for ~	…을 사과하다 I **apologize for** that. 그거 사과할게요. I just want to **apologize for** that. 내가 그거 사과할게요.
apologize to sby (for ~)	…에게 (…을) 사과하다 I came to **apologize to you.** 네게 사과하러 왔어. You've got to **apologize to me.** 넌 내게 사과해야 돼.
accept apologies	사과를 받아들이다 Please **accept my apologies.** 사과를 받아 주십시오. Will you **accept my apology?** 내 사과를 받아줄래요?

apply

v. 신청하다, 지원하다, 적용하다, 바르다

apply for sth	지원하다, 신청하다 I heard that you are going to **apply for** a scholarship. 네가 장학금을 신청할 거라던데.
apply to sb [sth]	지원하다 Is it a good idea to **apply to** many colleges? 많은 대학에 지원하는 게 좋은 생각이야?
apply to+V	…하기 위해 지원하다 My sister **applied to** study dentistry. 내 누이는 치의학을 연구하기 위해서 지원했어.
apply oneself to	열중하다 You must **apply yourself to** solving the problems. 그 문제들을 푸는데 힘을 쏟아야지.
apply sth to~	…을 …에 바르다 You'll need to **apply** some ointment **to** that wound. 넌 그 상처에는 연고를 발라야 될거야.

appreciate

v. 감사하다

appreciate +명사	…을 감사하다 Thank you. I **appreciate** the support. 고마워. 도와줘서 고마워. I **appreciate** your help. 도와줘서 고마워.

appreciate it [that, that]	…가 고마워 I really **appreciate this.** 정말 고마워.
appreciate you ~ing	네가 …해줘서 감사해 I **appreciate you giving** me a hand. 도와줘서 고마워. I really **appreciate you taking** the time to do this. 시간내서 이거 해줘서 정말 고마워.
I appreciate this, but ~	이거 고맙지만… I **really appreciate this, but** you don't have to go there. 고맙지만 네가 거기 갈 필요없어. I **really appreciate that but** I think I'd better not. 고맙지만 안 그러는게 낫겠어.
I just want to tell [say](sby) how much I appreciate~	…에 얼마나 감사하는지 말하고 싶어 I **want to tell her how much I appreciate** her love. 걔한테 내가 얼마나 걔의 사랑에 감사하는지 말하고 싶어.
I'd appreciate it if you~	…해주면 고맙겠어 I **would really appreciate it if you** didn't tell Dad about this. 아빠에게 그 얘기 안 했으면 정말 고맙겠어.

011

ask

질문하다, 묻다, 요구[청]하다

ask sby sth	…에게 뭔가 물어보다 I have to **ask you something.** 뭐 좀 물어봐야겠어. Is Jill around? I have to **ask her something.** 질 있어? 걔한테 뭐 좀 물어봐야 돼. Are you here to **ask me that?** 그거 물어볼려고 여기 온거야?

appreciate

ask (sby) a question
(…에게) 질문하다

Could I **ask you a question?** It's critical.
질문해도 돼? 중요한건데.

Do you mind if we **ask you a few questions?**
질문 몇 개 해도 될까요?

Let me **ask you a question.**
질문 하나 할게.

ask sby a favor
…에 호의를 부탁하다

I'm calling to **ask you for a favor.**
부탁 하나 하려고 전화했어.

Can I **ask you a favor?** 부탁 하나 해도 될까요?

ask sby about~
…에게 …에 관해 물어보다

Please, don't **ask me about** this again.
다시는 이런 부탁하지 말아줘.

ask sby to ~
…에게 …해달라고 부탁하다

I didn't **ask you to** do it! 너보고 그거 하라고 하지 않았잖아!

I need to ask you about~
…에 대해 물어볼게 있어

I need to ask you about your brother.
네 형에 대해 물어볼게 있어.

I'm going to (have to) ask you to+V
네게 …해달라고 할거야[해야 될거야]

I'm going to have to ask you to leave now.
그만 가보셔야 되겠네요.

I'm not asking you to+V
…해달라는 게 아냐

I'm not asking you to set me up.
만남을 주선해달라는 얘기가 아니야.

ask (sby) what [when~]~
(…에게) …을 물어보다

Can I **ask you what** happened here?
여기 무슨일인지 물어봐도 돼?

She will **ask me where** it came from.
그거 어디서 난건지 걔가 물어볼거야.

ask (sby) if [how]~
(…에게) …을 물어보다

Ask me if she was good in bed.
걔가 잠자리 잘하는지 내게 물어봐.

ask oneself~	…을 자문해보다
	You **ask yourself** why you're doing that. 왜 그러는지 스스로에게 물어봐.
ask (sb) for	(…에게) …를 부탁하다
	You don't have to **ask for** my permission. 내 허락을 부탁할 필요가 없어.
	She didn't really **ask for** you, he asked for me. 걘 네가 아니라 날 찾았어.
ask sby out	데이트신청하다 = ask sby out on a date
	I **asked Sara out** for dinner tonight. 새라한테 오늘밤에 저녁식사 하자고 했어.
	Are you asking me out on a date? 나한테 데이트 신청하는거야?
be asked to	…하도록 요청받다, 얘기를 듣다
	I **was asked to** go there instead of Karl. 칼 대신 내가 거기가라는 요청을 받았어.
	I thought you **were asked to** come home. 여기 오라는 얘기를 들었을텐데.
if you ask me	내 생각은, 내 생각을 말한다면
	If you ask me, you're making a huge mistake. 내 생각을 말하자면 넌 지금 큰 실수하고 있는거야.
Whatever you ask	말만해
	Whatever you ask, I will do. 뭐든지 부탁만 해. 내가 다 들어줄게.
All I'm asking is for you to~	내가 너한테 바라는 것은 …밖에 없어
	All I'm asking is for you to leave! 제발 좀 나가주라!
Feel free to ask~	뭐든 물어봐, 맘껏 물어봐
	Feel free to ask if you have any questions. 질문있으면 언제라도 해.

ask

back

n. 등, 뒷면 adv. 뒤로, 되받아, 과거로 v. 뒤로 물러서다, 지원하다

behind one's back
…가 없는데서
I went **behind my wife's back** to buy the computer.
아내 모르게 컴퓨터를 샀어.

get off one's back
…를 괴롭히지 않다
Please **get off my back,** and stop talking like this.
제발 그만 괴롭히고 그런식으로 말하지마.

give ~ back
…을 돌려주다
It's about time I **give something back.** 내가 좀 돌려줘야 될 때가 되었어.

take ~ back
…을 돌려받다
I'd give anything to **take that back.** 그걸 다시 되찾기 위해 뭐든 할거야.

get ~ back
…을 돌려받다
He has something of mine and I need you to **get it back.**
걔가 내걸 갖고 있는데 돌려받고 싶어.

look back (at)
(…을) 뒤돌아보다
Sometimes it's not good to **look back** in the past.
때로는 과거를 되돌아보지 않는게 좋아.

be back home
집에 돌아오다 *go back home 집에 돌아가다
Why did you decide to **go back home** early?
왜 집에 일찍 돌아가기로 한거야?

back up
도와주다, 지원하다, 백업하다
I used a USB drive to **back up** the documents.
난 서류를 백업하기 위해 USB 드라이브를 사용했어.

back off
뒤로 물러나다, 그만두다
Back off, all right? It's none of your business.
놔두라고, 알았어? 네가 상관할 일이 아니잖아.

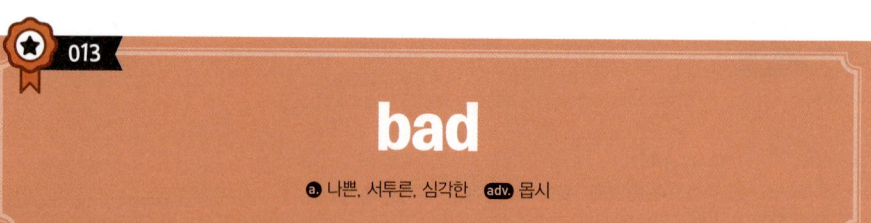

bad
a. 나쁜, 서투른, 심각한 **adv.** 몹시

go from bad to worse
악화되다
The situation **went from bad to worse.**
설상가상이야.

be bad at ~ing
…하는데 서투르다
He**'s really bad at** following directions.
걘 교통법규를 정말 안 지켜.

go bad
(음식, 상황) 변하다
Things **went bad** when I interviewed for the job.
내가 그 일을 위해 인터뷰했을 때 일이 틀어졌어.

feel bad about~
…을 미안해하다 *feel bad 몸이 안좋다
I'm really not happy that you **feel bad about** it.
네가 그거에 기분나쁘다니 정말 나도 기분이 안좋아.

in a bad way
(병, 상태) 위중하게, 어려운 상태로
My daughter's **in a bad way** right now.
내 딸은 지금 무척 어려운 상태야.

not bad
나쁘지 않은, 괜찮은
Not bad, but it was a little too long.
괜찮았는데, 좀 너무 길었어.

I feel (so) bad about (sb) ~ing
(…가) …하는 것은 정말 안됐어
I feel so bad about not attending the wedding.
결혼식에 못가서 기분이 속상해.
I feel bad about not signing your letter of recommendation.
네 추천장에 사인을 못해줘 속상해.

real bad
정말로
The party was **real bad,** and very boring.
파티는 정말로 아주아주 지루했어.

014

ball
n. 공, 무도회

the ball is in sby's court
…의 차례이다, …에 달려있다
This is the salary we're offering. **The ball's in your court.**
이게 우리가 제안하는 급여입니다. 이제 결정하시죠.

get[set] the ball rolling
(일이나 토의 등을) 시작하다, 진행시키다
I just thought I'd stop by and see her before I **get the ball rolling.** 내가 일을 계속 하기에 앞서 걔한테 들러서 잠깐 볼까 생각했었어.

have a ball
즐기다
Oh, honey, they're gonna **have a ball** with you.
오, 자기야, 걔들이 너랑 즐거운 시간을 보내게 될거야.

015

base
n. 아래부분, 기초(토대), 기반, 군사기지 v. 근거지를 두다 *basis n. 근거, 기준, 기반

on a first-come first-serve basis
선착순으로
No, it's **on a first come, first serve basis.**
죄송하지만, 저희는 선착순이라서요.

on a regular basis
정기적으로
Get into the habit of working out **on regular basis.**
규칙적으로 운동을 하는 습관을 들여 봐.

be on a first-name basis
이름부르는 사이다, 친한 사이다
We **are on a first-name basis.**
우리는 서로 야자하는 사이야.

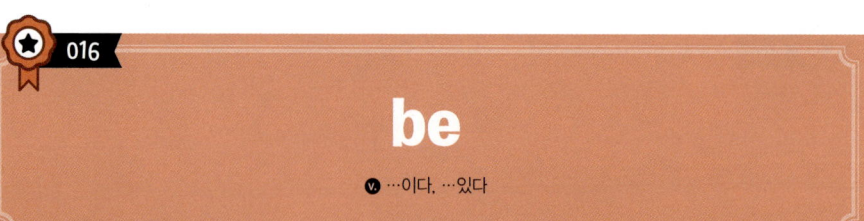

be

v …이다, …있다

be all right [OK] (with~)

(…가) 괜찮다 *be right하면 상대말이 맞다는 말.

Everything's going to **be all right[fine]**.
다 잘 될거야.

It's going to **be okay[fine]**.
잘 될거야, 괜찮을거야.

be there[here]

가다, 오다

They are going to **be here**.
걔네들 이리 올거야.

I'll (always) **be there for you**.
내가 (네게) 힘이 되어줄게.

I've **been there**. 무슨 말인지 알겠어, 정말 그 심정 이해해, 가본 적 있어.

We're almost **there**. 거의 다 됐어, 거의 끝났어.

The point is that~

중요한 것은 …야 *This thing is (that) S+V라고 해도 된다

The point is I don't need this right now.
핵심은 지금 싸울 필요가 없단거야.

(Don't) Be~

…해라(하지 마라)

Everyone please **be quiet** for a moment.
여러분 잠시 조용히 해 주십시오.

Don't be so hard on me.
날 너무 힘들게 하지마.

have been [gone] to[in]

…에 갔다 왔다

Where **have you been**?
너 어디 갔다 오는 거야?

I've **been to** his apartment and he wasn't there.
걔 아파트에 갔다왔는데 거기 없더라고.

be happy with [about]

…에 만족하다, 좋아하다

I'm very **happy with** my decision.
난 내 결정에 무척 만족해.

be

be glad to [that S+V]	…해서 기쁘다 **I'm glad to** hear that. 그 얘기를 들으니 기쁘네. **I'm glad** you feel that way. 그렇게 생각한다니 기뻐.
be worried about	…을 걱정하다 We **were all so worried** we were losing you. 우린 모두 너를 잃을 까 걱정했어.
be supposed to~	…하기로 되어 있다 **Am I supposed to** meet the client today? 내가 오늘 고객을 만나기로 되어있던가? **I am not supposed to** be here. 난 여기 있으면 돼.
be angry with	…에게 화나다 = be mad[upset] Why **are you so angry at** me? 왜 그렇게 나한테 화를 내는거죠?
be scheduled to	…할 예정이다 When **is he scheduled to** arrive at the airport? 그 사람이 공항에 언제 도착할 예정이니?
be interested in	…에 관심이 있다 I**'m not interested in** playing golf. 골프치는데 관심없어.
be disappointed at[about, to]	…에 실망하다 You must **be so disappointed in** me. 넌 나한테 실망을 많이 했음에 틀림없어.
be related to	…와 관련이 있다[친척이다] You**'re not related to** Kirk Smith, are you? 커크 스미스씨와 친척 정도 됩니까?
be surprised to	…하는 것을 보고 놀라다 **I'm surprised to** see you smoking. 너 담배피는 것을 보고 놀랐어.
be committed to+N[~ing]	…하는 데 전념하다 You**'re really committed to** making this family work. 넌 정말 이 가정을 제대로 만들려고 전념하고 있어.

27

be able to	…을 할 수 있다
	We hope you'll **be able to** join us. 우리와 함께 했으면 해.
be sorry about	…가 미안해 *I'm sorry to+V, I'm sorry (that) S+V의 형태로도 많이 쓰인다
	I'm sorry to hear that. 그렇다니 정말 유감이네요.
	I'm sorry I didn't get back to you sooner. 더 빨리 연락 못 줘서 미안해.
be ready	준비가 되다
	Your room won't **be ready** until one o'clock. 한 시간 후에 방이 준비됩니다.
be sure to	반드시 …하다
	You'll **be sure to** send me flowers first. 내게 꽃 먼저 꼭 보내.
be worth+N [~ing]	…만큼의[할만한] 가치가 있다 *be worthy of+N …의 가치가 있다
	This **isn't worth** the risk. 모험할 가치가 없어.
be better [worse]	더 좋다[나쁘다]
	It would **be better** if she didn't come. 걔가 오지 않으면 더 나을 수도 있어.
be available to+V	…할 시간이 있다
	Will you **be available to** grab a bite later? 좀 있다 좀 먹을 시간 있어?
be familiar with	…에 익숙해지다
	He's **familiar with** all phases of this business. 걘 이 사업의 모든 단계를 잘 알아.
It's not that ~	…한게 아니야
	It's not that we don't like you. 우리가 널 싫어한 건 아냐.
be the one who~	…가 …한 사람이야
	I'm the one who made him quit smoking. 걔 담배를 끊게 한 건 바로 나야.
	You're the one who ended it, remember? 그걸 끝낸 건 바로 너야, 기억해?

be

be in trouble
곤경에 처하다, 혼나다

We are really going to **be in trouble** now.
우리 이젠 정말 곤경에 처할거야.

be out of one's mind
제정신이 아니다 *be out of luck하게 되면 운이 없다라는 뜻

You'**re out of your mind!** 제정신이 아니구나!

You'**re out of luck.** 넌 운이 다 됐어.

be on sb
…가 부담이다

This one'**s on** me. 이번엔 내가 낼게.

be on the way
가는 중이다 *be on the phone call 통화중이다

She **is on her way** home. 걘 집으로 가고 있어.

The boss **is on the other line.**
사장님은 다른 통화중이세요.

be back
돌아오다

He won't **be back** in the office today.
걘 오늘 사무실에 돌아오지 않을거야.

be off
가다(leave)

I'm sorry! I must **be off** right now.
미안해! 나 지금 바로 나가야 돼.

I'**m off to** bed. 자러갈거야.

be over
…을 넘다, 끝나다, 도처에 보이다

The game[party] **is over.** 게임은[파티는] 끝났어.

The bathroom'**s over there.** 화장실은 저기에 있어.

She kissed me **all over** my face.
걘 내 얼굴 이곳저곳에 키스를 했어.

be with
…와 함께 있다, …와 지내다

I **haven't been with** a woman in some time.
한 동안 여자를 못사귀봤어.

be up
끝나다, 기분좋다, …을 꾀하다(be up to), …에 준비되다

What **have** you **been up to?** 뭐하고 지냈어?

I know what you'**re up to.** 네 속셈 다 알아.

All this stuff **is up for** auction. 이 모든 물건은 경매에 나온거야.

be into	…에 참여하다, …에 빠지다 I **am into** riding motorcycles. 난 오토바이를 타는데 흥미를 가지고 있지.
be in[out]	같이하다[하지 않다] Our card game will start at 8 pm tonight. **Are you in?** 카드게임 오후 8시에 할거야. 너도 할래?
be behind	…의 편이다, …을 지지하다　*be behind in one's work 일이 밀려있다 There's no way I **am behind in my work.** 내가 일이 밀려있을 리가 없어.
be on time	제시간에 오다 You'd better **be on time** tomorrow. 내일 늦지 않도록 해라.
be off base	틀리다 I'm sorry I called you lazy. I **was way off base.** 게으르다고 해서 미안. 내가 틀렸어.
be about to+V	…하려고 하다 I think I'**m about to** have a nervous breakdown. 신경쇠약에 걸릴 것 같아.
be to blame	…의 책임이다 If you dated other guys, you'**re to blame** for the relationship failing. 네가 다른 놈들과 데이트하면 관계를 망친게 네 책임이야.

017

bear

v. 참다, 견디다, (부정적 감정) 품다

can't bear to+V[~ing]	못참다 I **can't bear to** see her in such a pain. 걔가 그런 고통 겪는 걸 차마 볼 수없어.

be

can't bear the thought of~	…라는 생각을 못견디다
	You just **can't bear the thought of** a patient dying. 넌 환자가 죽어간다는 생각을 참을 수가 없는거야.

bear ~ in mind	…을 명심하다, 유의하다 *Bear in mind that S+V …을 명심해
	Bear in mind that you're under oath, Mr. Smith. 선서했다는 것을 명심하세요, 스미스 씨.

bear the responsibility	책임을 지다(be responsible for)
	You'll have to **bear the responsibility** for these mistakes. 넌 이 실수들에 대한 책임을 져야 할거야.

018 beat

n. 맥박, 박자   v. 이기다, 능가하다, 피하다, 때리다

feel the beat of one's heart	…의 심장박동을 느끼다
	We were so close that I could **feel the beat of her heart.** 우리는 아주 가까이 붙어 있어서 그녀의 심장박동을 느낄 수 있었어.

beat~	물리치다
	Nothing **beats** a cold beer at the end of the day. 하루를 끝내고 시원한 맥주만큼 좋은 것도 없어.

beat (sb) up	두들겨패다
	I don't **beat up** on weaker kids. It's cheap. 나보다 약한 애는 건드리지 않아. 너무 비열하잖아.

beat the world record	세계 신기록을 깨다
	The runner was not able to **beat the world record.** 그 주자는 세계 신기록을 깰 수 없었어.

beat the deadline	마감시간보다 먼저 마치다 *beat은 예정된 시간보다 먼저 하다, beat the traffic 교통혼잡을 피하다
	I usually try to get to the office by 6:45 to **beat the traffic.** 교통혼잡을 피하려고 보통 6시 45분까지 출근하려고 해.

beat around the bush	에둘러 얘기하다 Don't **beat around the bush.** What's your problem? 말 돌리지마. 문제가 뭐야?
You can't beat sth	…가 아주 대단하다 You can't do that. **You can't beat** them! 넌 그렇게 안돼. 걔네들을 당해낼 수가 없어.
It beats me	난 모르겠어 **Beats me.** Her car's still in the parking lot. 몰라. 걔 차가 아직도 주차장에 있어.

019 bed
n. 침대

get out of bed	일어나다 = get up He didn't even **get out of bed.** 걔는 일어나지 조차 못했어.
go (straight) to bed	자다 I can get it done before we **go to bed.** 자기 전에 끝낼 수 있어.
put sb in bed	재우다 My wife **put** the baby **in bed.** 내 아내는 아이를 재웠어.
make the [one's] bed	잠잔 후 침대를 정리하다 We'll need to **make the bed** before leaving. 우리는 나가기 전에 침대를 정리해야 돼.
get out of bed on the wrong side	기분이 안좋다 He's so grumpy, he **must have got out on the wrong side of bed.** 걔는 엄청 짜증부려. 아마 기분이 안좋은게 틀림없어.

go to bed with sb	…와 섹스하다 = sleep with sb
	I tried, but she wouldn't **go to bed with** me. 난 시도했지만, 그녀는 나와 자려고 하지 않았어.
get ~into bed	…와 잠자리를 하다
	She said our father **got into bed with** her. 그 여자는 우리 아버지와 잤다고 말했어.
be good in bed	밤일을 잘하다 ↔ be bad in bed
	If you want, I can tell people you'**re good in bed.** 네가 원한다면 네가 침대에서 끝내준다고 사람들에게 말할 수 있어.
B&B(bed & breakfast)	아침식사가 나오는 숙박
	They'll be staying at a **B&B** in Wales. 그들은 웨일즈의 아침식사가 나오는 숙박업소에 머물거야.

020 beg
v. 간청하다, 애걸하다

beg (sby) for sth	(…에게) …을 간청하다
	I am not gonna **beg for** forgiveness. 용서해달라고 빌지 않을거야.
beg sb (not) to+V	…에게 …해달라고(하지 말아 달라고) 간청하다
	I'm gonna have to run over there and **beg** him **to** love me. 난 그리로 달려가서 걔한테 날 사랑해달라고 애원할거야.
beg to+V	…하기를 간청하다
	Her life belongs to me, and she'll **beg to** keep it. 걔 목숨은 나한테 달렸는데 살려달라고 애원할거야.
I beg to differ	내 생각은 좀 다른데
	I beg to differ. There are some serious problems with it. 내 생각은 달라. 몇몇 중요한 문제가 있다고.

I beg your pardon	다시 얘기해줄래요?(Pardon? = Sorry?)
	I beg your pardon? Why do you think my son is dead? 뭐라구요? 왜 내 아들이 죽었다고 생각해요?
I'm begging you	제발 부탁이야
	Look, **I'm begging you,** don't do it. 이봐, 제발, 그러지마.

021 begin
v. 시작하다

begin sth	…을 시작하다
	Is everyone ready to **begin** the meeting? 다들 회의시작 준비됐어요?
begin to[~ing]	…하기 시작하다
	Tom pulls her toward him and they **begin to** kiss. 탐이 걜 자기 쪽으로 끌어당기더니 키스하기 시작한다.
begin with[by]	…부터 시작하다
	We would like to **begin with** that. 우선 그거부터 시작하고 싶어요.
	I'd like to **begin with** sex on the first date. 난 첫 데이트에서 섹스부터 하는 걸 원해요.
to begin with	무엇보다도 먼저, 우선
	They don't loved each other **to begin with.** 걔네들은 우선 서로 사랑하지 않았어.
in the beginning	맨 처음에
	That's true, **in the beginning.** 맨처음에는 사실야.

behave

v. 행동하다

behave very badly	못되게 행동하다
	Don't **behave badly** while I'm away.
	나 떠나 있는 동안 나쁘게 행동하지마.

behave like+ N(S+V)	…처럼 행동하다
	I thought you've seen him **behave like** that.
	걔가 그렇게 행동하는 것을 네가 본 적이 있다고 생각했어.

Behave yourself	예의바르게 행동해라
	Hey, make sure you **behave yourself** out there.
	야, 밖에 나가서는 올바르게 행동해야 해.

believe

v. 믿다

believe it	믿다 *앞서 말한 내용을 it이나 this[that]으로 받는 경우
	You'd better **believe it!**
	정말 맞는 말이야!
	I don't **believe this!** You talked to her about that?
	말도 안돼! 그걸 걔한테 말했단 말야?

believe sby	…을 믿다
	So **believe me,** I know exactly how you feel.
	그러니 날 믿어, 네 기분이 어떤지 잘 안다구.
	I didn't **believe him.** Because he's always lying to me.
	난 걜 안 믿었어. 늘상 거짓말하니까.

believe in+sby [sth or ~ing]	…의 존재를 믿거나 …을 사실이라 받아들이다 I'm still not sure I **believe in** God. 내가 신을 믿는지 아직 잘 모르겠어. I need you to **believe in** me. 네가 날 믿길 바래. I **believe in** being nice. 착하게 행동하는 게 옳다고 생각해.
I believe that~	…을 믿다, …라고 생각하다 I **believe** she is the best in her class. 난 걔가 자기 학급에서 최고라고 생각해. I **believe** he isn't guilty. 걔가 죄가 없다고 생각해.
I believe what~	…을 믿다 I really **believe what** I did was right. 난 정말 내가 한 일이 맞다고 생각해. I don't **believe what** I'm hearing. 내 귀를 믿을 수가 없네.
You're not going to believe what~	넌 …을 믿지 못할거야 **You are not going to believe what** I just did. 내가 방금 뭘 했는지 믿지 못 할거야. **You're not going to believe what** just happened. 방금 일어난 일 믿지 못 할거야.
I can't believe that [what, how~]	…가 믿겨지지가 않아 **I just can't believe** this is happening again! 이런 일이 또 생기다니 믿을 수가 없어! **I can't believe** you did that. 네가 그걸 했다니 믿을 수가 없어.
I can't believe what[how~]	…가 믿겨지지가 않아 **You can't believe how** sorry I am. 내가 얼마나 미안한지 모를거야.
Can you believe that S+V?	…라는 게 믿겨져? **Can you believe** she actually thought that? 걔가 그렇게 생각했다는 게 믿겨져? **Can you believe** she had a date with the teacher? 걔가 선생님이랑 데이트했다는게 믿겨져?

believe

It is hard [difficult] to believe that~	…를 믿기가 어렵다 **It's hard to believe** they didn't come to work. 걔네들이 출근하지 않았다니 놀랍네.
find it hard [defficult] to+V	…을 믿기 어렵다 Why do you **find it so hard to** believe? 왜 그게 그렇게 믿기 어려운거야? You may **find this very hard to** believe, but it's true. 이거 믿기 어렵겠지만 사실이야.
not believe a word of	…을 전혀 믿지 않다 No one is ever going to **believe a word of** that. 아무도 그거 조금도 믿지 않을거야.
believe so	그렇다고 믿다 I **believe so.** 그렇게 알고 있을게. I don't **believe so.** 난 그렇게 생각안해.
be believed to be ~	…라고 생각되다 (It's widely believed that S+V) It **is believed** that English is hard to learn. 영어는 배우기 어렵다고 생각돼.
believe ~ as ~	…을 …라고 믿다 Do you **believe** this **as** the truth? 그걸 사실이라고 믿습니까?

 024

belong

v. …에 속하다

belong (here)	(여기에) 속하다 You don't **belong here.** 넌 여기에 오면 안된다. I don't **belong here.** 내가 올 곳이 아냐.

belong to	…에 속하다
	I guess this **belongs to** you. And thank you for giving it to me. 이거 네꺼야. 내게 줘서 고마웠어.

belong together	연인사이이다
	It just seems that you two **belong together.** 너희 둘 연인사이인 것 같아.

belongings	소지품
	She came to get all of her **belongings** from the desk. 걔 와서 책상의 모든 소지품을 가져갔어.

025 best
n. 최선, 최상 **a.** 최고의 **adv.** 가장 잘

do one's best	최선을 다하다 = try one's best
	I'**m doing my best** to walk as fast as the others. 다른 사람처럼 빨리 걸으려고 최선을 다하고 있어.

make the best use of~	최대한 활용하다
	The police will **make the best use of** the evidence. 경찰은 그 증거를 최대한 활용할거야.

at best	기껏해야
	At best, he'll get a passing grade on the test. 잘해야 걔 시험통과학점을 받을거야.

the best man for[to] ~	…에 최적인 사람
	Anthony is **the best man to** lead the project. 앤소니는 그 프로젝트를 이끌 최적인 사람이야.

do sth as best as you can	최선을 다해 …하다
	I know you're tired, but **do it as best as you can.** 네가 시도한 것은 알지만, 최선을 다해서 해봐.

bet

v. 내기걸다, 단언하다

make a bet
내기를 걸다

Let's **make a bet** on which team is going to win this game.
이번 경기에서 어느 팀이 이길지 내기하자.

the bet
판돈

I'd like to raise **the bet** five bucks.
판돈 5달러 올리고 싶어.

bet sth
…을 걸다

I **bet** two dollars. 2달러 건다.

You **bet** your life[ass]! 물론!, 그럼!, 틀림없어!

You **bet** your ass! I'm going to fire you!
그럼! 널 해고 할거야!

bet sby+돈 that~
…에게 …한다고 돈을 걸다

I'll **bet you 50 bucks that** you can't stop smoking.
네가 담배 못 끊는데 50달러를 걸게.

I would bet sth on[that~]
…라는 건 확실해

I'd **bet my life on** it.
틀림없어, 확실해.

I'd **bet all my money that** he won't move to New York.
걔가 뉴욕으로 이사오지 않는다는 데 내 모든 돈을 걸겠어.

I('ll) bet (that)~
틀림없이 …해

I'll **bet.** 틀림없어, 정말이야, 확실해, 그러겠지.

I **bet you!** 정말야! 확실해!

I **bet** you will find a new boyfriend soon.
넌 곧 틀림없이 새로운 남자친구를 만나게 될거야.

You (can) bet (that)~
…가 틀림없어

You bet. 확실해, 물론이지.

You bet I'll be there. 꼭 거기에 갈게.

bet on ···에 돈을 걸다

I wouldn't **bet on** it. 그럴 일은 없을거야.
You can **bet on** it. 그럼, 물론이지, 정말야.
You can **bet on** me. 날 믿어봐.

027 better
ⓐ 더 좋은, 더 나은　adv. 더 잘

get the better of~ 능가하다, 이기다, 우세하다

You'll never **get the better of** me.
넌 결코 날 이길 수 없을거야.

had better+V ···하는 편이 낫다

I guess I'**d better** call and reschedule.
전화해서 일정을 재조정하는 편이 낫겠어.

had better not~ ···하지 않는 편이 낫다

You'**d better not** go outside. It's too cold.
나가지 마. 밖은 너무 추워.

get better 나아지다

Don't give up. Things will **get better.**
포기하지마. 상황이 좋아질거야.

better known as ···로 더 잘 알려진

Aspirin is **better known as** a headache remedy.
아스피린은 두통치료약으로 더 알려져 있어.

better than~ ···보다 나은

You'd better come up with something **better than** that.
그것보다 나은 뭔가를 제안하는 게 좋겠어.

bet

do better	더 잘하다
	Don't sweat it. You'll **do better** next time. 걱정마! 넌 다음 번에는 더 잘할거야.

like ~ better	…을 더 좋아하다
	This is great, but they **like** chocolate **better**. 이것도 훌륭하지만 걔들은 초콜릿을 더 좋아해.

be better off ~ing	…하는 편이 더 낫다
	He'd **be better off** going to medical school. 걘 의대에 가는 편이 더 나을지도 몰라.

much better	훨씬 더
	I know it was a cheap shot, but I feel so **much better** now. 치사했던 건 알지만 기분은 훨씬 좋네.

028 bid

n. 가격제시, 입찰 **v.** 경매에서 값을 부르다, 입찰에 응하다, 애쓰다

submit a bid for~	…에 가격제시를 하다, 입찰서를 제출하다
	The company plans to **submit a bid for** the new project. 회사는 새로운 프로젝트에 입찰서를 제출할 계획이야.

bid for sth [to do]	…에 대한 가격제시, 입찰하다
	You can **bid for** items on Internet auctions. 인터넷 경매를 통해 입찰할 수 있어.

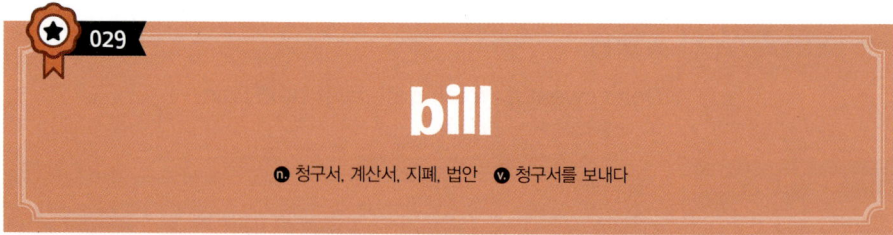

bill

n. 청구서, 계산서, 지폐, 법안 v. 청구서를 보내다

pay one's bill	청구서 돈을 내다
	My salary is so small that I can't **pay my bills.** 월급이 너무 적어서 공과금도 못내겠어.
foot the bill	비용을 부담하다
	I'll **foot the bill** this time around. 이번 건 내가 부담할게.
pick up the bill	돈을 지불하다
	Don't worry, Dad always **picks up the bill.** 걱정마, 아버지가 계산하셔.
fit the bill	꼭 들어맞다, 알맞다
	My guess is in this place you **fit the bill.** 내 생각으론 이 분야에서 네가 딱이야.

bit

n. 조금

a (little) bit of +N	약간의 …
	Can I have **a bit of** your chocolate bar? 네 초콜렛 바 좀 먹을 수 있겠니?
a bit	약간
	Well, maybe the weather will improve **a bit** this afternoon. 음. 오후에 날씨가 좀 좋아질거야.

a little bit	조금
	I have to warn you. This might hurt **a little bit**. 경고했잖아. 이건 좀 아플 수가 있다고.

just a bit	약간
	I'm **just a bit** depressed about my life. 사는 게 좀 막막해서 그래

031 bite
n. 물기, 한입 베어 문 조각 **v.** 물다

grab a bite	간단히 요기하다, 한입먹다
	Let's **grab a bite** to eat after the meeting. 회의 후에 간단히 요기하자.

have[take] a bite of	한입먹다
	Can I have a sip of your coffee and **a bite of** your muffin? 커피 한 모금과 머핀 한 조각 먹어도 돼?

be[get] bitten by ~	…에 물리다
	Were you **bitten by** some kind of rabid dog? 광견병같은 병걸린 개한테 물렸어?

bite the bullet	이를 악물고 참다
	Maybe we should just **bite the bullet** and go to Boston. 혹 우리가 싫어도 보스톤에 가야 될지도 몰라.

bite the dust	실패하다, 죽다
	What a terrible way to **bite the dust**. 참 끔찍하게 죽었네.

bites sby's head off	(별 이유없이) 호되게 혼내다
	You don't have to **bite my head off**! 그렇게 으르렁거리지 말라구요!

black
n. 검은색, 흑자

in the black	흑자의
	We're **in the black** again this month.
	이번달에 또 흑자야.
black out	의식을 잃다, 정전되다
	I didn't **black out.** My head doesn't hurt.
	난 의식을 잃지 않았어. 머리가 아프지 않아.

blame
n. 비난, 책임 **v.** 비난하다, 탓하다

take the blame for~	…에 대한 책임을 지다
	It was my fault. I **take the blame.**
	내 실수야. 내가 책임질게.
put[lay] the blame on sby	…을 탓하다
	Don't **place[lay] the blame on** me.
	내 탓하지마.
blame sth on ~	…로 …을 탓하다
	Finally, she will find a way to **blame this on** me.
	결국, 이게 내탓이라는 비난의 꼬투리를 잡을거야.
blame sth [sby] for sth	…을 …의 책임으로 돌리다
	I don't **blame you for** not returning my phone calls.
	내 전화한거 보고도 내게 전화해주지 않을 수도 있지.

I don't blame you	그럴 만도 하다
	I don't blame you. It was an accident.
	그럴 수도 있지. 실수였는데.

034 blow

n. 세게 때림, 코풀기 v. 불다, 코풀다, (기회) 날리다

blow one's nose	코를 풀다
	I have to **blow my nose.**
	나 코를 풀어야 돼.
blow it	기회를 날리다
	I blew it. I did the stupidest thing.
	망쳤어. 아주 멍청한 짓을 저질렀다고.
blow up	터지다, 화를 내다
	If you **blow up,** you'll blow it.
	화를 내면 일을 망쳐.
blow sby off	바람맞히다, 무시하다
	Don't **blow me off.** I want to talk with you personally.
	날 무시하지마. 개인적으로 얘기하고 싶어.
blow one's mind	…을 놀라게 하다, 충격을 주다
	Did that kiss just completely **blow her mind?**
	키스로 걔 마음을 뽕가게했어?

board

n. 널판지, 이사회 **v.** 승선하다, 탑승하다, 하숙하다

the board of directors	이사회
	The board of directors are going to meet next week. 이사회가 다음주에 열릴 예정이야.

board and lodging	식사를 제공하는 하숙 *room and board
	The airplane ticket is free, but you have to pay **boarding and lodging.** 항공료는 공짜이지만 숙박료는 지불해야 돼.

board the train	기차를 타다
	You can **board the plane** now. 이제 비행기에 탑승해 주십시오.

on board	승차한, 탑승한, 동참한 = aboard
	I'm glad that you're back **on board** with our plan. 네가 우리 계획에 다시 참여하게 되어 기뻐.

boarding pass	탑승권
	If you have your **boarding pass,** you can board the plane now. 탑승권 소지하신 분은 지금 탑승하십시오.

book

n. 책, 회계장부 **v.** 예약하다, 기록하다

(do, play sth) by the book	규정대로 (…을 하다)
	We **did** everything **by the book.** 우리는 모든 걸 절차대로 했어.

board

not in my books
내 생각[판단]으로는 아니다

You're all right in my book.
넌 완전히 내 타입이야.

book sth
예약하다

I booked a table for five.
5명 테이블을 예약했어.

book sby
…의 예약을 잡다(Sby is booked on[in]~)

I'm booked on AA Flight 335 to Boston.
보스톤행 AA 335편 예약했어.

I have no time. I'm booked all day.
나 시간이 없어. 일정이 꽉 찼어.

be booked up
예약이 꽉차다(be booked solid)

I'm sorry. We're all booked up tonight.
죄송하지만 오늘 밤 예약이 꽉 찼는데요.

We're booked solid for the next month.
담 달까지 예약이 꽉 찼어요.

 037

break

n. 휴식, 휴일, (TV)광고시간 **v.** 깨트리다, 깨다, 잠시 쉬다, 작은 돈으로 바꾸다

break+money
작은 돈으로 바꾸다

Would you please break this dollar bill for me?
이 달러를 잔돈으로 바꿔줄래요?

break
휴식, 휴식시간, 휴식시간을 갖다

Would you like to begin after a short break?
잠깐 쉬었다 시작할래?

How about we break for a while?
잠시 쉬는 게 어때?

Let's break for coffee.
잠깐 쉬면서 커피 마시자.

make a break for it	도망치다 Here they come. I say we **make a break for** it. 저기 걔네들이 와. 우리 도망쳐야 돼.
a big break	좋은 기회 I don't care! This is **a big break** for me! 상관없어! 이건 내게 아주 좋은 기회야!
break one's leg	다리가 부러지다, …의 다리를 부러트리다 I **broke my leg** skiing up last weekend. 지난주에 스키타다 다리가 부러졌어.
break one's promise	약속을 깨다 *break는 promise, rule, law, habit, record 등 추상명사를 목적어로 받는다. I will do my best not to **break my promise**. 약속을 지키도록 최선을 다할게. Every now and then, we have to **break the rules**. 가끔은 규칙을 깨야 돼.
break one's heart	실망시키다, 마음 아프게 하다 *heartbreaker는 그렇게 마음을 아프게 하는 사람 You **broke my heart**. 네가 내 맘을 찢어놨어. Don't **break my heart**. 내 마음을 아프게 하지마.
break the news to	…에게 (안좋은) 소식을 전하다 *break news 긴급뉴스 I imagine that you were pissed off when she **broke the news**. 걔가 소식을 전했을 때 너 열받아겠다.
break even	수지타산을 맞추다 This month, we barely **break even**. 이번 달에는 수지타산을 못 맞춰.
break the ice	어색함을 벗어나 대화를 시작하다 Okay, I've got to **break the ice** here. 좋아, 여기서 내가 이야기를 하지.
break for	…하러 잠시 쉬다 I'm about to **break for** lunch. 점심 먹으러 잠시 쉴거야. Shall we **break for** a snack? 잠시 쉬면서 스낵먹을까?

break

break away
떨어져나가다, 이탈하다, 독립하다, (관계) 끊다

My son's trying to **break away** from me with a girl.
내 아들이 여자애와 날 떠나려고 해.

break down
부서트리다, 없애다, 고장나다, 실패하다, 이해하기 쉽게 분리하다, 분류하다(into)

My car **broke down** again.
자동차가 다시 고장났어.

Everything can **be broken down** into three categories.
모든 건 3가지 분류로 나눠질 수 있어.

break in(to)
침입하다, 말하는데 끼어들다, 맞게 하다

We know who **broke into** your house.
누가 네 집을 침입했는지 알고 있어.

I **broke in** my new shoes.
새로운 신발에 적응했어.

break off
꺾다, 부러지다, 떨어져 나가다, (말, 관계 등을) 끝내다, 중단하다 *break it off 헤어지다

Did it **break off** or did someone break it?
그게 떨어져 나간거야 아니면 누가 깨트린거야?

My father **broke off** his affair with Cindy.
아버지는 신디와의 관계를 정리하셨어.

If you want, I'll just **break it off with** her.
당신이 원한다면, 그냥- 그냥 끝내지 뭐.

break out
일어나다, 발생하다, (발진, 종기 등이) 나다, 별안간 …하기 시작하다, 탈출하다(~of)

The fire **broke out** last night.
화재가 어젯밤에 발생했어.

I really want to **break out** of here.
난 정말 여기에서 벗어나고 싶어.

She **breaks out** into a smile and stands up.
걘 갑자기 웃더니 일어난다.

break up
부숴트리다, 해산하다, 헤어지다(with), 전화상태가 끊기다

I **broke up with** a girl who broke my heart.
내 맘에 상처 준 여자와 헤어졌어.

I'm going to **break up with** you.
우리 그만 만나자.

You're **breaking up**!
소리가 끊어져서 들려요!

break through	헤치고 나아가다, (난관을 딛고) 성공하다 *breakthrough 새로운 돌파구 That'll help me **break through** to her. 그게 내가 개한테 헤치고 가는데 도움이 될거야.
be broke	땡전 한푼 없다 The wedding is expensive. I**'m broke.** 결혼식 비용이 많이 나가 돈 한푼 없어.

breath
n. 숨 *breathe v. 숨을 쉬다

take a breath	숨을 쉬다 *take a deep breath 깊은 숨을 쉬다, 진정하다 Now all you have to do is **take a deep breath.** 넌 깊이 숨을 쉬기만 하면 돼.
don't hold your breath	너무 기대하지마 *hold your breath 숨을 참다 **Don't hold your breath.** That won't happen for a long time. 기대하지마. 한참 걸릴거야.
out of breath	숨이 찬 He was kind of **out of breath.** 걔는 조금 숨이 찼었어.
take one's breath away	…을 놀래키게 하다 I saw you, and you **took my breath away.** 널 봤는데 숨넘어가는 줄 알았어.
breathe down sby's neck	…을 화나게 가까이서 뭐하나 보다 My boss **is breathing down my neck** at work. 사장이 사무실에서 깐깐하게 굴어.
not breathe a word	비밀로 하다 Do **not breathe a word** of this. 이건 절대로 말을 꺼내지 마라.

bring

039

v 말을 하거나 듣는 사람이 있는 곳으로 뭔가를 이동하다

bring sby sth	…에게 …를 가져다 주다 = bring sth for~	
	We **brought** you some wine. 와인 좀 가져왔어.	
bring sby[sth] to~	…에(게) …를 데려가다, 가져가다	
	She **brought** another man **into** his bed again. 걘 또 다른 사내를 침대로 데려갔어.	
	Bring her **over** here. 걜 이리로 데려와.	
What brings [brought] ~?	…에 어쩐 일이야?	
	So, **what brings you** here at such a late hour? 이렇게 늦은 시각에 무슨 일로 오셨습니까?	
	What brings you to the hospital? 병원에는 어쩐 일이야?	
can't bring oneself to~	…할 마음이 내키지 않다	
	You **can't bring yourself to** give me one little kiss? 내게 살짝 키스할 마음도 없는거야?	
	I **can't even bring myself to** say it. 그걸 말할 수가 없어.	
bring sth to a close	끝나다 *come to a close 끝나다	
	Let's **bring this matter to a close.** 이 문제에 대해 결정을 내리자.	
which brings me to~	그래서 …하게 되다	
	I got divorced again. **Which brings me to** the strip bar. 난 다시 이혼했고 그래서 스트립바에 오게 됐어.	
bring sby to one's senses	제 정신으로 돌아오게 하다	
	It **brought me to my senses.** 그 덕에 제정신으로 돌아왔어.	

come to one's senses

제정신으로 돌아오다

She came to her senses finally.
걔가 마침내 제정신으로 돌아왔어.

bring around

데리고 오다, 가져오다, 화제를 바꾸다, 설득하다, 의식을 되찾게 하다

You can bring around your coworkers to the party.
파티에 네 동료들 데려와도 돼.

Why don't you bring the pizza around for us?
피자 좀 나주어주라.

bring back

다시 가져[데려]오다, 생각나게 하다, 반환하다

Bring her back here, will you?
걜 이리로 데려와 응?

They didn't bring back any food at all?
걔네들은 음식을 전혀 가져오지 않았어?

Can a relationship bring you back to life?
관계가 너를 기운나게 할 수 있을까?

bring down

끌어내리다, 파멸시키다, …을 붕괴시키다

What'd you bring me down here for?
날 왜 여기에 데려온거야?

I didn't mean to bring you down.
너희들 기분까지 망치게 할 생각은 아니었는데.

bring in

영입하다, (법)도입하다, 돈을 벌다

Did you send a man all the way to Chicago to bring me in?
나를 영입하려고 시카고까지 사람을 보냈어요?

My wife brings in a lot of money every month.
내 아내는 매월 많은 돈을 벌어.

bring on

가져오다, 초래하다 *Bring it on! 한번 해볼테면 해봐!

What brought this on? 이게 왜 그러는거야?

You want to hit me? Bring it on! 날 치고 싶다고? 어디 해봐!

What do you expect me to do? You brought this on yourself. 날더러 어찌라고? 네가 자초한거잖아.

bring out

갖고 나가다, 데리고 나오다, 밖으로 꺼내다, 나타내다, (제품을) 출시(발표)하다

I brought you out here because I want you to see this girl.
이 얘를 봤으면 해서 이리로 널 데려왔어.

The revised edition didn't bring out yet.
수정판은 아직 출간되지 않았어.

bring

bring up
(화제를) 꺼내다, 가르치다, 기르다

Are you going to **bring up** your child here while you go to school? 학교 다니는 동안에 여기서 아이를 기를거야?

I'm really kind of surprised nobody's ever **brought it up.**
아무도 그 얘길 하지 않아 좀 놀랐어.

bring about
…을 야기시키다, 일으키다(make sth happen; cause)

That might **bring about** the big trouble.
그로 인해 큰 어려움이 야기될 수도 있어.

bring along
…을 데리고 가다, 가져가다

Does he have a single friend that you could **bring along** for me? 날 위해 데려올 수 있는 독신친구가 있어?

bring into
어떤 상황에 빠트리다

I can't believe you **brought** my boss **into** this! I'm going to get fired! 사장님을 이런 상황에 빠트리다니! 해고시킬거야!

040

broke

ⓐ 무일푼의

be broke
빈털터리의

I can't go anywhere. I **am broke.**
난 어디도 갈 수가 없어. 빈털터리거든.

go broke
무일푼이 되다, 파산하다(go bankrupt보다 informal)

I know how the company **went broke.**
회사가 어떻게 거덜났는지 알아.

go for broke
위험을 무릅쓰고 전부를 걸다, 열심히 하다

I'm going to just **go for broke** here and say I like you.
이판사판으로 말해보는데 난 널 좋아해.

business

n. 사업(체), 직장일, 업무, 회사사업, 일

do business with
…와 거래를 하다, 사업을 하다
We stopped **doing business with** that firm.
우린 저 회사와 사업관계를 중단했어.

go into business
사업을 시작하다
She found a partner to **go into business** with.
걘 사업 파트너를 찾았어.

on business
사업차, 출장중
I'm going to China for a week **on business.**
사업상 일주일간 중국에 갈거야.

run a business
사업체를 운영하다
Mike's family **ran a small business.**
마이크 가족은 소규모 사업을 운영하고 있어.

start (up) one's own business
자기 사업을 시작하다
I**'m starting up my own business.**
난 내 사업을 시작할거야.

get down to business
본론으로 들어가다
We'll have some coffee before we **get down to business.**
일을 본격적으로 시작하기 전에 커피 좀 마시자.

business as usual
평상시와 다름없이
It was pretty much **business as usual.**
정말 평상시와 다름이 없었어.

mean business
진심이야
Don't laugh. I **mean business.** 웃지마. 진심이야

be none of sby's business
…의 일이 아니다
That**'s none of your business.** But it is my business.
남일에 신경꺼. 이건 내 일이야

business

business hours 근무시간, 영업시간

I wouldn't surf the Internet during **business hours** if I were you. 나라면 근무시간 중에는 인터넷을 하지 않겠어.

042

busy
ⓐ 바쁜

be busy with~ …로 바쁘다

I**'m busy with** a client at the moment.
지금은 손님 때문에 바빠요.

be busy (with) ~ing …하느라 바쁘다

They **were busy** traveling this weekend.
걔네들은 이번 주말에 여행하느라 바빴어.

get busy 뭔가 일을 시작하다

I was gonna call you back. I **got busy** on a case.
전화주려고 했는데, 사건으로 바빴어.

keep sb busy …을 바쁘게 하다 *keep myself busy 바쁘다

I **kept myself busy** by cleaning the house.
집안 청소하느라 바빴어.

too busy to~ 너무 바빠서 …을 못하다

Too busy to keep up with your schoolwork?
너무 바빠서 학교숙제를 따라갈 수가 없다구?

buy

n. 싸게 산 물건　**v.** 사다, 사주다, 상대방의 말을 믿다

---

buy — 싸게 산 물건

At 40 percent below market, this is **a good buy.**
싯가의 40%라면 잘 산 물건이지.

This was **a real buy.**
이건 정말 잘 산 물건이야.

---

buy sth — …을 사다

What kind of computer did you **buy?**
어떤 컴퓨터를 구입했어?

I **bought** this on impulse.
난 이걸 충동 구매했어.

---

buy sby sth — …에게 …을 사주다　*buy A B = buy B for A

Let me **buy** you a drink.
술 한잔 사죠.

I'll **buy** you something at the duty free shop, if you wan.
필요하면 면세점에서 뭐 좀 사올게.

---

buy sth on credit — …을 외상으로 사다

I'd like to **buy it on credit.**
외상으로 사고 싶은데요.

No one **bought this on credit.**
이걸 외상으로 사는 사람 없어요.

---

buy — 믿다

We **aren't buying your story.**
네 얘기 믿을 수 없어.

You're **not buying all this.**
이걸 곧이곧대로 믿지는 않지.

I **don't buy it.** 못 믿어.

---

buy off — 매수하다

You tried to **buy off** your friend with money.
넌 친구를 돈으로 매수하려고 했어.

call

n. 전화, 통화, 방문, 요청 **v.** 부르다, 외치다, 전화걸다

---

give sby a call — …에게 전화하다

Give me a call if you want.
전화하고 싶을 때 전화해.

You've got my number, **give me a call.**
내 번호 있지, 전화해.

make a call — 전화하다

You want me to **make a call?** 나보고 전화를 걸라고?

take a call — 전화받다

She had to step outside to **take a call.**
걘 전화받으려고 밖으로 나가야 했어.

expect one's call — …의 전화를 기다리다

I **was expecting your call.** 네 전화기다리고 있었어.

return one's call — 답신 전화를 하다

Leave a message, and I'll **return your call.**
메시지 남겨, 전화걸게.

transfer[direct] a call[one's call] — 전화를 돌려주다

How may I **direct you call?** 어디 바꿔드릴까요?

A phone call for you — 전화왔어 *You have[got] a call from~, There's a call from~

Phone call for you.
너한테 전화왔어. (= You have a phone call)

You got a call from the school.
학교에서 전화왔어.

Excuse me. **There's a phone call for** you.
실례합니다. 전화왔어요.

be one's call — …의 결정사항이다

That's your call. 네가 결정할 문제야, 네 뜻에 따르게.

be a close call

큰일날 뻔하다

That **was a close call.**
하마터면 큰일날 뻔했네. 위험천만이었어.

be on call

대기중이다

He **was on call** last night, so now he might be asleep.
어제 당직이었으니 어디선가 자고 있나 봐요.

I'm calling to~

전화한 건 다름이 아니라… *I called to+동사 …하려고 전화했어

I'm calling you because I saw that you called me.
네가 전화해서 전화하는거야.

I called to apologize. 사과하려고 전화했어.

call security

경비를 부르다

Please **call an ambulance.**
앰뷸런스 좀 불러주세요.

Could you **call a taxi** for me?
택시 좀 불러줄래요?

I **called security** to kick him out.
경비를 불러서 걜 쫓아냈어.

call sby sth

…을 …라고 부르다 *call sby names 욕을 하다

What do you **call** that in English?
저걸 영어로 뭐라고 하니?

Don't **call me names!**
욕하지 마!

call oneself sth

자칭 …라고 하다(실은 그럴 자격이 없다)

You **call yourself an actor.**
소위 배우라는 사람이.

call it a day

퇴근하다 = call it quits

It's coming up on 6:00. What do you say we **call it a day?**
6시 다 돼가. 그만 퇴근하자.

call in sick

아프다고 전화로 병가내다

What are you doing here? You **called in sick** this morning.
여기서 뭐해? 오늘 아침에 병가냈잖아.

call the shot

결정을 하다

I'**m calling the shots.** 내가 결정할래.

call

call on one's cell phone
…의 핸드폰으로 전화하다

They **called on my cell phone** to see where I am.
내가 어디있는지 알려고 핸드폰으로 전화했어.

call back
다시 전화하다 *call back later or in+시간

Could you **call back later**?
나중에 전화할래요?

I'll **call back** later.
나중에 전화할게.

I'll have him **call you back.**
네게 전화하라고 할게.

call for
요구하다(ask, demand), 소리쳐 부르다[청하다]

She already **called for** a consult.
이미 컨설트 요청을 하셨어.

Did anybody **call for** security?
누가 경비 불렀어?

call off
취소하다, 멈추다 =cancel

I want you to end it. I want you to **call off** the wedding.
네가 그걸 끝내. 결혼식을 취소하라고.

He told that Leo **called off** his engagement with Jane.
걔가 그러는데 레오가 제인과 파혼했대.

call out
큰소리로 외치다, 도움을 호소하다

She gets out of the car and **calls out** to Sam.
걘 차에서 나와 샘을 큰 소리로 불렀다.

call up
전화하다 *call up sby to+V or call up sby and+V 전화해서 …하다

Why don't you just **call up** Helen and invite her over.
헬렌에게 전화해서 오라고 해

call down
비난하다, 전화하다

The boss **called her down** for not working late.
사장은 야근을 하지 않는다고 걜 혼냈어.

call in
…에게 와서 도와달라고 전화하다, 도움을 구하다, 잠깐 방문하다

Call in the lawyers. We're getting a divorce.
변호사 좀 불러. 우리 이혼해.

 045

care

n. 돌보기, 근심 **v.** 관심을 갖다, 신경쓰다, 돌보다

take care of	…를 돌보다, …을 처리하다
	Let me **take care of** it. 나한테 맡겨.
	Let me t**ake care of** the bill. 내가 계산할게.
	I'll **take care of** your son while you're out. 너 외출할 때 애봐줄게.
~ for all I care [know]	…하든 말든 난 상관없다
	She could be his new secretary, **for all I care.** 걔가 그 사람의 새로운 비서이든 말든 상관없어.
care about	…을 걱정하다, 근심하다
	I can see how much you **care about** Becky. 네가 얼마나 베키를 생각하는지 알겠어.
	You still **care about** me. 너 아직 나 생각하는구나.
care for	(긍정) 돌보다, (부정/의문) …을 좋아하다, 원하다
	I got to love the nurse who **had cared for** me. 날 간호해준 간호사를 사랑하게 되었어.
	(Would you) **Care for** some coffee? 커피 드릴까요?
	I don't **care for** his style. 난 걔 스타일이 마음에 안 들어.
I don't care about~	난 …가 상관없어
	I don't care about any of that! 저거 아무런 상관없어!
	I don't care about your feelings. 네 감정 알 바 아냐.
I don't care what[if~]	…이든 아니든 상관없어
	I don't care if she's fat or thin. 난 걔가 뚱뚱하든 날씬하든 상관안해.
	I don't care who he sleeps with. 걔가 누구랑 자는지 관심없어.

care

Would[Do] you care if~ ?	…해도 돼?
	Do you care if I join you? 내가 껴도 돼요?

care less [if]~	(…에) 전혀 관심없다
	I couldn't **care less.** 알게 뭐람.
	I couldn't **care less if** she comes or not. 걔가 오든 말든 난 상관없어.

Who cares about[what~]~?	…을 누가 신경이나 쓰냐?
	Who cares what they think? 걔네들 누가 신경이나 쓰냐?
	Who cares! 누가 신경이나 쓴대!

046

carry

v. 나르다, 지니다

carry (sth)	…을 나르다
	The bed is too heavy to **carry** by myself. 침대는 너무 무거워 혼자 나를 수가 없어.
	The bus **carries** 40 passengers. 버스는 40명을 날라.

carry sth	…을 상점에서 팔다
	Do you **carry** DSLR batteries? DSLR 카메라 밧데리 파나요?
	I'm sorry, we don't **carry** that brand. 그 브랜드는 취급안해요.

carry on	계속하다 *carry-on 기내에 들고가는 수하물
	You're good. **Carry on.** 잘 하네요. 계속 가요.
	They **carried on** kissing when there was a knock at the door. 걔네들이 키스를 계속하고 있을 때 누가 문을 두들겼어.
	I'm just taking my **carry-on.** 기내수하물만 들고 가는거예요.

carry out	실행하다, …을 밖으로 끌어내다
	We need to **carry out** the plans we made. 우리가 짠 계획을 실천해야 돼.
	I'll be back after I **carry out** the trash. 쓰레기 밖에 버리고 올게.

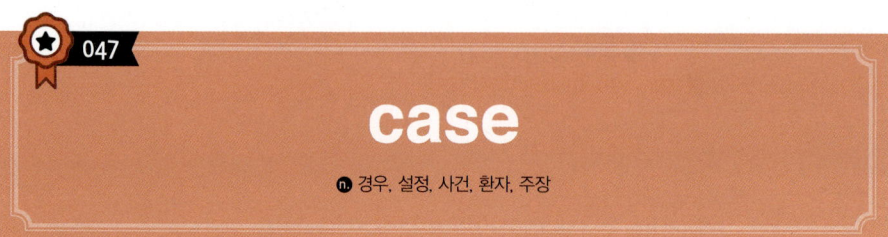

047 case
n. 경우, 설정, 사건, 환자, 주장

in some cases	어떤 경우에서는 *in most cases 대개의 경우에는
	In some cases we never solve the mystery. 어떤 경우에서는 우리는 전혀 미스테리를 풀지 못하고 있어.
if that is the case	그렇다면
	If that is the case, let's go out for a drink. 사실이 그렇다면 나가서 술한잔 하자.
in case of ~	…의 경우에 *in case S+V …하는 경우에
	In case I don't make it back in time, lock up before you leave. 시간내 못 돌아올 수도 있으니 가기 전 문잠그고 가.
in any case	어쨌든
	In any case, I'm not taking relationship advice from you. 어쨌든, 너로부터 어떤 인간관계에 대한 조언도 받지 않을거야.
in that case	그렇다면
	In that case I'll change the plans. 그렇다면 난 계획을 바꿀거야.
make a case for sth	…의 정당함을 입증하다
	The kids **made a case for** going to McDonalds. 아이들은 맥도날드에 가자고 주장했어.

catch

n. 포착, 포획(물), 멋진 상대 **v.** (붙)잡다, 병에 걸리다, 이해하다

catch
어획물, 대단한 것, 멋진 상대

What's the **catch**? 속셈이 뭐야?, 무슨 꿍꿍이야?

Nicole's a **catch**. 니콜은 꼭 붙잡고 싶은 여자야.

catch a cold
감기에 걸리다

I think I'm **catching a cold**. Achoo!
감기가 올려나봐. 에취!

It's too cold. Don't go out. You might **catch a cold**.
너무 추우니 나가지마. 감기 걸릴지도 몰라.

caught sby ~ing
…가 …하는 것을 잡다

You **caught me doing** it with Tammy. What's the big deal?
내가 태미와 그거하는거 들켰는데 그게 뭐 대수야?

She **caught me in** bed with Jill.
내가 질과 침대에 있는 걸 걔한테 들켰어.

be[get] caught in
…을 만나다, …에 잡히다

I **got caught in** a shower on my way home.
집에 오다 소나기를 만났어.

We **were caught in** a traffic jam.
우린 교통 혼잡에 꽉 막혔어.

catch
이해하다, 듣다

I didn't quite **catch** what you just said.
무슨 말하는 건지 잘 모르겠어.

catch on
…에 달라붙다, 걸리다 이해하다, 유행하다

Wow, you **catch on** quick.
와, 너 정말 이해 빠르네.

Excellent idea! You're **catching on**.
좋은 생각이야! 머리 잘 돌아가네.

catch up with	…을 따라잡다
	I'll **catch up with** you in the gym. 체육관에서 보자.
	Catch up with you later! 나중에 보자!

chance
n. 가능성, 기회

get[have] a chance	기회를 갖다
	We might actually **have a chance** of winning this. 우린 사실상 승산이 있어.
blow one's chance	기회를 날려버리다
	All you need to know is I **blew my chance.** 내가 기회놓친 것을 넌 알면 돼.
a second [another] chance	두번째 기회
	She gave me **a second chance.** 걘 내게 두 번째 기회를 줬어.
last chance	마지막 기회
	This was the **last chance** we had to make good on that promise. 이건 우리가 그 약속을 지켜야 되는 마지막 기회였어.
give[offer, provide] a chance	기회를 주다
	Give Susan a chance to do her job. 수잔에게 자신의 일을 할 기회를 줘라.
have a fifty-fifty chance of~	가능성이 반반이다
	Right now she **has a fifty-fifty chance of** surviving. 지금, 그녀가 살 가능성은 반반이야.

Is there any chance~ ?	…할 가능성이 있어? **Is there any chance that** you could stay home today? 오늘 너 집에 남아 있을 수 있어?
by chance	우연히　*by any chance (의문에서) 혹시라도, 만일 You said you found me **by chance?** 네가 날 우연히 찾았다고 말했지?
The chances are (that) S+V	…일 것 같아 **There's a chance** he can get better. 걔가 나아질 가능성이 있어.
take a chance	위험을 무릅쓰고 하다 = take chances on Chris **took a chance** and tried Internet dating. 크리스는 운걸고 인터넷데이트를 시도했어
not stand a chance of~	…할 것 같지 않다 Jill **doesn't stand a chance of** finishing on time. 질이 제때 일을 마칠 가능성은 없어.

 050

change

ⓝ 변화, 거스름돈[잔돈]　ⓥ 변화하다, 바꾸다, 환전하다

change	변화, 잔돈 There's been a **change** in the meeting schedule. 회의일정이 변경되었어. Here is your change and receipt. 여기 잔돈하고 영수증이요.
have a change of heart	마음[태도]을 바꾸다 I**'ve had a change of heart.** I don't want to see you anymore. 마음이 바뀌었어. 널 더 이상 보고 싶지 않아.
make a change	변경하다, 수정하다 Starting tomorrow, you have to **make a change.** 내일부터 변경해야 돼.

change	바뀌다, 변화하다, 옷을 갈아입다
	You **haven't changed.** 너 하나도 안 변했어.
	I'm going to go **change.** I've got a date. 가서 옷 갈아 입을게. 데이트 약속이 있거든.

change sth	…을 바꾸다
	I'd like to **change** my flight. 비행편을 바꾸고 싶어요.
	I recently **changed** jobs. 최근에 직업을 바꿨어.

change one's mind (about~)	(…에 대한) 마음을 바꾸다
	I guess she**'s changed her mind.** 걔가 마음을 바꿨나 봐.
	Why did you **change your mind?** 왜 네 마음을 바꿨어?

change A (to B)	A를 (B로) 바꾸다
	I have to **change** my ticket from economy **to** business class. 일반석 비행기표를 이등석으로 바꿔야겠어.

get changed	옷을 갈아입다
	I'm going to **get changed.** 옷 갈아 입을게.
	Go **get changed!** 가서 옷 갈아입어!

charge

n. 요금, 책임, 비난, 고소, 충전 **v.** 부과하다, 청구하다, 고소하다, 충전하다, 신용카드로 결제하다

be in charge of	…을 책임지고 있다
	Who **is in charge?** 누가 책임자야?
	Can I speak to someone **in charge** please? 책임자랑 통화하고 싶은데요.

change

put sby in charge of — …에게 …의 책임을 지우다

They **put** Brian **in charge of** organizing the party.
걔네들은 브라이언보고 파티를 준비하라고 했어.

take charge (of) — (…의) 책임을 지다

The way you**'re taking charge** is very impressive.
너의 책임지는 방식이 매우 인상적이야.

free of charge — 무료로

Take whatever you want. **Free of charge.**
마음에 드는 거 아무거나 골라. 무료야.

charge sby money — …에게 …을 청구하다

How much did you **charge?**
얼마예요?

I **charge** seven hundred dollars an hour.
시간당 7백달러 입니다.

charge sby [sth]for — …에게 …를 청구하다

They're going to **charge you for** that.
걔네들은 네게 그걸 청구할거야.

(Will that be) Cash or charge? — 현금요 아니면 신용카드로요?

Would you like to pay by **cash or charge?**
현금으로 낼래요 아님 신용카드로 낼래요?

I'll **charge** it, please.
카드로 할게요.

be charged with — …으로 기소되다

I **was charged with** stealing a cell phone.
핸드폰 훔친 죄로 기소됐어.

charge — 충전하다

I forgot my cell phone **charger.**
핸드폰 충전기를 두고 왔어.

Keep your cell phone **charged.**
네 핸드폰 충전시키고 다녀.

chat
n. 수다, 대화　**v.** 수다떨다, 채팅하다

have a chat with sb	…와 얘기하다 I'm having a little chat with her. 난 걔하고 잡담을 하고 있어.
have a chat about~	…에 대해 얘기하다 Let's chat about next month's schedule. 다음 달 일정에 대해 담소를 나눠보자.
chat about~	…에 대해 얘기하다 Call me and we'll chat about it. 전화해 우리 그에 관해 얘기하자.
chat with sb	…와 함께 얘기하다　*chat to sb …와 채팅하다, 얘기하다 I plan to chat to some friends tonight. 오늘밤 난 친구들과 채팅을 할거야. I wanted to chat with you before you did something foolish. 네가 어리석은 짓을 하기 전에 너와 얘기하고 싶었어.

cheat
n. 사기꾼, 속임수　**v.** 속이다, 부정행위하다, 바람을 피우다

cheating	컨닝, 부정 All right, you wanna win by cheating, go ahead. 좋아, 부정으로 이기고 싶다는거지, 그래 해봐.
cheat sb out of	…에게 사기를 쳐서 …빼앗다 You're trying to cheat me out of half of his fortune? 날 속여서 걔 자산의 반을 빼돌리려는거야?

cheat on sb	바람피다, 컨닝하다 *cheat on sb with~ …을 배신하고 …와 함께 바람을 피우다
	Greg was caught when he **cheated on** his wife. 그렉은 부인을 속이고 바람을 피다 잡혔어.
	Don't **cheat on** your final exam. 기말고사에서 컨닝하지마라.
feel[be] cheated	공정하게 대접을 받지 못하다
	I couldn't just let someone **get cheated** like that. 누군가 저렇게 배신당했다고 느끼게 놔둘 수가 없었어.

 054

check

n. 조사, 점검, 수표, (식당) 계산서 **v.** 제지하다, 확인하다, (짐)부치다, 체크인[아웃]하다

check	확인
	I get a cancer **check** once a year. 일년에 한번 암 검사를 해.
check	수표 *Check, please하게 되면 계산서 달라는 말이 된다.
	I'll pay **by check.** 수표로 낼게요.
	I'm going to pay for this **with a check.** 이거 수표로 낼게요.
	I'm sorry, we don't **accept checks** here. 죄송하지만 저희는 수표를 받지 않습니다.
check	확인하다
	Do you want me to **check** again? 다시 확인해볼까요?
	Where can I go to **check** my e-mail? 어디 가서 이메일을 볼 수 있나요?
Let me check~	…을 확인해볼게
	Let me check your blood pressure. 혈압 좀 재볼게요.

check if [whether]~

…인지 확인하다 *check to see if S+V

Could you check if she's still a virgin?
걔가 아직 처녀인지 확인해줄래?

check

(짐을) 부치다, (호텔 등에) 체크인(~in), 체크아웃하다(~out)

How many pieces of luggage are you checking?
부치실 짐이 몇 개 인가요?

How can I get to the check-in counter?
탑승수속 카운터는 어디로 가나요?

She's checking the coats.
걘 코트 맡기고 있어요.

double check

다시 확인하다

Be sure to double-check the alarm system.
반드시 경보장치를 다시 한번 점검해.

check in

(호텔 등에) 체크인하다, 입국수속하다, (가방) 맡기다

He checked in yesterday and paid with a credit card.
그 분은 어제 투숙했고 카드로 결제했어요.

check into

입원하다, 체크인하다, 조사하다

My father just checked into the hospital yesterday.
아버지가 어제 병원에 입원하셨어.

I need you to check into her background.
걔의 배경을 조사해봐.

check out

확인(조사)하다, 바라보다, (호텔)체크아웃하다, (책을) 대출하다

I'll check it out. 내가 확인해볼게.

Hey, check out that girl! She is really hot!
야, 저 여자애 봐봐! 정말 섹시하다!

Your wife checked out.
부인께서 퇴실하셨어요.

check on sb[sth]

…을 확인하다(제대로 되었는지, 안전한 지 등을)

Jack ran forward to check on what's going on.
잭은 무슨 일인지 확인해보려고 뛰어갔어.

check over

자세히 검토하다(특히 전문가들이)

It's time you had the doctor checked over.
의사의 검사를 받아야지.

check with	…에게 물어보다 *check with sb about sth …에게 …에 관해 물어보다
	You'd better **check with** the boss. 사장님께 확인해봐.
	Did you **check with** security? 경비에게 확인했어?
check up	조사하다, 확인하다, 의사가 건강진단하다 *check-up 건강진단
	I'm going to go **check up** on your friend. 네 친구가 어떤지 가봐야겠어요.
	The doctor can **check up** on him here. 의사는 여기서도 건강진단을 할 수 있어.
	I get a dental **check-up** every six months. 난 6개월마다 치과건강진단을 받아.

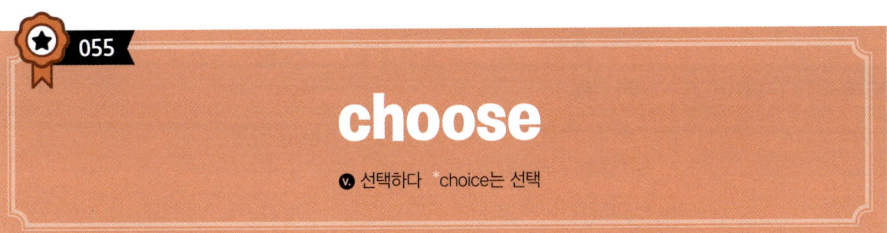

choose

선택하다 *choice는 선택

choose between [from~]	…사이에서 고르다
	I can't **choose between** you two! I love you both so much! 너희 둘 중 선택못해! 둘 다 정말 사랑해!
choose sby as[for]	…로 선택하다
	Jill **was chosen as** the president of our class. 질은 반장으로 뽑혔어.
choose sby[sth]	…을 선택하다
	Well, of course I **choose** you. 저기, 물론 널 고르지.
	Have you **chosen** your dessert? 디저트를 골랐어?
choose to ~	…하기로 선택하다
	He **chose to** live alone. 걘 혼자 살기로 했어.
	I **chose not to** hear that. 그 말 듣지 않기로 했어.

pick and choose	엄선하다, 신중히 고르다
	You can **pick and choose** the food you like at the buffet. 부페에서 원하는 음식을 고를 수 있어.
have a choice	선택권이 있다
	I didn't **have a choice.** 난 선택권이 없었어. I don't think you **have a choice.** 넌 선택권이 없어. What **choice** do I **have?** 내게 있는 선택권은 뭐야?
have no choice but to~	…할 수 밖에 없다
	I **had no choice but to** get divorced. 난 이혼할 수밖에 없었어.
make a choice	선택하다
	We are all responsible for **the choices** we **make.** 우리는 우리가 선택한거에 책임을 진다.
be sby's choice	…의 선택이다
	Your choice, but you can't have both. 네가 결정해, 하지만 두개를 다 가질 순 없어. I mean it **was your choice.** 내 말은 그건 네 선택이었어.

# 056

class

n. 학급, 수업, 특정해의 동창생, 계층, 등급 **a.** 일류의 **v.** 분류하다

take a class (in~)	…을 수업을 듣다, 공부하다　*miss a class 수업을 빼먹다
	We're gonna **take a French class.** 우리는 프랑스어 수업을 들을거야. I never **missed a class** before last night. 지난밤에 첨으로 수업을 빼먹었어.
have a class at+시간	…시에 수업이 있다
	We don't **have a class** today? 오늘은 휴강이에요?

choose

have got a English class (+시간)	…시에 영어수업이 있다
	I'm tired, but I **have got an English class at** 7 o'clock. 피곤하지만 7시에 영어수업이 있어.

skip a class	수업을 빼먹다
	That means I can **skip a class** this week. 그건 내가 이번주에 수업을 빼먹어도 된다는 말이네.

the class of 2010	2010년도 같이 공부한 동창생
	Now please join me in welcoming **the class of 2010**. 자 이제 함께 2010학년도 졸업생을 환영하도록 합시다.

be classed as~	…로 분류되다
	The waste from the plant **was classed as** toxic. 그 공장 폐기물은 독성물질로 분류되었어.

clean

ⓥ 청소하다, 정리하다 *cleaning ⓝ 청소

clean sth	…을 청소하다
	I just **cleaned** the bathroom. 방금 화장실을 청소했어.

clean up	…을 청소하다
	I'm just cleaning up. 막 청소 시작했어
	Can you help me **clean this up?** 이거 청소하는거 도와줄테야?

clean out	깨끗이 정리하다, 깨끗이 비우다
	Tammy **is cleaning out** the fridge. 태미는 냉장고를 깨끗이 정리하고 있어.
	My mother **is cleaning out** the trash container. 어머니가 쓰레기통을 깨끗이 비우고 계셔.

get sth cleaned	…을 청소하다, 깨끗이 하다
	Where can I get my dress cleaned? 어디서 내 옷을 깨끗이 할 수 있죠?

do the cleaning	청소하다 *cleaning lady 파출부
	What did you do after you've done the cleaning? 청소를 한 후에 뭘 했어?

058

clear

ⓐ 분명한, 확실한, 깨끗한　ⓥ 치우다, 내보내다, 혐의를 벗기다

make oneself clear	자기 의사를 분명히 하다
	Do I make myself clear? 내 말이 무슨 말인지 알겠어?
	Let me make myself clear. This is a mistake. 분명히 말하는데 이것은 실수야.

Is that clear?	알아들었어?
	No one is allowed inside. **Is that clear?** 아무도 안에 들어오면 안돼. 알아들었어?

be clear about	…에 대해 분명히 하다
	I thought I made it **clear about** all the extra work and everything. 모든 추가작업과 기타 등등에 대해 명확히 한 걸로 아는데.

be clear to sb	…에게 분명해지다　*make it clear to~ …에게 …을 확실히 하다
	How do I **make it clear to** my girlfriend? 어떻게 내 여친에게 그걸 확실히 하지?
	Are the regulations **clear to** you? 규정은 정확히 알아들었어?

clear sth up	문제를 해결하다, 미스터리를 해결하다, 청소하다
	We'll **clear it up.** I promise. 우리가 해결할게. 약속해.
	We just want to **clear up** a few things. 우린 단지 몇 가지를 정리하고 싶어.

clean

clear one's throat

목을 가다듬다

Professor Gumm **cleared his throat** before starting.
검 교수는 시작하기 전에 목을 가다듬었다.

059 close

ⓐ 가까운, 친근한, 유사한 ⓥ 닫다, 끝내다, 폐업하다

be close

근접하다, …와 가깝다(with), (정답) 거의 맞추다

You're **close.** [That's **close.**]
(정답에) 거의 근접했어.

I know you two **are close.**
두 사람이 가까운 거 알아.

close call

(위험 등에) 아슬아슬한 상황

That was **a close call.** 하마터면 큰일날 뻔했네, 위험천만이었어.

not even close

어림도 없다

You're **not even close.** 근처도 못 갔어.

get close

가까워지다 *stay close 가까이 있다

Alright, we're **getting closer.** 잘했어, 점점 가까워져.

Get closer. 가까이 와봐.

I told him to **stay close,** as usual.
걔보고 평상시처럼 가까이 있으라고 했어.

come close to

…에 거의 필적하다, …할 뻔하다, 가까이 오다

I **came close to** hitting my brother.
내가 내 형을 칠뻔했어.

His advice **came close to** home.
걔의 충고가 가슴에 와 닿았어.

bring ~ to a close

끝내다, 결정내리다

Let's **bring** this matter **to a close.**
이 문제에 대해 결정을 내리자.

close sth	…을 닫다, 마치다 Do you mind if I **close** the window? 창문을 닫아도 될까요? I'm sorry, but we**'re closed**. 죄송하지만 문 닫았는데요.
close up	닫다, 마무리하다 **Close up.** It's cold. 닫어. 추워. Will you **close up** for me? Thank you everyone. 마무리 해주시겠어요? 모두 수고했어요.
close down	닫다, 폐쇄하다 I**'m closing down** my office. I've lost all my clients. 사무실 문 닫을거야. 모든 고객을 잃었어.
close a deal	거래를 마무리하다 You told me you were going to Chicago to **close a deal**. 거래를 마무리하기 위해 시카고에 간다고 했잖아.
가게+**close at~**	…에 문을 닫다 That store **closes at** 7, come on. 저 상점은 7시면 닫아. 가자. Macy's **closes at** 7:30. 메이시 백화점은 7시 30분에 문 닫아.

060
cold
a. 추운, 차가운 **n.** 추위, 감기

stand outside in the cold	추운데 밖에 서 있다 If you **stand outside in the cold** you'll get sick. 추운데 밖에 서 있으면 병에 걸릴거야.
have (got) a cold	감기에 걸리다 She is at home because she **has a bad cold**. 걔 독감이 걸려서 집에 있어.

close

catch a cold	감기에 걸리다
	Stay inside or you'll **catch a cold**. 안에 들어가 있어 아니면 감기걸린다.
leave sb out in the cold	…을 냉대하다
	He **was left out in the cold** when the plan changed. 계획이 바뀔 때 걘 소외되었어.

061

come
v. 오다

come to+V	…하게 되다 (…하러 오다)
	She **came to** realize that she was stupid. 걘 자기가 멍청하다는 걸 깨닫게 되었다.
How come S+V?	어떻게 … 된거야?
	How come she didn't show up last night? 걔는 왜 어젯밤 안 왔대?
Here~ comes	여기 …가 온다
	Here comes the cocktail waitress. 칵테일 웨이트리스가 오네.
Come again?	뭐라고? = (I'm) Sorry? = Excuse me?
	Come again? I didn't hear you well. 뭐라고? 잘 못들었어.
come here to +V	…하러 여기에 오다
	I **came here to** let you know that I love you. 널 사랑한다는 걸 말하려고 왔어.
	Did you really **come here to** tell me about that? 정말 그거 말하려고 온거야?
come true	실현되다, 이루어지다
	I'm sure your wish is going to **come true**. 네 소망이 실현될거라고 확신해.

when it comes to+N	…에 관한 한 I've had some bad luck **when it comes to** relationships. 관계맺는 것에 관한 한 난 운이 없었어.
come to think of it	생각해보니 말야 **Come to think of it,** I don't need it anymore. 생각해보니, 난 그게 더 이상 필요하지 않아.
come first	…가 우선이다 What **comes first?** 뭐가 가장 소중해?
come and go	오고가다, 들락날락하다, 오락가락하다, 왔다가다 I have stomach aches. They **come and go** like every few minutes. 배가 아픈데 몇 분마다 통증이 왔다갔다해.
come as a schok	충격으로 받아들이다 Did that **come as a shock** to you? 이게 너한테 충격이었어?
come close to +N[~ing]	거의 …할 뻔하다 *come close to home 가슴에 와 닿다 His advice **comes close to** home. 그 사람의 충고가 가슴에 와닿았어.
come apart	산산히 찢어지다, 실패하기 시작하다 The right front tire started to **come apart.** 오른쪽 앞 타이어가 찢어지기 시작했어.
come across	우연히 만나다 = run across, bump into How did you **come across** this information? 이 정보는 어떻게 찾은거야?
come along	일이 진행되다, 함께 가다(~with sby) *Come along! 자, 어서! How **are** you **coming along with** your project? 네 프로젝트 어떻게 돼가? Can you **come along with** me to the post office? 우체국까지 같이 갈테야?
come around	들르다, 의식을 되찾다, 결국 …에 동의하다 How come you never **come around** anymore? 왜 넌 더 이상 들르지 않는거야? She **came around** here before? 걔 전에 여기 와본 적 있어?

come

come back to sby[sth]

돌아오다, …에게로 돌아가다, 회복되다 *come back to+V하면 …하기 위해 돌아가다

He didn't come back to help you.
걘 널 도와주기 위해 돌아오지 않았어.

come by

잠깐 들르다(drop by, stop by, swing by), 손에 넣다

Come by first in the morning if you can.
가능하면 내일 아침 들러.

come down

떨어지다, 혼내다, (병에) 걸리다(~with)

If you don't come down, I'm coming up.
네가 내려오지 않으면 내가 올라간다.

He's coming down with a really bad cold.
정말 심한 독감에 걸렸거든요.

come from

…의 출신이다, …로부터 오다[생기다]

This is a great bed. Where did it come from?
멋진 침대네. 이거 어디서 난거야?

Where does it come from?
왜 그런 말을 하는거야?

come in

들어오다, 유행하다 *come into는 …로 들어가다, …상태가 되다, (재산 등을) 물려받다

Come in and eat with us.
들어와서 우리랑 같이 먹자.

The shirts came in many colors.
이 셔츠는 여러 색깔로 나와.

You've recently come into a great deal of money.
넌 최근에 많은 돈을 물려받았지.

come off

떼어내다, 떨어지다, 예정대로 되다, 성공하다

Come off it! You were hitting on him!
그만해! 넌 걔한테 집적되고 있었잖아!

come on

(어떤 일이) 닥치다 *감탄사로는 힘내, 자 어서, 서둘레, 그러지마! *come on to 유혹하다

Why don't you come on in? 들어와.

So you're coming on to me!
너 나한테 추근거리고 있잖아!

come out

(사정, 결과) 밝혀지다, 출간되다, 나오다

When is that movie going to come out?
그 영화는 언제 나오는거야?

There's no way we come out of this.
우리가 여기서 벗어날 길이 없어.

come over
잠시 들르다[방문하다] *Sth come over sby하면 …가 …를 엄습한다

What's come over you?
대체 왜 이러는거요?

Hey, come over to my house Thursday.
야, 목요일날 우리 집에 와.

come through
통과하다, 해내다, (위기, 병)극복하다, 기대에 부응하다

She will come through this.
걘 이겨낼거야.

come to
…에 오다, …상황에 이르다 *come to an end는 끝나다, come to the conclusion은 결론에 이르다, come to a close는 끝내다

Did the movie finally come to an end?
드디어 영화 끝났어?

Well, let's hope it doesn't come to that.
저렇게 되지 않도록 희망하자.

I don't know how it's come to this.
그게 어떻게 이렇게 되었는지 몰라.

come up
올라오다, 다가개[오]다, 발생하다, (어떤 일이) 일어나다

Can you come up to my office for a second?
잠시 사무실로 올라올래?

She has a birthday coming up.
걔 생일이 다가와.

Something's come up. 예상치 못한 일이 생겼어.

come up with
…을 고안해내다[따라잡다]

I've tried and tried, but I can't come up with a solution.
계속 해봤는데, 답이 안 나와.

So how did you come up with this?
그래 이건 어떻게 생각해냈어?

come with
…와 함께 나오다, …와 함께 가다 *Sth comes with~ 하게 되면 이 제품(음식)에는 …이 달려 나온다

Who's coming with me? 같이 갈 사람?

What comes with that? 그거하고 딸린게 뭐야?

come

company

n. 회사, 손님, 함께 있는 사람들

have company	손님이 있다	
	We're going to **have company** this weekend. 우린 이번 주말 일행이 있을거야.	
	In a minute, Sweetheart. We **have company** right now. 조금 있다가, 자기야. 지금은 일행이 있어.	
expect company	손님이 오기로 되어 있다	
	I didn't **expect company** today. 오늘 같이 올 사람은 없었어.	
keep sby company	친구가 되어주다, 같이 있어주다	
	Would you **keep me company?** 나하고 같이 이야기하면서 있을래?	
keep company with sby	…와 함께 시간을 보내다	
	Wasn't Vicky **keeping company with** him? 비키는 그와 함께 있지 않았어?	

continue

v. 계속하다

continue	계속하다
	The birthday party **continues.** 파티는 계속되고 있어.
continue sth	…을 계속하다
	She hopes to **continue** her relationship with us. 걘 우리와의 관계를 계속하기를 바라고 있어.

continue to [-ing]	···을 계속하다 We **continue to** wait for the latest information. 우린 최신 정보를 계속 기다리고 있어. She **continued** talking on the phone. 걘 계속 전화로 얘기하고 있어.
continue with	···을 계속하다 Will you **continue with** your presentation? 발표를 계속해주실래요? I've decided I want to **continue with** the meeting. 난 회의를 계속하기로 결정했어.

064 cook
v. 요리하다 cook n. 요리사

cook sby sth (sth for sby)	···에게 요리해주다 I'll **cook** you dinner. 저녁 만들어줄게 My wife loves to **cook for** our children. 아내는 애들에게 요리해주는 걸 좋아해.
cook sth (for supper[dinner, lunch)	저녁[점심]으로 ···을 요리하다 We can go sailing and **cook** big lobsters. 우린 배타고 나가서 랍스터를 요리할 수 있어. You know how to **cook** it. 그거 어떻게 요리하는지 알잖아.
cook (sby) a meal[dinner, breakfast]	(···에게) 식사를 요리하다 How about I **cook dinner** at my place? 내가 우리 집에서 저녁을 하는 건 어때? She's **cooking Thanksgiving dinner**. 걘 추수감사절 만찬을 요리하고 있어.
cook up	요리를 빨리 준비하다, 변명, 이유 등을 빨리 고안하다 We just **cooked it up.** 어, 방금 지어낸거야. The evidence **was cooked.** 증거는 조작됐어.

What's cooking?	무슨 일이야?
	Come on. Let's see **what's cooking.** 이봐, 무슨 일인지 살펴보자.

065 cool

ⓐ 시원한, 침착한, 멋진 ⓥ 침착해지다

be cool with~	…가 좋다
	He's **not cool with** me moving in. 걔는 내가 이사 들어오는 걸 싫어해.
keep cool	침착하다 = stay cool
	Don't get too worked up, stay calm, **stay cool.** 흥분하지말고 진정해.
	All right! Everybody, **keep cool,** all right? 좋아! 모두들 차분해. 알았어?
lose one's cool	어려운 상황에서 흥분하다 ↔ keep one's cool 침착하다
	Sorry about the other day, kinda **lost my cool.** 요전날 미안했어. 좀 흥분했어.
cool down	진정하다, 진정시키다
	Okay, let's everybody just **cool down.** 자, 모두들 진정합시다.
	I'll give you a call when things **cool down.** 상황이 진정되면 네게 전화할게.
cool it	화를 가라앉히다, 차분해라
	Look, maybe we should just **cool it** for a while. 잠시 좀 진정하자고.

 066

cost

n. 비용, 가격, 원가, 희생, 손해 **v.** 가격이 …이다

cover the cost (of)	…의 비용을 대다
	Who's going to **cover the cost of** repairs? 수리비는 누가 댈거야?
	I'll **pay the cost of** a new computer. 새로운 컴퓨터 값 내가 댈게.
at all costs	어떤 희생을 치르더라도(at any cost)
	Your daughter needs to attend school **at all costs.** 네 딸은 어떻게 해서라도 학교에 가야 돼.
cost sby money	…에게 …의 비용이 들게 하다
	Your mistake **cost me a lot of money.** 네 실수 땜에 돈 많이 까먹었어.
	That's going to **cost you $5,000.** 5천 달러 들거야.
cost sby sth	…에게 …을 희생하게 하다, 잃게 하다
	It will **cost you your job.** 네 직장을 내놔야 할거야.
cost a fortune	비용이 엄청 들다
	It's so pretty. This must have **cost him a fortune.** 정말 예쁘네. 걔 돈 많이 들어갔겠다.
	It **must have cost you an arm and a leg** to buy it. 그거 사는데 돈 엄청 들어갔을거야.
How much does it cost to +V?	…하는데 비용이 얼마 들어요?
	How much does it cost? 이거 가격이 얼마예요?
	How much does it cost to fly to New York first-class? 뉴욕에 일등석으로 가면 얼마나 들어?

count

v. 세다, 포함하다

count
세다

Let me **count** the change in my pocket.
주머니에 있는 잔돈 세어볼게.

count to+숫자
…까지 세다

I said, "**Count to** ten!" 열까지 세라고 했어.

You **count to** five and you turn around!
다섯까지 세고 뒤로 돌아!

count sby (in[out])
포함[제외]하다

That sounds good. You can **count me in.**
좋아. 나도 끼워줘.

She's very upset with me. You can **count me out!**
걔 내게 무척 화났어. 난 빼줘!

count [for]
중요하다

Does that **count for** something?
그게 뭐 중요해?

Every minute[moment] **counts.**
모든 순간은 중요해.

It's ~ that counts
중요한 것은 …이다

It's the thought **that counts.**
중요한 건 생각이야.

count as
간주하다

It may **count as** a present. What do you think?
그건 선물로 간주될 수도 있어. 어떻게 생각해?

count on
…을 믿다, 의지하다

You can **count on** me.
나한테 맡겨.

Don't **count on** it. It's not going to happen.
믿지마. 그렇게 안될거야.

 068

cover

v 숨기다, 다루다, 보험에 들다, 은폐하다, …대신 일하다

cover sth[sby]
숨기다, 다루다, (보험에) 들다

Don't **cover** your mouth when you do that!
그거 할 때 입가리지마!

Haven't you and I **covered** that topic?
너하고 내가 그 문제를 다루지 않았어?

You know your insurance will **cover** that.
그거 보험으로 처리될 수 있다는 거 알잖아.

cover up
은폐하다, 감추다

You're making up new lies to **cover up** the old ones.
넌 지난 거짓말을 숨기기 위해 새로운 거짓말을 꾸며대고 있어.

cover for
…대신 일하다

Can you **cover for** me? I've got a date.
내 대신 좀 해줄테야? 데이트가 있었어.

That's it! I'm tired of **covering for** you two!
됐어! 너희 둘 대신 일봐주는데 지쳤어!

be covered with[in]
…로 가득차다

Tom **was covered with** snow when he came in.
탐은 들어올 때 눈으로 덮여있었어.

The children **were covered in** dirt after playing.
애들은 놀고 난 후에 먼지로 뒤범벅이 되었어.

Check it Out !

A: Make sure you ask John to **cover your shift** tomorrow.
B: Thanks for reminding me.

A: 존에게 내일 너 대신 교대근무를 해달라고 확실히 부탁해 놔.
B: 상기시켜 줘서 고마워.

credit

n. 신용거래, 융자금, 칭찬, 인정　**v.** 입금하다, …의 공으로 믿다, …로 여기다

buy sth on credit	외상으로 사다 I'd like to **buy it on credit**. 신용카드로 낼게요.
take credit for~	…에 대한 공을 가로채다 I am not gonna let you continue to **take credit for** all of my hard work. 내가 고생했는데 그 공을 네가 차지하도록 가만히 있지 않을거야.
give sby credit for sth	…에게 …에 대한 공을 인정하다 You have to **give me credit for** an original date. 독창적인 데이트를 한데 대해 나한테 공을 돌려야만해.
be a credit to~	…의 자랑거리이다　*be credited to~ …의 공이다 Chris **is a credit to** his university. 크리스는 걔 대학의 자랑거리야. The telephone's invention **is credited to** Edison. 전화기발명은 에디슨의 공이다.
be credited to your account	…가 계좌에 입금되다 The refund will **be credited to your account**. 환불금은 당신 계좌에 입금될 것입니다.

cut

n. 감소, 삭감, 벤상처　**v.** 베다, 자르다, 수량을 줄이다

cut corners	(시간, 경비 등을) 절약하다 I had to **cut corners** to save money. 돈을 저축하려고 절약해야 했어.

cut a deal	계약을 성사시키다
	I **cut Sally a deal** when she came to my shop. 샐리가 내 가게에 왔을 때 계약을 성사시켰어.
be cut out for~	…할 자질이 있다, …에 적합하다
	She's **cut out for** this job. 걘 이 일을 하는데 적합해.
	You're **not cut out to** be a physician. 넌 의사로서 적합한 사람은 아냐.
cut back on	줄이다
	It would be a good idea if we **cut back on** expenses. 경비를 줄인다면 좋은 생각일거야.
	We're going to **cut back on** shopping too. 쇼핑도 역시 줄일거야.
cut down on	줄이다, 삭감하다
	She's trying to get me to **cut down on** sugar. 걘 내가 설탕섭취를 줄이도록 하고 있어.
cut it out	잘라내다
	Don't do that! **Cut it out!** 그러지마! 그만둬!
	This is useless. We're going to have to **cut it out.** 이건 필요없어. 잘라내야 돼.
cut off	잘라내다, 중단하다
	I **was cut off.** 전화가 끊기다.
	I don't mean to **cut you off.** 말을 끊으려고 했던 건 아니에요.

071

damage

ⓝ 손해, 피해, pl. 손해배상금 ⓥ 손해를 입히다, 훼손하다

do damage	손해를 끼치다
	It could **do some serious damage to** our firm's image. 그건 우리 회사의 이미지에 꽤 심각한 피해를 줄 수 있어.

The damage is done	이미 일어난 일이야 Look at the bright side. **The damage is done.** 긍정적인 면을 봐라. 이미 손해를 봤잖아.
brain damage	뇌손상 Don's **brain damage** was caused by a head injury. 돈의 뇌손상은 머리 부상에서 기인한거야.
What's the damage?	얼마예요?, 피해규모가 어때? That was a good meal. **What's the damage?** 식사 맛있었어요. 얼마죠?
Sth has been damaged	…가 훼손되었다 *강조하려면 badly, seriously 등의 부사를 삽입한다. The building **has been damaged by** the fire. 그 빌딩은 화재로 파손되었어.

date

ⓝ 날, 약속[데이트], 데이트 상대 ⓥ 날짜를 적다, 데이트하다

set a date	날짜를 정하다 Well, make sure you let me know when you **set a date.** 그럼, 날짜가 잡히면 내게 꼭 알려줘야 돼.
have a date with sby	…와 데이트가 있다 I'**ve got a date with** Jane this evening. 오늘 저녁에 제인이랑 데이트하기로 했거든.
go (out) on a date (with sby)	…와 데이트를 하다 You **went on a date with** my boyfriend! 내 남친하고 데이트했지! I **went on a date with** Alan last night. 지난 밤에 앨런하고 데이트했어.
date	데이트 하는 사람, 상대, 데이트 I'm not sure if **this date** will be successful. 이번 데이트가 성공할런지 잘 모르겠어.

make a date with sby[to+V]	만날 주선을 하다 I **made a date with** Ann **to** see a movie. 난 앤과 데이트하면서 영화보기로 했어.
to date	지금까지 = until now **To date,** she hasn't been here. 현재까지 걘 여기에 오지 않았어.
out of date	구식의 *up to date 최신의 This is the most **up to date** computer software. 이건 가장 최신 컴퓨터소프트웨어야.
date sby	…와 데이트하다 That's because you'**re dating** Scott. 그건 네가 스캇하고 데이트하기 때문야.
date back to sth	…까지 거슬러 올라가다 The Chinese furniture **dates back to** the last century. 이 중국가구는 지난 세기 것이야.

073 day
n. 날, 요일, 낮

day-to-day	하루하루의, 일상의 How are the **day to day** operations going around here? 매일 하는 일은 잘되나?
daytime	주간의 Which do you prefer, nighttime or **daytime?** 밤과 낮 중에어 어떤 게 더 좋아?
every other day	이틀에 한번씩 He exercises in the gym **every other day.** 걘 격일로 체육관에서 운동을 해.

date

have one's day	때를 만나다, 전성기를 누리다
	Life is tough, but you'll **have your day.**
	인생은 험하지만, 넌 때를 만나게 될거야.
in one's day	한창 때에는
	I've been with many women **in my day.**
	내가 젊었을 때에는 많은 여성들과 놀았어.
later in the day	(그날 중으로) 나중에, 그날 늦게 *rest of the day 남은 하루
	Please call her **later in the day.**
	오후늦게 걔에게 전화해.
	Take the rest of the day off and go home.
	오늘은 그만 하고 집에 가지 그래.
some[one] day	언젠가
	Maybe **one day** you will change your mind!
	언젠가는 네 마음이 바뀔거야!
the day after tomorrow	모레 *the day before yesterday 그저께
	Work will commence again **the day after tomorrow.**
	근무는 내일모레 다시 시작될거야.
these days	요즈음
	Everything's fine **these days.** What's new with you?
	잘 지내고 있어. 너는?

074
deal
n. 거래, 취급   **v.** 거래하다, 취급하다, 다루다

a great deal (of~)	많은(…)
	We earn **a great deal of** money working for a company.
	우린 회사에서 일하면서 많은 돈을 벌고 있어.

a deal	거래
	(That's a) **Deal.** 좋아, 그렇게 하자.
	A deal's a deal. 약속한 거야.
	Here's a[the] deal. 이렇게 하자, 이런거야.
	It's a deal? 그럴래?, 좋아?
	(It's a) **Done deal.** 그러기로 한거야.
have a deal	합의하다
	We **have a deal?** 동의하니?, 그럴래?
	I thought we **had a deal.** 얘기가 다 됐다고 생각했는데.
make a deal	거래하다, 타협하다
	I'll **make a deal with** you. 너와 거래할게.
	Let's **make a deal.** 이렇게 하자.
make a big deal out of	…을 과장하다
	Don't **make a big deal out of** it. 과장하지마.
be no big deal	큰 일이 아니다
	What's the big deal? 별거 아니네?, 무슨 큰 일이라도 난거야?
	Don't worry! **It's no big deal.** 걱정 마! 별거 아냐.
deal with	…을 다루다
	He's a difficult man to **deal with.** 걔는 거래하기 어려운 사람야.
	Deal with it. 정신차려, 왜 이렇게 눈치가 없어.
	I can **deal with** it. 가능해.
	I can't **deal with** the raw stuff. 날 음식은 못 먹어.

decide

v. 결정하다　decision 결심, 결정

decide sth
···을 결정하다

They're just trying to **decide** something.
걔네들은 뭔가 결정하려고 하고 있어.

Okay, so how do we **decide** that?
좋아, 그걸 어떻게 결정하지?

decide to+V
···하기로 결정하다

I'**ve decided to** break up with Helen.
나 헬렌하고 헤어지기로 했어.

decide that ~
···하기로 결정하다

I **decided** I wanted to come to your party.
네 파티에 가기로 결정했어.

decide what~ [what to~]
···을 결정하다

Now let's **decide who** has the nicest ass.
자 이제 누구 엉덩이가 가장 멋진지 결정하자.

decide (up)on
···으로 결정하다

She is trying to **decide on** a new couch for his place.
걘 집에 놓을 새로운 소파를 결정하려고 해.

You need to **decide on** which university you'll attend.
어느 대학에 진학 할건지 결정해야 돼.

You decide
네가 결정해

You decide when.
언제 만날지 네가 결정해.

I don't know what I'm going to do. **You decide.**
어떻게 해야 할지 모르겠어. 네가 결정해.

make a decision
결정하다

She's trying to **make a decision** about something.
걘 뭔가 결정을 하려고 해.

deserve

v. …할 자격이 있다

deserve sth

…을 받을 만하다

Does she not **deserve** love?
걘 사랑받을 자격이 없어?

I just think you **deserve** some respect.
넌 존경을 받을 만하다고 생각해.

deserve more than~

…을 받을 자격이 되고도 남는다

You **deserve more than that.**
넌 그럴 자격이 되고도 충분해.

deserve that [this, it]

그럴 자격이 된다

You don't **deserve this.**
넌 이럴 자격이 없어.

If you want to punch me, go ahead, I **deserve it.**
날 치고 싶으면 어서 쳐. 맞아도 싸.

deserve to~

…할 자격이 되다

It's Saturday night. They **deserve to** have a little fun.
토요일 밤이야. 걔네들 좀 즐겨도 돼.

Your colleague **deserved to** win.
네 동료들이 승리할 자격이 돼.

die

v. 죽다　dead **a.** 죽은　death **n.** 죽음

die of[from]
…으로 죽다

My dad **died of** a heart attack when I was a kid.
아버지는 내가 어렸을 때 심장마비로 돌아가셨어.

be dying for sth
몹시 …을 하고 싶어하다

It's not worth you **dying for** it.
네가 그것을 하고 싶어할 가치가 없어.

be dying to+V
몹시 …를 하고 싶어하다

I can't believe how much I**'m dying to** see her.
정말이지 갤 보고 싶어 죽겠어.

to die for
너무 좋아서 몹시 갖고 싶은

You look wonderful! That dress is **to die for.**
너 멋져 보여! 그 옷 정말로 탐난다.

would rather die~
차라리 죽겠다

I**'d rather die than** go back.
돌아가느니 죽는게 낫겠어.

never say die
죽는 소리 하지마라

Never say die. Just keep on trying and eventually you'll succeed. 기운차리라고, 계속 시도하다 보면 결국 성공할테니까.

go dead
장비가 죽다, 저리다

My battery **went dead** and it stopped working.
배터리가 다 돼서 작동이 안돼.

drop dead
돌연사하다

Do me a favor and tell Jack that he can **drop dead!**
부탁인데 잭에게 돌연사할 수도 있다고 말해줘!

deadly
치명적인

We are taught that there are seven **deadly** sins.
우린 7개의 치명적인 죄가 있다고 가르침을 받았어.

 078

difference

n. 차이, pl.불화 *different **a.** 다른 *differ **v.** 다르다

---

difference between~

···사이의 차이

What's the **difference between** English and French?
영어와 프랑스어의 차이점이 뭐야?

major[minor] difference

큰[사소한] 차이

Having a new computer made **a major difference.**
새로운 컴퓨터를 갖게 되는 건 큰 차이가 있었어.

settle[resolve] one's differences

불화를 해소하다

You and I can **settle our differences** on the court.
우리는 법으로 우리 문제점을 해결할 수 있어.

tell the difference

차이점을 구분하다

I can never **tell the difference** between the two.
난 그 두 개의 차이점을 절대 구분못할거야.

make a difference

차이가 나다

Time won't **make a difference.**
시간이 흐른다고 달라지지 않을거야.

make no difference

차이가 나지 않다, 문제가 아니다

I don't really give a damn, it **makes no difference** to me.
난 정말 알바아냐, 나한테는 전혀 상관없는 일인데.

be different from[to]

···와 다르다

This food **is different from** the type I normally eat.
이 음식은 내가 통상적으로 먹는 타입과 다른 거야.

difference

079

discuss

v. 토의하다 discussion 토의, 논의

discuss with sby	…와 토의하다
	What did you want to **discuss with** me? 나와 무슨 얘기를 하고 싶었어?

discuss sth with sby	…와 함께 …을 토의하다
	My boss says I'm good at **discussing things with** clients. 사장은 내가 고객들을 잘 응대한대.

can't discuss sth	…는 말 못한다
	She **can't discuss** this with her parents. 그녀는 부모님과 이걸 상의는 못해.

have a discussion with	…와 토의하다
	We need to **have a discussion with** the landlord. 우리는 집주인과 상의를 해야겠어.

End of discussion	얘기 끝, 더이상 왈가왈부하지마
	You get money, you get laid. **End of discussion.** 돈이 있으면 섹스해. 더이상 말마.

080

do

v. 하다

do well (with~)	(…을) 잘하다
	You **did it very well.** 아주 잘 했어요. You'**re doing great!** Don't you give up! 너 잘하고 있어! 포기하지마!

사물주어+will do	족하다, 쓸만하다 = That'll be fine, That's fine
	Anything **will do.** 뭐든 됐어.
	Either **will do.** 아무거나 괜찮아.

do a good job	일을 잘하다 *Good job! 잘했어!, Good for you! 잘됐다!
	You **did a good job!** I was very impressed.
	정말 잘 했어! 매우 인상적이었어.

do one's job	…의 일을 하다
	I**'m just doing my job.** 내 일을 할 뿐인데.
	I **do my job,** you **do yours.** 난 내 일을 하니까 넌 네 일을 해.
	Do your job right. 일에 차질없이 제대로 해.

do one's best	최선을 다하다
	I **did my best to** do my homework
	난 최선을 다해서 숙제를 했어.

do one's hair	머리손질하다
	I**'m doing my hair.** 머리 손질 중이에요.

do wrong	잘못하다
	What **am** I **doing wrong?**
	내가 지금 뭘 잘못하고 있는거지?

do (sby) a favor	…에게 호의를 베풀다
	Could you **do me a favor** and bring me a drink?
	부탁인데 마실 것 좀 갖다 줄테야?

do sb good	…에게 도움이 되다
	Fresh air will **do you good.**
	신선한 공기가 도움될거야.

do sth	뭔가를 하다
	Tom, can you **do something** about this?
	탐, 이거 좀 어떻게 해볼래?
	You guys! We have to **do something!**
	얘들아! 우린 뭔가 해야 돼!

would anything for~	…을 위해서라면 뭐든지 하다
	I**'d do anything for** you. 널 위해서라면 뭐든지 하겠다.

do

I didn't do~	난…하지 않았어
	I didn't do anything. 난 아무 짓도 안 했어.
	I didn't do anything wrong. 난 잘못한 게 없어.

do everything in one's power	힘껏 다하다
	I **did everything in my power.** 내 힘껏 다했어.

do the dishes	요리하다 *do lunch 점심먹다
	Why don't you let her **do the dishes?** 걔가 설거지하게 해.

do the laundry	세탁하다
	Just go **do the laundry.** 가서 세탁해.

be done with	…을 끝내다
	I'**m done with** the work. 일 끝냈어.
	I'**m done with** my choices. 선택했어.
	Are you **done with** this? 이거 끝냈어?

do this[that, it]	…을 하다
	I can't **do this.** 나 이건 못해.
	I can **do it** better. 내가 더 잘 할 수 있어.
	You can't **do that!** 그러면 안되지!
	I'll **do that.** 그렇게 할게.
	You'll **do that.** 그렇게 해.
	You **do that.** 그렇게 해라.
	You can't **do this** to me. 나한테 이러면 안되지, 이러지마.
	I **do this** all the time. 이런 일엔 이골이 났다.

~ I can do	내가 할 수 있는…
	I did all **I could do.** 내가 할 수 있는 건 다했어.
	That's all **I can do.** 그게 내가 할 수 있는 다야.
	It's the least **I can do.** 최소한의 제 성의예요.
	It's the best **I can do.** 그게 내가 할 수 있는 최선야.
	There's nothing more **I can do.** 내가 더 이상 할 수 있는 게 없어.

do with	(어떻게) …을 처리하다, 다루다, …으로 때우다, …가 필요하다(could do with)
	What will Peter **do with** that? 피터가 그걸로 뭘 하겠니?
	I know what to **do with** a woman. 여자를 어떻게 다루는 지를 알아.
do without	…없이 지내다, …은 없어도 좋다(can do without)
	You'll have to **do without** bread for a few days. 넌 며칠간 빵없이 지내야 할거야.
Neither did I	나도 안그랬어
	You had a such a great time? **So did I!** 멋진 시간 보냈다고? 나도 그래!
Why don't you~?	…하자 = I want you to~ *Why don't I~?= Let me~, Why don't we~? = Let's~
	Why don't you stay here and just hang out with me. 여기 남아 나랑 놀자.
	Why don't we get together on Saturday? 토요일에 좀 만나죠.

081

doubt

 의심, 의혹　 v. 의심하다, 믿지 않다

have no doubt that S+V	…할 의심의 여지가 없다
	I **have no doubt** she's highly capable. 난 걔가 출중한 능력을 가진 걸 의심치 않아.
There is no doubt that S+V	…라는거에 의심의 여지가 없다
	There is no doubt about it. 확실히 그래.
	There is no doubt we'll get there on time. 거기에 제시간에 도착할 것은 틀림없어.
No doubt S+V	…일 것이다
	No doubt the neighborhood is dangerous. 이웃이 위험한 것은 의심의 여지가 없어.

do

No doubt (about it)	당연하다
	Chris's having affair with her secretary. **No doubt about it.**
	크리스는 자기 비서하고 불륜을 저지르고 있어. 확실해.

No one doubts~	아무도 …의심하지 않는다
	No one doubts that he is guilty of the crime.
	그가 유죄라는데 아무도 의심하지 않는다.

without a doubt	의심없이
	This is **without a doubt** the dirtiest hotel ever.
	이건 의심의 여지 없이 최악의 더러운 호텔이야.

beyond doubt	의심의 여지없이
	It's **beyond doubt** that she will be back.
	그녀는 분명히 돌아올거야.

I doubt S+V	…가 아닐거라고 생각하다
	I doubt that it's possible.
	그게 가능할거라 생각하지 않아.
	I doubt you will be able to get baseball tickets.
	너 야구 경기 표 구할 수 없을 것 같아.

I doubt very much whether [if]~	…일지 매우 의심스럽다
	I doubt very much whether Jason will learn the truth.
	제이슨이 진실을 알게 될지 매우 의심스러워.

draw

n. 추첨, 무승부, 인기를 끄는거 **v.** 그리다, 끌어당기다, 추첨하다, 비기다, 인출

a draw	무승부(tie), 추첨(draw straws)
	The hockey game ended in **a draw.**
	하키경기는 무승부로 끝났어.

draw (sby) a picture of~	…을 그리다
	She **drew a picture of** you! 걔가 널 그렸어!

draw sby a map	…에게 약도를 그려주다	
	Why don't you **draw me a map to** your office? 네 사무실 약도 좀 그려주라.	
draw a line	선을 긋다, 구분하다, 한계를 두다	
	And that's where I **draw the line.** 그리고 거기가 내 한계를 둔 곳이야.	
draw (sby's) attention to	(…의) 주의를 끌다	
	The guide **drew our attention to** the famous painting. 가이드는 유명 그림에 우리의 주의를 기울이게 했어.	
draw near [closer]	가까이 가다	
	She was shy at first, but she **drew near** later on. 걘 처음엔 수줍어했지만 나중에는 가까이 왔어.	
draw out	끌어내다, 은행에서 인출하다	
	I think you have to **draw him out.** 네가 걜 끌어내야 할 거 같아.	
	She will **drew out** money to pay you back. 걘 네게 돈을 갚기 위해 돈을 인출했어.	
draw up	(문서를) 작성하다, 입안하다	
	It took me two days to **draw up** those plans! 이 계획서 만드는 데 이틀 걸렸어!	
draw back	뒤로 물러서다	
	The group **drew back** from the volcano. 사람들은 화산으로부터 뒤로 물러섰어.	
be drawn to	…에게 끌리다	
	I don't know what it is. I'**m strangely drawn to** him. 난 그게 뭔지 모르겠지만 걔한테 이상하게 끌렸어.	
draw straws	제비뽑기하다	
	You want to **draw straws?** 제비뽑을까?	
	We'll **draw straws** if you want. 원한다면 제비를 뽑을게.	

dress

n. 옷, 드레스 v. 옷을 입(히)다, 상처를 치료하다

in that dress — 그 옷을 입고
You look good **in that dress**. 그 옷 입으니 멋져.

get dressed — 옷을 입다
It only takes us two minutes to **get dressed**.
옷 입는데 2분이면 돼.

dress up — 성장하다, 꾸미다
Why **are** you **all dressed up?** 왜 그렇게 차려 입었어?

undress — 옷을 벗(기)다
They **are** both **getting undressed.** 걔네들은 둘 다 옷을 벗었어.

drink

n. 마실 것, 한 잔, 음료, 술 v. (음료, 술) 마시다, 축배하다(~to)

a drink — 음료, 술
How about **a drink?** 술 한잔 어때?
Drop by for **a drink** (sometime). 언제 술하러 한 번 들러.

have[get] a drink — 한잔 마시다
Let's go **have a drink** together, tonight.
오늘 밤 같이 술 한잔 하러 가자.
He**'s a heavy drinker.** 걘 술을 많이 마셔.
Do you want to go **get a drink** or something?
어디 가서 한잔할래요?

have drinks with~

…와 함께 술을 마시다

She's **having drinks with** her date.
걘 데이트 상대와 술 마시고 있어.

She's out **having drinks with** David.
걘 나가서 데이빗과 술 마시고 있어.

I'll **having drinks with** friends. 난 친구들과 술 마시고 있어.

Let's **get some drinks,** shall we?
술 좀 마시자, 그럴래?

get[buy] sby a drink

…에게 술을 주(사)다

Come on in, Betty. Can I **get you a drink?**
베티야 어서 들어와. 술 한잔 줄까?

Let me **buy you a drink.** 내가 술 살게.

take a drink (of)

(…를) 한잔 마시다

She **took a drink of** wine with Jack.
걘 잭과 와인 한잔을 마셨어.

He's **taking a drink of** water from the bottle.
걘 병에든 물을 마시고 있어.

(go out) for a drink

술마시러 (나가다)

How about **going out for a drink** tonight?
오늘 저녁 한잔 할까?

I want to **take you out for a drink** tonight.
오늘 밤 같이 한잔 했으면 하는데.

How about we **get together for a drink?**
만나서 한잔 어때?

Sally, **join us for a drink?** 샐리, 같이 한잔 할까요?

You want to **meet for a drink?**
만나서 술먹을래?

freshen one's drink

새로 잔에 따르다

May I **freshen your drink?** 잔을 다시 채워줄까요?

drink

마시다

What would you like to **drink?** 뭐 마실래?

What are you **drinking?** 뭐 마실래?

I'd like something to **drink.** 뭐 좀 마시고 싶어.

I don't **drink.** 난 술 안 해.

How much do you usually **drink?** 보통 얼마나 마셔?

drink

drink and drive	음주운전하다
	Don't **drink and drive.** 음주운전 하지마라.
	You're **drunk** right now. 너 지금 취했어.
	I can't drive. I've **been drinking.** 나 운전 못해. 술먹었어.
	I wasn't drinking. I mean I wasn't **under the influence.** 술 안마셨어. 내 말은 술 안 먹었다고.

drink to	…을 위해 건배하다
	I'll **drink to** that! 옳소! 찬성이오!
	Let's **drink to** Mr. Kim's future. 김씨의 미래를 위해 건배하자.

drink coffee [tea, wine]	커피[차, 와인]를 마시다
	I am not supposed to **drink coffee.** 난 커피를 마시면 안돼.

get[want] sth to drink	마실 것을 갖다주다[원하다]
	Would you **like something to drink?** 뭐 좀 마실래요?
	Can I **get you something to drink?** 마실 것 좀 줄까?

got drunk	술 취하다
	I **got drunk** easily. 난 쉽게 취해.
	He's **drunk as a skunk[lord].** 고주망태로 취해있어.

085

drive

n. 드라이브, 추진력, 조직적 운동 **v.** 운전하다, 몰다, …하게 만들다

go for a drive	드라이브하러 가다
	Would you like to **go for a drive?** 드라이브 갈래?

drive+특정모델	…차를 몰다 Randall **drove a BMW** to the beach. 랜달은 BMW를 몰고 해변으로 갔어.
drive to +장소명사	…로 차를 몰고 가다, 차를 몰고 …에 도착하다, 가다 I'm going to **drive to Seattle** tonight. 오늘밤 차로 시애틀에 갈거야.
drive back to +장소명사	…로 차를 몰고 돌아오다 We can **drive back to** your apartment later. 우리는 나중에 차몰고 네 아파트로 가면 돼.
drive oneself to+장소명사	차를 몰고 …에 가다 Jerry **drove himself to** the hospital after the accident. 제리는 사고 후에 직접 차를 몰고 병원에 갔어.
drive sb to +장소명사	…을 차로 데려가다 He's gonna **drive me to** the park. 걘 차로 날 공원에 데려다 줄거야.
drive sb to+V	…하게 하다 This can **drive you to** be isolated. 이건 널 고립되게 할 수 있어.
drive me home	나를 집에 차로 데려다주다 Do you have someone to **drive you home?** 너 집에 운전해줄 사람있어?
drive sb crazy [mad]	…을 미치게 하다 That was gonna **drive me crazy** all night. 그게 날 밤새 미치게 만들었어.
drive sb up the wall	…을 돌게 만들다 That secretary is going to **drive me up the wall.** 저 비서가 내 성미를 건드리고 있어.

drop

n. 방울, 액체의 소량, 하락(in) **v.** 떨어지다, 떨어뜨리다, 줄어들다, 차로 데려가 내려주다

drop
방울, (액체의) 소량(of), (수량) 하락(in)

The waiter poured the coffee neatly without spilling a drop. 웨이터는 한 방울도 흘리지 않고 깨끗하게 커피를 따랐다.

Not a drop. Not even half a drop.
전혀 그렇지 않아.

drop sth
그만두다

Can you[we] drop this? 이 얘기 좀 그만 할 수 없니?

Drop the subject! 그 얘기는 그만하자!

drop a line [note]
짧은 편지를 쓰다, 연락하다

Drop me a line. 나한테 연락 좀 해.

I'll drop you a line. 편지할게.

drop the ball
실수하다

I guess I dropped the ball. 큰 실수를 한 것 같아.

I think that you dropped the ball on the project.
네가 그 프로젝트 건 실수한 것 같아.

drop by
(아는 사람을 불시에) 방문하다, 들르다

Drop by for a drink (sometime).
언제 한번 들러 술마시자.

Drop in sometime.
근처에 오면 한 번 들러.

drop off
내리다, 내려주다

I'll drop you off at your house tonight.
오늘밤에 집에 내려주고 갈게.

Why don't you just drop me off, and you can come back?
날 내려주고 넌 다시 돌아와라.

drop out
탈락하다, (학교) 그만두다

You're really dropping out? 너 정말 학교 그만 둘거야?

due

a. adv. 마땅히 치러져야 하는, …에 기인하다, 지급기일이 된, (교통수단) 도착예정인, …하기로 되어 있는, **n.** 회비

due+시간부사	**…가 만기인** Our electric bill **is due** tomorrow. 우리 전기료 고지서가 내일이 마감일이야.
be due on [in, at]	**…까지이다** The bills **are due on** the first day of the month. 청구서는 그달 첫날에 지불 기한이죠. The team's report **is due on** January 4. 그 팀 보고서는 1월 4일이 마감이야. The mortgage money **is due in** a week. 모기지 대출금은 일주일 내에 내야 돼.
be due in	**(열차·비행기가) 도착 예정인** Our guests **are due in** a few hours. 우리 손님들은 몇시간 안에 도착할거야.
be due to sb	**…에게 치러져야 한다** A lot of money **is due to** the person who invented this. 이걸 발명한 사람에게 많은 돈이 주어져야 해.
be due to +동사원형	**…할 예정이다** The plane **is not due to** arrive for another hour. 한 시간 더 있어야 비행기가 도착할 거라는군.
(be) due to	**…때문에** = because of Kerry can't be here **due to** getting sick. 케리는 아파서 여기 올 수가 없어.
in due course	**적절한 때에** We'll discuss the salary **in due course.** 우리는 적절한 때에 급여에 대해 토의해야 돼.
dues	**회비** **The membership dues** are very expensive for this club. 이 클럽 회원 회비는 아주 비싸.

ear
n. 귀, 청각

have a very good ear for~	…을 잘 알다, …에 소질이 있다	
	Ramon **has a very good ear for** talented singers.	
	레이몬은 재능있는 가수들을 잘 알아봐.	
be all ears	경청하다	
	If you have a better idea, **I'm all ears.**	
	더 나은 아이디어가 있다면 열심히 들을게.	
keep your ears open for~	…에 신경을 쓰다	
	Keep your ears open for some new ideas.	
	새로운 아이디어에 귀를 기울여봐.	
I couldn't believe my ears when~	…때 내 귀를 믿을 수가 없었어	
	I couldn't believe my ears when he lied.	
	걔가 거짓말을 할 때 내 귀를 믿을 수가 없었어.	
sby's ear are burning	…의 귀가 간지럽다	
	My ears are burning.	
	(남이 험담하는 것 같아) 귀가 가렵다.	
sth goes in one ear and out the other	한쪽 귀로 듣고 한쪽 귀로 흘리다	
	You know our kids. I love them dearly, but **that goes in one ear and out the other.**	
	우리 애들 알잖아. 난 걔들을 무지 사랑하지만 걔들은 한 귀로 듣고 한 귀로 흘려.	

easy

a. 쉬운, 편안한 *ease **n.** 쉬움, 편안함

be easy to+V
…하기 쉽다
It's just so easy to get off the subject.
주제를 벗어나 다른 얘기를 하는 건 쉬워.

make sth easier
…을 더욱 쉽게 하다
I left Chicago to make life easier for everyone.
난 다들 편하게 살도록 시카고를 떠났어.

feel easy
편안함을 느끼다
I hope you feel easy about these plans.
이 계획들에 네가 불편하지 않기를 바래.

I'm easy
(다른 사람의 결정을 받아들이면서) 난 어떤 것도 괜찮아
She is so easy to please.
걔는 대하기 편한 사람이야.
Can I have a glass of water? I'm easy to please.
물 한잔 줄래? 난 까다롭지 않아.

with ease
쉽게
This can be completed with ease.
이건 쉽게 완성될 수 있을거야.

feel at ease
안심하다 *put one's mind at ease …의 마음을 편하게 하다
I'm going to put your mind at ease about these problems.
난 이 문제에 대해 네 맘을 편하게 해줄게.

ill at ease
불편한, 거북한
Neighbors feel ill at ease since the robbery.
이웃들은 도난사건 이후에 불편해 해.

eat
v 먹다

eat (sth)	먹다 I **eat** a lot of raw vegetables. 난 생야채를 많이 먹어.
get sth to eat	…을 먹다 Do you want to **get something to eat**? 너 뭐 좀 먹을래? Let's **have something to eat.** 뭐 좀 먹자.
eat lunch [dinner]	점심[저녁]을 먹다 The children are very active after they **eat lunch**. 애들은 점심 후에 무척 활동적이야. What do you want to **eat for lunch** today? 오늘 점심으로 뭘 먹을테야?
eat out	외식하다 We've **been eating out** a lot lately. 우린 최근에 외식을 아주 많이 했어. We're **eating out** tonight. 오늘 저녁 외식한다.
eat up	먹어 치우다 It **eats up** the batteries. 배터리가 빨리 닳아요.
eat like a horse	대식하다 *eat like a bird 조금먹다 He **ate like a horse** after working all day. 그는 종일 일하고 난 후 엄청 먹어댔어.
What's eating you?	무슨 일이야? *eat sb …을 감정을 사로잡다 You look sad. **What's eating you?** 슬퍼보이네. 무슨 걱정거리가 있어?

end

n. 끝, 결말, 최후, 목적 **v.** 끝내다, 끝나다

---

go off the deep end

근거없이 화를 버럭내다

You **went off the deep end.** What is your problem?
버럭 화를 내던데 무슨 문제야?

---

bring[put] an end to

…을 끝내다

Why don't we **put an end to** this right now.
지금 당장 그만두자.

---

at the end of

…의 끝에

I finally got home **at the end of** the day!
마침내 일을 마치고 집에 돌아왔다!

---

in the end

결국

In the end, I didn't leave for New York.
결국 난 뉴욕으로 떠나지 않았어.

---

make (both) ends meet

수지타산을 맞추다

With his low salary, he couldn't **make ends meet.**
걘 그의 낮은 급여로는 수지타산을 맞출 수가 없었어.

~end

끝나다

It **ended** very well. 잘 끝났어.

We know that **ends** well.
그거 잘 끝났다는 걸 알고 있어.

---

end sth

…을 끝내다

Just **end** your relationship with Tony.
토니와의 관계를 끝내.

---

end up with [~ing]

결국 …으로 끝나다

I **ended up** getting married and having kids.
결혼도 하고 아이들도 낳게 됐어.

You're not going to **end up** alone.
넌 결국 외롭게 끝나지 않을거야.

enjoy 092

v. 즐기다, 누리다, 즐겁게 보내다(enjoy oneself)

enjoy+명사
…을 즐기다

We **enjoyed** it very much. 우린 매우 즐거웠어.

I hope you **enjoyed** your meal. 식사 맛있게 하길 바래.

We **enjoyed** your company. 같이 있어서 즐거웠어.

Enjoy+명사
즐겁게 …해

Enjoy your meal! 맛있게 드세요!

Enjoy yourself. 즐겁게 지내.

Enjoy your stay in Korea. 한국에 있는 동안 즐겁게 지내.

enjoy ~ing
…을 즐기다

I don't **enjoy** being with you. 너랑 있는 게 즐겁지 않아.

I **enjoyed** talking with you. 너랑 얘기해서 즐거웠어.

enjoy oneself
신나게 놀다

We took a vacation and **enjoyed ourselves.**
우린 휴가가서 즐겁게 놀았어.

I **enjoyed myself** very much.
무척 즐거웠어.

envy 093

n. 부러움, 시샘 **v.** 부러워하다

(green) with envy
부러워하는

You're the one who's **green with envy.**
샘이 나서 죽을 지경인 사람은 바로 너야.

envy sby (for~)	…을 부러워하다 I really **envy you for** living overseas for so long. 그렇게 오랫동안 외국에서 살다니 정말 부러워.
envy people who~	…한 사람들을 부러워하다 I **envy somebody who** can be so in touch with their dreams. 자신들의 꿈을 이렇게 이룰 수 있는 사람이 부러워.
envy sby sth	…의 …를 부러워하다 I **envy** you your childhood. 네 어린 시절이 부러워.

094 ever

adv. 언제든, 여느때보다(비교급강조), 도대체(의문사 뒤)

Have you ever +pp?	…해본 적이 있어? Let me ask you something. **Have you ever been** in love? 뭐 좀 물어볼게. 사랑해본 적 있어?
hardly ever	거의 …하지 않는 = almost never I **hardly ever** get to see you. 너 보기가 힘드네.
never ever	(강조어구) 전혀, 절대로 I promise I will **never ever** use charts again. 다시는 절대로 그 챠트를 쓰지 않는다고 약속할게.
비교급+than ever	여느때보다 …한 (과거와 비교하여 최고임을 강조하기 위한) Wow, it's raining **harder than ever** before. 와, 그 어느 때보다 더 비가 오네.
as ever	여전히, 변함없이 He's as great a salesman **as ever** lived. 그 사람은 제일 가는 판매사원이야.

ever since	…이후로 줄곧
	You've been acting strange **ever since** I got back. 내가 돌아온 이후로 너 좀 이상하게 행동해.

095 every
a. adv. 모든, 가능한 모든, …때마다

every single	(강조) 단 하나의 …도
	You're putting **every single** one of us at risk. 넌 우리 모두를 한 명도 빠짐없이 위태롭게 하고 있어.
every other day	격일로
	Every other day we attend English class. 이틀에 한번씩 우리는 영어수업을 들어.
every day	매일 *everyday 매일의
	I work overtime almost **every day.** 거의 매일 야근야.
every now and then	때때로, 가끔
	It was okay to accept help **every now and then.** 가끔 도움을 받는게 좋았어.
every once in a while	가끔
	I water the plants **every once in a while.** 난 가끔 화초에 물을 줘.
have every reason to~	…할만한 충분한 이유가 있다
	I've given you **every reason to** hate me. 네가 날 싫어하는 것은 당연하지.
every time S +V	…할 때마다
	I'm getting angrier **every time** I think of it. 난 그걸 생각할 때마다 화가 더 나.

expect

v. 기대하다, 예상하다, 임신하다

---

expect sby

…가 오기를 기다리다

I'm **expecting** somebody. 누가 오기로 되어 있는데요.
I'm **expecting** company. 더 올 사람 있어요.
I've been **expecting** you. 기다리고 있었어요.

expect (a child)

임신하다

I heard Eva **is expecting.** 에바가 임신했대.
Are you **expecting** (a child)? 너 임신했어?

expect sby back

…가 돌아오는 걸 예상하다

When do you **expect him back?**
언제 돌아오실까요?

expect to+V

…하기를 기대하다

I didn't **expect to** see you here.
여기서 널 만날 줄 생각도 못했어.

expect sby to~

…가 …하기를 기대하다

Do you **expect me to** believe that?
내가 그말을 믿을 것 같니?

expect that ~

…을 기대하다

I **expect that** she will make a recovery.
걔가 회복될거라 생각해.

be expected to+V

…할 것으로 예상되다

She **was expected to** attend the meeting.
걘 회의에 참가할 것으로 예상되었어.

What do you expect to~?

뭘 …하기를 바라는 거야?

What do you expect to see there?
가서 뭘 보길 바라는거야?

expect

~than I expected

내가 예상했던 것 보다 더

She's more cute than I expected.
걘 내가 예상했던 것 보다 더 예뻐.

097

excuse

ⓝ 변명, 사과, 이유, 용서 ⓥ 변명하다, 용서하다, (자리비우는걸)허락하다

There is no excuse for~

…에 대한 이유가 안된다

There's no excuse for it.
그거에 대한 변명의 여지가 없어.

There's no excuse for trying to hit her.
걜 때리려고 한 건 변명의 여지가 없어.

have no excuse for

…에 대해 변명할 말이 없다

I just ran out of excuses. 이젠 변명거리도 다 떨어졌어요.

I have no excuse for not coming home yesterday.
어제 외박한거 변명할 말이 없어.

make an[one's] excuse for

…에 대한 이유를 대다

He always finds an excuse for anything that he does.
걘 항상 자기가 하는 일 무엇이든 변명거리를 대.

Jamie made an excuse for being late.
제이미는 늦은 거에 대해 변명거리를 댔어.

excuse me

(주의환기) 실례합니다, 미안합니다, 뭐라고요?

Excuse me, where's the bathroom?
죄송하지만 화장실이 어디죠?

Excuse me, what did you say? 미안하지만 뭐라고 말했어?

excuse sby

…를 양해하다

May I be excused for a moment?
잠깐 자리를 비워도 될까요?

Could you excuse us for a second? 자리 좀 비켜줄래요?

You're excused now. 이제 가봐도 좋다.

If you'll excuse me	양해를 해주신다면, (자리를 뜨면서) 괜찮다면 **If you'll excuse me,** I have other things to do. 괜찮으시다면 다른 할 일이 있어서요. **If you'll excuse me,** I'm going to go back to the office. 괜찮다면 사무실로 돌아갈게요.
excuse A for B	A에게 B를 용서하다 Please **excuse me for** being late. 늦어서 미안해. **Excuse me for** being so selfish. 너무 이기적이어서 미안해.

098

eye
n 눈

can't take one's eyes off	…에게서 눈을 떼지 못하다 He said he **couldn't keep his eyes off** me. 걘 내게서 눈을 뗄 수가 없다고 말했어.
have an eye for	…을 보는 눈이 있다　*have an[one's] eye out for~ …을 감시하다 I tend to **have a bit of an eye for** these things. 난 이런 것들을 보는 눈이 좀 있는 편이야.
have one's eyes on sth	갖고 싶거나 사고 싶어 눈찍어두다, 실수를 피하기 위해 계속 주시하다 Did you get that sexy bra you **had your eyes on?** 네가 눈독들이던 그 섹시한 브라자 샀어?
have one's eye on sby	뭔가 잘못된 일을 할까 지켜보다 I'll have to **keep my eye on** you. 네게서 눈을 떼지 않고 지켜봐야 돼.
keep an eye on	돌보다 He's gonna **keep an eye on** the apartment until I get there. 내가 도착할 때까지 걔가 아파트를 잘 봐줄거야.

excuse

see eye to eye (with sby)	(…와) 동의하다 We **see eye to eye** on this. 이 문제에 대해서 우리는 의견의 일치를 보았어.
hit sby in the eye	…의 눈을 때리다 Mark **hit Gary in the eye** during the fight. 마크는 싸우는 도중에 게리의 눈을 때렸어.

099 face
n. 얼굴, 표면 **v.** 마주보다, 직면하다, 직시하다

in the face of~	어떤 어려운 상황에 직면하여 Mary succeeded **in the face of** a very difficult situation. 메리는 아주 어려운 상황에 직면하여서도 성공을 해냈어.
make a face	인상을 찌푸리다 Don't **make a face.** 이상한 표정 짓지마.
face each other	서로 마주보다 They turn over and **face each other.** 걔네들은 몸을 뒤집고 서로를 쳐다봤어.
be faced with~	…에 직면하다 I'**ve been faced with** an ethical dilemma. 난 윤리적인 딜레마에 직면해있어.
Let's face it	사실을 직시하자, 까놓고 말해서 **Let's face it,** you're not good enough for him anyway. 현실을 직시해. 넌 어쨌거나 걔한테는 턱없이 부족해.

# fall

n. 떨어짐, 폭포, 가을, 감소 **v.** 떨어지다, 감소하다, 어떤 상태로 …되다

fall asleep
잠들다 *fall asleep ~ing하면 …하다 잠들다

Don't **fall asleep** at the wheel.
운전하면서 자지 마라.

I can't forgive you for **falling asleep** during sex.
섹스 중에 잠든 널 용서할 수가 없어.

fall in love (with sby)
사랑에 빠지다

I've got to stop **falling in love with** strange women.
낯선 여자와 사랑에 빠지는 일은 그만해야겠어.

fall short of
…이 부족하다 = be[run] short of

We help people who **fall short of** cash.
우린 돈이 부족한 사람들을 도와.

At least they **fell short of** hitting me.
적어도 걔네들은 날 치기까지는 안했어.

fall apart
산산조각나다, 엉망이 되다, 상태가 안 좋아지다

My entire body **is falling apart.**
몸살에 걸려 온몸이 쑤셔.

My life **is falling apart.**
내 인생이 엉망진창이 되고 있어.

Things **were falling apart** at home.
집의 일들이 엉망야.

fall down
넘어지다, 무너지다, 실패하다 *fall down a cliff하면 절벽에서 떨어지는 것을, fall down the stairs하면 계단에서 넘어지는 것

I **fell down** the stairs and broke my tooth.
계단에서 떨어져 이가 부러졌어.

fall for
(트릭 등에) 속아 넘어가다, 사랑하기 시작하다

Don't **fall for** it. He'll only steal your money.
혹하지마. 네 돈을 훔칠려는거야.

You **fall for** it every time!
넌 매번 넘어가나!

120

fall

fall into
안기다, 침대에 …에 빠져들다, …하기 시작하다, 구분되다 *fall into place 이야기가 제대로 맞다, 앞뒤가 들어맞다, fall into the hands of …의 수중에 넘어가다

I just **fell into** bed with my clothes on.
난 그냥 옷을 입은 채 침대에 누워버렸어.

She **has fallen into** a black hole of debt.
걘 엄청난 빚더미에 빠져있어.

Do you want to **fall into** the trap?
속임수에 빠지고 싶은거야?

fall flat on one's face
앞으로 꼬꾸라지다

She **fell flat on her face** and broke her nose.
걘 앞으로 꼬구라져 코가 부러졌어.

fall victim [prey] to ~
병이 걸리다, …에 속다, 공격당하다

We **have fallen victim to** an epidemic.
우린 전염병에 걸렸어.

fall off
…에서 떨어져나가다, (가격 등) 내려가다

Nothing big, I **fell off** my bike
별일 아냐. 자전거에서 떨어졌어.

fall on
…(위)로 넘어지다, (생일, 기념일이) 언제 …이다

My birthday will **fall on** a Sunday this year.
내 생일은 금년에 일요일이야.

Why does it always **fall on** us to help you?
왜 널 돕는 걸 내가 책임져야 해?

Sam **fell on** top of her and they began kissing again.
샘은 걔 위에 누워 다시 키스를 하기 시작했어.

The lunar new year **falls on** a different day each year.
음력 새해는 매년 날이 달라.

fall out
일어나다, …결과가 나오다, 싸우다(~with)

It wasn't my ring! It **fell out** of his jacket!
그건 내 반지가 아니라 걔의 옷에서 떨어져 나온거야

My hair started **falling out.**
내 머리가 빠지기 시작했어.

We had some kind of big-time **falling out.**
우린 좀 크게 한바탕 싸웠어.

fall back on
기대다, 의지하다

She took off her shirt and **fell back on** the couch.
걘 셔츠를 벗고 소파에 기댔어.

fall behind sby[sth]	뒤지다 *fall behind on[with]~ 늦어지다, 체납하다 I've just **fallen behind** on my housework. 숙제가 늦어졌어.
fall over	꼬꾸라지다, 발에 걸려 넘어지다(trip over) Mike punched her and the waitress **fell over.** 마이크가 걜 한때 때리니까 걔가 넘어졌어. Jill looks sick and starts to **fall over.** 질은 아파보이고 넘어지려 해.
fall through	실패하다, 수포로 돌아가다 How come he didn't **fall through?** 어떻게 걔가 실패한거야? This plan **fell through** the cracks. 이 계획은 수포로 돌아갔어.
fall in with	우연히 만나 어울리다, 동조하다, 동의하다 I was just a kid and I **fell in with** the wrong crowd. 난 그냥 애였고 안 좋은 애들과 어울렸어.

101

far

ⓐ 멀리, …만큼 떨어져, (강조) 훨씬, 아주

be far from	…와는 크게 떨어져 있다, 관련이 없다 That's **not far from** the airport. 공항에서 멀지 않아.
as far as I know	내가 아는 한 *as far as possible 가능한 한 **As far as I know** they sent it yesterday. 내가 아는 한 그거 어제 보냈대는데.
go too far	지나치다 The fighting couple **went too far** and upset their parents. 그 싸우던 커플은 선을 넘어서 부모들을 당황시켰어.

fall

by far

훨씬 = far and away

You are **by far** the most handsome student.
넌 단연코 가장 잘생긴 학생야.

102 feel
ⓥ 기분이 …하다, …같은 느낌이다, …하고 싶다

feel+형용사

…해

I **feel** really sick today.
오늘 무척 아파요.

I **feel** weird about what happened the other day.
요전날 일어났던 일이 좀 이상해.

I don't really **feel** right about doing this.
이거 하는게 영 찜찜해.

feel okay

괜찮아 = feel all right

You're **feeling okay,** David?
데이빗, 괜찮아?

How can you **feel okay** about this?
어떻게 이게 괜찮다는거야?

feel better [good, great]

기분이 좋아

I'm not **feeling very good.**
기분이 그리 좋지 않아요.

I'd **feel better** if I slept with Diane.
내가 다이안과 자면 기분이 좋아질텐데.

It **feels good** to be taken care of.
누가 돌봐주면 기분이 좋아.

feel well[bad]

기분이 좋다[나쁘다] *기분이 나쁜 이유를 부가하려면 feel bad about~

I don't **feel well** these days. 요즘 몸이 안 좋아.

Leave me alone. I'm not **feeling well.**
가만 놔둬. 기분이 별로 안 좋아.

Don't **feel so bad about** it. 너무 속상해하지마.

feel like+명사
…같은 느낌이야

I **feel like** a new person.
다시 태어난 기분이야.

You **made me feel like** an idiot.
너 때문에 바보가 된 기분이야.

feel like S+V
…같은 느낌이야

I **feel like** you are not listening to me.
네가 내 말을 듣지 않는 것 같아.

I still **feel like** something's not right.
뭔가 잘 못된 것 같다는 생각이 들어.

feel like ~ing
…하고 싶다

I **feel like** having a cup of coffee.
커피 먹고 싶어.

I **don't feel like** going to work.
저 말야, 출근하기 싫어.

I **don't feel like** it. 사양할래.

feel free to~
마음대로 …해

Feel free to stay here as long as you like.
있고 싶을 때까지 있어.

Feel free to ask if you have any questions.
질문있으면 언제라도 해.

feel the same way
똑같이 생각하다, 공감하다

I **feel the same way.**
나도 그렇게 생각해.

I don't **feel the same** way about you.
너에 대해 난 달리 생각해.

feel for
…을 동정하다 *feel for sby …의 고통을 동정하다, feel for sth …을 안타깝게 생각하다

She suffers from depression. We all **feel for** her.
걘 우울증을 앓고 있어. 우리 모두 걜 동정해.

I **feel for** the loss of one of our own.
우리 것을 하나 잃어 안타까워 하고 있어.

feel up to+명사 [~ing]
…할 정도로 힘이 있다

I don't **feel up to** it. 나 그거 못할 것 같아.

I just don't **feel up to** working on the project.
그 프로젝트를 못할 것 같아.

feel

feel the need to~
…할 필요성을 느끼다

You don't **feel the need to** apologize to me.
내게 사과할 필요성을 못 느끼는구나.

have the[a] feeling~
…인 것 같아, …라는 기분이 들다

I **have the feeling** you had something to do with it.
네가 그것과 관련있었다는 느낌야.

I **got the feeling that** your wife's coming on to me.
네 마누라가 날 유혹한다는 생각이 들어.

I **have a feeling** he's going to be very angry.
걔가 무척 화낼 것 같아.

I **got a feeling** he'll be back.
걔가 돌아올 것 같아.

have feelings for~
…을 좋아하다

I **have (strong) feelings for** her.
나 쟤한테 마음이 (무척) 있어.

You'**ve had feelings for** me?
나한테 특별한 감정을 느꼈다구?

You **still have feelings for** me, don't you?
아직도 날 좋아하지, 그렇지 않아?

have a good [bad] feeling about~
…에 기분이 좋다[나쁘다]

I **had a bad feeling about** this.
난 이거에 대해 기분이 안 좋았어.

I'**ve got a good feeling about** this.
난 이거에 기분이 좋았어.

I **have a really good feeling about** her.
난 걔한테 정말 좋은 감정이야.

I **have a weird feeling about** this place.
난 이곳 기분이 이상해.

(There's) No hard feelings
악의는 아냐

There's **no hard feelings for** firing you.
널 해고한거 기분나쁘게 생각마.

No hard feelings about you leaving behind me.
네가 날 두고 가버린거 기분 나쁘게 생각안해.

What are your feelings about~?
…을 어떻게 생각해?

What are your feelings about us divorcing?
우리 이혼하는거 어떻게 생각해?

spare one's feelings	감정을 상하지 않게 하다 I was trying to **spare your feelings.** 네 감정을 상하지 않게 하려고 했어.
hide one's feelings	…의 감정을 숨기다 Yeah, at least you **hid your feelings** well about it. 그래, 적어도 넌 그거에 대해 네 감정을 잘 숨겼어.
hurt one's feelings	…의 감정을 상하게 하다 She's too afraid of **hurting your feelings.** 엄마의 감정을 상하게 할까봐.

103
foot
n. 발, …의 바닥부분, (단위) 피트

on foot	도보로 Even **on foot,** it's no more than 10 minutes. 걸어서라도 10분 이상 안 걸려요.
get back on one's feet	다시 일어서다 We fixed everything and now we're **getting back on** our feet. 다 고쳤고 이젠 다시 좋아지고 있어.
stand on one's own feet	자립하다 Chris **stood on his own feet** after graduating. 크리스는 졸업 후 자립했어.
get cold feet	긴장하다, 떨다 Many people **get cold feet** before a big decision. 많은 사람들이 큰 결정에 앞서 겁먹어.
put one's foot in one's mouth	실언하다 Jeff really **put his foot in his mouth** at the meeting. 회의 때 제프가 정말 큰 실수를 했어요.

fight

n. 싸움 v. 싸우다

have a fight (with)

(…와) 싸우다

We **had a fight.** 우린 싸웠어.

I**'ve just had a fight with** my husband.
남편과 싸웠어.

get in(to) a fight (with)

(…와) 싸움을 하다

My parents **got into a big fight** and got divorced.
부모님은 크게 싸우시고 헤어지셨어.

put up a (good, bad) fight

싸움을 계속하다, 선전[고전]하다

Honey, you **put up a very good fight.**
자기야, 정말 잘 싸웠어.

give up without a fight

순순히 물러나다

Don't **give up without a fight.**
싸워보지도 않고 물러나지마.

pick a fight (with)

(…에게) 싸움을 걸다

Why do you want to **pick a fight with** me?
왜 내게 싸움을 걸고 싶은거야?

start a fight

싸움을 시작하다 *miss the fight 싸움을 못보다

Just get over here. I don't want you to **miss the fight.**
이리와. 싸움구경 놓치면 안 되지.

I didn't **start a fight.**
내가 싸움을 시작하지 않았어.

win a fight

싸움에서 이기다 ↔ lose a fight

You won't **win a fight** with your teacher.
선생님과의 싸움에서 질거야.

fight over [about]

…로 싸우다

We**'ve been fighting about** this all week
우린 한 주 내내 이 문제로 싸웠어

fight with	…와 싸우다
	She'll never **fight with** her mother again. 걘 엄마랑 다신 안 싸울거야. You're **fighting with** me about stupid shoes. 넌 지금 고작 신발로 나와 싸우고 있는 거야.

fight a lot	많이 싸우다
	They didn't **fight a lot.** 걔네들은 많이 싸우지 않아. We've been **fighting a lot** more than we used to. 우린 예전보다 많이 싸우고 있어.

fight sth	…와 싸우다
	Every day we're **fighting** traffic. 우린 매일 교통지옥과 싸우고 있어. We're going to **fight** this and we're going to win. 우린 이거와 싸우지만 이기지 못할거야.

fight sby on sth	…와 …문제로 싸우다
	Why **are** you **fighting me on** this? 왜 이걸로 나와 싸우는거야? I'll **fight you on** this. 이 문제로 너와 싸울거야.

fight for	…위해 싸우다
	Do you want to **fight for** us? 우릴 위해 싸울거야? I **am fighting for** a principle. 난 원칙을 위해 싸우고 있어.

figure
n. 수치, 인물   v. 생각하다

put a figure on sth	…의 가격을 정확히 말하다
	Let's **put a figure on** the building being restored. 복원되는 빌딩의 가격 수치를 정확히 정해놓자.

fight

reach six figures	6자리 숫자에 이르다 *six figures 여섯자리수	
	Dock workers rake in over **six figures** a year.	
	부두 근로자들은 연간 많은 돈을 긁어모아.	
keep your figure	몸매유지하다 *watch your figure 살찌지 않도록 먹는거에 조심하다	
	How do you **keep your figure** as you age?	
	나이가 들어가면서 너는 몸매를 어떻게 유지해?	
I figure that S+V	사실일거라 생각하다	
	I figure I'll be recruited by the FBI any day now.	
	난 곧 FBI에 채용될거라 생각해.	
That[It] figures	그럴 줄 알았어, 당연해	
	He never called you? **That figures.**	
	걔가 너한테 결코 전화하지 않았지? 그럴 줄 알았어.	
figure out	생각끝에 이해하다, 알아내다	
	You go ahead and talk while I **figure it out.**	
	내가 알아내는 동안 넌 어서 말이나 해봐.	

106

fill

ⓥ 채우다

fill sth	…을 채우다
	She **filled** a glass with water from the tap.
	걘 꼭지에서 물 한 컵을 받았어.
be filled with	…로 가득차다(fill A with B)
	The house **is filled with** guests. 집에는 손님들로 가득찼어.
fill in	서류에 적어 넣다, 채우다, 알리다, 대리하다
	You can **fill in** all the information on the form.
	양식서에 모든 정보를 적어.
	Whatever you've got going on, **fill me in.**
	뭘 하든 내게 알려줘.

fill out

기입하다

Could you tell me how to **fill out** this form?
이 양식서 어떻게 적는지 알려줄래요?

I've got some paperwork for you to **fill out**.
네가 작성해야 하는 서류가 있어.

fill up

(기름) 넣다

I ran out of gas. Where can we **fill up**?
기름이 없어. 어디서 기름넣지?

Please **fill it[her] up**. 기름 넣어주세요.

107 find

v. 찾다, 구하다, 발견하다, …하다는 것을 알다

find sby

…을 찾다 *find sby sth하면 …에게 …을 찾아다주다

Where will I **find** you?
널 어디서 찾지?, 어디 있을건데?

You know where to **find** me.
내 연락처는 알고 있지.

find sby[sth]+ 형용사[pp,~ing]

…을 …하다고 생각하다

I **found them** kissing in my car!
걔네들이 내 차에서 키스를 하는 거야!

I **find it difficult to** get the job done by tomorrow.
그 일을 내일까지 끝마치는 건 힘들어.

find oneself

…에 있다, …을 구하다, 갖추다

You're going to **find yourself** very alone.
넌 매우 외로워질거야.

find a way to

길을 찾다, 방법을 찾다

She'll get through this. She'll **find a way to** survive.
걔는 이걸 견딜거야. 생존방법을 찾아낼거야.

We've got to **find a way to** make this work.
이거 작동하게 하는 방법을 찾아야 돼.

find out
사실을 알아내다 *find가 구체적인 물체를 찾아내는 것임에 반해 find out~는 …라는 사실이란 추상적인 개념을 목적어로 받는다. find out 다음에는 명사, that 절, if절 등 다양하게 올 수 있다.

If you find the document, you'll **find out** the truth.
그 서류를 찾으면 진실을 알아내게 될거야.

She **found out** that Jimmy is not her own son.
지미가 자기의 아들이 아니라는 걸 알아냈어.

I want you to **find out** if my daughter is using drugs again.
내 딸이 약을 다시 하는지 알아봐줘.

find fault with
…을 비난하다

Please stop **finding fault with** people around you.
주변 사람 탓하는 것 좀 그만해라.

I can't **find fault with** the kitchen.
부엌이 흠잡을 데가 없어.

lost and found
분실물 보관소

I have got to go and check in the **lost and found.**
분실물 보관소에 가서 확인해봐야겠어.

108

fine

ⓐ 좋은, 괜찮은, 미세한 adv. 잘, 괜찮게 ⓝ 벌금 ⓥ 벌금을 내리다

be fine with [by]
…가 괜찮다

I think anything that makes you happy **is fine by** me.
난 널 기쁘게 하는 거라면 뭐라도 좋아.

be fine for sby
…에게 좋다

Friday **is fine for** me. 나도 금요일이 좋아.

be doing fine
잘 지내다

To date, the business **has been doing fine.**
현재까지 사업은 잘 되고 있어.

pay a fine
벌금을 내다

What do I have to **pay a fine?** 벌금내려면 어떻게 해야 해요?

get a ~ fine for ~	…에 대한 벌금 …을 맞다
	The company **got a large fine for** polluting. 그 회사는 환경오염으로 엄청난 벌금을 맞았어.

be fined+돈+ for~	…로 벌금 …을 맞다
	The student **was fined over $500 for** traffic violations. 그 학생은 교통위반으로 500 달러가 넘는 벌금을 받았어.

109 finish
v. 끝내다, 마치다

finish	끝내다, 마치다, 완성하다
	Have you **finished?** 다 했어? I**'ve just finished** work. 방금 일을 마쳤어.

finish sth	…을 끝마치다
	When can you **finish** the project? 언제 프로젝트를 끝낼 수 있어? Is it urgent that I **finish** this? 이거 급히 끝내야 하는거야? How long does it take to **finish** it? 이거를 마치는데 얼마나 걸려?

finish (food)	…을 마치다
	Just let me **finish** my lunch and we can start. 점심 좀 마저 먹고 나서 시작하면 돼. Is it okay if I **finish** the orange juice? 오렌지 주스 마저 다 마셔도 될까?

finish on time	…을 제시간에 마치다
	I expect him to **finish on time.** 난 걔가 제시간에 마칠거라 예상하고 있어.

finish ~ing	…을 끝내다
	Did you **finish** checking in to your room? 투숙절차는 다 끝났어?

fine

be finished with	…을 끝내다

I've **finished with** the work.
난 일을 끝냈어.

I'm **not finished with** you.
아직 할 얘기가 남았어.

finish off	끝내다, 마무리하다

Why don't you **finish off** these pies?
이 파이 마저 먹어

The guys **finished off** all of the beer in the fridge.
걔네들이 냉장고에 있는 모든 맥주를 끝냈어.

finish up	…로 끝나다, 결국 …으로 되다

Did you **finish up** the work you were doing?
하던 일 끝냈어?

110

fire

n. 화재, 발사 **v.** 사격하다, 해고하다

start a fire	화재가 시작되다

The campers **started a fire,** but the wind blew it out.
캠핑자들이 불을 냈는데 바람이 불어 꺼졌어.

put out a fire	불을 끄다

The fireman arrived quickly to **put out a fire.**
소방관이 재빨리 도착해서 불을 껐어.

set fire to	불을 지르다

The crashed cars **set fire to** the trees.
충돌한 차로 인해 나무들에 불이 붙었어.

Where's the fire?	어디를 그렇게 급히 가?

Hey Chris, **where's the fire?** You seem to be in a big hurry today. 애, 크리스, 어디 불이라도 났어? 오늘 무척 서두르는 것 같아.

fire[shoot] questions at sby	…에게 질문을 던지다　★Fire away 질문을 해봐
	The reporters **shot questions at** the murderer.
	기자들이 살인자에게 질문을 쏟아부었어.
get[be] fired for~	…로 해고되다
	Bill **got fired for** stealing.
	빌이 횡령으로 회사에서 잘렸대.

111 first

a. 첫째의　**adv.** 첫째로, 처음으로　**n.** 최초의 것

come first	…가 우선이다
	Work **comes first.** I always have a lot to do.
	일이 우선이야. 난 늘 할 일이 많아.
at first	우선
	My roommate and I didn't see eye to eye **at first.**
	룸메이트와 나는 첨에 의견일치를 못봤어.
first of all	무엇보다도
	First of all, let me check my schedule.
	먼저, 일정 좀 보고.
first thing (in the morning)	아침에 제일 먼저
	I'll call him **first thing in the morning.**
	아침에 가장 먼저 걔한테 전화할게.
put the first thing first	가장 중요한 일을 하다
	Let's **put the first things first** and complete the survey.
	가장 중요한 일을 먼저 해서 조사를 끝내자고.
in the first place	맨먼저
	I'm annoyed that the whole thing happened **in the first place.**
	무엇보다 그 모든 일이 일어나서 짜증났어.

put ~ first	…을 가장 중요시하다
	The lawyer **puts** his clients **first.** 변호사들은 의뢰인들을 가장 중요시해.

for the first time	최초로
	That night, **for the first time,** Chris spent the night at my place. 그날 밤 처음으로 크리스는 내 집에서 밤을 보냈어.

not know the first thing	아무 것도 모르다
	I **don't know the first thing about** accounting. 회계의 회자도 몰라.

be the first to +V	최초로 …하다
	I didn't think she'd **be the first to** go. 걔가 제일 먼저 가리라고는 생각 못 했어

112 fit

ⓐ 건강한, 적합한   ⓝ 발작   ⓥ 맞다, 설치하다, 적합하다

fit for[to]	…에 적절한
	I don't think he'**s fit for** being a soldier. 걔가 군인으로 적합치 않은 것 같아.

see fit	적절하다고 생각하다
	I will help you in any way I **see fit.** 어떤 방식이든 내가 적절하다고 생각하는 방법으로 도와줄게.

have[throw] a fit	발작하다
	Jason **had a fit** when I wouldn't buy him a CD. 제이슨은 CD를 사주지 않으려하자 발작을 일으켰어.

fit (sby)+(well, perfectly)	(…에게 옷이) 맞다
	It **fits** me perfectly. 내게 완벽하게 맞아. It doesn't quite **fit.** 옷이 전혀 맞지 않아. How'**s** the dress **fitting?** 옷이 맞아?

fit into

…에 어울리다, 적합하다

The vacation will **fit well into** my schedule.
휴가가 내 일정과 안맞아.

113 fix
n. 위치, 곤경   **v.** 고정시키다, 준비하다, 수리하다

get a fix on

알아내다, 파악하다

Can you **get a fix on** our location?
우리 장소를 알아냈어?

Rescuers **got a fix on** the lost camper.
구조대는 실종된 캠핑자들의 위치를 파악했어.

fix

수리하다, 고치다

How long will it take to **fix** it?
이거 고치는데 얼마나 걸려?

fix one's hair [make-up]

머리[화장]을 손질하다

Sally **is fixing her hair** in her room.
샐리는 자기 방에서 머리만지고 있어.

My sister **is just fixing her makeup.**
내 누이는 화장을 손질하고 있어.

get fixed

수리되다   *get sth fixed …을 수리하다

That's how it **got fixed!**
그렇게 수리되는거야!

I never did **get** my shoes **fixed.**
내 신발을 수선한 적이 없어.

fix

고정시키다, 정하다

My attention **is fixed on** earning money these days.
요즘 내 관심은 돈 버는데 집중되어 있어.

fix+요리, 식사

준비하다

She is fixing lunch in the kitchen.
걘 부엌에서 점심을 준비하고 있어.

I'm going to fix you a drink.
술 한잔 준비해줄게.

fix up

회의 일정등을 잡다, 방이나 건물 치장하거나 수리하다

The landlord's trying to fix up the place for the new tenant. 집주인은 새로 세들어오는 사람을 위해 집을 수리하고 있어.

She agreed to be fixed up on a blind date.
걘 소개팅을 하기로 날을 잡는데 동의했어.

fix up with

소개시켜주다, 제공하다

Yesterday he asked me to fix him up with somebody.
어제 걘 내게 사람을 소개시켜달라고 했어.

You've fixed him up with his perfect woman!
넌 걔한테 완벽한 여자를 소개시켜준거야!

114

follow

v 따라가다, 지키다, 이해하다

follow sby

…의 뒤를 따르다, 알아듣다, 이해하다

Why do you always follow me?
왜 날 항상 따라다니는거야?

Are you following me?
알아듣고 있지?

I can't follow you. Please speak slower.
이해가 안되니 좀 천천히 말해줘요.

follow suit

선례를 따르다

She went back to eating and her guests followed suit.
걘 다시 먹기 시작했고 손님들은 걔를 따라했어.

follow the rules [example]	규칙[선례]를 따르다 **We expect you to follow Jeff's example.** 제프의 선례를 따랐으면 해. **Follow the rules,** and we should get along fine. 규칙을 따르면 우린 괜찮을거야.
follow one's heart	마음가는대로 하다, 기분대로 하다 Jack, you have to **follow your heart.** 잭, 마음가는대로 해야 돼.
follow up	후속조치를 하다 Did the doctor **follow up** after your operation? 의사가 네 수술 후의 후속조치를 했어?

115

forget

 잊다, 기억못하다, …을 잊고 두고 오다

forget sby[sth]	…을 잊다, …을 두고 오다 We had to go back because I **forget** my jacket. 자켓을 두고 와서 돌아가야 돼.
forget about sb[sth]	…을 잊다, 신경 안쓰다, …하기로 한 걸 잊다 You should just **forget about** what I said in the office. 내가 사무실에서 한 말은 다 잊어. You can **forget about** Tammy, she left us. 태미는 잊어버려, 우릴 떠났잖아.
forget to~	…할 것을 잊다 I **forgot to** pick up my dry cleaning! 세탁물 가져오는거 잊었어! I **just forgot to** return his call. 걔 전화와서 한다는 걸 잊었어.
forget that~	…을 잊다 **You just forget that** I told you this? 내가 이거 너한테 말한 거 잊었어? **I forgot** you were here. 네가 여기 있다는 걸 잊었어.

follow

forget what~	…을 잊다
	Don't **forget what** we talked about last night. 간밤에 우리가 얘기한거 잊지마.
	I always **forget how** beautiful you are. 네가 얼마나 예쁜지 늘 잊어.
Don't forget to~	…하는 것을 잊지마라
	See you later. **Don't forget to** e-mail me. 나중에 봐. 잊지말고 메일 보내고.
	Please **don't forget to** make a backup of those files. 그 파일의 복사본을 꼭 만들어 놓아.
Forget (about) it	잊어버려, 신경쓰지마, 됐어
	Let's just **forget it.** 잊어버리자고.
	Forget it. You can't understand. 됐어. 넌 이해못해.
I'll never forget sb[sth]	절대 …을 잊지 않을거야
	I'll never forget you. 널 영원히 잊지 못할거야.
	I will never forget this. 이걸 절대 잊지 않을 거야.
I almost forgot~	깜박 잊을 뻔했어
	Oh, **I almost forgot.** Your file. Here. 어, 깜박할 뻔 했어. 자 여기 네 파일야.
	I almost forgot about her present. 걔 선물을 깜박할 뻔 했어.
I totally [completely] forget~	…을 깜박 잊었어
	We totally forgot about lunch! 점심 깜빡했어!
before I forget	잊기 전에 말해두는데
	Before I forget, you got a call from Sam. 잊기 전에 말해두는데 샘이 전화했었어.
Aren't you forgetting~?	뭐 잊지 않았어?
	Look Peter, **aren't you forgetting** anything? 피터야, 뭐 잊은 거 없어?
be forgetful	깜박 깜박하다
	I'm afraid I**'m becoming forgetful.** 점점 깜박하는게 걱정돼.
	She**'s very forgetful.** Older than she looks. 걘 무척 깜박깜박해. 겉모습보다 더 늙었어.

forgive
v. 용서하다, …해서 죄송하다

forgive sby for ~ing	…가 …한 것을 용서하다
	Did she **forgive him for** dating other women?
	그가 다른 여자와 데이트한 걸 그녀가 용서했니?

forgive sby for what~	가 …한 것을 용서하다
	Can you ever **forgive me for what** I did to you?
	내가 네게 한 짓을 용서해줄 수 있어?

forgive sby sth	…의 …를 용서하다
	Helen **forgave** her husband's cheating.
	헬렌은 남편의 바람을 용서했어.

forgive and forget	잊고 용서하다
	Let's **forgive and forget** it. 그냥 잊고 용서해주자.
	Forgive and forget. That's my motto. 잊고 용서하는게 내 모토야.

free
a. 자유로운, 무료의, …없는 **adv.** 무료로 **v.** 석방하다, 풀어주다

have free time	시간이 되다
	Come up my way when you**'ve got free time.**
	시간나면 나 사는 곳으로 와봐.

set sby free	…을 석방하다
	The court **set** the prisoner **free.**
	법정은 그 죄수를 석방시켰다.

free from[of]	…이 없는	
	It would be nice to be **free from** debt. 빚이 없다면 좋을텐데.	
free of charge	무료로 = for free	
	It's **free of charge.** 무료입니다.	
fat-free	지방이 없는, 무지방의	
	People who are dieting eat **fat-free** yogurt. 다이어트하는 사람들은 무지방 요구르트를 먹어.	

118 fun

ⓐ 재미있는 ⓝ 재미, 장난 *funny 우스운, 재미있는, 이상한

have fun	즐거운 시간을 보내다, 재미보다
	He **is having fun** at the beach. 걘 해변에서 즐거운 시간을 보내고 있어.
have much [a lot of] fun	아주 즐건 시간을 보내다
	I can't remember the last time I **had so much fun.** 내가 마지막으로 그렇게 재미있었던 때가 기억이 안나.
be fun	재미있다
	This is going to **be so much fun.** 이건 무척 재미있을거야.
for fun	재미삼아
	I wish I had a little time **for fun.** 놀 시간이 좀 있으면 좋겠어.
it's no fun ~ing	…하는 것은 재미없다
	It's no fun sitting at home all alone. 혼자서 집에 앉아 있는 것을 지루해. .

make[poke] fun of~	…을 놀리다 You're **making fun of** me? 너 지금 나 놀리냐?, 장난하냐?
What's so funny?	뭐가 그렇게 우스워? **What's so funny?** I just called you a stupid jerk. 뭐가 그렇게 우스워? 널 멍청한 놈이라고 불렀는데.

119 get
v. 얻다, 사다, 취하다, 걸리다, 듣다

get a new job	새 직장을 구하다 *get a reputation 명성을 얻다 She **got a new job.** 걔 새 직업을 구했어.
get a refund	환불받다 *get a discount 할인받다 I'd like to **get a refund,** please? 환불받고 싶은데요?
get it at a bargain	세일 때 사다 *get it at the flea market 벼룩시장에서 사다 I **got it at a bargain.** 난 세일 때 그거 샀어.
get it on a sale	세일 때 사다 She **got** the necklace **on a sale.** 걔 세일 때 목걸이를 샀어.
get it from the gift shop	선물가게에서 사다 I **got it from the gift shop.** 선물가게에서 샀어.
get that (from)	(…로부터) 그 얘기를 듣다 Where did you **get that?** 그거 어디서 들었어? I **get that** a lot. 난 그런 얘기 많이 들어. You **get that** from a doctor? 의사한테 들었어?
get some rest	휴식을 취하다 Why don't you **get some rest?** 좀 쉬시지 그러세요?

fun

get enough sleep	숙면하다
	I didn't **get any sleep** last night. 어젯밤에 잠을 한숨도 못잤어.
get the runs	설사하다 *get a cold 감기에 걸리다
	I**'ve got the runs.** 나 설사해.(= I have diarrhea)
get a sore throat	목이 아프다 *get stomach ache 배가 아프다
	I**'ve really got a sore throat.** 목이 정말 아파.
get it	이해하다, 알다
	I **got it.** 알았어.
	You **get** that we hate you, right? 우리가 널 싫어하는 거 알지, 그지?
	You **got it.** 맞아. 바로 그거야. 알았어.
got it[that]?	이해했어?
	You **got it?** 알았어?
	You **got that?** 알아 들었어?
not get it[that]	이해안되다, 모르다
	I **don't get it.** Why are you late again? 이해가 안돼. 왜 또 늦은거야?
get sby	…을 이해하다
	I need to be with someone who **gets** me. 날 이해해주는 사람과 있어야 돼.
get it	울리는 전화나 문소리에 내가 가겠다
	Honey, I'm taking a shower. Would you **get that?** 자기야, 샤워중인데 전화 좀 받아줄래?
	I'll **get it.** I guess it's for me. 내가 받을게. 내 전화일거야.
get this	맡다, 처리하다
	Don't worry. I **got this.** 걱정마. 내가 알아서 처리할게.
get sb	(전화로) 바꿔주다
	Please **get** me Susan. 수잔 좀 바꿔줘요.
	Get me Chris on the phone! 크리스 좀 바꿔주세요!
get sb	체포하다
	The police finally **got** her. 경찰이 마침내 걜 체포했다.

get sb	확보하다
	That's the last time I**'ve got** him on camera. 그 때 이후로 카메라에서 걜 못봤어.
get the idea	이해하다, …라는 생각을 하다
	I just never **got the idea** that they were really happy. 걔네들이 행복하다는 생각 해본 적 없어.
I will get you ~ sth	…에게 …을 사주다[갖다 주다]
	I will get you a present as soon as I get some money. 돈이 생기는 대로 너한테 선물을 사줄게.
Let me get you sth	…에게 …을 사주다[갖다 주다]
	Let me get you a beer. 맥주 갖다 줄게.
Can I get you sth ~?	…을 갖다 줄까?
	Can I get you something? 뭐 좀 사다줄까?
Can you get me sth~ ?	…을 갖다 줄래?
	Can you get me a taxi, please?(= Can you call a cab for me?) 택시 좀 불러줄래요?
	Can you get me a glass of water, please? 물 한잔 주실래요?
Please get me sth~	…을 갖다주라
	Please get me some coffee. 커피 좀 주세요.
I want you to get sth~	…을 갖다주라
	I want you to get me a present. 선물 사다 줘.
Would you get sth for sby?	…에게 …을 갖다줄래?
	Would you get that for me? 내게 그거 좀 가져다줄래요?
I('ve) got ~ for sby?	…에게 줄 …가 있어
	I('ve) got something **for** you. 네게 줄 게 있어.
	I got news **for** you Chris. 크리스에게 새로운 소식이 있어.
	I got this **for** you. 이게 네꺼야.

get

What did you get sby for+ 기념일~ ?	…때 …에게 뭐 사줬어?	
	What did you get her for her birthday? 걔 생일 선물로 뭘 줬어?	
get angry with[at] sby	…에 화내다	
	I think you're **still angry with** me. 너 아직 내게 화났지.	
get mad at sby	…에게 화내다	
	Don't **get mad at** me! 나한테 화내지마!	
get upset about [with] sby	…에 화나다	
	I know you're **still upset about** me. 너 아직 나한테 화나있지.	
	Why **are** you **upset with** me? 왜 나한테 화를 내는거야?	
get serious (about)	진지[심각]해지다, 진지하게 사귀다	
	I think it's time we **get serious.** 이제 진지해져야 될 때라고 생각해.	
get sleepy	졸리다	
	My father is a wonderful man who just **gets a little sleepy.** 아버지는 좀 졸려하지만 훌륭한 사람이야.	
get busy	바쁘다, 뭔가 일을 시작하다	
	Well, you'd better **get busy.** 저기, 넌 좀 바빠야겠다.	
get sick	아프다, 병들다	
	Did Mindy **get sick?** Was there an accident? 민디가 아팠어? 사고가 있었던거야?	
	He **got sick.** He died a couple of weeks ago. 걘 아팠어. 2,3주전에 죽었어.	
get full	배부르다 *get thirsty 목마르다 get hungry 배고프다	
	Don't worry. I never **get full.** 걱정마. 난 얼마든지 먹을 수 있어.	
get fat	살이 찌다	
	Jen **got fat** because she ate too much. 젠은 너무 먹어대더니 뚱뚱해졌어.	
get better	나아지다	
	I know it's tough now, but things will **get better.** 지금 힘들지만 상황이 좋아질거야.	

get worse
악화되다

Let's just stop this before things **get worse.**
상황이 악화되기 전에 이거 그만두자.

get more~
더 …해지다

We're gonna have to **get more** creative than them.
우리는 그것들보다 더 창의적이어야 될거야.

be getting better
점점 좋아지다

We think the baby'**s getting better.**
아기가 점점 좋아지는 것 같아.

You hear that? I'**m getting better.**
들었지? 난 점점 좋아지고 있어.

be getting worse
점점 나빠지다

I could tell his illness **was getting worse.**
걔의 병세가 악화되는 것을 알 수 있었어.

be getting more~
점점 …해지다

I'**m getting more and more** confident by the day.
난 하루하루 점점 더 자신감이 생기고 있어.

be getting+비교급+and+비교급
점점 …해지다

Is my daughter **just getting crazier and crazier?**
내 딸이 점점 더 미쳐가는거예요?

keep getting better
점점 계속 좋아지고 있다

It just **keeps getting better!**
점점 나아져가는구나!

keep getting worse
점점 계속 나빠지고 있다

I was too depressed. It just **kept getting worse and worse.**
넘 실망스러워. 계속 나빠지고만 있어.

get lost
길을 잃다 *get drunk 술에 취하다

If you **get lost,** just give me a call.
혹시 길을 잃으면 내게 전화해.

get hurt
다치다 *get dressed 옷을 입다

I just don't want her to **get hurt** again.
난 걔가 다시 상처받기를 원치 않아.

get

get screwed — 망하다

They **got screwed** when they bought an apartment.
그들은 아파트를 샀을 때 망했어.

get tired of — 피곤하다 *get exhausted 지치다

You'll **get tired of** hearing her complain.
넌 그녀의 불평소리를 듣는데 지겨울거야.

get going — 출발하다, 떠나다, 착수하다 *get ~ going …을 시작하다

Come on, honey! Let's **get going.**
서둘러, 자기야! 출발하자구.

Get the party **going** by playing some music.
음악 좀 틀고 파티를 시작하자고.

get started — 시작하다 *get started on …을 시작하다

We're running out of time, we need to **get started.**
시간이 다 됐습니다. 시작하겠습니다.

I got to **get started on** my speech!
연설을 시작하겠습니다!

get caught (for)~ing — …하다 잡히다, 들키다.

My teacher **got caught** watching porns on the internet.
선생님이 인터넷으로 포르노를 보다 들켰어.

I **got caught for** speeding. 속도위반으로 걸렸어.

get caught in~ — …를 만나다, 마주치다

We **got caught in** the storm at the lake.
호수에서 폭풍을 만났어.

get stuck ~ing[in] — …하느라 꼼짝달싹 못하다

I **got stuck in** traffic this morning.
아침에 교통체증에 걸렸어.

get past — 통과하다, 지나다, 잊다

Can we please **get past** this? 제발 지나간 일로 치면 안될까?

Check it Out!

A: Why don't we go to the movies tonight?
B: Why don't you **get lost**?

A: 오늘 영화보러 갈래?
B: 좀 사라져 줄래?

get married

결혼하다 *get divorced 이혼하다

I can't believe they're **getting married.**
걔네들이 결혼한다는게 믿기지 않아.

I don't want to **get married** yet.
아직 결혼 안할거야.

get me wrong

나를 오해하다

Don't **get me wrong.** I do this all the time.
오해하지마. 난 늘상 이래.

get sth straight

…을 바로잡다, 사실인지 확인해보다

So let me **get this straight.** You divorced again?
그러니까 네 말은 또 이혼했다는거야?

get sby pregnant

…을 임신시키다

I was stupid enough to **get her pregnant.**
난 멍청하게도 걔를 임신시켰어.

How'd you **get her pregnant?**
어쩌다가 걔를 임신시켰어?

get sby so hot

…을 흥분시키다 *get sby sober 술을 끊게 해주다

You **got me so hot,** I just came.
넌 날 정말 흥분시켰어. 난 방금 사정했어.

You **got me sober.** 너 때문에 내가 술을 끊게 됐어.

get sby to~

…에게 …하도록 하다

You can't **get her to** understand it.
넌 걔에게 그걸 이해시키지 못할거야.

I'm going to **get you to** talk to her.
네가 걔랑 얘기하게끔 할거야.

got sby thinking

생각하게 하다

Our anniversary is coming up and it **got me thinking.**
기념일이 다가오고 있어 그 때문에 생각이 났어.

get ~ done

…을 마치다

Please **get it done** by the afternoon.
오후까지는 끝내주세요.

We'd like to **get this thing done** today.
우리는 오늘까지 이것을 끝내고 싶어요.

get sby arrested	체포되게 하다	
	You think this is a joke? You **got me arrested**!	
	이게 장난같아? 너 때문에 내가 체포됐다고!	
get sby started on	…얘기는 꺼내지도마	
	Don't **get me started on** lady drivers.	
	여성운전자얘기는 꺼내지도마.	
get sby drunk	취하게 하다	
	What are doing? Trying to **get me drunk?**	
	뭐해? 나 취하게 할려고?	
get here [there]	여기에 오다, 거기에 가다	
	Can I **get there** by bus? 거기 버스로 갈 수 있어요?	
	What's the best way to **get there?**	
	거기 가는 최선의 방법은 뭐야?	
get to+장소명사	…에 가다	
	How long does it take to **get to** the Stadium?	
	경기장에 가려면 시간이 얼마나 걸리죠?	
get nowhere with	성과를 못내다 *get sb nowhere 효과가 없다	
	I'**m getting nowhere with** this report.	
	보고서를 작성하는 게 잘 안돼요.	
	This **is getting us nowhere!**	
	이래선 아무 결말도 안난다!	
get sby to~	…을 …로 데리고 가다	
	We have to **get her to** a hospital.	
	걜 병원에 입원시켜야 돼.	
	The subway will **get you to** the museum.	
	이 전철을 타면 박물관으로 가.	
get sby in trouble	곤경에 처하게 하다 *get sby out of trouble 곤경에서 …을 구하다	
	She can **get you in trouble.**	
	걘 너를 곤경에 빠트릴 수 있어.	
get sby into bed	…와 섹스하다	
	He really wants to **get you into bed**.	
	걘 정말 너와 섹스를 하고 싶어해.	

get to+V	…하게 되다	
	You are so cute! How did you **get to** be so cute? 넌 참 귀여워! 어떻게 그렇게 귀여운거야?	
get to know	알게 되다 *get to meet 만나게 되다	
	I was hoping to **get to know** you better. 난 너를 더 잘 알게 되기를 바랬어.	
go get	…을 가지러[사러] 가다	
	Do you want to **go get** something to eat? 밖에 나가서 뭘 좀 먹을래?	
come get	와서 …하다	
	I'll **come get** you and I'll explain everything. 와서 널 보고 모든 걸 설명할게.	
I've got~	…가 있어	
	I'm gonna go change, **I've got** a date. 나 옷갈아 입어야 돼. 데이트가 있어.	
You've got [You got]~	넌 …가 있어	
	Your agent called. **You got** that audition. 에이전트가 전화했었어. 오디션이 있대.	
I've got to+V	…해야 돼	
	All right, look. **I've gotta** tell you something. 좋아, 이봐, 난 네게 할 말이 있어.	
You've got to +V	…넌 …해야 돼	
	You gotta help me out! 넌 나를 도와야 돼!	
get to sby	짜증나게 하다	
	I guess the stress **is getting to** me. 스트레스 때문에 짜증나는 것 같아.	
get ~ back	되찾다	
	She wants to **get** her boyfriend **back.** 걘 남친을 되찾고 싶어해.	
get back+장소	…로 돌아가다	
	I need to **get back to** the office. 사무실로 돌아가야 돼.	

get

get back home	집에 돌아가다 When can we **get back home**? 우린 언제 집에 돌아갈 수 있어?
get back at sby	복수하다 She is using you to **get back at** me! 걘 나한테 복수하려고 널 이용하는 거야!
get back to sby	나중에 얘기하다 *get back to sby on sth I'll **get back to** you when you're not so busy. 안 바쁘실 때 연락할게요. I'll **get back to** you first thing in the morning. 내일 아침 바로 연락할게.
get back to sby(on~)	…에게 …에 대해 연락하다 Let me **get back to** you tomorrow on that. 그 건으로 내일 내가 연락할게.
get back to sth	처음화제로 돌아가다 Today we are going to **get back to** basics. 오늘 우린 기초로 돌아가려고.
get back to work	다시 일하러 가다 I'd like to **get back to work** as soon as I can. 가능한 한 빨리 다시 일하고 싶습니다.
get back to the way~	…하던 방식으로 돌아가다 So let's **get back to the way** we were. 자 그럼 우리 하던 방식으로 돌아가자.
get back to ~ing	…으로 돌아가다 I'm gonna **get back to** retraining. 난 다시 교육을 받을거야. I'll **get back to** painting eventually. 난 결국 그림을 그리게 될거야.
get one's act together	정신을 차리다 = get a grip, get a life, get real You gotta **get your act together.** 똑똑하게 굴어야 돼.
get a minute [second]	시간이 있다 You **got a minute?** I really need to talk to you. 시간있어? 얘기 좀 하자.

get the feeling	…라는 느낌이 든다
	I **got a feeling** he'll be back. 걔가 돌아올 것 같은 느낌이야.
get a hold of	…을 잡다, 연락하다 = get ahold of
	How can he **get a hold of** you? 걘 너한테 어떻게 연락해?
get together (with)	만나다 *get-together 만남, 모임
	I have to **get together with** my mother. It's her birthday. 우리 엄마 만나야 돼. 엄마 생신이거든.
	How did you two **get together**? 두 분은 어떻게 만나셨어요?
get in touch with	연락을 취하다
	Where can I **get in touch with** her? 어디로 연락해야 그 여자와 연락이 될까요?
	I tried to **get in touch with** you. 네게 연락하려고 했어.
get in the way	방해되다
	I think they're **getting in the way** of our friendship. 난 그것들이 우리 우정에 방해되는 것 같아.
get along with	…와 잘 지내다
	I want to **get along with** everyone. 사람들 모두와 다 잘 지내고 싶어.
get used to +N[~ing]	…에 익숙해지다 = be accustomed to *used to~ …하곤 했다
	You'd better **get used to** it. 거기에 익숙해져야 해.
get on	버스나 기차를 타다
	Where did you **get on** the bus? 버스 어디서 타셨어요?
get off	버스나 기차에서 내리다
	Could you tell me where to **get off**? 어디서 내리는지 알려줄래요?
get in	택시나 차에 타다
	Come on, **get in**, it's cold out there. 자, 어서 들어와, 밖이 춥다

get

get out	택시나 차에서 내리다
	I saw them **get out of** the car. 난 걔네들이 차에서 내리는 걸 봤어.
get out of	…에서 나가다, 떠나다
	I thought I told you to **get out of** here. 나가라고 말했던 것 같은데.
	I'**m getting out of** here. 여기서 나가야겠다.
	Get out of my house! 집에서 나가!
get out of the way	비키다
	The tree is falling. **Get out of the way!** 나무가 넘어져. 비켜서라!
get down to~	진지하게 …을 하기 시작하다
	We need to **get down to business.** 본론으로 들어가야겠어요.
	Let's **get down to business.** 자 일을 시작합시다.
get through	어려운 일을 해내다, 어려운 시기를 잘 지내다, 사람과의 관계를 끝내다
	I'm not sure we can **get through** this difficult time. 우리가 이 어려운 시기를 헤쳐나갈 수 있을지 모르겠어.
	I'll never **get through** this. 난 결코 이 일을 해낼 수 없을거야.
get through to	…와 연락이 닿다
	I'd like to **get through to** Mr. James. 제임스씨와 연락하고 싶은데요.
get away (from)	멀어지다, 벗어나다, 휴식을 취하다
	I'm glad you were able to **get away** today. 네가 오늘 쉴 수 있어 다행야.
	Hey, get back! **Get away from** her! 야, 물러서! 걔한테서 꺼지라고!
get over sth	극복하다, 이겨내다
	I can't **get over** losing you. 널 잃고는 못 견뎌.
get over sby	잊다
	I slept with Chris to **get over** you. 난 너를 잊기 위해 크리스와 잠을 잤어.

get over with sth[get sth over with]	끝내다 I just want to **get it over with.** 난 그냥 빨리 해서 끝내버렸으면 좋겠어요. Let's **get it over with.** 끝내자.
get over (to+장소)	(…에) 오다 I've got to **get over to** Jack's. 잭의 집에 가야 돼.
get on with sth	…을 계속하다 You **get on with** it. I quit. 넌 계속해. 난 그만둔다. Never mind. Let's **get on with** the game. 신경쓰지 말고 게임이나 계속하자.
get on with sby	…와 지내다(get along) How're you **getting on?** 어떻게 지내?
get right on sth	…을 바로 시작하다　*get it on 시작하다, 섹스하다 I'll **get right on** it. 당장 그렇게 하겠습니다.
get off (of)~	떨어지다, 그만두다 Would you please **get off** the phone? 전화 좀 그만 쓸래?
get off on the wrong foot	잘못 시작하다 We **got off on the wrong foot.** 우리는 잘못 시작했어.
get off work	퇴근하다, 결근하다 I need to **get off work** early on Friday. 금요일날 조퇴를 해야 해.
get into~	들어가다, 관심갖다, …하다, (학교에) 들어가다 Can we **get into** this another time? I was sleeping. 나중에 통화하면 안될까. 자던중이었어. I can't **get into** this with you now. 지금은 당신과 이 문제를 따질 수 없어. I will never **get into** medical school. 난 절대로 의대에 안 갈거야. What **are** you **getting into?** 무슨 일을 하려는거야?

get

get into fight	싸우다
	You guys **get into a fight?** 너희들 싸우니?
get carried away	빠지다, 넋을 잃다
	I'm understanding, but let's not **get carried away.** 이해하지만 너무 빠지지는 말자.
get away with it	나쁜 짓하고 벌받지 않다, 무사하다
	I will not let you **get away with this.** 네가 그걸 피할 수 없게 할거야.
	Trust me, she'll never **get away with it.** 날 믿어. 걘 무사하지 못할거야.
get around sby[sth]	돌아다니다, 피하다
	You can **get around** the rules if you are careful. 넌 조심하면 규정을 피할 수 있을거야.
get around to~	시간내서 …시작하다
	Did you **get around to** fixing the fridge? 너 시간내서 냉장고를 고쳤어?
get ahead	앞서다
	People always want to **get ahead of** each other. 사람들은 항상 서로 앞서가길 원해.
get by	겨우 살아가다, 지나가다
	Could I **get by** please? 좀 지나갈 수 있을까요?
get on one's nerve	신경에 거슬리다
	It doesn't mean you **get on my nerves.** 너 때문에 짜증난다는 말은 아냐.
get wind of~	…의 소문을 듣다
	I **got wind of** the possibility that the store would be sold. 가게가 팔릴 수도 있다는 얘길 들었어.

Check it Out!

A: Come off it! You're really getting on my nerves.
B: What's wrong with you this morning?

  A: 그만해! 너 정말 신경거슬린다.
  B: 너 오늘 아침 왜 그러는거야?

get a crush on~	…에게 반하다 Sure, she **had a crush on** Chris. 물론, 걘 크리스에게 홀딱 반했어.
get a thing for	…을 좋아하다 He **has (got) a thing for** her. 걘 그 여자를 맘에 두고 있어.
get a move on	서두르다 I'd better **get a move on** it. 빨리 서둘러야겠어.
get help	도움을 받다 We have got to **get help**. 도움을 받아야 해.
get out of hand	상황이 걷잡을 수 없게 되다 Listen, This **is totally getting out of hand.** 이 사태는 걷잡을 수 없어졌어.
get the hang of	손에 익다 I think I'**m getting the hang of** it. 난 점점 요령이 붙는 것 같아.
get the hint	눈치채다 = take the hint **Take the hint,** she doesn't want to go out with you. 정신차려, 걘 너랑 데이트하기 싫어하는거야.
get a taxi	택시를 타다 Where can I **get a taxi?** 어디서 택시를 탈 수 있나요?
get cold feet	겁먹다 What's the matter? **Are** we **getting cold feet?** 왜 그래? 우리 긴장하는거야?
get back on one's feet	자립하다 I want you to **get back on your feet.** 난 네가 빨리 재기하길 바래.
get one's own way	자기 하고 싶은대로 하다 What a bitch! She always **gets her own way.** 나쁜 것 같으니라구! 그 앤 항상 자기 맘대로라니까.

get sby down	실망시키다, 비난하다
	You can't let the boss **get you down.** 사장 때문에 괴로워하지마.

get worked up	흥분하다
	He **got really worked up.** 정말 열 받았지

get even with	복수하다
	Did you **get even with** him yet? 그에게 복수했나요?

give
v 주다

give sby sth	…에게 …을 주다
	Your aunt **gave** you this shirt. 숙모가 너한테 이 셔츠를 사주셨어. For my last birthday you **gave** me a hug! 지난 내 생일에 넌 날 포옹해줬어!

give sth to sby	…에게 …을 주다
	I'll **give it to** him the moment he walks in. 그 사람이 들어오자마자 전해 줄게요.

You gave me~	넌 …을 내게 줬어
	I'm upset about the advice **you gave me.** 난 네가 한 충고에 화가 났어.

I gave you~	너에게 …을 줬어
	I gave you a key for emergencies! 비상시를 위해 열쇠를 줬잖아!

Give me~	…을 내게 해주다
	Have a good day. **Give me** a kiss. 잘 지내. 키스해주고.

Can you give me ~ ?	내게 …해줄래요? **Can you give me** any discount? 좀 깎아줄래요?
Did you give sby ~ ?	…에게 …을 줬어? **Did you give** him a beer? 걔에게 맥주줬어?
You didn't give sby~	넌 …에게 …을 주지 않았어 Wait, **you didn't give** me your gift yet. 잠깐, 넌 아직 내게 네 선물을 주지 않았어.
give (sby) a call	전화하다 *call 대신에 ring, buzz라고 해도 된다 If you have any questions, **give me a call.** 혹 물어볼거 있으면 전화하고.
give (sby) a hand (with/ ~ing)	도와주다 Do you think you can **give me a hand** today? 오늘 저 좀 도와주실 수 있으세요? **Give me a hand with** this, Tom. 탐, 이것 좀 도와줘.
give (sby) a chance (to~)	기회를 주다 I'll **give you another chance.** 한번 더 기회를 주지.
give (sby) a ride[lift]	태워주다 How about I **give you a ride** home? 내가 집에까지 데려다 줄까?
give (sby) an answer	대답하다 Could you **give me an answer** by tomorrow? 내일까지 알려주시겠어요?
give (sby) a raise	월급을 올려주다 We need to **give the secretary a raise.** 비서 봉급을 올려줘야겠어요.
give sth a try	시도해보다 Why don't you **give it a try** right now? 지금 당장 한번 해 보는게 어때?

give

give my love [regards] to	안부를 전하다 **Give my best regards to** him for me when you see him. 걜 만나면 안부 좀 전해 주세요. Make sure you **give my love to** Cindy. 신디에게 안부 꼭 좀 전해 주세요.
give (sby) one's word	약속하다 = I'll promise I will **give you my word** I will not touch her. 내 약속하는데 걜 만지지 않을게.
give sth a break	그만하다 **Give it a break.** I hardly drink at all. 그만 좀 해라. 거의 술 안 마시잖아.
give sby a break	그만하다, 봐주다 **Give me a break.** I haven't done this before. 좀 봐줘요. 이런 적 처음이잖아요.
give it a rest	그만하다 You have to **give it a rest.** 그만 좀 해야지.
give sby a hard time	힘들게 하다 Please don't **give me a hard time.** 나를 곤란하게 하지 마세요.
give oneself a hard time	자책하다 Don't **give yourself a hard time.** 너무 자책하지마.
give sth some thought	생각 좀 해보다 You should **give it some thought.** 그거 생각 좀 해봐.
give me some time	시간을 좀 주다 I just need you to **give me some time.** 내게 시간을 좀 더 줘.
not give a damn[shit] (about)	상관하지 않다 I **don't give a damn** who slept with your wife. 누가 네 마누라하고 잤는지 난 알바 아냐.

159

give sby that	…의 말을 인정하다
	Don't **give me that.** I know all the details. 그런 말마. 속속들이 다 알고 있다고.
give it to sby straight	단도직입적으로 말하다　*give it to sby 혼내다, 섹스하다
	Give it to me straight. 솔직하게 말해줘.
I'd give anything to [for]	기필코 …하다　*anything 대신에 my right arm을 넣어도 된다.
	I'd give anything to be with you again. 다시 너랑 있을 수 있다면 뭐든지 하겠어.
	I'd give the world to go out with Jane. 무슨 일이 있어도 제인과 데이트하고 싶어.
give away	거저주다, 기회를 놓치다
	I think you should **give away** the money. 넌 돈을 기부해야 될 것 같아.
	I don't want it and I'm going to **give it away.** 난 그게 필요없어서 줘버릴거야.
give me back sth	내게 …을 돌려주다
	Give back the money you owe me. 내게 줄 돈 돌려줘.
give you back sth	네게 …을 돌려주다
	I came to **give you back** your stuff. 네 물건 돌려주려 왔어.
give in (to)	받아들이다, 따르다, 제출하다
	You're going to **give in** eventually. 너도 결국에는 받아드릴거야.
give sth over	넘겨주다, 내주다　give oneself for 몰두하다, 굴복하다
	I'll **give** the money **over** to Charles. 찰스에게 돈을 건네줄게.

Check it Out!

A: Could you **give** these keys **back to** John?
B: Sure, I'll see him at lunch.

　A: 이 열쇠 존에게 돌려줄래?
　B: 그래. 점심 때 만날거야.

give

give out
배포하다, 발표하다

The hospital won't **give out** any information.
병원은 어떠한 정보도 발표하지 않을 겁니다.

give up sth
…을 포기하다 *give up for ~ …을 포기하다

He's trying to **give up** cigarettes.
걘 담배를 끊으려고 해.

give way to
양보하다

We'll have to **give way to** the new method of production.
우리는 새로운 생산방식으로 바꿔야 될 것 같아.

give rise to
어떤 결과를 낳다, 일으키다

This decision will **give rise to** a lot of negative publicity.
이 결과는 부정적인 선전 효과를 많이 낳을거야.

give a party
파티를 열다

Let's **give Chris a retirement party.**
크리스의 퇴임파티를 열어주자.

give sth priority
우선권을 주다

Dr. Paulson **gave** the sick patients **priority.**
폴슨 의사는 중환자를 우선시했다.

give oneself a treat
몰두하다, 즐겨보다

I think I'm going to **give myself a treat!**
큰 맘 먹고 한번 즐겨볼까 해!

give off
(냄새, 빛) …을 발하다

That rotten cabbage **is giving off** an awful smell.
저 썩은 양배추에서 아주 끔찍한 냄새가 나.

give an inch
양보하다

Neither party in the divorce would **give an inch.**
이혼에서 어느 한쪽도 물러서려 하지 않고 있어.

give specifics
세세히 설명하다

Describe her room, and **give specifics.**
걔 방을 묘사하고 자세하게 설명을 해봐.

121

go
v 가다

go to+장소명사
…에 가다
I'm **going to** Florida for a couple of weeks.
몇 주간 플로리다에 갈거야.

go to+V
…하러 가다
I need to **go to** see a doctor.
의사한테 가봐야겠어.

go ~ing
…하러 가다
I'm **going shopping** today. Want to come along?
나 오늘 쇼핑가는데 같이 갈래?

went to+N
…에 갔었어
I **went to** a party last night.
어젯밤에 파티에 갔었어.

went to+V
…하러 갔었어
I don't know when she **went to** sleep.
걔가 언제 잠자러 갔는지 몰라.

go get+V
가서 …하다
Let's **go get** some ice cream.
가서 아이스크림 좀 먹자

go have+V
가서 …하다
Do what you like. You **go have** fun with the guys.
맘대로 해. 가서 얘들하고 재미있게 보내.

go take+V
가서 …하다
I have to **go take** a shower.
가서 샤워해야겠어.

go see+V
가서 …을 만나다
You'd better **go see** a doctor.
가서 진찰받아봐.

go

go meet+V	가서 …을 만나다
	Suit yourself. I have to **go meet** Sam anyhow.
	멋대로 해. 어쨌든 난 샘을 만나러 가야 돼.
go for a walk	산책하러 가다
	Want to **go for a walk?** 산책 갈래?
	How about you and I **go for a walk?**
	너와 나 산책하면 어때?
go for a drive	드라이브하러 가다
	Let's **go for a drive.** 드라이브 하자.
go for a ride ~	…을 타러가다
	Want to **go for a ride on** my boat?
	내 배 타볼래?
go for a swim	수영하러 가다
	Would you like to **go for a swin?**
	수영하러 갈래?
go for a drink [coffee]	술[커피] 마시러 가다
	Would you two girls like to **go for a drink?**
	두 여자분들 술 한잔 할래요?
go on a trip	여행하다[가다]
	I wanted to **go on a little trip.**
	가까운 여행을 가고 싶어했어.
	I can't **go on a trip** with you.
	너랑 여행못가.
go on a cruise	크루즈여행하다
	I've always wanted to **go on a cruise.**
	항상 크루즈 여행을 해보고 싶어했어.
go on a date	데이트하다
	Would you like to **go on a date** sometime?
	언제 한번 데이트할래요?
go on a diet	다이어트하다
	He needs to **go on a diet** for a while.
	걘 잠시 다이어트를 해야 돼.

go on a vacation
휴가가다

I'm thinking of **going on a vacation.**
휴가 갈 생각이야.

~ go well
…가 잘 되다

The meeting **went well.** 회의가 잘 됐어.

Well, that **went well.** 어, 그거 잘 됐어.

How's ~ going?
…가 어때?

How's your business **going?**
하는 일 어때?

How did ~ go?
…가 어땠어?

How did it **go** with Erin? 에린하고 어때?

be going to ~
…할거야

I**'m going to** be thirty in a few years.
몇 년이면 나 서른 살 돼.

I**'m not going to** take your word for that.
네 말을 믿지 않을거야.

I'm going
나 가, 나 참석해 *I'm not going 난 안가

I promise. **I'm going.** I'll meet you out there.
정말 갈게. 거기서 보자.

I'm not going. I don't want to see her.
난 안가. 걔 보기 싫어.

go wrong
잘못되다 *go bad 상하다

Something **has gone wrong.**
뭔가 잘못됐어.

Where did we **go wrong?**
우린 어디서 잘못된거지?

Milk **goes bad** quickly in hot weather.
우유는 더운 날씨에 쉽게 상해.

go grey
머리가 희어지다

You'll **go grey** if you don't dye your hair.
머리염색을 하지 않으면 머리가 희어질거야.

go mad
미치다

If you lock me up, I'll **go mad.** 날 가두면 나 미칠거예요.

go

go digital — 디지털화하다 *go international 국제화되다, go global 국제화하다

Samsung **went global** about 30 years ago.
삼성은 30여년 전에 국제화했어.

go naked — 발가벗다 = get naked

We **get naked** and have hot crazy sex.
우리는 옷 다 벗고 미친듯 섹스했어.

go too far — 지나치다 = go overboard

You'**ve gone too far.** 넌 너무 지나쳤어.

Her joke **went too far.** 걔 농담은 지나쳤어.

have+N+to go — 아직 …가 남았어, 더 …을 해야 돼

We **have** another 10 miles **to go.**
우린 아직 10마일 더 가야 돼.

Just one week **to go** to my birthday.
내 생일까지 단 일주일 남았어.

I'd like+음식 +to go — …을 포장해주세요

(I'd like) Two sandwiches **to go.**
샌드위치 두 개 포장해주세요.

(Will this be/Is that) For here or **to go?**
여기서 드실거예요 아니면 포장예요?

Will that be **to go?** 가져가실 건가요?

go easy — 서두르지 않다, 여유를 갖다

All I'm saying is I think we should **go easy.**
내말은 내 생각에 우리가 여유를 가져야 한다는거야.

go easy on sby — 살살 다루다

Go easy on me. This is my first time.
살살해 줘. 나 처음이거든.

go easy on sth — 적당히 하다

You've got to **go easy on** butter and cheese.
버터하고 치즈를 적당히 먹어야 돼.

Here goes — 한번 해봐야지, 자 이제 간다

I'm not sure if this will work. **Here goes.**
이게 될지 모르겠어. 한번 해봐야지.

Here we go	자 간다, 여기 있다
	You are going to love these. Ok, **here we go.**
	이거 좋아하게 될거야. 자 시작한다.
Here we go again	또 시작이군
	Oh no! **Here we go again!** 맙소새 또 시작이군!
Here you go	자 여기 있어요
	I made your favorite, tacos. **Here you go.**
	네가 젤 좋아하는 타코 만들었어. 자 여기.
There you go	자, 받아, 거봐, 내 말이 맞지, 그래 그렇게 하는거야
	There you go! That's the spirit I'm looking for!
	바로 그거야! 저게 바로 내가 바라던 정신이야!
There you go again	또 시작이군
	There you go again. Don't be critical of yourself.
	또 시작이군. 그만 네 얼굴 타령해라.
	There you go again! Always looking for a girl!
	또 시작이군! 맨날 여자나 찾아다니고!
There goes sth[sby]	…가 멀어져가다, 사라지다, 놓치다
	There goes your theory, Chris. Good try, though.
	크리스, 네 이론은 다 틀렸어. 그래도 시도는 좋았어.
go about	…을 풀어가다, …을 시작하다, 자기 일에 계속하다
	I don't even know how I would **go about** it.
	난 그걸 어떻게 풀어나가야 할지도 모르겠어.
	How are you going to **go about** doing that?
	그거 어떻게 시작할거야?
go after	…을 뒤쫓다, 추적하다, …을 구하려 하다
	Jim wanted to **go after** her again but I talked him out of it.
	짐은 걔를 쫓아가려 했는데 내가 말렸어
go at	공격하다, 덤벼들다, (덤벼들 듯 열심히) …일에 착수하다
	After the insult, Greg **went at** his brother.
	모욕을 받더니, 그렉은 동생을 공격했어.
go beyond	능가하다, …보다 낫다
	The facts in the report **go beyond** all reason.
	보고서사항은 전혀 사리에 안맞아.

go

go into effect	(새 법이) 실시되다 New traffic laws **go into effect** this year. 새로운 교통법이 금년에 발효돼.
go against	…에 반하다, …에 거슬리다, …에 불리해지다 You can't **go against** your classmates. 넌 학급 아이들의 의견에 반대할 수 없어
It goes against	…에 어긋나다 **It goes against** everything we stand for. 우리 주장하는 모든 것에 위배돼.
It goes against +N+to+V	…하는 것은 …에 어긋난다 **It goes against** my beliefs **to** skip church services. 교회예배를 가지 않는 건 내 신념에 어긋나.
go ahead	(재촉하며 혹은 허락하며) 어서 해, 계속해 **Go ahead** and tell them about that. 어서 걔네들한테 그거 말해줘.
go ahead with~	…을 시작[계속]하다 I don't think I can **go ahead with** it. Because it's wrong. 그걸 계속 못하겠어. 잘못됐으니까.
go ahead of~	…을 앞서가다 Let's **go ahead of** the cars that are waiting here. 여기서 기다리고 있는 차들을 앞서가자고.
go along (with)	(…에) 찬성[동의]하다, 나아가다, 해 나가다 I'll **go along with** that. 그 점에 동의해. I'm learning about it as we **go along.** 그냥 해 나가면서 그걸 배웠어.
(News or rumors) go around	…가 돌아다니다, 퍼지다 There's a rumor **going around** that she's gay. 걔가 게이라는 소문이 퍼지고 있어.

Check it Out!

A: How **are** things **going around** here?
B: They couldn't be better.

A: 여기 일이 어떻게 돼가니?
B: 아주 좋아.

go around ~ing	끊임없이 …하다
	There's plenty of fruit and fish to **go around**. 다들에게 돌아갈 만큼 과일과 고기가 많아.
	I'll **go around** and cover the back. 내가 돌아갈 테니 뒤를 커버해.
	I don't ordinarily **go around** kissing guys at parties. 난 보통 파티에서 남자애들에게 키스나 하며 돌아다니지 않아.
be plenty of+명사 +to go around	골고루 차례가 돌아갈 만큼 많다
	Do we have **enough food to go around?** 모든 사람에게 돌아갈 정도로 음식이 충분해?
go away	가다, 가버리다, (고통, 아픔 등) …가 사라지다
	Will the pain ever **go away?** Will I feel better? 아픔이 없어지긴 할까요? 나아질까요?
go away for +기간	…동안 떠나다 (leave for a period of time)
	We should **go away for** the weekend together. 우리 함께 일주일간 떠나자.
go back to some place	…로 돌아가다
	Go back to your seats. 너희들 자리로 돌아가라.
go back to+ sth[~ing]	다시 …하기 시작하다
	We'll have to **go back to** eating meat. 우린 다시 고기를 먹기 시작해야 돼.
~ go back+시간	…는 얼마된 것이다
	Our relations **go back** at least 20 years. 우리들 관계는 20년으로 거슬러 올라가.
go back on one's word [promise]	…을 어기다
	I promised to marry her, but I **went back on my word**. 걔랑 결혼하겠다고 약속했지만 없던 걸로 했어.
go by	시간이 흘러가다, …가 지나가다, 들르다, …을 흘려보내다
	I worked ten hours today. I'll **go by** tomorrow. 오늘 10시간 일했어. 내일 들를게.
	Let's just **go by** the party for a little while. 잠시 파티에 들르자.
	You used to **go by** the name of "Sam." 넌 '샘'이란 이름으로 통했었어.

go

go for
…을 얻고자 최선을 다하다, …을 좋아하다

I never thought you'd **go for** me.
네가 나를 원하는지 생각못했어.

The same **goes for** you.
너도 마찬가지야.

I would[could] go for sth
…을 원하다

I could go for some Mexican tonight.
오늘 밤은 멕시칸 음식 좀 먹어보지.

That[The same] goes for sth[sby]
…마찬가지이다

You have to stay here. **The same goes for** her.
넌 여기 있어야 돼. 걔도 마찬가지이고.

go into
…에 들어가다, (일, 직업) …을 시작하다, …을 자세히 조사[설명]하다

I have to **go into** intensive therapy right now.
지금 강력한 치료를 받아야 해.

Never **go into** business with somebody you're sleeping with.
함께 자는 사람하고는 절대로 일하지마.

go into details
자세히 검토하다   *go into labor 진통을 시작하다

As a gentleman, I would prefer not **going into details**.
신사로서 난 세부적으로는 들어가지 않을게.

(The gun, The alarm, The air bag) go off
…가 발사되다, 울리다, 터지다

I was late again today because the alarm didn't **go off**.
알람이 안울려서 오늘 또 늦었어.

go[be] off to~
…로[…하기 위해] 가다

Well, I'**m off to** China in the morning.
난 아침에 중국으로 떠나.

I'**m off to** meet Cindy's friend. How do I look?
난 신디의 친구 만나러가는데 내 모습 어때?

go off with sby
…와 함께 가다(go away with)

You **went off with** her and you never called.
넌 걔랑 가버리더니 전화도 안했어.

go off with sth
…을 허락없이 가지고 가버리다

Pete **went off with** a large bag of groceries.
피트는 식료품이 든 커다란 봉투를 들고 가버렸어.

go on with [~ing]	…을 계속하다 What's **going on with** him? 그 사람 무슨 일 있어?
go on to sth [V~]	다음으로 넘어가다, 계속해서 …하다 Shall we **go on to** the next item on the agenda? 다음 안건으로 넘어갈까요?
go on (and on) about sth[sby]	…관해 이야기를 늘어놓다 She **went on about** her sexual adventures. 걘 자신의 섹스경험을 늘어놓았다.
go out (with)	…와 데이트하다(go out on a date) I can't believe Jim **went out with** my wife! 짐이 내 아내와 데이트했다는게 안 믿겨져! He's **going out with** Jane. 그 사람은 제인하고 사귀어.
go out for ~	…하러 나가다 I came by to see if you could **go out for** dinner with me. 나랑 저녁먹을 수 있는지 확인하러 왔어.
go out to[and] +V	…하러 나가다 Let's **go out to** dinner tonight. 오늘 저녁, 외식하자.
go out ~ing	…하러 나가다 I can't **go out** tonight. Something's come up 오늘 밤 못 가. 일이 좀 생겨서
go over	검토하다(think over), 들여다보다(examine) We'll **go over** your idea during lunch. 점심먹으면서 네 생각을 검토해볼게. You want me to **go over** there now? 나보고 거기 가라고?
go through sth	어려움 등을 겪다, 경험하다, 뒤지다 I'm sorry you had to **go through** that. 네가 그 일을 겪게 돼서 안됐어. You mind if we **go through** Peter's belongings? 우리가 피터의 소지품을 뒤져봐도 괜찮니?

go

go through with sth	(내키지 않는 일을) 끝내다, 하다	
	I'd appreciate it if we don't **go through** this again. 다시는 이 일을 겪지 않았으면 좋겠어.	
go through the roof	격노하다(=hit the roof=hit the ceiling), 고점을 찍다	
	The price of fuel **has gone through the roof**. 기름값이 엄청 올랐어.	
go (well) with	…와 (잘) 어울리다, …로 선택하다, …와 함께 가다	
	This skirt and this blouse **go together well**. 이 치마와 이 블라우스가 잘 어울려요.	
go without	…없이 지내다, …없이 해나가다	
	The college students will **go without** alcohol for a week. 대학생들은 일주일간 술안마시고 지낼거야.	
go for the day	퇴근하다	
	It looks as if Sam **has gone for the day**. 샘이 퇴근한 것 같은데.	
go to the trouble	사서 고생하다	
	Who would **go to the trouble** of killing someone that way? 누가 그렇게 고생을 해가면서 사람을 죽이려할까?	
go down	…로 (내려)가다(to~), 내리다, 떨어지다	
	I told you not to **go down** there! 거기 가지 말라고 했잖아!	
	Why don't we **go down to** the bar? 바에 가자.	
go together	함께 가다	
	Let's **go together** and grab dinner before. 같이 가서 그 전에 저녁부터 먹자.	
go behind one's back	뒤통수치다	
	She **went behind my back** to the boss. 걘 내 뒤에서 사장에게 날 비난했어.	
go under	(사업이) 파산하다, 실패하다	
	It **went under** because it was a poor restaurant. 레스토랑은 형편없었기 때문에 망했어.	

go up	오르다, 올라가다
	You need to **go up** one more floor. 한 층 더 올라가셔야 해요.
Don't go there	(그 얘기) 꺼내지마
	Don't go there. She won't talk about it. 그 얘기는 하지마. 걔 말하려고 하지 않을거야.
let go of	…을 놔주다
	Get your hands off me! **Let go of** me. You don't own me. 나 건드리지마! 날 놔둬. 난 네 소유가 아냐
go nuts	…을 좋아하다, 화내다
	He's going to **go nuts.** 걔가 무척 화낼거야.
	She's going to **go nuts** for it. 걔가 엄청 좋아할거야.
go abroad	해외로 가다
	I'd like to **go abroad** for a few years. 난 몇 년간 해외로 가고 싶어.
let sby go	…을 가게 하다, 해고하다
	Are you still sad Mom wouldn't **let you go** to Paris. 엄마가 파리 못가게 해서 아직도 화났어?
go all the way	갈데까지 가다
	They went **all the way** the other night. 걔들은 요전날 갈데까지 갔다.
go from bad to worse	설상가상이다
	The situation **went from bad to worse.** 설상가상이야.
go out of one's way to~	…하기 위해 애를 많이 쓰다
	He **goes out of my way to** help me. 그는 날 돕기 위해 애를 많이 썼다.

good

a. 좋은, 효과적인, 수나 양이 충분한　**adv.** 잘　**n.** 선, 도움, 소용　goods 상품

be good at~
…에 능숙하다

What **are** you **good at**? 너 뭐 잘하니?

She'**s really good at** singing. 쟤는 진짜 노래를 잘해.

be good for~
…에 좋다

What time would **be good for** you?
몇시가 좋으시겠어요?

Good for you!
잘됐어!

Good for you! You deserve it.
잘됐네. 넌 자격이 있잖아.

be in a very good mood
기분이 무척 좋다

I thought he **was in a particularly good mood.**
걔가 무척 기분이 좋다고 생각했어.

it's good (for sby) to+V
…가 …하는 것은 좋은 일이야

It's not good for you to stay up too late.
너무 늦게까지 안자고 있는 건 좋지 않아.

It's good for you to eat some vegetables.
야채를 먹는게 너한테 좋아.

it's a good thing that~
…은 다행이야

That's a good thing to do while the weather is nice.
날씨 좋을 때 세차하는게 좋지.

not good enough
충분하지 못한

He's **not good enough** to raise a child.
걔는 애를 키우기에는 부족해.

do sby good
…에게 득이 되다

I won't be driving you to school. The walk will **do you good.**
차로 학교 데려다 주지 않을거야. 걷는게 네게 도움이 될거야.

| What's the good of~ ? | …하는게 무슨 소용이 있어?
What's the good of working a job you hate?
네가 싫어하는 일을 해봤자 무슨 소용이 있어? |

123 grow
v. 자라다, 성장하다, 재배하다

grow up	성장하다 You have to **grow up** and act like an adult. 철 좀 들어서 어른처럼 행동해라.
grow up and +V	자라서 …되다 *grow up to be~ He will **grow up and** work for the government. 걔는 자라서 공무원이 될거야.
grow+숫자	…만큼 자라다 The tree **grew** three times taller this year. 그 나무는 올해 3배나 컸어.
생각+grow in sby	…에서 …라는 생각이 자라다 Thoughts of getting married **grew in** her mind. 결혼해야겠다는 생각이 그녀 맘속에서 자랐어.
grow+형용사	점점 …해지다 *grow old, grow cold We **grew** anxious when the flight was delayed. 우리는 비행편이 지연됐을 때 걱정이 됐어.
grow out of+옷	커서 옷이 맞지 않다 Most kids **grow out of** playing with toys. 대부분의 애들은 크면 장난감을 갖고 놀지 않지.
sth[sb] grow on you	…을 좋아하기 시작하다 Well, hopefully, it'll **grow on** you. 저기 바라건대, 네가 그걸 좋아하게 될거야.

good

guess
n. 추측 **v.** 추측하다, …라고 생각하다

take a guess
짐작하다(venture a guess)

I will **take a guess** on who had the nerve to do that.
누가 그걸 할 용기가 있는지 알아 맞춰볼게.

anybody's guess
예상하기 어려운 것

That's **anybody's guess.**
아무도 몰라.

How much longer is **anybody's guess.**
얼마나 긴지는 아무도 몰라.

Your guess is as good as mine.
모른긴 나도 매한가지야.

I guess (that)~
…라고 생각하다

I guess I fell asleep at the wheel.
운전 중에 존 것 같아.

Do you have the time? **I guess** I'm late.
몇 시야. 늦은 것 같아.

I guess so
그렇다고 생각한다

I guess so. Wish me luck. 그럴 걸. 행운을 빌어줘.

Let me guess
가만있자, 추측해보건데, 말 안해도 알아

Let me guess. You don't want to go there?
말 안해도 알아. 넌 거기 가고 싶지 않은거지?

hand

n. 도움, 일손 **v.** 건네주다, 도와주다

need a hand	도움이 필요하다 I thought you might **need a hand**. 네가 도움을 필요로 할지 모른다고 생각했어. Do you **need a hand** with that? 그거 도와줄까?
give (sby) a hand	(…을) 도와주다 Can you **give me a hand**? 좀 도와줄래? It's my turn to **lend a hand**. 지금 내가 도와줄 차례인 걸.
have one's hand full	무척 바쁘다 I **have my hands full**! 너무 바빠서 다른 일을 할 겨를이 없어!
put sth in the hands of	…의 수중에 맡기다 Don't **put** your fate **in the hands of** others. 네 운명을 다른 사람의 손에 맡기지마.
hold one's hand	…의 손을 잡다 I don't need anyone to **hold my hand**. 누가 내 손 잡아줄 필요없어.
get your hands on	…을 얻는데 성공하다 How did you **get your hands on** the secret? 그 비밀을 어떻게 얻어냈어?
have[get] sby [sth] on one's hands	…가 수중에 있다 I've **got** a little time **on my hands**. 지금 시간이 별로 없어. I **don't have** anything **on my hand**! 난 빈털터리야!

hand

put one's hand(s) on …손을 대다, 붙잡다

He **put his hand on** my chest and kissed me.
걘 내 가슴에 손을 얹고 키스를 했어.

get[take] one's hands off …에서 손을 떼다

Stop it! **Get your hands off** me!
그만해! 내게서 손을 떼!

Would you just **take your hands off** me?
내게서 손 좀 치워줄래?

put one's hand together for~ …에게 큰 박수를 보내다

Put your hands together for our next speaker.
다음 연사에게 큰 박수를 보내주십시오.

hand sby sth …에게 …을 건네주다

Can you **hand** me the salt? 소금 좀 줄래?

Hand me the tissues. 티슈 좀 줘요.

have (got) to hand it to sby …에게 손들다

I've **got to hand it to** you!
너 정말 대단하구나!

I've **got to hand it to** you. You are a strong man.
너 정말 대단해. 넌 강한 남자야.

hand down 내리다, 전해주다, 물려주다

Grandma **handed down** some of her jewelry to me.
할머니는 보석 몇 개를 내게 물려주셨어.

hand in 제출하다(submit)

Did you **hand in** the report you were working on?
네가 작업하던 레포트 제출했어?

hand out (사람들에게) 나누어주다, 배포하다(give out)

I stood in the doorway **handing out** pamphlets.
문에 서서 팜플렛을 나눠줬어.

hand over (권리 등을) 양도하다, 넘겨주다

Hand over some money to pay the bill.
계산서 지불하게 돈 좀 줘.

hang

n. 요령 **v.** 매달다, 놀다

get the hang of
…을 다루는 법을 알다, 요령을 터득하다

Don't worry. You'll **get the hang of** it.
걱정마. 곧 익숙해질거야.

hangover
숙취, 후유증

I have a **hangover.**
술이 아직 안 깼나봐.

She woke up with the worst **hangover** of her life.
걘 최악의 숙취상태로 깨어났어.

hang around
(…와) 어울리다, 어슬렁거리다

He's just really great to **hang around** with.
걘 같이 어울리기 정말 좋은 애야.

hang in there
(어려운 상황) 참고 견디다

I'll be right back. **Hang in there.**
바로 돌아올게. 참고 견뎌.

hang on
잠시 (끊지 않고) 기다리다, …을 꼭 붙잡다(~to)

We're going to take care of you. Just **hang on.**
저희가 잘 돌봐드릴게요, 기다려요.

Hang on, don't do this.
잠깐, 이러지마.

hang out (with)
…와 친하게 지내다

Just **hang out with** me.
나랑 그냥 놀자.

Do you know of any cool places to **hang out?**
가서 놀 만한 데 어디 근사한 데 알아?

hang up
전화를 끊다

Please **hang up** the phone.
제발 전화 좀 끊어.

Don't **hang up.** Just listen.
전화 끊지 말고 내 얘기 들어.

hang with	사귀다, 어울리다

It's my last chance to **hang with** my girlfriends.
내 여자친구들과 어울릴 수 있는 마지막 기회야.

I'm going to let you **hang with** Cindy.
신디와 어울리는거 허락해줄게.

127 happen
ⓥ 일어나다, 우연히 …하다

happen	(무슨 일이) 일어나다

Let's see what **happens.** 어떻게 되나 보자고.

Tell me what **happened.** 무슨 일이 있었는지 말해.

How did it **happen?** 이게 어떻게 된거야?

be happening	(무슨 일이) 일어나다, 벌어지다

This can't **be happening.** 이런 일은 있을 수가 없어.

How can this **be happening?** 어떻게 이런 일이 일어나는거지?

What happened?	무슨 일이야?, 어떻게 된거야?

I can't believe it! **What happened?** 말도 안돼! 무슨 일이야?

What's happening? You're OK? 무슨 일이야? 너 괜찮아?

happen to [with]~	…에게 일어나다, …가 어떻게 되다

What happened to[with] you? 너 무슨 일이야?, 왜 그래?

How could this **happen to** me? 나한테 어떻게 이런 일이 생긴단 말야?

can[could] happen	그럴 수도 있다

It **could happen.** 그럴 수도 있겠지.

That **can't happen.** 말도 안돼, 그렇지 않아.

It was a simple mistake. It **could happen** to anyone.
단순한 실수였어. 누구나 그럴 수 있어.

What's the worst that **could happen?** 무슨 나쁜 일이야 나겠어?

never happen	절대 그렇지 않다
	That **has never happened** before. 이런 적 처음이야.
	That **never happened** to me. 이런 경험 처음이야.
	It **never happened.** 이런 적 한번도 없었어.
	It**'s never going to happen.** 절대 그런 일 없을거야.

happen to+V	우연히 …하다
	I **happened to** be there last night. 지난 밤에 마침 거기에 있었어.
	Haven't we met before? Do you **happen to** know about Jane? 우리 만난 적 있어? 혹시 제인 아니?

If anything happens	무슨 일이 생기면
	If anything happens to that child, you're a dead man. 저 아이에게 무슨 일 생기면 넌 끝장야.

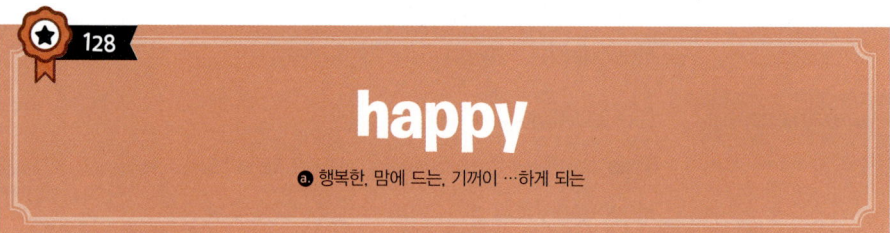

128 happy

ⓐ 행복한, 맘에 드는, 기꺼이 …하게 되는

be happy about~	…에 기쁘다
	Aren't you **happy about** this promotion? 이번 승진이 기쁘지 않아?

be happy ~ing	…해서 기쁘다
	You**'re not happy** living in Boston? 너 보스톤에서 사는게 좋지 않구나?

be happy with~	…에 만족하다
	She**'s not happy with** her sex life. 걔는 자기 성생활에 불만이야

be happy to+V	…하게 되어 기쁘다, 기꺼이 …하다
	I **was happy to** spend time with you. 함께 시간 보내서 즐거웠어.

happen

be happy for sby	…가 잘돼서 기쁘다
	That is great. I'm **so happy for** you.
	잘됐네. 잘돼서 나도 기뻐.
make sb happy	…을 기쁘게 하다
	Now it's your turn to make an effort to **make** Kate happy.
	이제 네가 노력해서 케이트를 기쁘게 해줄 차례야.

hard
ⓐ 단단한, 곤란한   **adv.** 열심히, 몹시

It's hard (for sby) to+V	…가 …하는 것은 힘들다
	We tried following you, but **it was hard to** keep up.
	널 따라갈려고 했지만 쫓아가기 힘드네.
be hard on sby	…에게 심하게 굴다
	Don't **be so hard on** yourself.
	너무 자책하지마.
	You shouldn't **be so hard on** her.
	넌 걔한테 넘 심하게 하면 안돼.
hard to believe	믿기 어려운
	You may find this very **hard to believe,** but it's true.
	이건 좀 믿기 어렵지만 사실이야.
do sth the hard way	고생하면서 …을 하다
	I guess we're gonna have to **do this the hard way.**
	우리가 이걸 고생하면서 해야될 것 같아.
give sb a hard time	…을 힘들게 하다
	Don't **give her a hard time.** 걔 너무 심하게 대하지마.
have a hard time	힘든 때를 보내다
	I'm still **having a hard time** accepting the decision.
	난 그 결정을 받아들이는데 아직도 어려움이 있어.

learn the hard way	많은 실수를 해가면서 배우다 He's just gonna have to **learn the hard way.** 걘 고생하면서 배워야 할거야.
no hard feelings	반감, 나쁜 감정 **No hard feelings** about you leaving me behind. 날 두고 간거 기분 나쁘게 생각안해.

130

hate

n. 싫어함   v. 싫어하다, 미워하다, …하고 싶지 않다

hate to~[~ing]	…하기를 싫어하다 I **hate to** disturb you, but this is important. 방해하고 싶진 않지만 중요한 일이라서요.
I hate it when~	…할 때 정말 싫더라 I **hate it when** they do that. 걔네들이 저럴 때 싫어.
hate sby ~ing	…가 …하는게 싫어 I **hate** people getting down on themselves. 난 자책하는 사람들이 싫어.
I hate to think~	…라고 생각하기가 싫어 I **hate to think** how lonely he was when he died. 난 걔가 죽었을 때 얼마나 외로웠는지 생각하기 싫어.
I hate to say it, but ~	말하기 정말 싫지만… I **hate to say it, but** we just wasted a lot of time. 말하지 정말 싫지만, 우리는 많은 시간을 낭비했을 뿐이야.

have

131

v. 먹다, 마시다, (병에) 걸리다

---

have a drink — 술마시다

Let's go **have a drink** together, tonight.
오늘 저녁 함께 술 마시자.

---

have the same — 같은 걸로 먹다

I'll **have the same.** 같은 걸로 주세요.

I'll **have what she's having.**
저 여자가 먹는 걸로 주세요.

---

have dinner [lunch] (with~) — …와 저녁[점심]하다

I thought we could **have dinner** some night.
언제 밤에 저녁을 먹을 수 있을거라 생각했어.

---

have high blood pressure — 고혈압이다

I **have high[low] blood pressure.**
고[저]혈압이야.

---

have a high temperature — 열이 많이 나다

I **have a high temperature.** 열이 많이 나.

---

have food poisoning — 식중독에 걸리다

I **have food poisoning.** 식중독이야.

---

have a hangover — 숙취가 있다

I **have a hangover.** 술이 아직 안깼나봐.

---

have diarrhea — 설사하다

I **have diarrhea.** 나 설사해.

---

have a nervous breakdown — 신경쇠약에 걸리다

I think I'm about to **have a nervous breakdown.**
신경쇠약에 걸릴 것 같아.

have one's hands full	바쁘다	
	I **have my hands full!** 너무 바빠서 다른 일을 할 겨를이 없어요!	
have a lot on one's mind	마음이 복잡하다	
	I just **have a lot on my mind.** 신경쓸게 많아요, 할 일이 많아요.	
have A in mind	…을 염두에 두고 있다	
	Do you **have** any particular restaurant **in mind?** 특별한 식당 생각해둔데 있어?	
	What do you **have in mind?** 뭘 생각하고 있어?	
have sth going	뭔가 돌아가고 있다	
	You two really **have something going,** don't you? 너희 둘, 정말로 뭔가가 잘되고 있는 거지, 그지 않아?	
have everything ready	모든 준비를 하다	
	We're going to **have everything ready.** 우리는 모든 준비를 할거야.	
have+사람+V [~ing]	…시키다, …하게 하다	
	I'll **have** him **call** you back. 걔보고 네게 전화하라고 할게.	
	I will **have** my secretary **work** on the file. 비서보고 그 서류 작업하라고 할게.	
	You **had** it **coming!** 네가 자초한거야!	
have+사물+pp	…가 …되도록 하다	
	Call the police! I **had** my bag **stolen!** 경찰불러요! 가방 소매치기 당했어요!	
	She **had** her teeth **pulled out.** 이를 뽑았어.	
I have to+V	나는 …해야만 한다	
	I'm sorry, but I **have to** cancel my reservation. 미안하지만 예약을 취소해야 돼요.	
I have to admit that ~	…한 것을 인정하지 않을 수 없다	
	I have to admit that it's pretty tough. 정말이지 쉽지 않네요.	

have

You have to+V	넌 …해야 돼	
	You have to be honest with me. 너 나한테 솔직히 말해.	
You don't have to+V	…할 필요없어, …하지 않아도 돼	
	It's all right. **You don't have to** explain. 괜찮아. 설명 안해도 돼	
Do I have to ~?	내가 …해야 하나요?	
	Do I have to spell it out for you? 다시 분명히 설명해야 돼?	
What do I have to ~?	내가 무엇을 …해야 하나요?	
	What do I have to do to get you to shut up? 너 입다물게 하려면 어떻게 해야 돼?	
You'd better +V	…하도록 해	
	You'd better hurry up. We might be late. 서둘러. 늦을지 몰라.	
You'd better not+V	…하지 마	
	You'd better not go outside. It's raining. 나가지마. 밖에 비와.	
have a big sale	빅세일을 하다	
	We**'re having a big sale** this week. 이번 주중에 세일을 크게 해요.	
have a talk	얘기를 나누다	
	Can we **have a talk?** 이야기 좀 할 수 있겠니?	
have a fight	싸우다	
	You guys **have a fight?** 너희들 싸웠어?	
have a little chat with~	…와 수다를 좀 떨다	
	I**'m having a little chat with** her. 난 걔와 수다를 떨고 있어.	
have a suggestion	제안을 하다	
	I **have a suggestion** that was given to me by a colleague last week. 지난 주 제 동료 한사람이 알려준 건의사항이 하나 있습니다.	

have a[the] feeling	…라는 생각이 들다 *have feelings for~ …에게 맘이 있다
	I **have a feeling** that she is not going to show up. 걔가 안 올 것 같아.

have a hunch	…라는 느낌이 들다
	I **have a hunch** he's lying to me. 걔가 거짓말하는 느낌이 들어.

have a problem with	…에게 불만이 있다 *have no problem with …에게 불만이 없다
	I **have no problem with** that. 난 괜찮아요. Do you **have a problem with** me? 나한테 뭐 불만있어?

have a question	질문이 있다
	I **have a question** about your report. 네 보고서 물어볼 게 있어.

have a chance to+V[of ~ing]	…할 가능성이 있다
	I'm sorry I didn't **have a chance to** call. 전화 못 해서 미안해. We might actually **have a chance of** winning this. 이걸 이길 가능성이 있을지 몰라.

have an appointment (with sb, to+동사)	(…와, …할) 약속이 있다 *병원약속, 미장원약속, 손님약속
	I **have an appointment to** see Dr. Kim 김선생님 진찰 예약되어 있어요.

have a[no] plan	계획이 있다[없다]
	It looks like she might **have a plan.** 걔 계획이 있는 것 같아.

have a heart	동정을 베풀다 *have no heart 인정사정없다
	Have a heart. I really need a vacation. 좀 봐줘요. 정말 휴가 가야 돼요.

have a point	일리가 있다, 맞다
	I think he might **have a point.** 내 생각에 걔가 일리가 있는 것 같아.

have a baby	애를 낳다
	I'm going to **have a baby.** 난 애를 낳을거야.

have

have an appetite for~	…을 좋아하다	
	She **has an appetite for** rap music. 걔는 랩 음악을 좋아해.	
have a shot [try]	한번 해보다	
	Let me **have a shot[try/stab] at** it. 내가 한번 해볼게.	
have an affair	바람피다	
	I have no doubt he **was having an affair with** Jane. 걔가 제인하고 관계를 가졌다는데 의심의 여지가 없어.	
have a bad connection	전화가 혼선이다	
	We **have a bad connection.** 혼선이야.	
have a flat tire	타이어가 펑크나다	
	I **have a flat tire.** 타이어가 펑크났어요.	
have an eye for~	…을 보는 눈이 있다	
	She **has an eye for** it. 그 여자도 안목이 있어요.	
have a little fender-bender	가벼운 접촉사고가 나다 *have an accident 사고가 나다	
	I **had a little fender-bender.** 작은 접촉 사고가 있었어.	
have an understanding	서로 이해하다	
	I thought we **had an understanding.** 우린 약속된 거 아니었어.	
have a fit	발작하다	
	She almost **had a fit.** 까무러칠 뻔했다.	
have a reputation	명성이 있다	
	You **have a reputation** for driving a hard bargain. 당신은 어려운 거래를 잘 성사시킨다는 명성을 가지고 있어요.	
have a bad day	재수없는 날이다	
	I **had a bad day.** 진짜 재수없는 날이야.	
have a hectic day	바쁜 날이다	
	I **had a pretty hectic day.** 정신없이 바빴어.	

have a rough day	힘든 하루이다	
	I **had a rough day.** 힘든 하루였어.	
	I **had a big day.** 내겐 오늘 중요한 일이 있었어.	
have a good time	즐거운 시간을 보내다	
	I really **had a good time.** 정말 즐거웠어.	
	I'm just here with my friends **having a good time.** 그냥 친구들과 놀러 온 거예요.	
have time to [for]	…할 시간이 있다	
	I don't **have time for** this. 이럴 시간 없어.	
	Do you **have time to** go there for me? 날 위해 거기 갈 시간 돼?	
have enough (+명사)	(…가) 충분하다	
	I don't **have enough** help. 충분한 도움을 못 받고 있어.	
have enough of+명사	…가 충분하다	
	I**'ve had enough of** you. 이제 너한테 질렸어.	
have enough to+V	…할 것이 충분하다	
	I hope you **had enough to** eat. 충분히 먹었길 바래.	
have fun	재미있다	
	Did you **have fun** with her? 걔하고 재밌었어?	
have second [another] thought	(번복이나 수정하기 위해) 다시 생각하다 *부정으로 쓰면 다시 생각하지 않다, 걱정하지 않다	
	We**'re having second thought about** it. 우리는 그걸 다시 생각하고 있어.	
have one's word	…의 말을 믿다 *give one's word는 약속을 하다	
	You **have my word.** 내 약속하지.(= You have my promise)	
have company	일행이 있다	
	You want to come over now? You **have company.** 지금 오겠다고? 손님있는데.	
have money	돈이 있다	
	I **have a lot of money** on me now. 난 지금 돈이 많아.	

have

have the nerve [guts] — 용기가 있다
I can't believe she **had the nerve to** kiss Chris.
걔가 크리스에게 키스할 용기를 냈다니.

have every right to+V — …할 만하다, …하는 게 당연하다 *every가 빠지면 …할 권리가 있다
You **have every right to** be angry with me
네가 내게 화낼만 해.

have faith in — …을 믿다
My father doesn't **have any faith in** me.
우리 아빠는 나한테 아무런 신뢰를 갖고 있지 않으셔.

have one's own way — …의 방식대로 하다
She won't always **get her own way.**
걘 항상 자기 방식대로만 하지는 않을거야.

have no idea — 모르다
I **had no idea** you are into this stuff.
이런 걸 좋아하는지 몰랐군.

I have no idea 의문사 S+V [의문사 to+V~] — (…인지) 몰라
I **have no idea what** it is. 그게 뭔지 모르겠어.
I **have no idea what** you are talking about.
네가 무슨 말을 하는 건지 모르겠어.

You have no idea 의문사 S+V [의문사 to+V~] — (넌 …인지) 모를거야
You have no idea what she did the last time.
넌 걔가 지난번에 뭘 했는지 모를거야.

Do you have any idea 의문사 S+V [의문사 to+V]? — 넌 (…인지) 알아?
Do you have any idea when it might arrive?
언제 도착할 지 아시나요?

Check it Out!

A: Can you pick up dinner on the way home?
B: No, I don't **have time to** get it.
  A: 집에 가는 길에 저녁을 사갈 수 있니?
  B: 아니, 그럴 시간 없어.

have no doubt	틀림없다, 의심의 여지가 없다
	I **have no doubt** you'll do well. 분명 네가 잘 할거야.
have no choice	선택의 여지가 없다 *have no choice but to+V 어쩔 수 없이 …해야 한다
	You **have no choice** in this matter. 이 문제에서 넌 선택의 여지가 없어.
have no reason for[to+V]~	…할 이유가 없다
	I **have no reason to** trust you. 내가 널 믿을 이유는 하나도 없어.
Rumor has it~	…라는 소문을 들었어
	Rumor has it the store's going to shut down. 소문에 의하면 그 가게가 문닫을거래.
May I have~?	…을 주실래요?
	May I have your email address? 이메일 주소 알려줄래요?
have to do with	…과 관련이 있다
	What does that **have to do with** you? 그게 너와 무슨 상관이야? Does it **have to do with** your family? 그게 너희 가족과 관련이 있어?
have something to do with	…와 관련이 있다
	Our accident **had something to do with** the weather. 우리가 당한 사건은 날씨와 관련이 있었어.
have nothing to do with	…와 아무 관련이 없다
	I **had nothing to do with** hurting you. 난 너를 다치게 한 것과 전혀 관련이 없었어
have something to+V	…할 것이 좀 있다
	We **have something to** show you. 너한테 보여줄 게 있어.
have nothing to+V	…할 것이 아무 것도 없다
	I **have nothing to** complain about. 아무 불만 없어.
have any+명사	…가 있다
	I don't think she **has any** intention of doing that. 걔가 그걸 할 생각이 전혀 없을 것 같아.

have

don't have any~	…가 하나도 없어 I **don't have any** plans for now. 지금으로선 아무 계획이 없어.
Do you have any~ ?	혹은 …가 있어? **Do you have any** identification? 혹 신분증 있나요?
have had it with~	…에 질리다 I**'ve had it with** you guys. 너희들한테 질려버렸다.
have had it up to here (with~)	…에 진절머리 나다 I**'ve had it up to here with** you! 너라면 이제 치가 떨려, 너한테 질려버렸어!
I've had+명사	…해왔어 I**'ve had** some personal problems 개인적인 문제가 좀 있어
I've never had+명사	…을 해본 적 없어 I**'ve never had** a one-night stand. 원나잇스탠드 해본 적 없어.
It's been+명사 [형용사]	…였어 **It has been** fun. 재밌었어. **It has been** a while. 오랜 만이야.
It has been+ 시간+since ~	…한지 …나 됐다 **It has been four years since** we last met. 이거 안지가 얼마나 됐어? **It has been 5 months since** I left Korea. 결혼한지 얼마나 됐어?
have everything sby needs	…가 원하는 모든 것을 갖다 You seem to **have everything you need**. 네가 원하는 건 다 갖은 것 같아.
have sth in stock [out of stock]	재고가 있다[없다] I'll check to see if we **have any in stock**. 재고가 있는지 찾아 볼게요.

head

n 머리 **v** 특정방향으로 가다, 책임지다

be out of one's head	제정신이 아니다 What are you doing? **Are you out of your mind?** 너 뭐하는 거야? 미쳤냐?
be[get] in over one's head	감당할 수 없는 일에 연루되다 I think I might **be in over my head.** 난 감당이 안될 것 같아.
keep one's head above water	어려운 상황을 간신히 꾸려 나가다 You'll need to work hard to **keep your head above water.** 망하지 않고 꾸려가려면 열심히 일해야 될거야.
keep one's heads up	기운내다 It was a bad time, but we **kept our heads up.** 안좋은 때지만 우리는 기운을 냈어.
get ~ out of one's head	…을 잊다, 그만 생각하다 I haven't been able to **get her out of my head** all summer. 난 여름내내 걔를 머릿속에서 지울 수가 없었어.
give sb the heads up on~	…대해 미리 일러주다 *heads up 사전충고 Just **give me a heads up on** the new product line. 신상품군에 대해 내게 미리 좀 알려줘.
head for	…로 향하다 We'll grab a bite to eat before we **head for** the airport. 우린 공항에 가기 전에 식사를 조금 할거야.
head toward	…로 향하다 You might as well **head toward** the library. 넌 도서관으로 가는게 나을거야.

hear

v. 들리다, 듣다

hear sby
…의 얘기를 듣다

I'm sorry I can't **hear** you. 미안하지만 안들려요.

It's good to **hear** your voice. 네 목소리 들으니 좋아.

I can't[couldn't] **hear** you. 안 들려.

You heard me
명심해

You heard me, son, turn it down!
시키는대로 해, 자식아. 소리줄이라고!

I hear you
너랑 동감이야

I hear you. It isn't fair that all this falls on you.
동감이야. 이게 다 네탓이라는 건 부당해.

Do you hear me?
내 말 듣고 있니?, 알았어?

I need you to pay attention. **Do you hear me?**
주목해봐. 내말 듣고 있니?

hear sby[sth] +V[~ing]
…가 …하는 것을 듣다

I**'ve never heard** him **make** that sound.
걔가 그런 소리를 내는거 못 들어봤어.

I**'ve never heard** her **talk** like this.
걔가 이렇게 말하는거 못 들어봤어.

I heard you say that S+V
네가 …라고 말하는 걸 들었어

I heard you say that she was emotionally unstable.
네가 걔 정서적으로 불안정하다고 한 말 들었어.

You never heard me say that S+V
넌 내가 …라고 하는 말을 들은 적이 없어

You never heard me say that I love you.
넌 내가 널 사랑한다는 말을 들어본 적이 없어.

You never heard me say that.
넌 내가 그렇게 말하는 걸 들은 적이 없어.

I('ve) heard that S+V	…라고 들었다 *hear that S+V …을 듣다	
	I hear you've been promoted. 너 승진했다며.	
	I heard you had some fun with her last night. 지난 밤에 걔하고 재밌게 보냈다며.	
	I heard you were going to get married. 너 결혼할거라며.	
Have you heard [Did you hear] that ~?	…라는 소식 들었니?	
	Did you hear that she went to China for study? 걔가 공부하러 중국에 간거 알아?	
never heard	…을 전혀 듣지 못하다	
	I can't believe it. I**'ve never heard** of such a thing. 말도 안돼. 그런 얘기 들어본 적이 없어.	
I didn't hear~	…을 못 들었다	
	I didn't hear you come in. 네가 들어오는 소리 못 들었어.	
	I didn't hear you leave the hotel room. 네가 호텔 나갔다는 얘기 못 들었어.	
I have never heard~	…을 들어본 적이 없다	
	You've never heard that before? 그거 전에 못 들어봤어?	
hear sby out	…의 말을 끝까지 듣다	
	Please, **hear me out.** This is important. 좀 잘 들어봐. 중요하다고.	
hear about	…에 관한 듣다 *hear about sby ~ing …가 …한다는 이야기를 듣다	
	How did they **hear about** my divorce? 걔들이 내가 이혼한 걸 어떻게 알았대?	
	I **heard about** you **getting** married next month. 네가 다음 달에 결혼한다는 이야기 들었어.	
hear of	…의 소식을 듣다	
	I **never heard of** such a thing. 말도 안돼.	
	I**'ve never heard of** you until this morning. 오늘 아침까지 네 소식 들은 게 없었어.	
	You ever **hear of** it? 그거 들어본 적 있어?	

hear

hear from | …로부터 듣다
I haven't **heard from** him since the divorce.
이혼 이후에 걔 소식 몰라.
Unfortunately, I never **heard from** him.
안됐지만 걔한테서 들은 소식 없어.

From what I hear(d) | 내가 듣기로
From what I hear, that's going to take a while.
내가 듣기로는 시간이 좀 걸릴거야.

hear it through the grapevine | 소문으로 듣다
I **heard it through the grapevine** the other day.
요전날 소문으로 들었어.

134 heart
n. 심장, 마음, 핵심.

have a good [big] heart | 마음이 좋다[넓다]
He's **got such a good heart.** 걘 무척 자상한 얘야.

have a heart | 인정이 있다
That was a little girl! Don't you **have a heart?**
어린 소녀였잖아! 인정도 없어?

have one's heart set on ~ing | …하기로 마음먹다
My son **has his heart set on** going to Africa.
내 아들은 아프리카에 가려고 작심을 했어.

not have the heart to+V | …할 용기를 내지 못하다
I **didn't have the heart to** tell her to stop that.
난 걔한테 그걸 그만두라고 할 용기가 없었어.

learn~ by heart | 암기하다
Gina **learned** the song **by heart.**
지나는 그 노래를 외웠어.

help

n. 도움 **v.** 돕다, 도움이 되다

---

need (some) help

도움이 (좀) 필요하다

I **need help** with this. 이 문제에 대해서 도와주었으면 좋겠어.

We got to **get help**. 도움을 받아야 해.

You **want help** or not? 도움을 원하는거야 원하지 않는거야?

---

be a great[big] help (to)

(…에게) 큰 도움이 되다

Thanks. You've **been a great help.** 고마워. 도움 많이 됐어.

Actually you **were a big help tonight.** 정말 넌 오늘밤 큰 도움이 됐어.

Thank you. You've **been very helpful.** 고마워. 넌 정말 도움이 많이 됐어.

It would be very helpful to+V [if S+V]

…하면 무척 도움이 될거야

It would be helpful to know his email address.
걔 이메일주소를 알면 도움이 될텐데.

---

with the help of sby

…의 도움을 받아, …덕택에

I could solve the problem **with the help of** Hellen.
헬렌의 도움으로 이 문제를 풀 수 있었어.

---

help sby do

…가 …하는 것을 돕다

I'll **help** you **finish** washing the dishes if you like.
괜찮으면 설거지 도와줄게.

---

help sby with

…가 …하는 것을 돕다

Can I **help** you **with** anything? 도와드릴까요?

Let me **help** you **with** that. 내가 그거 도와줄게.

---

help

도움이 되다 *help+V …하는데 도움이 되다

It will **help** solve the traffic problems.
교통문제를 해결하는 데 도움이 될거야.

(Sometimes) That **helps.** (간혹) 도움이 돼.

Leave me alone. You're **not helping.** 나 혼자 내버려 둬. 넌 도움이 안돼.

help

help yourself (to~)	(…을) 마음껏 들어요 Go ahead, **help yourself.** Take whatever you want. 어서 편히 들어. 뭐든 다 갖다 먹어. **Help yourself to** the cake. 케익 마음껏 들어. **Help yourself to** whatever's in the fridge. 냉장고에 있는 거 아무거나 들어.
can't help ~ing	…하지 않을 수 없다 = can't help but+V I'm sorry, but I **can't help** myself. 미안. 나도 어쩔 수 없어. I **can't help but** pay her the money. 걔한테 돈을 갚을 수밖에 없어.
help sby out (with sth)	…을 도와주다 Somebody **help me out!** 누구 나 좀 도와줘! I'm trying to **help you out** here. 널 도와주려고 하고 있어.
So, help me (God)	맹세컨대 **So help me,** I will win this lottery. 맹세컨대, 이 복권에 당첨될거야.

136

hell
n. 지옥

go through hell	물불을 가리지 않다. 지옥같은 시간을 보내다 Ray **went through hell** in the hospital. 레이는 병원에서 지옥같은 시간을 보냈어.
put sb through hell	…을 매우 힘들게 하다 Officers in the military **put** new soldiers **through hell.** 군 장교들은 신병들을 매우 힘들게 했어.
as hell	대단히, 매우 They're cheap and dangerous **as hell.** 걔네들은 매우 야비하고 위험해.

give sby hell	…에게 대노하다
	She **gave** her boyfriend **hell** over the other woman. 걔는 다른 여자문제로 남친에게 엄청 화를 냈어.

get the hell out	빨리 빠져나오다
	Get the hell out and don't ever come back! 빨리 빠져나오고 다시는 돌아오지마!

scare the hell out of sby	죽을 정도로 무섭게하다
	You **scare the hell out of** me, baby. 자기야, 난 정말 무서워죽는줄 알았어.

go to hell	지옥에 가다, 망치다, (명령문) 뒈져라
	The plan **went to hell** when you killed her. 네가 그 여자를 죽였을 때 계획은 망쳤어. **Go to hell.** You are just a jerk. 꺼져. 머저리 같은 놈.

like hell	맹렬히, 결코 …이 아닌
	Right now, it just hurts **like hell.** 지금, 끔찍하게 아파.

What the hell~ ?	도대체…?
	What the hell are you trying to prove? 이런 젠장, 도대체 뭐하자는거야?

hit

n. 성공, 타격, 안타, (사이트) 방문수 **v.** 때리다, 치다, 득점을 올리다

hit the road	출발하다
	I am going to **hit the road.** 나 출발할거야. I'd better **hit the road.** 그만 출발해야겠어.

hit the jackpot	대박을 터트리다(win a lot of money)
	She went to the casino hoping to **hit the jackpot.** 대박 터질 희망을 갖고 카지노에 갔어.

hell

hit the ceiling	격노하다(to get angry) Get it finished or the boss will **hit the ceiling.** 그거 끝내 그렇지 않으면 사장이 격노할거야.
hit the nail on the head	정확히 맞히다 You'**ve hit the nail** right **on the head!** 바로 맞혔어!
hit it off (with)	(…와) 금세 친해지다 They really **hit it off.** 쟤네들은 바로 좋아하더라고. We **hit it off.** 우린 서로 잘 맞았어.
hit on	갑자기 어떤 생각이 떠오르다(come up with), 유혹하다 **Are** you **hitting on** me? 지금 날 꼬시는거냐? You already **hit on** me an hour ago. 한 시간 전에 이미 유혹했는데요.
It hit me that~	…라는 생각이 갑자기 들다 **It hit me that** this isn't going to work. 갑자기 이 결혼은 제대로 될 수가 없을거라는 생각이 들었어.

138

high

a. 높은, 고위의 **n.** 최고 *highly 대단히, 매우

give high priority to~	…에 최우선 순위를 두다 The firm **gives high priority to** finding new workers. 회사는 새로운 직원을 찾는데 최우선순위를 뒀어.
it's high time that~	…해야 할 때이다 **It's high time** we took a vacation and enjoyed ourselves. 휴가를 얻어 즐길 때가 되었다.
speak highly of~	…을 칭찬하다 The president **spoke highly of** you. 사장이 너를 매우 칭찬했어.

highly recommended	적극적으로 추천받은
	It's **highly recommended** that you stop smoking.
	금연을 적극 추천합니다.

hold

ⓥ 손에 쥐다, 소유하다, (모임) 열다, 붙잡다, 유지하다, 수용하다

hold still	가만히 있다, 기다리다
	You're drunk. **Hold still.** 당신은 취했구나. 좀 가만히 있어.
	How can I **hold still** when you're touching me?
	네가 날 만지는데 어떻게 가만히 있어?

hold good	유효하다
	Her promises **have held good** over the years.
	그녀의 약속은 오랫동안 유효했어.

hold true	사실이다
	Whatever it is, one thing **holds true.**
	그것이 무엇이든 간에 한 가지는 진실야.

hold sby	…을 가지 못하게 잡아두다
	Hold them right there. I'm on my way.
	걔네들 거기 잡아둬. 지금 가고 있어.

hold sby hostage	인질로 …을 잡아두다 *hold sby prisoner 투옥시키다
	The girl **was held hostage.** 걔는 인질로 잡혀있어.

hold sby responsible	…가 책임이라고 생각하다
	I'm going to **hold you responsible.**
	네가 책임져야 된다고 생각해.

hold sth[sby] steady	계속 …하다
	Hold it **steady.** 움직이지 않게 계속 잡고 있어.
	Hold her **steady.** 걔를 꽉 잡고 있어.

high

hold sby still
…을 가만히 있게 하다

Hold him **still!** 걔 어디 가지 못하게 해!

hold a meeting
회의를 갖다

Every year, they **hold** this underground bike race.
사람들은 매년 이 지하 자전거 경주를 한대.

hold your breath
숨을 죽이다, 숨을 참다

So how long can you really **hold your breath** for?
그래 진짜 얼마 동안이나 숨을 참을 수 있어?

hold your tongue
닥치고 있어

Hold your tongue! The walls have ears!
말 조심해! 낮말은 새가 듣고 밤말은 쥐가 듣잖아!

hold water
이치에 맞다

That'll never **hold water.** 그런 건 통하지 않아.

hold your horses!
속도를 줄여!, 진정해! (말고삐를 잡으라는 데서 유래)

Just **hold your horses!** We have a lot of time.
천천히 해! 우리 시간 많다고.

hold a grudge
원한을 품다

Don't **hold a grudge against** me.
내게 원한을 품지마.

hold sth against sby
(과거에 받은 상처로) 잊지 않고 계속 싫어하다

I won't **hold it against** you.
널 원망하진 않을거야.

I don't think you should **hold that against** him.
걔 말 꽁하게 마음 속에 담아두지마.

hold back
저지하다, (감정) 억제하다, 자제하다, 망설이다, 감추다

She could barely **hold back** the tears.
걔는 눈물을 참을 수가 없었어.

Did he **hold back** information on this issue?
이 문제에 대한 정보를 걔가 숨겼어?

hold down
제지하다, 억누르다, (직업 등을) 계속 유지하다 = hold down a job

Hold him **down** before he runs away.
걔가 도망가기 전에 잡아.

201

hold off (on sth/~ing)	미루다, 연기하다 Can you just **hold off** for a second? 잠시 미룰 수 있어? I can't **hold off on** talking to him anymore. 걔한테 말하는 걸 더 이상 미룰 수 없어.
Hold on (a minute/ a second)	잠깐 기다려, 잠깐만 **Hold on,** let me think it over. 잠깐, 생각할 시간 좀 줘. Could you **hold a second**? 잠시 기다리실래요?
hold on[hold the line]	전화를 끊지 않고 잠시 기다리다 Could you just **hold the line** for a second? 잠깐 기다리시겠어요?
hold on to sby [sth]	…을 계속 갖다, 고수하다, 지니다 She had a breakdown and couldn't **hold on to** her job. 걔 신경쇠약에 걸려서 직장을 계속 다닐 수 없었어.
hold it	잠시만, 잠깐 기다려 Betty, **hold it** for ten minutes. We have to get through this. 베티야, 10분만 기다려. 이거 끝내야 돼.
hold out	(손 등을) 내밀다, (희망 등을) 주다, 버티다, 저항하다 She **held out** her arms to hug me. 걔 나를 안으려고 팔을 뻗었어. They can't **hold out** much longer. 걔네들은 더 오래 버티지 못할거야. Looks like she'**s been holding out on** me. 걔가 내게 뭔가 숨겨왔던 것 같아.
hold out hope of~[that~]	…하리란 기대를 주다 She **is holding out hope that** she'll see her son again. 걔 아들을 다시 볼거라는 희망을 갖고 있어.
hold out against	굴복하지 않다 They can't **hold out against** that army. 그들은 그 군대에 굴복하지 않을 수 없어.
hold out for sth	…을 끝까지 요구하다 You should just **hold out for** something else. 넌 뭔가 다른 것을 요구해야 돼.

hold out on sby	…에게 중요한 이야기를 하지 않다
	You **aren't holding out on** us, are you? 넌 우리에게 비밀로 하지 않잖아, 그지?
hold to+약속 [주의]	…을 믿다, 신뢰하다, 고수하다
	She didn't **hold to** her promise. 걘 약속을 지키지 않았어.
hold sby to~	…가 …을 지키도록 하다
	I **hold you to** a higher standard. Don't let me down again. 넌 더 높은 기준을 충족시켜야 돼. 날 다시 실망시키지마.
	I going to **hold you to** that. 네가 꼭 그 약속 지키게 만들거야.
hold up	손들다, 지탱[지]하다, 미루다, 늦게 하다, 강탈하다
	What **held you up?** 왜 늦었어?
	What's **the hold up?** 왜 지체해?, 왜 이리 늦는거야?
hold in	자제하다
	You'll need that to **hold in** your feelings. 네 감정에서 그걸 자제해야 돼.

140 hope

n. 희망, 바람 …하기를 바라다, …라면 좋겠다

There is hope	희망이 있다
	She's going to continue to think that **there's hope.** 걘 희망이 있다고 계속 생각할거야.
	Don't say that there is hope when **there is no hope.** 희망이 없는데 희망이 있다고 말하지마.
get one's hopes up	기대를 올리다, 기대를 부추기다
	You don't **get her hopes up** like that. 걔가 그렇게 기대하게끔 하지마.
	Don't **get your hopes up,** honey. You'll just be disappointed. 자기야 너무 기대하지마. 실망할 수도 있어.

hope for the best	잘 되기를 희망하다	
	All we can do is to wait and **hope for the best.** 우리가 할 수 있는 일은 기다리면서 잘 되기를 바라는거야.	
lose hope	희망을 잃다	
	I just can't do it anymore. I**'ve lost hope.** 난 더 이상 못하겠어. 희망을 잃었어.	
have high hopes of[for]~	…에 큰 기대를 하다	
	You **had high hopes for** a relationship with this man. 넌 이 남자와 관계에 큰 기대를 했어.	
be one's last [only, best] hope of	…의 마지막[유일한, 최고의] 희망이야	
	Your only hope is to somehow get him alive. 네 유일한 희망은 어떻게든 걔를 살리는거야.	
hope to~	…하기를 바라다	
	You are the kind of woman I **hope to** marry. 넌 내가 결혼하고픈 그런 여자야.	
	You **hope to** do that? 그렇게 하고 싶어?	
hope that ~	…이길 바라다	
	I **hope** you enjoyed your meal. 식사 맛있게 했길 바래.	
	I **hope** I haven't disturb[disturb] you. 방해하지 않았길 바래.	
I'm hoping~	…하면 좋겠어, …하고 싶어	
	I'm hoping to sleep with her tonight. 오늘 밤 걔랑 자고 싶어.	
hope so	그러길 바라다 *I hope not 그렇지 않기를 바래	
	I **hope so,** but I can't forget my ex. 나도 그러길 바라는데 옛 남친을 잊을 수가 없어.	
	Well, you better **hope so.** 저기, 그렇게 되기를 바래라.	
	I **hope not,** but I think so. 그렇지 않기를 바라는데 그렇게 생각해.	
	Let's **hope not.** 그렇지 않기를 바라자고.	
Hopefully!	바라건대, 잘하면, 아마 *hopeless 희망없는, 구제불능인	
	Hopefully I won't need to do that. 그럴 일이 없었으면 좋겠어.	
	You're **hopeless.** 넌 구제불능야.	

hope

hurt

v. 아프게하다, 아프다, 손상시키다

(Sby) hurt sby | (…가) …을 아프게 하다
You're hurting me. 네가 날 아프게 해.
Did I **hurt** you in some way? 어떻게 내가 당신을 아프게 했나요?

신체부위+hurt | …가 아프다
My leg still hurts. 다리가 아직도 아파.
My head hurts. 머리가 아파.

It[This, That] hurt | …가 아프다
It hurts. (like hell) 너무 아파.
That hurts. 그거 안됐네, 마음이 아프겠구나.
That had to hurt! 아팠겠다!
Does it still hurt? 아직도 아파?

It[This, That] hurt sby | (…을) 아프게 하다
It hurt her so much when she left.
걔가 떠났을 때 무척 아팠어.
Okay, **that hurt** us. 응, 저게 날 아프게 했어.

Sby is hurting | …가 상심이 크다, 마음이 아프다
You're angry. **You're hurting.** 화도 나고, 상심도 크겠지.
I'm not sure **she's hurting.** 걔가 마음이 아픈지 모르겠어.

Sby is hurt | …가 아프다
I'm hurt. 아파.
I know **you're hurt.** 네가 아프다는거 알아.
She is just trying to see where **you're hurt.**
걔는 네가 어디가 아픈지 보려는거야.

It won't [doesn't] hurt to~	…하는데 지장을 주다
	Go ahead! **It won't hurt to** try. 해봐! 손해 볼 것 없잖아.
	It doesn't hurt to ask. 물어본다고 손해 볼 것 없어. 그냥 한번 물어본 거예요.
	It wouldn't hurt. 밑질 것 없다.

get hurt	다치다(hurt oneself)
	You **got hurt** playing golf with my dad? 우리 아빠랑 골프치다 다쳤어?
	I don't want to see her **get hurt.** 걔가 다치는 걸 원치 않아.

hurt one's feelings	…의 감정을 상하게 하다
	I'm sorry if I **hurt your feelings.** 네 감정을 상하게 했다면 미안.
	It really **hurt my feelings.** 그게 정말 내 기분을 상하게 했어.

142
injure

v. 부상을 입(히)다, 해치다 *injury n. 부상

injure one's back	허리를 다치다
	Remember when you **injured your leg?** 네가 다리 부상을 당했을 때를 기억해?

be injured in the accident	사고에서 부상을 당하다
	I heard that John **was injured in a car accident.** 존이 교통사고나서 다쳤다며.

be badly injured	중상을 입다
	Cary **was badly injured** in the explosion. 캐리는 그 폭발에서 중상을 입었어.

suffer an injury	부상을 입다
	The athlete **suffered an injury** during the soccer game. 그 운동선수는 축구경기에서 부상을 입었어.

hurt

recover from injuries	부상에서 회복하다 Do you think she'll **recover from her injuries**? 걔가 부상에서 회복될 것 같아?
get injured	부상을 당하다 Are you sure I'll **get injured** while skiing? 내가 스키타다 부상당할거라고 확신하는거야?

impress
v. 감동을 주다, 깊은 인상을 주다

impress sby	…에게 감동을 주다 How can I **impress** a girl I want to date? 데이트하고 싶은 애에게 어떻게하면 관심 끌 수 있니?
be impressed by~	…에 감동받다 I'**m impressed with** the amount of money you made. 네가 번 돈 규모가 매우 인상적야.
have[get] the impression that~	…라는 인상을 받다 I **get the impression** that's a little tough for you. 그건 너한테는 좀 벅차다는 느낌이야.
give the impression	…라는 인상을 주다 She **gives the impression of** being smart. 걔는 영리하다는 인상을 줘.
make an impression	감명을 주다, …라는 인상을 주다 You **made quite an impression** at the poker game. 넌 포커게임에서 정말 강한 인상을 남겼어.
first impression	첫인상 **My first impression of** Tom was not good. 탐에 대한 내 첫인상은 좋지 않았어.

introduce
v. 소개하다, 도입하다

introduce sby (to sby[sth])

…에게 …을 소개하다

I'd like to **introduce** you **to** my boss.
우리 사장님이셔.

Let me **introduce** our newest member.
우리 새로운 멤버야.

introduce sby as

…을 …로 소개하다

Is it okay if I **introduce** you two **as** 'my girlfriend?'
널 내 애인으로 소개해도 돼?

He **introduced** me to his mother **as** a friend.
걘 날 자기 어머니한테 친구로 소개했어.

introduce oneself

자기 소개하다

Let me start by **introducing myself.** I am Professor Smith.
내 소개부터 할게요. 스미스 교수입니다.

invite
v. 초대하다

invite sby

…을 초청하다

Thank you for **inviting us.** 우릴 초대해줘서 고마워.

I just wanted to thank you for **inviting me.**
날 초대해줘서 고마워.

Who **invited you,** anyway? 어쨌든 누가 널 초대한거야?

invite sby to

…을 …로 초대하다

I'm going to **invite** them **to** dinner.
난 걔네들은 저녁에 초대할거야.

introduce

invite sby over (for)	…로 초대하다 She **invited** me **over for** dinner. 걘 저녁먹자고 날 초대했어. **Invite** her **over.** It'll be fun. 걔 초대해. 재미있을거야.
be[get] invited to	…에 초대되다, …하라고 요청받다 We **weren't invited.** 우린 초대받지 못했어. I can't believe that I'**m not invited to** her party! 내가 걔 파티에 초대받지 못하다니!
invite sby to +V	…하자고 초대[권]하다 Let's **invite** him **to** go hiking this weekend. 이번 주말에 하이킹하러가게 걔 오라고 해.

job
n. 일, 직장, 일자리, 과제, 책임

apply for a job	구직하다 When's the best time to **apply for a job?** 언제가 구직지원을 하기에 가장 좋은 때야?
get a job	취직되다, 일자리를 얻다 It's just so tough to **get a job** these days. 요즘엔 취직하기가 너무 어려워.
find a job	일자리를 찾다 It is getting so hard to **find a job** right now. 이제 구직은 갈수록 어려워져.
take a job	일자리를 받아들이다 Paula **took a job** at the factory. 폴라는 공장에 취업했어.
offer sby a job	…에게 일자리를 제의하다 We want to **offer you a job** as a general manager. 당신에게 총지배인 자리를 권하고 싶어.

leave one's job	직장을 그만두다
	Carl **left his job** to return to university.
	칼은 직장을 그만두고 대학으로 돌아갔어.
lose one's job	일자리를 잃다
	You don't know what it's like to **lose a job.**
	넌 실직한다는게 뭔지 몰라.
out of a job	백수상태인 = without a job = between jobs
	Oh my God, are you **out of a job** again?
	맙소사, 너 또 백수야?
do the job	효과가 있다, 그 일을 하다
	This new computer really **did the job.**
	이 새로운 컴퓨터는 정말 잘 해냈어.
it's one's job to~	…하는 것은 …의 일이다
	It's my job to offer advice. 조언을 하는게 내 일인걸.
do a good job	일을 잘하다
	You **did such a good job** today. 넌 오늘 아주 잘했어.

join
ⓥ 연결하다, 가입[입사]하다, 합류하다

join the firm	회사에 입사하다
	I was meant to **join the firm.** 난 그 회사에 들어가기로 되어 있었어.
join the army	입대하다
	I may **join the army** later this year.
	금년말에 군대에 입대할지도 몰라.
join sby	…와 합류하다
	Why don't you ask her to **join** us?
	쟤도 함께 하자고 물어봐

job

| join sby in sth [-ing sb] | …와 함께 행동하다
I suggest you **join** me **in** the bathroom.
나와 함께 욕실로 가지 그래 |

148

joke
n. 농담 **v.** 농담하다

make a joke	농담하다 Don't **make a joke** of your life. 인생을 낭비하지 마세요.
play a joke on sby	놀리다 Let's **play a joke on** Lenny today. 오늘 레니 좀 놀려먹자.
have a joke with sby	장난하다 Pete **had a joke with** his friends. 피트는 친구들과 장난을 쳤어.
tell a joke	농담을 하다 Did your father ever **tell a joke** to you? 네 아빠가 네게 농담해본 적 있어?
get the joke	농담을 이해하다 I don't think anyone **got the joke.** 난 누구도 그 조크를 이해못했다고 생각해.
it's no joke ~ing	…하는 건 장난이 아냐 It seems silly, but **it's no joke** seeing people fall down. 우스꽝스럽게 보이지만 사람들이 넘어지는 것은 위험한 것이야.
can't take a joke	농담을 못알아듣다 **Can't** you **take a joke?** 농담도 못하나?
You're joking	농담마 *I'm not joking! 농담아냐! **You're joking!** That's impossible! 농담마! 그건 말도 안돼!

keep

n 생활비　**v** …한 상태로 두다, 보존하다, 기르다, 지키다, 일기쓰다

keep ~ing
계속해서 …하다

Are you going to **keep** doing that? 계속 그렇게 할거야?

You can't **keep** doing this to me. 나한테 계속 이렇게 하지마.

keep going
계속하다

Should we go back or **keep going**?
돌아가야 될까 아니면 계속해야 될까?

keep sby[sth] +형용사
…을 …한 상태로 놓아두다

Sorry to **kept** you waiting so long. 오래 기다리게 해서 미안해.

I'll **keep** it private. 비밀로 할게.

I **kept myself** busy. 그동안 바빴다.

keep one's fingers crossed
행운을 빌다

I'll **keep my fingers crossed** (for you)!
행운을 빌어줄게!

keep sby company
…와 같이 있다, …와 동무하다 *keep me company (다른 사람이) 나와 같이 있다
keep you company (내가) 너와 함께 있다

Please **keep me company** for a while.
나랑 잠시 같이 있어줘.

Mind if I **keep you company** for a bit?
잠깐 당신과 같이 있어도 돼요?

keep sby[sth] from+~ing
…가 …하는 것을 막다 *keep sby[sth]+~ing하게 되면 …을 …하게 하다

I was just trying to **keep you from** doing something stupid.
난 단지 네가 어리석은 짓을 못하도록 했던거야.

keep oneself from
자신을 …못하게 하다

She can barely **keep herself from** smiling.
걘 간신히 웃음을 참을 수 있었어.

keep

keep sby[sth] +~ing	…을 …하게 하다 He's trying to **keep** me **from** talking to anybody. 걔는 내가 다른 누구와도 얘기하지 못하도록 하려고 해.
keep sth from sby	…에게 …을 알리지 않다 I'm going to find out eventually, so why **keep it from** me? 내가 결국 알아낼텐데 왜 내게 말하지 않는거야?
keep one's promise[word]	약속을 지키다 Don't worry. Bill always **keeps his word.** 걱정하지마. 빌은 언제나 약속을 잘 지켜.
keep a secret	비밀을 지키다　*keep a diary 일기쓰다 Could you **keep a secret?** 비밀로 해줄래요?
keep early hours	일찍자고 일찍 일어나다 Neil **keeps early hours** and is in bed by nine. 닐은 일찍 자고 일찍 일어나서 9시에는 잠들어.
keep a record	기록하다 They **keep a record** of all activity. 걔네들은 모든 행동들을 기록하고 있어.
keep the change	잔돈을 갖다 Here's twenty dollars, and **keep the change.** 여기 20달러요. 잔돈은 가지세요.
keep an eye on	돌보다, 주의깊게 보다, 지켜보다 Would you **keep an eye on** this for me? 이거 좀 봐줄래요? You want me to **keep an eye on** her? 걔를 감시할까요?
keep a straight face	진지한 표정을 짓다 I couldn't **keep a straight face.** 웃음을 참을 수 없었어.
keep an open mind	편견을 갖지 않다 I'm trying to **keep an open mind.** 편견을 갖지 않으려 해.

keep in touch with	…와 연락하다
	You still **keep in touch with** her? 걔랑 아직 연락하고 있어?
	Keep in touch, okay? 연락하자, 응?
keep in mind	명심하다
	I'll **keep** that **in mind.** 명심할게요.
Keep in mind (that) S+V	…을 명심해
	Keep in mind that Mindy is always late. 민디는 항상 늦는다는 것을 기억해.
Let's keep in mind(that) S+V	…을 잘 기억해두자
	Let's keep in mind this is out last chance to do that. 이게 우리가 그걸 할 수 있는 마지막 기회라는 걸 명심하자고.
keep down	(…가 늘어나는 것을) 억제하다, 줄이다, (소리를) 낮추다
	Please **keep** your voices **down.** 제발, 목소리 좀 낮춰.
	Would you **keep** it **down?** 조용히 좀 해줄래요?
keep sth off ~	…에 가까이 못하게 하다, 떨어져 있게 하다
	I think it's a good idea to **keep** children **off** drugs. 애들이 마약에 손대지 못하도록 하는 것이 좋겠다는 게 내 생각이야.
keep up	(좋은 상태로) 유지하다
	keep up the good work. 계속해서 열심히 해.
	Keep it up! 꾸준히 하세요!
keep up with	뒤처지지 않다
	I've got to **keep up with** him. 난 걔한테 뒤처지지 않아야 돼.
keep away from	…을 멀리하다
	You can't **keep away from** her. 넌 걜 멀리 할 수 없어.
keep track of	…을 기록하다, …을 놓치지 않다, …의 소식을 알고 있다
	Some parents don't **keep track of** their children. 일부 부모들은 자식들을 따라가지 못해.

keep your chin up	기운내다
	Keep your chin up. Things will be getting for you.
	기운내. 네 사정이 더 좋아질거야.

keep pace with	…와 보조를 맞추다, …에 뒤지지 않게 하다
	I couldn't **keep pace with** the other workers.
	난 다른 직원들을 따라갈 수가 없었어.

keep sth to oneself	…을 혼자 간직하다
	There are some things I like to **keep to myself.**
	내가 혼자 간직하고 싶은 것들이 있어.

150 kick
n. 차기, 쾌감 v. 발로 차다

kick sby in the face[head, stomach]	…의 얼굴[머리, 배]을 발로 차다
	During the bar fight, he **kicked** someone **in the face.**
	바에서 싸움이 일어났을 때 걔는 누군가의 얼굴을 발로 찼어.

kick the habit	습관을 버리다
	They were trying to **kick the habit.**
	걔네들은 습관을 끊으려고 노력했었어.

be kicked out of~	…로부터 쫓겨나다
	My son **got kicked out of** high school.
	내 아들은 고등학교에서 퇴학당했어.

kick one's ass	혼내다, 물리치다
	I'll **kick your ass** right out of my house.
	내가 널 내 집에서 쫓아버릴거야.

for kicks	재미삼아
	I do that sometimes, Chris. I do it just **for kicks.**
	크리스, 난 가끔 그래. 그냥 장난삼아 그래.

151 kid
n 아이 **v** 농담하다, …를 속이다, 착각하다

kid brother	남동생
	That's my **kid sister,** Julie. Why? What's she got to do with it? 여동생 줄리예요. 왜요? 걔가 그거와 무슨 상관이죠?
You're kidding me	너 **농담하는거지** *You got to be kidding me 농담하는거지
	Oh, come on, **you got to be kidding me.** 이러지마, 너 나 놀리는거지.
kid sby about sth	…에게 …에 대한 **농담하다** = make jokes about
	Linda's friends **kid** her **about** her boyfriend. 린다의 친구는 린다의 친구에게 린다에 대해 거짓말을 했어.
No kidding	정말이야
	No kidding? So why are you out here? 농담해? 그럼 넌 여기 왜 있는데?
Are you kidding?	정말이야?
	Are you kidding me? I'm not a whore! 그걸 말이라고 해요? 난 창녀가 아녜요.
I kid you not	정말이야, 농담아냐
	He'll kick your ass. **I kid you not.** 걘 널 혼낼꺼야. 농담아냐.

152 kind
a 친절한 **n** 종류

it's kind of sby to+V	…하다니 고맙다
	It's kind of them to bring a gift. 걔네들이 선물을 가져오다니 고맙다.

kid

kind of	약간 = sort of
	We **kind of** had a plan tonight, remember?
	우리 오늘 저녁에 계획이 좀 있었잖아, 기억나?
What kinds of ~?	무슨 종류의…?
	What kind of woman do you want to date?
	어떤 타입의 여자와 데이트하고 싶어?
one of a kind	유일한, 독특한
	It's **one of a kind.** I paid a lot for it.
	아주 희귀한거야. 돈 엄청 지불했어.
two of a kind	비슷한 것[사람]
	You and your brother are **two of a kind.**
	너와 네 형은 아주 비슷해.

 153

know
ⓥ 알다

know about	…에 대해 알다
	Do you **know about** this?
	그거 알고 있어?
	Who is she? What do we **know about** her?
	걔 누구야? 걔에 대해 뭐 알고 있는 것 있어?
I don't know anything about~	…에 대해 전혀 모르다
	I didn't know anything about this, I swear.
	난 이거에 대해 전혀 몰라, 정말야.
	You **don't know anything about** me, do you?
	나에 대해 아무것도 모르지, 그지?
I don't know any+명사	아무런 …도 몰라
	I don't **know any** people around here.
	여기 아는 사람 하나도 없어.

Do you know anything about ~?	…에 관해 뭐 알고 있는 거 있니? **Do you know anything about** women? 여성에 대해 뭐 아는거 있어?
Do you know any+명사?	아는 …가 좀 있어? **Do you know any** good restaurants? 근사한 식당 아는데 있어?
I know (that) S+V	…을 알아 Please stop. **I know that** you're lying to me. 그만둬. 거짓말하는거 알아.
I don't know (that) S+V	…을 몰라 **I don't know that** I can do that. 내가 그걸 할 수 있을지 모르겠어.
Do you know (that) S+V?	…을 알아? **Do you know that** there's no liquor in this house? 집에 술이 없다는 걸 알아?
know when [where] S+V	…을 알다 I **know exactly what** you need. 네가 원하는 게 뭔지 알겠어. Do you **know where** the train station is located? 기차역이 어디 있는지 알아?
You don't know what[how]~	넌 …을 몰라 You don't know that. **You don't know** me anymore. 넌 그걸 몰라. 넌 더 이상 날 몰라.
know when [how, where] to+V	…하는 것을 알아 I **don't know when** I'm gonna see you again. 내가 언제 널 다시 볼지 모르겠어.
I don't know how[what] to~	…하는 방법(것)을 몰라 **I don't know how to** say it in English. 그걸 영어로 어떻게 말하는지 몰라. **I don't know what else to** do. 달리 어떻게 해야 할지 모르겠어.
Do you know how to ~?	어떻게 …하는지 알아? **Do you know how to** use it? 그걸 어떻게 사용하는지 알아?

Know

let sby know	…에게 알려주다 If you need any help, **let me know.** 도움이 필요하면 알려줘.
Let me know if [what]~	…을 알려줘 **Let me know if** she likes it, okay? 쟤가 그걸 좋아하는지 아닌지 알려줘, 응?
I'll let you know~	…을 알려줄게 **I'll let you know** as soon as he's in recovery. 걔가 회복 되는대로 알려줄게.
I'd like to let you know ~	…을 알려줄려고 **I'd like to let you know** about a problem we've been having. 우리가 직면한 문제에 대해 알려줄려고.
I want to let you know~	…을 알려주고 싶어 **I wanted to let you know** you did okay. 네가 잘 했다는 걸 알려주고 싶었어.
know the answer (to)	(…을) 알다 I think I **know the answer to** this question. 그 문제의 답을 알 것 같아.
know the whole story	…을 잘 알고 있다, …에 밝다 I **know the whole story.** 자초지종은 알아.
not know the first thing about	…에 대해 아무 것도 모르다 I **don't know the first thing about** how to use it. 그걸 이용하는 방법을 전혀 몰라. You **don't know the first thing about** it. 쥐뿔도 모르면서.
I(You) don't know the half of~	…을 잘 몰라 You **don't know the half of** it. 얼마나 심각한지 네가 아직 몰라서 그래.
happen to know~	우연히 알다 I **happen to know** you kissed her in the car. 네가 차에서 걔한테 키스하는거 봤어. Do you **happen to know** about Jane? 너 혹시 제인 아니?

I happen to know (about) sth[that S+V]	어쩌다 …알게 되었어 **I happen to know that** Chris has really high expectations for this birthday. 크리스가 이번 생일에 정말 큰 기대를 하고 있다는 걸 우연히 알게 됐어.
Do you happen to know (about) sth[that S+V]?	혹시 …알아? **Do you happen to know if** there is a good restaurant around here? 이 근처에 혹 좋은 식당 아시나요?
know better than	…할 만큼 어리석지 않다 You **know better than** that. 알만한 사람이 왜 그런 짓을 하니. I **know better than** that. 난 그런 짓을 할 만큼 어리석지 않아.
As you know, ~	알다시피 **As you know,** it's my job to interview people. 알다시피 인터뷰하는게 내 일이야.
know the feeling	그 심정 이해하다 I **know the feeling.** The same thing happened to me. 그 심정 알지. 나도 같은 일을 겪었어.
know one's way around~	…에 대해 잘 알다 You **know your way around** a gun. 너는 총에 대해 잘 알잖아.
You know what?	그거 알아?, 근데 말야? **You know what?** I'm going to finish this later. 저말야. 이거 나중에 끝낼게.
Not that I know of	내가 알기로는 그렇지 않아 **Not that I know of** but I haven't been working here that long. 내가 알기로는 아냐. 하지만 난 여기 온지가 얼마 안됐어.
for all I know	아마 …일지도 몰라 **For all I know,** she's trying to find me. 걔가 날 찾으려고 했는지 모르지.
before you know it	금세 I'll be back **before you know it.** 금세 다녀올게.

Know

God[Lord] knows what S+V!	…은 아무도 몰라! **God only knows what** your parents is going to say. 네 부모가 뭐라 할지 누가 알겠어.
God[Lord] knows that S+V	정말이지 …해 **God knows** I owe you so much. 정말이지 네게 신세진 게 많아.
Nobody knows~	아무도 …을 몰라 **Nobody knows** what she's doing. 걔가 뭘하는지 누가 알겠어.
Who knows~?	누가 …알아? **Who knows** anything about that guy? 저 사람에 대해 뭐 좀 아는 사람?
be known to [for]	…로 유명하다, …으로 알려지다 She **was known for** her cooking. 걔는 요리로 유명했어.
know for sure	확실히 알다 I don't **know for sure.** 난 확실히 몰라.

 154

last

ⓐ 마지막의, 최근의 ⓐⓓ 마지막에, 가장 최근에 ⓝ 최후의 것[사람] ⓥ 계속되다

at the last moment [minute]	마지막 순간에 Can I count on you not to cancel **at the last second?** 마지막 순간에 취소하지 않을 거라고 믿어도 돼?
at last	마침내 Jamie gave up smoking **at last.** 제이미는 마침내 담배피는걸 포기했어.

last but not least	마지막이지만 중요한 **Last but not least,** remember to be nice to other people. 끝으로 중요한 말 더하자면 다른 사람들에게 착하게 대하는 걸 기억해.
be the last to +V	가장 …하지 않을 사람이다 I don't believe this. Why **am I the last to** know? 이건 말도 안돼. 왜 내가 맨 나중에 알게 돼?
last for~	…동안 계속되다 The test is supposed to **last for** hours. 시험은 몇시간 계속 될거야.

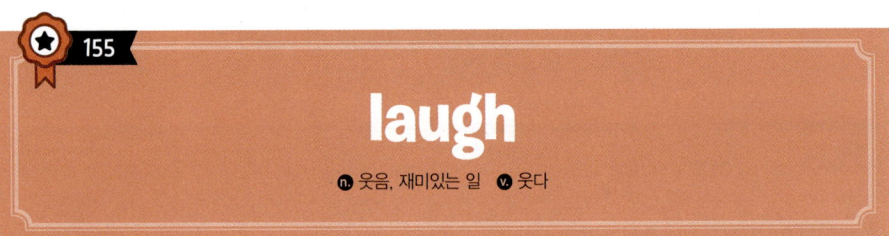

155 laugh
n. 웃음, 재미있는 일 **v.** 웃다

have the last laugh	마지막으로 웃다 Who **got the last laugh?** 누가 최종 승자야?
laugh at [about]	웃다 It's hard not to **laugh at** her. 걔를 비웃지 않는건 어려워. We **laughed at** her arrogant behavior. 우린 걔의 건방진 행동을 비웃었지.
laugh at (sby behind one's back)	(…가 없는데서) 비웃다 Everyone **laughed at** the old car Keith was driving. 다들 키스가 모는 낡은 차를 비웃었어.
make sb laugh	…을 웃게 하다 *Don't make me laugh 나 웃기지마 One of the reasons I came back here Mark, you **make me laugh.** 마크, 내가 여기 돌아온 이유중의 하나는 네가 내게 웃음을 줘서 그래.

last

lay
v. 놓다, 눕히다

lay sth on
…을 …에 놓다

I went over and **laid my head on** her lap.
난 다가가 머리를 걔의 무릎에 올려놨어.

lay the groundwork
기반을 다지다

This report will **lay the groundwork** for the new rules.
이 보고서는 새로운 규칙을 세우는데 기반을 다질거야.

lay emphasis [stress] on
…을 강조하다

Parents should **lay emphasis on** being honest.
부모는 정직함을 강조해야 한다.

lay a finger on
…에 손대다

I'll call the police if you **lay a finger on** me.
내게 손끝하나 대면 경찰을 부를거야.

lay (~) low
때려눕히다, 축 쳐져 있다, 녹초가 되다

I'm kind of into **laying low.** 요즘 축 쳐져 있어.

Go back to school and **lay low.** 학교로 돌아가서 얌전히 있어라.

lay down
내려놓다, 눕히다, 규정하다, 세우다

I just want to **lay down** a couple of ground rules.
몇몇 기본 원칙을 세워놓고 싶어.

lay off
그만두게 하다, 그만두다

We're going to **be laying off** people in every department
모든 부서별로 몇 사람씩 자를거야.

Could you **lay off,** please?
그만 좀 할래요?

lay out
가지런히 늘어놓다, 펼쳐놓다

I **have laid out** clean towels on the floor of the bathroom.
화장실 바닥에 깨끗한 타올을 늘어놓았어.

lead

n. 선두, 우세, 선례 **v.** 앞장서 이끌다, 연결되다, …하게 되다

have [hold] the lead	앞서고 있다, 주도권을 갖다 My team **has the lead,** but that may change. 우리 팀이 앞서고 있지만 바뀔 수도 있어.
take the lead	앞장서다, 솔선수범하다 She **took the lead** in everything. 그 여자는 모든 일에 선두에 섰어. Who's gonna **take the lead?** 누가 선두에 설거야?
lead the way	안내하다, 앞장서다 Fantastic! **Lead the way,** I'm coming in. 끝내주네! 앞장서, 들어갈게.
lead a good [happy] life	행복한 삶을 영위하다 I've been trying to **lead a better life.** 좀 나은 삶을 살려고 하고 있었어.
lead to	…하게 되다 Does this road **lead to** the beach? 이 길이 해변으로 이어지나요? Poor planning **leads to** failure. 기획을 부실하게 하면 실패로 이어져.

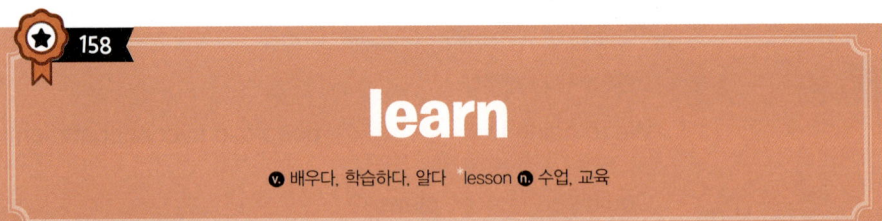

learn

v. 배우다, 학습하다, 알다 **lesson n.** 수업, 교육

learn a[one's] lesson	교훈을 얻다 **Haven't** you **learned your lesson** yet? 아직 따끔한 맛을 못 봤어? I**'ve learned my lesson.** 교훈을 얻었어.

lead

lesson learned	교훈을 얻었어	
	You're right. **Lesson learned.** 네 말이 맞아. 교훈을 얻었어.	
	Well, **lesson learned!** My teacher is mean! 그래, 교훈을 얻었어! 우리 선생님은 비열해!	
learn by heart	암기하다	
	We **learned** the poem **by heart.** 우린 그 시를 암기했어.	
learn about	…에 관해 배우다	
	You have a lot to **learn about** men. 넌 남자에 대해 알아야 될게 많아.	
	I'm here to **learn about** cooking. 요리 배우러 여기 왔는데요.	
learn how to +V	…하는 법을 배우다	
	Learn how to hide your feelings! 네 감정을 숨기는 걸 배워!	
give[take] a lesson	수업을 하다[듣다]	
	She**'s giving me scuba lessons** every weekend. 매주 갠 내게 스쿠바 타는 법을 알려줘.	
Let this[that] be a lesson to~	이걸 교훈 삼아라	
	Let this be a lesson to all of you, all right? 이거 너희 모두 교훈으로 삼아, 알았지?	
	Let that be a lesson to you. 저게 네 교훈이 되도록 해.	
You never learn	구제불능이야	
	You're always late. **You never learn!** 넌 항상 늦어. 구제불능이야!	
fast learner	빨리 배우는 사람	
	Sam was a **fast learner** and was promoted quickly. 샘은 빨리 배우는 타입이라 금세 승진했어.	

least

a. 가장 적은 **ad.** 가장 적게

to say the least

줄잡아 말해도

That was very awkward, **to say the least.**
아무리 좋게 말해도 저건 너무 어색했어.

at least

적어도

At least you put the money to good use.
적어도 넌 돈을 좋은 데에 썼잖아.

at the very least

아무리 못해도, 적어도

At the very least, submit a basic proposal.
적어도, 기본적인 제안서를 제출해.

leave

n. 휴가 **v.** 출발하다, 그만두다, 남겨놓다, 깜박두고 오다, …한 상태로 놓아두다

be on leave

휴가중이다 *go on leave 휴가를 가다

He **is on leave.** 걔 휴가 중이야.

leave for~

…을 향해 출발하다 *leave+장소명사 …을 떠나다, 나가다

He **left** New York **for** Seoul.
걔 뉴욕을 출발해 서울로 향했어.

He **left for** Boston yesterday.
걔 어제 보스톤으로 출발했어.

I **leave for** work at 7 o'clock in the morning.
아침 7시에 출근해.

He got up to **leave** the room.
걔 일어나 방을 나갔어.

least

leave sth ~	(…에) 두고오다, 남겨놓다, 깜박 놓고 오다	
	How much should I **leave** on the table? 테이블에 얼마 만큼 남겨두어야 돼?	
leave sby	…을 떠나다, 헤어지다, 남겨두다	
	I told her I was going to **leave** her. 난 걔한테 떠날거라고 말했어.	
	Where does that **leave** me? 그럼 난 어떻게 되는거야?	
	I **left** you a note. 너한테 노트를 남겨놨어.	
leave sth to sby	…에게 …을 맡기다	
	Leave it **to** me to find her. 걔 찾는 건 내게 맡겨.	
	I'll **leave** them **to** you when I die. 내가 죽을 때 그것들 네게 맡길게.	
	I think we can just **leave it at that.** 우리 이제 그만 둘 수 있을 것 같아.	
leave sth~	…한 채로 두다, …상태가 되다	
	Don't **leave** things half done. 일을 하다 말면 안돼.	
	I **left** the door open and she must have gotten out. 난 문을 열어놔서 걔가 나갔음에 틀림없어.	
leave sby alone	…을 내버려두다	
	Could you please just **leave me alone**? 나 좀 가만히 둘래요?	
	I **left her alone** out there. 난 걜 그곳에 혼자 남겨뒀어.	
	They're even, so just **leave it alone.** 공평하니까 그냥 놔둬.	
leave a message	메시지를 남기다	
	Could I **leave a message**? 메모 좀 전해주세요.	
	They **left us a message** saying they were getting married. 걔네들이 결혼할거란 메시지를 남겼어.	
leave a job	회사를 그만두다 *leave work 퇴근하다(=get off work)	
	I can't **leave this job** at the moment. 지금은 회사 그만 두지 못해.	
	He **left work** in the middle of the day to have a date. 걘 데이트하려고 근무 중 퇴근했어.	

227

have sth left	…가 남았다 *leftover 남은 것(음식)
	We don't **have** much time **left.** 시간이 얼마 남지 않았어.
	It**'s left over.** From the wedding. 남은 거거든요. 결혼식에서요.
leave sby[sth] behind	데려가지 않다, 떨쳐버리다, 남겨두다
	The four kids run off, **leaving** Parker **behind.** 4명의 아이들은 파커를 뒤에 남겨놓고 도망쳤어
	That why he **left** you **behind?** 그래서 걔가 널 남겨두었구나?
leave out	고려하지 않다, 제외하다 *be[feel] left out 소외당하다, 환영받지 못하다
	Have fun. Just **leave me out** of it. 즐겁게 보내. 난 빠질게.
	Frankly, I didn't want you to **feel left out.** 솔직히 네가 소외감을 느끼길 않길 바랬어.
leave off	하던 일을 그만두다 *continue[pick up, take up] where we left off 지난번 하던 데서 다시 시작하다
	Let's **pick it up where we left off.** 지난번 하던 데서 다시 시작하자.
	Shall we **continue where we left off** last night? 지난밤 하다가 만 걸 계속하자
leave much [something] to be desired	불만족스럽다
	Your manner **leaves something to be desired.** 네 매너가 좀 그렇다.
leave room for	…의 여지를 남겨두다
	Don't get too full. You have to **leave room for** dessert. 과식하지마. 디저트 먹을 자린 비워둬.
leave sby in the cold	제외시키다, 소외시키다
	We can't **leave** her **out in the cold.** 걔를 제외시킬 수는 없어.
Better left unsaid	말 안하는 게 좋겠어, 입다물고
	I think some things are **better left unsaid.** 어떤 것들은 말을 아예 안 하는게 좋은 것 같아.
Take it or leave it	하던지 말던지 해라
	I'll give you $30 for your MP3. **Take it or leave it.** 네 MP3 30달러 줄게. 하던지 말던지 해.

161 lend

v. 빌려주다   borrow 빌리다

lend sth
…을 빌려주다

We're a team. I'**m just lending** support.
우린 팀이야. 단지 도움을 줄 뿐이야.

lend sby sth
…에게 …을 빌려주다

If you want, I can **lend** you some money.
원한다면 돈 빌려줄 수 있어.

Lending friends money is always a mistake.
친구에게 돈을 빌려주는 건 항상 실수야.

lend a hand
도움을 빌려주다

Can you **lend me a hand?** 나 좀 도와줄래?

She asked if I could **lend a hand.**
걘 내가 도와줄 수 있는지 물어봤어.

borrow sth from sby
…에게서 …을 빌리다

I need to **borrow** some money. 돈 좀 빌려야겠어.

I'**m never borrowing** a dress **from** you again.
다신 절대로 네게서 옷을 빌리지 않을게.

162 let

v. …하게 하다

let me check~
…을 확인해보다

Would you mind **letting me check** your bag?
가방을 확인해봐도 될까요?

let me know~	…을 알려줘 E-mail me to **let me know** how you're doing. 어떻게 지내는지 궁금하니까 이메일보내.
let me think ~	…을 생각해볼게 **Let me think** it over again. 그거 다시 한번 생각해볼게.
let me try~	…을 해볼게 **Let me try to** explain it to you, okay? 네게 설명을 하도록 할게, 알았지?
Let me see	(잠깐 생각해보며) 어디 보자, 봐봐 **Let's see,** how about four o'clock? 글쎄요, 4시는 어때요?
Let me see if~	…을 확인해보다, …을 알아보다 *Let's see if~ **Let me see if** I can reschedule the appointment. 약속을 다시 조정할 수 있는 지 알아볼게. **Let me see what** I can do. 내가 할 수 있는게 뭔지 볼게. **Let me see if** I can reschedule the appointment. 약속을 다시 조정할 수 있는지 알아볼게.
Let me[Let's] see what [how]~	을 알아보다 **Let me see what** is going to happen. 어떤 일이 벌어질지 보자.
Let me (just) say	말하자면 **Let me say,** I am a great lover of soccer. 말하자면, 난 축구를 아주 즐겨봐.
I will let you +V	네가 …하도록 할게 **I will not let you** get away with this. 넌 무사히 넘어가지 못하게 할거야. **I will let you** know when I find her. 내가 걜 찾으면 알려줄게.
I'm not going to let you+V	네가 …하지 못하도록 할게 **We're not going to let** that happen. I promise you. 다시 그런 일 없을거야, 약속해.

let

let that[this, it] happen
그런 일이 일어나게 하다

How can you **let this happen?**
어떻게 이런 일이 일어나도록 놔뒀어?

Don't let sby [sth]+V
…가 …하지 못하게 해

Just **don't let** it happen again, all right?
다시 그런 일 없도록 해. 알았지?

Don't let her drink anymore!
걔가 술 더 못 마시게 해!

Let's+V
…하자

Let's call it a day and get some beer.
그만하고 맥주 좀 먹자.

Let's go inside for a while. 잠시 들어가 있자.

Let's (just) say~
…라고 하자, …라고 가정해보자

Let's say we leave him here. What will happen?
우리가 걜 여기다 두고 가면 무슨 일이 벌어질까?

Let's face it
받아들이자, 현실을 직시하자

Let's face it. She's going to leave someday
현실을 직시하자고. 걘 언젠가 떠날거야

let ~ go
해고하다, 잊어버리다 *let go of 놓아주다, 해고하다

Don't **let him go!** 걜 가게 하지마!, 놓아주지마!

Let go of me! 날 놔줘!

let alone~
…는 말할 것도 없이

We were barely speaking, **let alone** having sex.
우린 섹스는 말할 것도 없이 말도 거의 안해.

let sby in[out]
…을 들여보내다, 내보내다

Let me out of here right now. You **let me out.**
지금 당장 날 내보내줘. 내보내줘.

let sby down
…를 실망시키다

I'll try not to **let you down.**
실망시키지 않도록 할게요.

You **let me down** this year, Jimmy.
지미야 넌 올해 날 실망시켰어.

231

let sby off	…을 놓아주다, …을 봐주다, 내보내다
	My boss **let me off** early, so I took the plane. 사장님이 일찍 보내줘서 비행기를 탔어. **Let her off** the plane! 비행기에서 걔 내려줘요!

let sth out	밖으로 내보내다, (맘속을) 털어놓다, (소리) 지르다
	Honey, you can **let it out.** 자기야, 털어놔봐.

let it slip	무심결에 말해버리다
	Cindy **let it slip** that you're in love with Jane. 신디가 실수로 네가 제인을 사랑한다고 말했어.

let sby in on	…에게 …의 비밀을 누설하다
	I'm going to **let you in on** a little secret. 작은 비밀 하나 알려줄게.

let up	멈추다
	The rain outside **hasn't let up.** 밖의 비가 멈추지 않았어.

163 lie
v. 눕다, 거짓말하다 **n.** 거짓말

tell a lie (to)	(…에게) 거짓말하다
	You shouldn't **tell a lie to** a client. 고객에게 거짓말해선 안돼.

lie on[in]	…에 눕다(과거형은 lay)
	Tony **is lying on** the couch watching TV. 토니는 TV를 보면서 소파에 누워있어. She **lay back** with her eyes closed. 걔 두 눈을 감고 반듯이 누워있었어.

let

lie down	드러눕다, 굴복하다, 감수하다
	I need to **lie down.** 좀 누워야겠어.
	You're injured, you need to **lie down.** 부상당했으니 누워있어야 돼.
lie back	반드시 눕다, 뒤로 기대다
	I need you to **lie back.** 뒤로 누워야 돼.
	Will you **lie back** and let me examine for me? 진찰을 할 수 있게 누워주시겠어요?
lie in	…에 있다
	My happiness **lies in** being with my family. 나의 행복은 나의 가족과 함께 있는거야.
lie to[about]	…에게[…에 관해] 거짓말하다
	You **lied to** me! 넌 거짓말했어!
	You have never **lied to** me. 한 번도 내게 거짓말 안했잖아.
	She even **lied about** her job. 걘 직업에 대해서도 거짓말 했어.

line

n. 선, 줄, 라인

stand in line	일렬로 서다
	I saw you **standing in line.** 네가 줄 서 있는 걸 봤어.
get in line	줄을 서다
	Yeah, well, **get in line** behind all the other ladies! 저기, 다른 여자들 뒤에 다들 줄서요!
be in line for (a promotion)	곧 (승진) 할 예정이다
	I'm also **in line for a promotion.** 내가 승진할 차례야.

like

● 좋아하다

I (don't) like to+V	…하는 것을 좋아한다[좋아하지 않는다] **I don't like to** spend money on jewelry. 난 보석류에 돈을 낭비하고 싶지 않아.
Do you like to +동사[~ing]?	…하는 걸 좋아해? **Do you like** playing online computer games? 온라인 컴퓨터 게임 하는거 좋아해?
I don't like you to~	네가 …하지 않기를 바래 **I don't like you to** complain all the time. 난 네가 늘상 징징대지 않기를 바래.
I would like +명사	…로 할게, 난 …로 할래, …를 주세요 **I'd like** a cup of coffee with my dessert. 디저트와 곁들여 커피 한 잔 주세요.
Would you like +명사?	…줄까요? **Would you like** some more of this? 더 드실래요? **Would you like** a glass of lemonade? 레모네이드 한 잔 하실래요?
I would like to +V	…하고 싶어 **I'd like to** propose a toast. 축배를 듭시다.
Would you like to+V?	…할래? **Would you like to** come for dinner? 저녁 먹으러 올래요?
I would like you to+V	네가 …해줬으면 좋겠어 **I'd like you to** stay with me tonight. 오늘 밤 안 갔으면 좋겠어. **I'd like you to** meet my friend, Jim. 내 친구 짐하고 인사해.

like

Would you like me to+V?
내가 …할까?

Would you like me to close the window?
창문 내가 닫을까?

Would you like +명사+pp [전치사구]?
…를 …하게 할까요?

Would you like cheese on your spaghetti?
스파게티 위에 치즈를 올려드릴까요?

like sth about ~
…에 대해 …을 좋아하다

You know what I **like about** you?
내가 너의 어떤 점을 좋아하는지 알아?

This is what I **like about** New York.
이게 바로 내가 뉴욕을 좋아하는거야.

take a liking to
…이 좋아하기 시작하다

I**'ve never taken a liking to** junk food.
난 정크푸드를 좋아해본 적이 없어.

if you like
원한다면

If you like it so much, why don't you buy it?
그렇게 좋다면 사지 그래.

whether you like it or not
좋든 싫든

Whether you like it or not, she is a suspect.
네가 좋든 싫든간에 걘 용의자야.

I'd like to think ~
…이길 바래

I'd like to think you'd set me up with someone like him.
걔 같은 사람 소개시켜주었으면 해.

How do you like ~?
…은 어때?

How do you like this snowy weather?
이렇게 눈이 내리는 날씨 어때?

How do you like to+V[~ing]?
…하는 건 어때?

How would you like to pay for this?
이거 어떻게 지불하시겠어요?

How do you like being married?
결혼하니까 어때?

How would you like+명사?	…은 어떻게 해드릴까요, …는 어떠세요? **How would you like** your steak? 고기 어떻게 해드릴까요? **How would you like** your steak cooked? 고기를 어떻게 해드릴까요?
How would you like it if ~?	…한다면 어떻겠어? **How would you like it if** I had dinner with your wife? 내가 네 아내하고 저녁을 한다면 어떻겠어?
What would you like to~?	무엇을 …할까요? **What would you like to** talk about first? 먼저 뭘 얘기하고 싶어?
What's ~ like?	…가 어때? **What's** the new manager **like**? 새로 온 부장님 어때?
It's like+명사 [~ing, S+V]	…하는 것과 같아, …하는 셈야 **It's like** something's changed. 뭔가 바뀐 것 같아. **It's like** he hates me. 걔가 날 싫어하나 봐.
I know [understand] what it's like to~	…하는 것이 어떤 건지 알아 **I know what it's like to** be a teenager. 10대라는게 어떤 건지 알아.
You don't know [You have no idea] what it's like to~	…하는 것이 어떤 건지 넌 몰라 **You don't know what it's like to** be out of work. 넌 실직하는게 어떤 건지 몰라.
It's not like sby to+동사	…하는 것은 …답지 않다 **It's not like you to** have a one-night stand. 하룻밤 즐기는 것을 하다니 너답지 않아.
things like that	그런 것들 You shouldn't say **things like that**. 그렇게 말하면 안되지.

like

something [anything] like that[this]
그런 것

I knew **something like this** was going to happen.
이런 일이 일어날 줄 알았어.

Have you ever seen **anything like this?**
이런 거 본 적 있어?

I've never felt **like this before.** 이런 느낌 처음이야.

like I said
내가 말한 것처럼

Like I said, it's none of your concern.
내가 말했잖아, 네 일 아니라고.

act like
…처럼 행동하다

Stop **acting like** you're all that. 잘난척지마.

like hell
무척, 엄청나게

It hurts **like hell.** 너무 아프네요.

166 listen
v. 주의깊게 듣다

listen
(주의 깊게) 듣다

I**'m listening.** 듣고 있어. 어서 말해.

You**'re just not listening.** 내 말 안 듣고 뭐하냐.

listen carefully
주의 깊게 듣다, 경청하다

Listen carefully. This is very important.
잘 들어. 이거 중요한거야.

listen to
…말을 듣다

Are you **listening to** me? 내 말 듣고 있어?

He **listens to** me. 제가 알아듣게 말할게요.

Will you **listen to yourself?** 방금 뭐라고 했지?

listen for	귀를 기울여 듣다
	They **listened for** a response and heard nothing. 걔네들은 귀를 기울였지만 아무 것도 듣지 못했어.
listen up	잘 듣다, 귀 기울여 듣다　*Listen 이봐
	All right, everybody, **listen up.** 좋아, 다들 잘 들어. **Listen,** I'm broke, okay? 이봐, 나 빈털터리야, 알았어?

167 live

ⓐ ⓐⓓⱽ 살아있는, 생중계의   ⓥ 살다   living 살아있는, 생존, 삶

live ~ life	…한 삶을 살다
	I'm trying to **live a healthier life** these days. 요즘 더 건강한 삶을 살려고 노력 중야.
live in[on]	…에서 살다, …으로 살아가다(on)
	I **live on** the second floor of an apartment building. 아파트 건물 2층에 살아.
	I have to **live on** a budget. 예산에 맞춰 살아가야 돼.
live up to~	…에 충족시키다, 부응하다, 실천하다
	I have to **live up to** my reputation. 난 명성에 맞게 살아야 돼.
	We're trying to **live up to** our word. 우린 우리가 한 말을 지키며 살려고 해.
live with	…와 함께 살다, …을 참다(~sth)
	I can **live with** that. 괜찮아, 참을 만해.
	Can you both **live with** that? 그 정도 선에서 둘이 합의하면 안 되나요?

live without	…없이 살다
	It's difficult to **live without** a cell phone. 휴대폰 없이 살긴 힘들어.
	I can't **live without** you. 너 없이는 못살아.
earn[make] a living	생계비를 벌다
	I have to **earn a living** and pay the rent. 생계비도 벌고 임대료도 내야 돼.
do for a living	생계비를 벌다
	What do you **do for a living?** 직업이 뭐예요?
	We're just saying what we **do for a living.** 우린 직업이 뭔지 서로 얘기하고 있었어.

168 look
n. 보기, 눈길, 표정 **v.** 바라다보다, 쳐다보다

take[have] a look	쳐다보다
	Do you mind if I **take a look** around here? 내가 여기 좀 둘러봐도 괜찮겠니?
have[get] a close look	자세히 쳐다보다
	The technician needs to **have a close look** at the machine. 그 기술자는 그 기계를 자세히 쳐다볼 필요가 있어.
give sby a worried look	…을 걱정스럽게 쳐다보다
	She turned and **gave us a worried look.** 걔는 돌아서서 우리를 걱정스럽게 쳐다봤어.
be looking to +V	…할 생각이다, 예정이다
	You **were looking to** pick a fight. 넌 싸움 걸려고 하고 있었어.
look+형용사	…처럼 보이다
	You don't **look** happy right now. 넌 지금 행복해보이지 않아.

look as if [though] S+V	마치 …인 것처럼 보인다 He does **look as if** he has something else on his min. 걘 뭔가 다른 생각을 품고 있는 것처럼 보여.
look the other way	다른 쪽을 보다, 외면하다, 모른 척하다 The businessman **looked the other way** when offered a bribe. 그 비즈니스맨은 뇌물을 받을 때 모른 척을 했어.
look at	…을 쳐다보다 Oh, **look at** the time. I gotta fly. 어휴, 시간 좀 봐라, 가야 돼.
look for	…찾다, 구하다 Sounds like it's time to **look for** another mate. 다른 짝을 찾아볼 때가 된 것 같구나.
look like	…인 것 같다 You **look like** you eat enough food for 2 people. 너 2인분 식사는 충분히 할 것 같아 보여.
look forward to~	학수고대하다 I'm **looking forward to** getting to know you. 널 빨리 알게 되고 싶어.
look into	조사하다 We have to **look into** the matter right now. 우린 지금 당장 그 문제를 조사해야 돼.
look over	검토하다 Please **look over** the contract before you sign it. 사인하기 전에 계약서를 검토하세요.
look out (for)	조심하다, 경계하다 Why do you **look out for** him? 왜 걜 주시하는거예요?
look back (on)	되돌아보다 Try not to **look back on** the past. 과거를 회상하지 않도록 노력해라.

lose

v 잃다, 지다, 손해를 보다 | loss **n** 잃음, 분실, 손실

lose sth
…을 잃다, 지다

I **lost** my passport. 여권을 잃어버렸어.

She **lost** her job last month. 지난 달에 직장을 잃었어.

You're not going to **lose** him. 걘 잃지 않을거야.

lose weight
살이 빠지다 ↔ gain weight

If I eat less, I'll **lose weight**. 소식하면 살이 빠질거야.

You look like you've **lost weight** lately. 너 최근에 살이 빠진 것 같아.

lose face
망신당하다

He doesn't want to **lose face**. 걘 자기 자존심 구겨지는 꼴 못 봐.

lose time
시계가 늦다, 시간을 낭비하다

We'll **lose time** if we stop to eat now.
지금 먹기 위해 멈추면 시간을 낭비할거야.

lose sight of
…을 못보다, 놓치다

Greedy people **lose sight of** the importance of family.
탐욕스런 사람은 가족의 중요성을 놓친다.

lose track of
…을 놓치다, 연락이 끊기다

I **lost track of** you, but I always heard about you.
너와 연락이 끊겼지만 네 얘기 항상 들었어.

Yeah. I guess I **lost track of** time.
그래. 내가 시간을 놓친 것 같아.

lose a chance
기회를 놓치다

I don't want to **lose a chance** to go to Hollywood.
할리우드에 갈 수 있는 기회를 놓치고 싶지 않아.

lose touch with
…와 접촉이 없어지다

I **lost touch with** many of my old friends.
많은 오랜 친구들과 연락이 끊겼어.

lose one's temper	화를 내다 (get angry)
	I am sorry I lost my temper, but I was upset. 화를 내서 미안하지만 열받았어.
	I lost my temper with the boss. 내가 참지 못하고 사장에게 버럭 화를 냈어.
be[get] lost	길을 잃다
	Get lost! 꺼져버려!
	I think I**'m lost.** 길을 잃은 것 같아요.
have[get] nothing to lose	잃을 게 없다
	You've got nothing to lose. 밑져야 본전인데 뭐.
	I've got nothing to lose except you. 널 빼면 난 잃을게 없어.
You lost me	못 알아들었어
	You lost me. I'm not sure what you mean. 못 알아들었어. 무슨 말인지 모르겠어.
	You lost me. Say that again please. 못 알아들었어. 다시 한번 말해줘.

170

love

n. 사랑 **v.** 사랑하다, 좋아하다, …하고 싶어하다(I'd love to+V)

be[fall] in love with	…와 사랑하다, 사랑에 빠지다
	I**'m madly in love with** you. 미치도록 널 사랑하고 있어.
	Your dad**'s in love** big time. 네 아빠는 사랑에 푹 빠져있어.
make love to	사랑을 나누다
	She **made love to** me that night. 걘 그날 밤 나와 사랑을 나눴어.
	I **made love to** her, and I left. 난 걔와 사랑을 나누고 가버렸어.

lose

love sby[sth]	…을 사랑[좋아]하다
	I **love** you but I can't marry you. 널 사랑하지만 결혼할 수 없어.
	I **love** this cake! 이 케익 좋아!

love ~ing[to~]	…하기를 좋아하다
	He's a great guy and I **love** being with him. 걘 멋지고 같이 있는게 좋아.
	I just **love to** sing! 난 그냥 노래부르는게 좋아!

I'd love to+V	…하고 싶어하다
	I'd love to leave but I have to stay. 가고 싶지만 남아 있어야 돼.
	I'd love to go to France someday. 언젠가 프랑스에 가고 싶어.

love at first sight	첫눈에 반한 사랑
	My parents say it was **love at first sight** when they met. 부모님은 만났을 때 첫눈에 반했다고 말하셔.

be going to love~	…을 좋아하게 될거야
	My wife **is going to love** it. 내 아내가 좋아하게 될거야.

171

luck

n. 운, 운명

wish sby luck	…에게 행운을 빌어주다
	My interview is at the end of the week, so **wish me luck!** 면접이 이번 주말에 있거든, 행운을 빌어줘!

Good luck	행운을 빌어
	Good luck on your date. 데이트 잘 되기를 바랄게.
	Good luck with that! 행운이 있기를!

Just my luck	내 운이 그렇지 뭐 That's **just my luck!** I have never had any success when it comes to women. 그럼 그렇지! 난 여자 문제와 관련해서는 성공하는 법이 없다니까.
You're out of luck	운이 없네 **I'm out of luck.** The tickets were sold out. 운이 없어. 표가 다 매진되었대.
luck out	운이 좋다 Man, did I **luck out** marrying you. 야, 나 너랑 결혼해서 정말 땡잡은거지.

172

make

v 만들다, …가 되도록 하다, …하게 하다

make+sby[sth] +동사	…하게 하다, …가 …하도록 만들다 There are ways to **make this work.** 이걸 되게 하는 방법이 있을거야. You'll **make it happen.** 성공할거야. Don't **make me go** in there! 내가 꼭 그리로 가야겠니!
make me feel +형용사	내 기분을 …하게 만들다 You're just saying that to **make me feel** better. 나 기분 좋으라고 하는 말이지. You **make me feel** special. 넌 날 특별하다고 생각하게 해줘.
make you feel +형용사[feel like~]	네 기분을 …하게 만들다 We can at least **make you feel** more comfortable. 우린 적어도 네가 더 편하도록 할 수 있어.
Don't make me feel~	날 …하게 하지마 **Don't make me feel** bad. 나 기분 나쁘게 하지마.

luck

What makes you think (that) S+V?	어째서 …라고 생각해? **What makes you think** he's seeing someone? 왜 걔가 다른 사람을 만나고 있다는거야?
make+sby[sth] +형용사[명사]~	…를 …하게 만들다 It'll only **make** a bad situation worse. 단지 사태를 더 어렵게 할 뿐이야. What **makes** you so special? 자네는 뭐가 그리 특별한가? What **makes** you so sure? 너 무슨 믿는 데라도 있니?
make oneself clear	…에게 자신의 말을 이해시키다 Do I **make myself clear?** 내 말을 알아 들었어? I didn't **make myself clear.** 내 말 뜻을 이해 못했구만.
make oneself understood	자신의 말을 이해시키다 Can he **make himself understood** in Japanese? 일본어는 좀 할 수 있나요?
make oneself at home [comfortable]	편히 하다 Please feel free to **make yourself at home.** 집처럼 편히하세요.
make sby+음식	…에게 …을 만들어주다 I am going to **make** you some coffee. 커피 좀 만들어줄게.
make an effort	노력하다 I am serious about this. I want you all to **make an effort**. 난 이거 장난아냐. 난 너희들 모두가 노력하기를 바래.
make an agreement	합의하다 Will we have time to **make an agreement?** 우리가 합의할 시간이 있을까?
make an attempt	시도하다 I'm going to **make an attempt to** date Patty. 난 패티와의 데이트를 시도해볼거야.
make a bargain	매매계약을 하다 You can't **make a bargain with** Mr. Burns. 넌 번즈 씨와 거래를 할 수 없어.

make a choice	선택하다 I'm sorry, but I had to **make a choice.** 미안하지만 난 선택을 해야 했어.
make a confession	고백하다 I have **a confession to make.** I damaged your car. 고백할 게 있어. 네 차를 망가트렸어.
make an offer	제의하다 I think that we should **make an offer** on the property. 그 부동산 매입가를 제시해야 할 거 같은데.
make a proposal	제안하다 He **made a proposal** that we start a business. 걔는 우리가 사업을 시작하자고 제안했어.
make a purchase	구매하다 You can **make a purchase** in the duty-free shop. 넌 면세점에서 구매를 할 수 있어.
make a request	간청하다 Several people **made a request** for some beer. 몇몇 사람들이 맥주 좀 더 달라고 했어.
make a speech	연설하다 I have to **make a speech** next week. 다음 주에 연설해야 해요.
make a reservation	예약하다 What time can we **make a reservation?** 몇 시에 예약가능해요?
make an appointment (with)	(…와) 약속을 잡다 I'll **make an appointment with** the agent for later today. 오늘 늦게 부동산 중개업자하고 약속을 잡을게.
make a difference (to sby)	…에게 상관이 있다, 중요하다 A few more people isn't going to **make a difference.** 사람 몇 더 온다고 달라질 건 없어. **What difference does it make?** 그래서 달라지는게 뭔데? , 그게 무슨 차이가 있어?

make

make no difference
전혀 중요하지 않다, 상관없다 = not make any difference

My girlfriend's friends **make no difference to** me.
여친의 친구들은 내겐 중요치 않아.

make a mistake
실수하다

I **made a mistake.** It's my fault. 내가 실수했어. 내 잘못이야.

make a deal
거래하다

Let's **make a deal** never to fight over again.
다시 싸우지 않기로 거래하자.

make a scene
소란을 피우다 *make a noise 시끄럽게 하다

Let's not **make a scene.** It's not worth it.
소란피지마. 그럴 가치도 없어.

make an excuse
변명하다

No need to **make an excuse** for your absence.
네가 오지 못한 이유를 댈 필요가 없어.

make a face
인상짓다

Don't **make a face.** 이상한 표정 짓지마.

make a call
전화를 걸다 *take a call 전화받다

I have to go **make a call,** I'll be back.
전화좀 걸고, 곧 돌아올게.

Your friend went out to **make a call.**
네 친구는 전화걸러 나갔어.

make a move on
추근대다 *make a move 이동하다

They don't **make a move** without Jack's say so.
잭이 허락하지 않으면 걔네들은 시작하지 않아.

Don't be afraid, **make a move on** her!
겁내하지 말고, 걔한테 대쉬해봐!

make a pass at
추근대다

I saw Carla **make a pass at** my man.
칼라가 내 남자에게 추근대는걸 봤어.

make a mess of
…을 그르치다

I'm afraid I've **made a mess** here on your desk.
이 책상을 어질러놓은 것 같아.

make a run for it	도망가다, 서둘러 피하다 Let's **make a run for it.** 도망가자, 빨리 피하자.
make a match	잘 어울리다 She will **make a perfect match for** you. 그녀는 너와 완벽하게 어울린다.
make a killing	많은 돈을 벌다 We are going to **make a killing** tonight. 오늘 밤 떼돈 벌겠어.
make a fortune	떼돈을 벌다 You're too lazy to **make a fortune.** 넌 부자가 되기에는 너무 게을러.
make a living	생활비를 벌다 How are you planning to **make a living?** 어떻게 해서 생계를 유지할 계획이야?
make a fool of oneself	어리석게 행동하다 I just **made a completely fool of myself.** 내가 아주 멍청한 짓을 했군
make the grade	필요한 기준에 다다르다, 성공하다 Only a few of you will **make the grade.** 너희들 중 극소수만이 기준에 달성할거야.
make sure	…을 확인하다, …을 확실히 하다 **Make sure that** you arrive on time tomorrow. 내일 정시에 꼭 도착하고. I'll **make sure that** I keep in touch. 내가 꼭 연락할게.
Let me make sure that S+V	…을 확인해볼게 **Let me make sure** I understand. You don't love her? 확인해볼게. 걔를 사랑하지 않는거야?
Please make sure (that)~	반드시 …하도록 해라 **Please make sure** they comes. 걔들이 꼭 오도록 해.

make

I want to make sure~	…를 꼭 확인하고 싶어
	I want to make sure that you're okay. 네가 괜찮은지 확인하고 싶어서.

I want you to make sure~	네가 …을 확실히 해라
	I want you to make sure she doesn't name names. 걔가 이름을 불지 않도록 네가 확실히 해라.

make sense	말이 되다
	Does that **make any sense to** you? 너한테는 이게 말이 돼?

make money	돈을 벌다
	I can't find a way to **make money.** 어떻게 해야 돈을 벌 수 있는지 모르겠어.

make time	시간을 내다
	I can **make time** for you this Friday. 이번 금요일에 네게 시간 낼 수 없는데.

make love (to sby)	(…와) 사랑을 나누다
	He **made love to** me. 그 사람과 난 사랑을 나눴어.

make friends with	…와 친구를 사귀다
	You have to **make friends with** him. 걔랑 친구해라.

make it	해내다, 성공하다
	When can you **make it?** 몇 시에 도착할 수 있겠니? Can you **make it?** 어디 약속에 올 수 있어?

make it to+명사	시간에 늦지 않게 …에 도착하다
	I almost didn't **make it to** the party. 그 파티에 못갈 뻔했어.

Check it Out!

A: Don't forget to drop me a line.
B: **I'll make sure that** I keep in touch.
   A: 잊지 말고 꼭 연락해.
   B: 내가 꼭 연락할게.

make it on time	제 시간에 오다	
	I wonder if she **made it on time**. 제 시간에 도착했는지 모르겠네.	
make it on one's own	혼자 해내다, 자립하다	
	You'll never **make it on your own**. 넌 절대로 혼자 해내지 못할거야.	
make it through	(어려운 상황을) 잘 넘기다, 해내다	
	So don't worry about it. You'll **make it through**. 그럼 걱정마. 넌 해낼거야.	
make it up to sby	보상하다	
	I want to try to **make it up to** you. 내가 다 보상해줄게.	
make fun of	…을 놀리다	
	Don't **make fun of** me, okay? 너 지금 나한테 장난치나?	
make nothing of	…을 무시하다	
	I can't **make nothing of** it. 전혀 이해 못하겠어요.	
	Oh, **make nothing of** his question. 저런, 그 사람 질문 무시해버려.	
make much of	…을 중시하다	
	You shouldn't **make much of** her remarks. 걔의 말들을 너무 중시하지마.	
make little of	…을 경시하다	
	Why does he always **make little of** my work? 왜 그는 늘 나의 업무를 무시할까요?	
make the most of~	…을 최대한 활용하다	
	The most you can do is **make the most of** it. 네가 할 수 있는 최선은 그걸 최대한 활용하는거야.	
make the best of~	(어려움 속에서도) 최대한 노력하다, 극복하다	
	I know this move has been hard on you, but try to **make the best of** it. 이 조치가 네게는 힘들었겠지만 최대한 이용하도록 해.	

make

make up one's mind
결심하다, 결정하다

I **haven't made up my mind** yet. 아직 결정을 못했어.

Hurry up and **make up your mind.**
어서 마음을 결정해.

make out
이해하다, … 인 척하다, 애무하다

Can you **make out** what it says on the map?
지도에 뭐라고 써있는지 알아보겠어?

I want to **make out with** my girlfriend.
애인하고 애무하고 싶어.

make up
구성하다, (속이기 위해) 진짜 인 척하다, 새로 만들어내다, 준비하다, 화장하다, 화해하다(~with)

Is that something you're **making up?**
이게 네가 꾸미고 있는거야?

He didn't recognize me at first without my **make up.**
걘 처음에 내 화장 안 한 얼굴을 못알아봤어.

make up for sth
보상하다, 벌충하다

You want to do this to **make up for** the past?
과거를 보상하기 위해 이걸 하고 싶은거야?

make off with
…을 가지고 도망가다

They **made off with** my MP3 player.
걔네들은 내 MP3 플레이어를 가지고 도망갔다.

be made of [from]
…으로 만들어지다

You people **are made of** stone!
너희들 정말 냉정하구나!

make do with
…으로 때우다 *make do without …없이 때우다

You'll have to **make do with** it. 이걸로라도 때워야 하겠는데.

make believe
…인 척하다

You don't have to **make believe** you're going to call.
넌 전화를 할 것처럼 할 필요가 없어.

make like
…인 척하다, 흉내내다

He **made like** he had been invited.
걘 자기가 초대된 것처럼 행동했어.

market

n. 시장 **v.** 시장에 내놓다

be in the market for sth	…을 살려고 하다(= want to buy sth) **Are** you **in the market for** some luggage? 가방 살거야?
on the market	판매중인(available to buy) The house was **on the market** for more than a year. 그 집은 매물로 일년이상 나와있어.
put sth on the market	시장에 내놓다 We'll **put** the company **on the market** next year. 우리는 내년에 회사를 매물로 내놓을거야.
come onto the market	시장에 나오다 More properties will **come onto the market** soon. 더 많은 부동산들이 곧 시장에 나오게 될거야.

matter

n. 문제, 상황 **v.** 중요하다, 문제되다

as a matter of fact	사실 **As a matter of fact** I didn't go to bed last night. 사실은 간밤에 잠을 못 잤어.
for that matter	그 문제에 대해 **For that matter,** we may as well give up. 그 문제에 대해, 우리는 포기하는게 낫겠어.

market

| the heart of the matter | 문제의 핵심

It takes a while to get to **the heart of the matter.**
문제의 핵심에 들어가는 것은 시간이 걸려. |

| it matters that ~ | …것이 문제이다, 중요하다

I don't really think that **it matters** to Alexis.
그게 알렉스에게 중요하다고 생각하지 않아. |

| to make matters worse | 설상가상으로

To make matters worse, it began to rain.
설상가상, 비가 내리기 시작했어. |

175

mean

v. 의미하다 **a.** 야비한

| I mean~ | 내 말은 …야

I mean I lost weight. 내 말은 내가 살이 빠졌다고.
I mean today, not tomorrow. 내 말은 내일이 아니고 오늘 말하는거야. |

| (Do) You mean~ ? | …라는 말이지?

Do you mean he might like me? 걔가 날 좋아할지도 모른단 말야?
You mean he got fired? 그 친구가 해고당했단 말이야? |

| What do you mean~? | …가 무슨 말이야?

What do you mean you're not so sure?
확실하지 않다니 무슨 말이야?
What do you mean by that? Am I fat?
그게 무슨 말이야? 내가 뚱뚱하다고? |

| It doesn't mean that~ | …라는 말은 아니야

It doesn't mean he's great in bed.
걔가 밤일을 잘한다는 말은 아니야.
I guess that means we got something in common.
그게 의미하는 건 우리가 공통점이 없다는거야. |

mean to

…할 작정이다

I **meant to** say thank you.
네게 고맙다고 말할 생각이었어.

I **meant to** tell you, I don't love you anymore.
진작 말할려고 했는데, 난 너 더 이상 사랑하지 않아.

You **mean to** tell me you can't find a room?
방을 구할 수 없다는거야?

I didn't mean to~

…하려던 게 아니었어

I **didn't mean to** offend[insult, upset] you.
널 기분나쁘게[모욕, 화나게] 하려는 게 아니었어.

I'm sorry! I **didn't mean to** do that!
미안! 그럴려고 그런게 아니었어!

I **didn't mean to** hurt you.
너에게 상처 줄 의도가 아니었어.

I **didn't mean to** say that.
그렇게 말할려는게 아니었어.

mean it[that]

진심이다, 정말이다   *I don't mean it 그럴 생각은 아냐

Don't be upset. I didn't **mean that.**
화내지마. 그럴려고 그런게 아니야.

You don't **mean that.** 농담이지.

I **mean it.** I didn't know about that.
정말야. 난 정말 그거에 대해 몰랐어.

You **mean it?** That would be so fun!
정말야? 굉장히 재미있겠다!

mean a lot

…에게 큰 의미가 있다, 중요하다, 친숙하다

It **means a lot** to me that you came.
네가 왔다는게 나한테는 큰 의미가 있어.

That **means a lot** to me. 건 내게 매우 중요해.

I'm sure it would **mean a lot** to her
그게 걔한테 의미가 클거라 확신해.

mean everthing to sby

…에게 가장 중요하다

You **mean everything to** me. 넌 나의 모든 것이야.

That **means nothing to** me. 그건 내게 중요하지 않아.

It **doesn't mean anything to** me. 난 상관없어.

mean

~what sby mean
…가 의미하는 것

That's not **what I mean.**
실은 그런 뜻이 아냐.

I know[see] **what you mean.**
무슨 말인지 알아.

I'm not sure[I don't know] **what you mean.**
무슨 말인지 모르겠어.

You know **what I mean?** 무슨 말인지 알겠어?

See **what I mean?** 내 말 무슨 말인지 알겠어?

If you know **what I mean.** 내가 무슨 말 하는지 안다.

mean no harm
나쁜 뜻으로 그런게 아니야

I really **didn't mean any offence.**
기분나쁘게 하려는 건 아니었어.

I **didn't mean any harm.**
다치게 할 생각은 없었어.

I **mean no disrespect,** doctor.
의사선생님, 불쾌하게 듣지 않았으면 해요.

be meant to~
…하기로 되어 있다

I **was meant to** spend the rest of my life with you.
난 남은 여생을 너와 함께 보내도록 되어 있어.

I feel like I **was meant to** pick this up.
내가 이걸 선택하도록 되어 있는 것 같았어.

by all means
물론이지, 그렇고 말고, 그 정도야

By all means, let's hear your opinion.
물론이지. 자 네 의견을 들어보자.

mean maybe
그럴 수도 있다

I don't **mean maybe!** 대충 하는 말 아냐. 진심으로 하는 말이야!

Check it Out!

A: If I were you, I wouldn't go in there.
B: I'm not sure **what you mean.**

  A: 내가 너라면 거기 안 들어갈거야.
  B: 무슨 얘긴지 잘 모르겠는데.

meet

ⓥ 만나다, 맞서다, (요구, 주문) 충족시키다 *meeting 회의, 만남

meet sby	…을 만나다 What time would you like to **meet**? 몇 시에 만날래? Haven't we **met** before? 우리 만난 적 있나요?
I'd like you to meet~	…을 소개할게 **I'd like you to meet** my boyfriend. 내 친구 한 명 소개할게. Everybody, there's someone **I'd like you to meet**. 너희들한테 소개할 사람이 있어.
meet the deadline[goal]	마감[목표]을 맞추다 You'll need to hurry to **meet the deadline**. 마감하려면 서둘러야 돼.
meet the need [satisfaction]	필요를 충족시키다, 만족시켜주다 The hotel didn't **meet our satisfaction**. 그 호텔은 만족스럽지 못했어.
make ends meet	수지타산을 맞추다 We need to save money to **make ends meet**. 수지타산을 맞추기 위해 돈을 저축해야 한다.
meet with	회의하다, 만나다, 경험하다, 겪다, 우연히 만나다 I'd like to **meet with** you this afternoon. 오늘 오후에 만나고 싶어.
meet up with	(우연히) 만나다 They walked into the restaurant to **meet up with** her. 그들은 걔 만나기 위해 식당으로 들어갔어.
have[attend] a meeting	회의가 있다, 회의에 참석하다 Are you going to **attend the meeting**? 회의에 참석할거야? Did you **have a meeting** with her yesterday? 걔랑 어제 회의했어? He'**s in a meeting** right now. 걘 지금 회의중이야.

mention

v. 언급하다, 말하다

mention (sby[sth])

(…을) 언급하다

Did I not **mention** that? 내가 그거 말하지 않았어?

You **mentioned** that. 네가 그걸 언급했어.

How could you not **mention** it? 어떻게 그걸 언급하지 않을 수 있어?

mention sth to sby

…에게 …을 언급하다

Don't **mention** it **to** anyone. 그거 아무한테도 말하지마.

She never **mentioned** it **to** you? 걔가 네게 그걸 말한 적이 없다고?

mention that~

…라고 말하다

Did I **mention** I'm sleeping with her?
내가 걔하고 잔다고 말했어?

He **mentioned that** maybe I might quit.
걘 내가 그만두어야 할지 모를거라고 말했어.

mention earlier [before]

미리[전에] 말하다

He **should've mentioned** his wife **earlier.**
걘 아내에게 미리 말했어야 했어.

As I mentioned before, I'm not going to the office party.
내가 전에 말했듯이, 사무실 파티에 안갈거야.

now that you mention it

그 얘길 해서 말인데

Now that you mention it, I remember meeting her.
그 얘길해서 말인데 걜 만난게 기억나.

not to mention sth

…은 말할것도 없고

You can go surfing, **no to mention** swimming.
수영은 말할 것도 없고 서핑갈 수도 있어.

be worth mentioning

언급할 가치가 있다

It's **not even worth mentioning.** 그건 언급할 가치도 없어.

I know, but it's **still worth mentioning,** I think.
알아, 하지만 내 생각엔 언급할 가치가 있어.

mess

v. 지저분하게 만들다 **n.** 엉망

make a mess (of)	(…을) 엉망으로 만들다
	She's **made a mess of** her personal life. 걘 자신의 개인적인 삶을 망쳐버렸어.

be in a mess	엉망이 되다
	She i**s in a mess** because she got pregnant. 걘 임신을 해서 엉망이야.

mess up	엉망으로 만들다
	I plan to **mess up** his life big time. 걔 인생을 완전히 망쳐버릴 계획이야.

mess with	장난치다, 놀리다
	Don't **mess with** me. I get angry easily. 나 건드리지마. 나 화 잘 내.

mind

v. (부정, 의문문) …에 거슬리다, 화나다, 상관하지 않다 **n.** 마음, 정신, 생각

Do[Would] you mind ~ing?	…해도 될까요?
	Would you mind letting me check your bag? 손님 가방 속을 확인해 봐도 될까요? **Do you mind** picking me up tomorrow? 내일 나 좀 태워 줄 수 있겠니?

mess

Do[Would] you mind if ~?

…해도 될까요?

Would you mind if I smoke here?
여기서 담배펴도 돼요?

Do you mind if we ask you some questions about her?
걔에 대해 몇 가지 질문해도 돼?

I don't mind~

…해도 상관없어

That's all right. **I don't mind** waiting.
괜찮아. 기다려도 괜찮아.

I don't mind her hanging around with you.
걔가 너랑 같이 놀아도 상관없어.

I don't mind if you ask. 네가 물어봐도 상관없어.

Never mind~

…을 신경쓰지마

Never mind that. 그거 신경쓰지마.

Well, **never mind** me. 그래, 나 신경쓰지마.

Never mind that we don't have it. 그게 없다고 신경쓰지마.

I wouldn't ~ mind

…하고 싶다, …하면 좋겠다

I wouldn't mind a cup of coffee. 커피한잔 마시고 싶어.

I wouldn't mind having some real food sometime.
언젠가 한번 진짜 음식을 먹고 싶어.

Do you mind?

그만할래?, 괜찮겠어?

I'd like to go for a walk. **Do you mind?**
산책하고 싶은데, 괜찮겠어?

I really have to go to the bathroom. **Do you mind?**
나 정말 화장실가야 하는데 괜찮겠어?

mind one's own business

남의 일에 간섭하지 않다 = mind one's manners, mind one's P's and Q's

Mind your P's and Q's! 행동거지 조심해!

I'll thank you to **mind your own business.**
남의 일에 참견 말아줬으면 고맙겠네.

if you don't mind

괜찮다면

If you don't mind, I'd like to ask you both a few questions.
괜찮다면 너희 둘에게 질문 좀 할게.

If you don't mind me asking, why were you so interested in this? 내가 물어봐도 괜찮다면 왜 넌 이거에 관심있었어?

change one's mind	마음 바꾸다, 변심하다
	What made you **change your mind?**
	왜 맘이 바뀐거야?
take sby's mind off	…을 잊게 하다
	Maybe it'll **take your mind off** Betty.
	아마 그게 베티 생각을 잊게 해줄거야.
	Just try to really **keep Tom's mind off** of it.
	탐이 그 생각에서 벗어나게끔 힘써봐.
put sth[sby] out of one's mind	…을 일부러 잊다, 신경쓰지 않다
	I just **got** that jerk **out of my mind!** 그 자식 잊어 버렸어!
	So just **put** it **out of your mind.** 그냥 잊어버려.
lose one's mind	정신을 잃다, 미치다 = go[be] out of one's mind
	I'm **losing my mind.** 내가 제정신이 아니야.
	What are you doing? **Are** you **out of your mind?**
	뭐해? 너 미쳤어?
have half a mind to~	…을 할까말까 하다
	I **have half a mind to** throw this martini right in your face!
	이 마티니를 네 얼굴에 부을까 생각중야!
	I **got half a mind to** contract the company.
	이 회사와 계약을 맺을까 망설이고 있어.
have sth in mind	…을 염두에 두고 있다 *keep[bear] ~in mind 명심하다
	What do you **have in mind?** 뭘 생각하고 있어?
	Do you **have** something else **on your mind?**
	뭐 다른 생각있어?
make up one's mind	결정하다(decide)
	I **haven't made up my mind** yet. 아직 결정을 못했어.
slip one's mind	…을 깜박 잊다
	It (completely) **slipped my mind.** 깜박 잊었어.
cross one's mind	…가 …의 생각에 떠오르다
	The thought never **crossed my mind.**
	그 생각이 전혀 나질 않았어.
	It hasn't even **crossed my mind.** 난 그 생각이 나지도 않았어.

mind

come to mind	갑자기 …생각이 나다
	Nothing **comes to mind,** but I'll check my files. 아무것도 생각나지 않지만 파일을 확인해볼게.

blow one's mind	…을 당황케하다, 놀래키다, 흥분시키다
	It **blew my mind.** 당황스러웠어.

go[run, flash] through sby's mind	잠시 생각하다
	I wonder what **was going through her mind** when she stood there. 걔 거기 서있었을 때 무슨 생각을 했는지 궁금해.

set[put] sby's mind at rest [ease]	…의 마음을 편하게 하다
	You can **put your mind at rest.** 안심해도 돼.

keep your mind on~	…에 전념하다
	Then stay here and **keep your mind on** your job, you hear me? 여기 남아서 네 일에 전념해. 알았어?

~ be the last thing on one's mind	…을 별로 생각하기 싫다
	Oh, please, that'**s the last thing on my mind.** 오, 제발. 그건 별로 생각하기 싫어.
	Children **were the last thing on her mind.** 걘 아이들을 별로 생각하고 싶지 않아했어.

180

miss

v. 놓치다, 그리워하다, …할 뻔하다

miss	…을 놓치다
	I heard you **missed** the train this morning. 오늘 아침 열차를 놓쳤다며.
	I **missed** my stop. 내가 내릴 정거장을 놓쳤어.
	I wouldn't **miss** it (for the world). 어떤 일이 있어도 초대에 응할게.
	I'll never **miss** it. 꼭 갈게요.

miss	…가 부족하다
	We're missing $50. 50달러가 부족해.
	This food is missing salt. 이 음식은 소금이 부족해.
miss sby	보고 싶어하다
	I'm going to miss you. 보고 싶을거야.
	I miss you already. 벌써 보고 싶어져.
	I miss you so much. 정말 널 보고 싶어.
You can't miss it	쉽게 찾을 수 있다
	Go straight for two blocks. You can't miss it. 2블록 곧장 가요. 쉽게 찾을거예요.
miss out on	(기회 등) 놓치다
	I don't want to miss out on the holidays with my kids. 애들과 함께하는 명절을 놓치고 싶진 않아.
	You're going to be missing out. It's a fun game. 좋은 기회를 놓치는거야. 재미있는 게임인데.

181

mix

 섞다, 혼동하다　 혼합, 섞인거

mix A with B	A와 B를 섞다 = mix together
	I don't like to mix business with pleasure. 공과사를 혼동하는 걸 안좋아해.
mix up with	…와 혼동하다 *get mixed up with 혼동하다, 엮이다
	Obviously, you've got me mixed up with someone else. 분명히 날 다른 사람과 혼동한거야.
	My daughter got mixed up with drugs. 내 딸은 마약에 빠졌어.
mix-up	혼동, 실수
	There was a little mix-up when I traveled overseas. 해외여행 중에 약간 혼선이 있었어.

money
◎ 돈

make money	돈을 벌다	
	I have to do whatever it takes to **make money.**	
	돈벌기 위해서는 뭐라도 해야 돼.	
spend money on sth[~ing]	…하는데 돈을 쓰다	
	The family **spent its money on** food and rent.	
	가족은 음식과 월세로 돈을 쓰고 있어.	
	The church **spends money** helping others.	
	교회는 다른 사람들을 돕는데 돈을 써.	
cost sby money	돈이 …들다	
	Your mistake **cost me a lot of money.** 네 실수 때문에 돈많이 까먹었어.	
save money	저축하다	
	We won't cut corners just to **save money.**	
	단지 돈을 절약하기 위해 편법을 쓰지는 않을거야.	
lose money	돈을 잃다	
	We all **lost our money** investing in mutual funds.	
	우리 모두 뮤츄얼 펀드 투자에서 돈을 잃었지.	
waste money	돈을 낭비하다	
	They **waste money** buying comic books.	
	걔들은 만화책을 사는데 돈을 낭비하고 있어.	
raise money	돈을 마련하다	
	We want to **raise money** for poor people.	
	우리는 불쌍한 사람들을 위해 돈을 마련하고 싶어.	
be right on the money	맞다, 정확하다	
	Your suspicion **was right on the money.**	
	네가 의심하던게 딱 맞았어.	
be out of money	돈이 떨어지다	
	For the most part, we **are out of money.** 주로 우리는 돈이 부족해.	

most

a. adv. 최고의, 대부분의, 가장, 거의

most of all	무엇보다도
	Sam liked my present **most of all**.
	샘은 무엇보다도 내 선물을 좋아했어.
at most	많아봐야, 기껏해야
	At most it is only worth a hundred dollars.
	기껏해야, 그건 겨우 100 달러 짜리야.
for the most part	대개, 보통
	Their marriage is a failure **for the most part**.
	걔네들 결혼은 거의 실패야.
most of the time	보통 = usually
	Lisa puts others before herself **most of the time**.
	리사는 대부분 자신보다 남을 우선시해.
make the most of~	…을 최대한 활용하다
	Why don't we just **make the most of** it? 그걸 최대한 이용하자.

mouth

n. 입

big mouth	수다쟁이
	You've got a **big mouth**. 너 참 입이 싸구나.
keep one's mouth shut	입을 다물다, 비밀을 지키다
	Keep your mouth shut about that. I don't want her to find out. 아무한테도 말하지마. 걔가 몰라야 되잖아.

open one's mouth	입을 열다	
	You had better **open your mouth** and talk. 입열고 비밀을 말하는게 좋아.	
watch your mouth	말 조심하다	
	Maybe you should **watch your mouth**. 넌 입조심해야 할 걸.	

185

move

ⓥ 움직이다, 이사하다, 제안하다, 감동시키다   ⓝ 움직임, 이동, 이사

move	움직이다
	Don't **move**. 꼼짝마, 움직이지마.
	Stay right where you are. Don't **move**. Freeze! 거기 꼼짝마, 움직이지마, 한발 짝도!
move	가다
	(It's) Time to **move**. 이제 그만 가봐야겠어.
	Let's **move** it. 가자.
	Let's **move** out. 떠납시다.
move in (out)	이사해오다(가다), 동거하다, 이사가다(move to)
	I want you to **move in with** me. 나랑 함께 살자.
	You can't **move in with** me. 넌 나랑 동거 못해.
move on (to)	진행하다, 옮겨가다, 앞으로 계속 나아가다
	I failed at this job, so I'm going to **move on.** 이 일에 실패해서 다음 일로 넘어갈거야.
be moved by	…에 감동받다
	She **was so moved by** Jack's story. 걘 잭의 이야기에 감동받았어.

get a move on	서두르다 **Get a move on!** 빨리 움직여!, 시작해! I'd better **get a move on** it. 빨리 서둘러야겠어.
make a move on	…에게 말을 걸다, 추근대다 He **made a move on** me. 그 사람이 내게 추근댔어.

186 much
a. adv. 많은, 매우, 정말, 많이

much the same	거의 같은 (almost the same) Well, I'm pretty **much the same.** 저기, 난 거의 똑같아.
(very) much like	매우 유사한 방식으로 She's a little girl, **very much like** our daughter. 걔는 어린 여자애이고 우리 딸과 무척 닮았어.
too much	너무 과하게 Eating **too much** meat causes cancer? Is that a fact? 고기를 많이 먹으면 암을 유발한다고? 그게 정말이야?
as much as	…만큼 I've never loved anybody **as much as** I love you. 내가 다른 사람 누구도 너만큼 사랑해본 적이 없어.
How much~?	얼마만큼…? **How much** should I spend for a new car? 새 차 뽑으려면 돈을 얼마나 써야 돼?
not much of a~	대단한 …은 아닌 Tammy is **not much of a** driver. She's had several accidents. 태미는 운전을 잘 하는 편이 아냐. 사고를 여러 번 냈어.

not so much as~	…조차도 못하는 It's **not so much as** most people believe. 그건 대부분의 사람들이 믿는 것보다 못해.
not think much of	대수롭지 않게 생각하다 I **didn't think much of** it. 난 그걸 별로 대수롭지 않게 생각했어.

187 name
n. 이름, 명성 **v.** 명명하다, 이름을 대다, 임명하다

call sby names	…의 욕을 하다 Come on, don't **call him names.** 왜 그래. 걔한테 욕하지마.
in the name of~	…의 이름으로 The room was reserved **in the name of** Helen Brown. 그 방은 헬렌 브라운의 이름으로 예약되었어.
the name of the game	핵심 That's right, friend, that's **the name of the game.** 맞아, 친구야. 그게 핵심이야.
under the name of~	…라는 미명하에, …라는 이름으로 Do you have a table **under the name of** Barton? 바튼이라는 이름으로 예약된 좌석이 있어요?
name your price	가격을 말해봐, 얼마를 원해 I want to buy it. **Name your price.** 그거 사고 싶은데, 가격을 제시해봐요.
be named (to)~	…로 임명되다 *name 이름을 …라 짓다 We **named** our dog Rich. 우린 강아지 이름을 리치라고 지었어.
you name it	기타 등등 **You name it.** What can I do for you? 말해 봐. 뭘 도와줘야 하지?

need

v. 필요하다, 해야 한다 **n.** 필요, 요구, 의무

need sth
…가 필요해

I **need** your help. 네 도움이 필요해.

If you **need** anything, just ask. 뭐든 필요하면 말만 해요.

I **need** more time to think. 생각할 시간이 더 필요해.

need sby
…을 원해, 필요해

I don't **need** you anymore. 난 더 이상 네가 필요없어.

We **need** you back. 우린 네가 돌아오길 바래.

need to~
…해야 해, …할 필요가 있어

Hey, I **need to** talk to you. 저기, 얘기 좀 하자.

I **need to** borrow some money. 돈 좀 빌려야겠어.

We **need to** talk about something.
우리 얘기 좀 해야 할 것 같아.

You need to~
넌 …해야 돼

You need to call her right now. 지금 당장 걔에게 전화해야 돼.

You need to talk with your teacher.
네 선생님하고 얘기해봐.

Do you need to get up early tomorrow morning?
내일 아침 일찍 일어나야 돼?

need sby to~
…가 했으면 해

I **need you to** get this done by tomorrow.
내일까지 이걸 끝내야 해.

I **need you to** leave right now.
지금 당장 떠나줘.

Do you **need me to** pick you up from the airport?
공항에서 널 픽업해줄까?

need

don't need to~
…할 필요가 없어

I don't need to think about it.
난 그걸 생각할 필요없어.

I don't need to know the details.
자세한 건 알 필요없어.

I don't need you doing me any favors.
내게 호의를 베풀지 않아도 돼.

All I need is~
내가 필요한 건 …뿐이야

All I need to do is get some more fun.
내가 필요로 하는 건 더 재미를 보는거야.

All I need you to do is sign here.
넌 여기에 사인만 하면 돼.

(There's) No need to~
…할 필요가 없다

There's no need to be embarrassed.
당황할 필요 없어.

There's really no need to explain.
정말이지 설명할 필요 없어.

No need to talk about it. 얘기할 필요 없어.

No need to lie. 거짓말 할 필요는 없어.

That's all I need to
내가 필요한 건 …뿐이야

That's all I need. 이게 내가 필요한 전부다.

That's all I need to know. 내가 알고 싶은 건 그게 다야.

be in need of~
…가 필요하다

I'**m in need of** a real friend.
난 진정한 친구가 필요해.

see a need to~
…할 필요성이 있다

I don't **see a need to** go there.
거기 갈 필요가 없어 보여.

meet a need ~
…필요를 충족시켜주다

I'm unable to **meet your needs.**
난 네 필요를 충족시켜줄 수가 없어.

next
a. adv. n. 다음의, 그 다음에

the next best thing	그 다음으로 최고의 것 (the next+최상급+N) Then being close to him was **the next best thing**. 그런데 걔와 가까이 있는 것이 차선책이었어.
the next thing I knew	깨닫고 보니, 어느 틈엔가 **The next thing I knew,** smoke was coming from the building. 어느 틈엔가, 건물에서 연기가 나오고 있었어.
next to	…의 옆에 My car is **next to** the post office. 내 차는 우체국 옆에 있어.
next to nothing	거의 …없는 I got it for **next to nothing.** 거의 거저에 샀어.
next time	다음번에 **Next time** I think I'll bring some coffee to keep me awake. 다음 번에는 계속 깨어있으려면 커피 몇 잔은 있어야 할 것 같아.
the next in line	다음 차례 The cashier will take **the next person in line.** 캐셔는 다음 차례의 손님을 처리할거야.

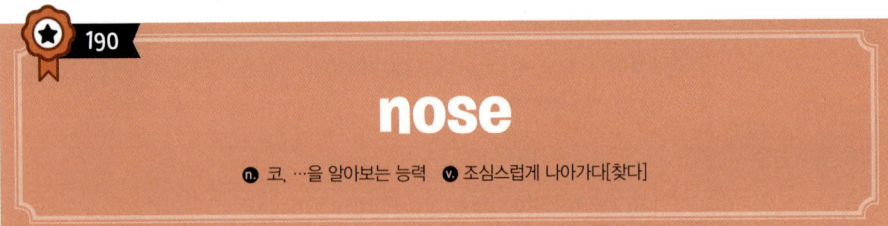

nose
n. 코, …을 알아보는 능력 **v.** 조심스럽게 나아가다[찾다]

blow one's nose	코를 풀다 Kevin **blew his nose** at the table. 케빈은 테이블에서 코를 풀었어.

pick one's nose	코를 후비다 Cindy went to the bathroom to **pick her nose.** 신디는 코를 후비려고 화장실로 갔어.
~nose is running	코가 흐르다 My **nose won't stop running.** 코가 멈추지 않고 계속 흘러.
keep one's nose clean	행동거지를 바로 하다 I've made it a point to **keep my nose clean.** 난 다른 일에 휘말리지 않도록 참견하지 않아.
have a good nose for	…에 식견이 있다 Ken always **had a good nose for** solving crimes. 켄은 범죄를 해결하는데 일가견이 있었어.
punch sb on the nose	…의 코를 때리다 She **punched** her boyfriend **on the nose.** 걘 남친의 코를 때렸어.
nose around	…의 정보를 알아내려고 하다 Let's **nose around** while we wait for him to show up. 걔가 오기를 기다릴 때까지 둘러보자.

 191

nothing

pron. 아무것도 (아니다)

There's nothing+형용사	…한 것이 하나도 없다 **There's nothing** wrong with the plane. 비행기에는 아무 이상도 없어.
There's nothing to+V[S+V]	…한 것이 아무 것도 없다 **There's nothing to** be afraid of, Charlie. 찰리, 무서워할게 아무 것도 없어.

There's nothing better[more, worse]~ than~	…보다 더 …한 것은 아무 것도 없다	
	There's nothing worse than a foolish advisor. 어리석은 조언자보다 더 최악인 것은 없어.	
mean nothing to sby	…에게 아무런 의미가 없다	
	You're not so special. Men **mean nothing to** her. 넌 특별한게 없어 걔한테 남자는 별 의미가 없을거야.	
Nothing much	별로 없는	
	Nothing much. How about you? 그냥 그래. 넌 어때?	
nothing like~	전혀 …같지 않은	
	For the record, she's **nothing like** Sam. 참고로 말해두는데, 그 여자는 샘이랑 전혀 달라.	
for nothing	거저, 아무일도 아닌 것에 *all for nothing 수포로 돌아가	
	So I apologized **for nothing?** 그래 난 아무 이유도 없이 사과했단 말야?	
	I will work **for nothing.** It can be like an internship. 난 무보수로 일해. 인턴쉽같은거야.	
	It was all **for nothing.** 모든 일이 수포로 돌아갔어.	
think nothing of it	별거 아닌 것으로 생각하다, 경시하다	
	Think nothing of it. It was a simple problem. 마음쓰지마. 간단한 문제였는걸	
nothing but	그저 …일 뿐	
	I have **nothing but** respect for Chris. 난 크리스를 존경할 뿐이야.	

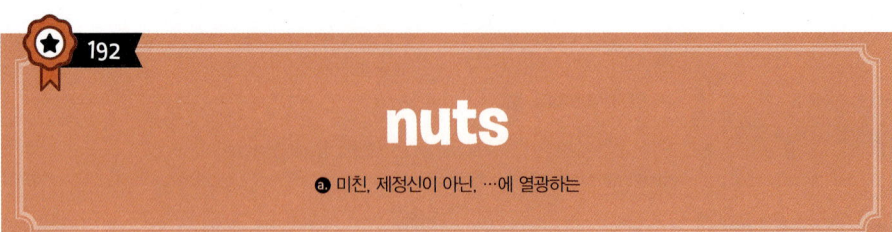

192 nuts

ⓐ 미친, 제정신이 아닌, …에 열광하는

~nuts	광	
	Sports nuts come to watch games on the weekend. 스포츠 광들은 주말에 게임을 보러 와.	

drive sb nuts	…을 열받게 하다
	Doesn't Rick **drive you nuts?** 릭이 널 화나게 하지 않니?
go nuts (~ing)	미치다, 열광하다, 화내다
	He's gonna **go nuts** for you. 걔는 너를 미치도록 좋아할거야.
be nuts to+V	…을 아주 좋아하다
	I'd **be nuts to** refuse his offer of money.
	난 기꺼운 맘으로 걔의 돈을 주겠다는 제의를 거절할거야.
be nuts about [over]	열광하다, 끌리다 *be nuts 미치다
	Carla **is nuts for** turning down the job.
	칼라가 그 직업을 거절하다니 미쳤구만.
in a nutshell	간단히 말해서
	In a nutshell, we had to fire him.
	간단히 말해서, 우린 걔를 해고해야 돼.

offer

v. 제안하다, 제공하다 **n.** 제의

offer sby sth (for~)	…에게 …을 제안하다
	Who **is offering** you the job with such a high salary?
	누가 네게 그런 고임금의 일자리를 권하고 있어?
offer sth to sby	…에게 …을 제안하다
	I'm not one to **offer** advice **to** others.
	난 다른 사람들에게 충고를 하는 사람은 아니야.
offer to+V	…하겠다고 제의하다
	Well, then, I might as well **offer to** stay.
	그러면 머물러 있겠다고 제의하는게 낫겠어.
make an offer	제의하다
	I think we need to **make an offer** on the house.
	우리가 그 집 구매제안을 해야 될 것같아.

take[accept] an offer	제안을 수락하다, 받아들이다 Would you **accept an offer** of ten thousand dollars? 만 달러를 주겠다는 제의를 받아들일거야?
turn down an offer	제의를 거절하다 **Turn down that offer** because it's too low. 그 제의는 너무 낮기 때문에 거절해라.

194 open
v. 열다 **a.** 열린, 공개된

open sth	…을 열다 My mother **is opening** her gifts. 어머니가 자신의 선물들을 뜯어보고 있어. I **opened** the door for them. 난 걔네들에게 문을 열어줬어.
open one's mind	마음을 열다 I'm trying to **keep an open mind.** 편견을 갖지 않으려 해.
open up	열다, 시작하다 **Open up.** We want to talk to you. 문 열어. 너랑 얘기하고 싶어. I'm thinking about **opening up** my own restaurant. 내 식당을 낼까 생각중이야.
open an account	계좌를 만들다 Teach him how to **open a bank account.** 은행계좌 어떻게 만드는지 알려줘.
(be) open	(문이) 열리다, 열려있다 The banks **open** at 9:30 from Monday through Friday. 은행은 월~금요일까지 9시 30분에 문을 열어.

offer

be open to	…을 받기 쉽다, …에 개방되어 있다
	A lot of opportunities **are open to** young kids. 어린 애들에게는 많은 기회가 열려져 있어.

get sth open	…을 열다, …을 드러내다
	Dad, will you just please let me **get this out,** okay? 아빠, 말할 기회를 주세요.
	The car is locked. Help me **get it open.** 차가 잠겼어. 여는 것 도와줘.

out in the open	백일하에
	Let's get this **out in the open.** 백일하에 드러내놓자.

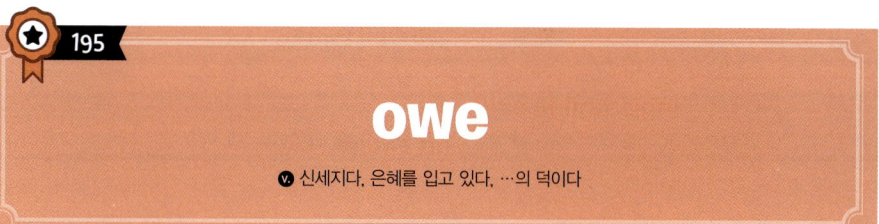

owe
ⓥ 신세지다, 은혜를 입고 있다, …의 덕이다

owe sby + (money or sth)	…에게 …만큼의 빚을 지다
	How much do I **owe** you? 내가 얼마를 내면 되지?
	Now, you **owe** me fifteen bucks. 이제 내게 15달러 빚졌어.
	You didn't **owe** me anything. 넌 내게 빚진 게 없어.

owe A B (B to A)	A에게 B를 빚지고 있다, …은 …의 덕택이다
	I **owe** you the truth. 사실대로 말해야겠어.
	We **owe** them an explanation. 그들에게 해명을 해야 해.

owe it to sby (to+V)	…의 덕택이다, …하는 것이 …에 대한 의무이다
	I **owe** it **to** my colleagues. 동료 덕이에요.
	I felt like I **owed** it **to** him. 이거 걔 덕택인 것 같아.

owe sby an apology	…에게 사과해야 된다
	You **owe** me **an apology.** 너 나한테 사과해야 돼.
	I **owe** you **an apology.** 네게 사과해야 돼.
	Do I **owe** her **an apology?** 내가 걔한테 사과해야 하는거야?

I owe you one	신세가 많구나
	It was a great idea. **I really owe you one.** 좋은 생각였어. 네게 정말 신세졌어.
	Thanks for coming over. **I owe you one.** 와줘서 고마워. 신세 많이 졌어.
I owe sby big time	…에게 신세를 많이 지다
	You guys **owe me big time.** 너희들 내게 신세 많이 졌어.
	She says you **owe her big time.** 걔가 그러는데, 네가 걔한테 신세 많이 졌다고 해.

196 part

n. 일부, 부분 **v.** 헤어지다, 갈라놓다 **ad.** 반쯤, 어느 정도

easy part	쉬운 부분 *hard part는 어려운 부분
	You've already done **the hard part.** 이미 어려운 부분은 마쳤어.
as a part of	…의 일환으로, 일원으로
	I stayed on **as a part of** the research team. 난 조사팀의 일원으로 계속 남았어.
be part of~	…의 일부[원]이다
	Henry **is part of** our study group. 헨리는 우리 스터디그룹 멤버야.
play the part of	…의 역을 하다
	He always **plays the part of** a sad old man. 걘 항상 슬픈 노인의 역을 해.
play a part in sth	…에서 역할을 하다
	Larry **played a part in** the crime and went to jail. 래리는 범죄에 가담을 해서 감옥에 갔어.

Part of me+V~	내 맘속 일부는 …하다
	There's a part of me that doesn't want to know. 내 맘속 일부는 그걸 알고 싶지 않아.

take part in	참여하다
	I know she took a part in the problem. 난 걔가 그 문제에 개입한 것을 알고 있어.

want no part of sth	…에 참여를 원치 않다, 관여하고 싶지 않다
	I want no part of this. 난 이거에 관여하고 싶지 않아.

part	헤어지다
	Are you going to part from your spouse? 너 네 배우자와 헤어질거야?

pass

v 지나가다, 건네주다, 통과하다　**n** 입장(통행)권, 합격, 패스

pass sby sth	…에게 …를 넘기다
	Hey Jimmy, could you pass me those cookies? 지미야, 저 쿠키 좀 건네줄테야?
	Could you pass me that please? 그것 좀 줄테야?

pass the exam	시험에 통과하다
	You'll pass the exam if you study. 넌 공부하면 시험에 붙을거야.

pass away	사망하다, 돌아가시다
	I'm very sorry to tell you your mother has passed away. 이런 말을 하게 돼서 유감이지만 어머님이 방금 숨을 거두었습니다.

pass out	실신하다
	He passed out behind the wheel. 걘 운전대에서 실신했어.
	Oh, gosh, you got drunk and you passed out. 오 맙소사. 너 취해서 실신했어.

pass by	…의 옆을 지나가다
	You just **passed by** me without a kiss? 키스도 안해주고 지나가는거야?

pass up	거절하다, (기회를) 놓치다
	Don't **pass up** your chance. 기회를 놓치지 마라.

pass through	지나가다, 통과하다, 경험하다
	The last train **passed through** here an hour ago. 마지막 열차가 1시간 전에 지나갔어요.

make a pass at	추근되다, 집적대다
	He **made a pass at** me. 걔가 나한테 추근거렸어. Did he **make a pass at** you? 걔가 너한테 집적댔어?

198

pay

Ⓥ (물건, 세금) 지불하다, (결과, 이익) 가져오다, 수지맞다   Ⓝ 지불, 지급, 급여

pay for	…의 비용을 지불하다, …의 대가를 치르다(혼나다)
	I'll **pay for** dinner. 저녁 내가 낼게. He will **pay for** my lawyer. 걔가 내 변호사 비용 댈거야. You get what you **pay for**. 땀을 흘린 만큼 얻는거야.

pay for that	그 비용을 지불하다
	You'll **pay for that**! 어디 두고 봅시다!. 너 대가를 치러야 할거야! How would you like to **pay for this**? 이거 어떻게 지불하실건가요? How much did you **pay for that**? 그거 얼마 줬어?

pay money for [to]~	…하는데 돈을 지불하다
	I **paid $500 for** this dress. 이 옷 사는데 500 달러 지불했어. He **paid a lot of money for** it. 걔 그거 사는데 많은 돈을 지불했어.

pass

pay sby money (to~)	…에게 돈을 지불하다 She **paid me 50 dollars** not to tell. 걘 얘기하지 말라며 내게 50 달러를 줬어. You couldn't **pay me to** do it. 이걸 하라고 돈으로 시킬 수는 없어.
pay in cash	현금으로 지불하다 I'm just going to **pay for this with a check.** 이거 수표로 낼게요. Can I **pay in** Korean won? 한국 돈으로 내도 돼요?
pay the bill	계산서를 지불하다 I'd like to **pay the bill,** please. 계산을 좀 하려고요. I just **paid my credit card bill.** 신용카드 대금을 냈어.
pay a fine	벌금을 내다 I have to **pay a fine** for speeding. 속도위반으로 벌금내야 돼.
pay the price	대가를 치르다 Why should I **pay the price?** 왜 내가 대가를 치러야 돼. You commit a crime, you **pay the price.** 죄를 지었으면 벌을 받아야지.
pay rent	임대료를 내다 I got to **pay rent!** 임대료를 내야 돼!
get paid (for+ N, to+V)	지불받다, 임금을 받다 We work. We **get paid.** You don't owe me anything. 우린 일하고 돈을 받아. 네가 신세진거 없어.
pay attention	주의를 기울이다 She ignored me. She didn't **pay any attention to** me. 걘 날 무시해. 내게 주의를 기울이지도 않았어.
pay back	돈을 되갚다, 복수하다 I promise I'll **pay you back.** 다음에 갚을게. You can **pay me back** whenever you like. 편할때 갚아. You don't have to **pay me back.** 돈 갚을 필요없어.

pay off	이익을 내다, 좋은 결과가 되다, 빚을 갚다
	Don't worry about me **paying off** your debt. 내가 네 빚을 갚는거 걱정마.
	I'**ve paid off** all my debt. 내 빚을 모두 다 갚았어.
	Sending an e-mail **has finally paid off.** 이메일을 보낸게 좋은 결과를 낳았어.
pay a visit to	방문하다
	I'll **pay a visit to** the Paul's on my way home. 집에 오는 길에 폴 사무실에 방문할거야.
pay one's dues	책임을 다하다, 대가를 치르다
	I'**ve paid my dues.** 난 대가를 치루었어.
pay raise	임금인상 ↔ pay cut 임금삭감
	I got a big **pay raise!** 난 월급이 엄청 올랐어!
pay check	월급
	I got my first **pay check** yesterday. 어제 첫 월급을 탔어.

199 pick

v. 고르다, 선발하다 n. 선택, 선택한 사람, 정수(최고의 것)

pick out	고르다, 선택하다
	Can you help me **pick out** an engagement ring? 약혼반지 고르는거 도와줄래?
	I'm here to **pick out** my Christmas tree. 크리스마스트리 고르러 왔어.
pick up	들어올리다, 사다, 차로 태워주다, 향상하다, (속도) 내다
	I **picked it up** at a flea market for $5. 벼룩시장에서 5달러에 샀어.
	Let me **pick you up** in the morning. 아침에 픽업할게.
	Who's going to **pick it up?** 술값은 누가내지?
	I think things **are picking up.** 상황이 나아질거에요.

pay

pick up the tab	돈을 지불하다
	Jim said that he'd **pick up the tab.** 짐이 자기가 계산한다고 했어.

pick up the pieces	재기하다, 다시 일어서다
	Her friends came to help **pick up the pieces.** 걔 친구들이 와서 다시 시작하는 걸 도와줬어.

pick on	괴롭히다
	Why **are** you **picking on** me? 왜 날 괴롭히는거야? **Stop picking on** me. 날 못살게 굴지마, 놀리지마.

take one's pick	마음대로 고르다
	Take your pick. It's free of charge. 맘대로 골라. 무료야. You can **take your pick.** 골라서 가져가.

picky	까다로운
	He's really **picky** about his food. 걘 음식고르는데 까다로워.

200

place

n. 장소, 곳, 집 v. 두다, 알아보다, 평가하다

one's place	살고 있는 집
	How about coming over to **my place** tonight? 오늘밤 우리집에 놀러올래?

all over the place	도처에, 곳곳에
	These are from **all over the place.** 이것들은 도처에서 온 것들이야.

there's no place for	…할 여지가 없다, …할 자리는 없다
	There's no place for truth on the internet. 인터넷에 진실이 있을 곳은 없어.

in place	제 자리에 놓인
	Let me know as soon as they're **in place**.
	그것들이 준비 되는대로 알려줘.
in place of~	…의 대신에 = in sby's place
	The waiter brought soup **in place of** a salad.
	웨이터는 샐러드 대신에 스프를 가져왔어.
put oneself in one's place	…의 입장이 되어보다
	He's stressed. **Put yourself in his place.**
	걔가 스트레스를 받았나 봐. 한번 걔 입장이 되어 봐.
take sb's place	…을 대신하다(take the place of sth)
	Nothing can **take the place of** good health.
	건강보다 더 좋은 것은 없어.
go places	성공하다
	I feel that I am going to **go places** after I graduate from Yale.
	예일대를 졸업만 하면 내 인생이 활짝 필 것 같아.
place emphasis on~	…에 강조하다
	The school **places an emphasis on** science and math.
	학교에서는 과학과 수학을 강조하고 있어.

201

plan

ⓥ 계획을 세우다, …할 작정이다   ⓝ 계획, 도면, 약도

plan sth	…을 계획하다
	He's **planning** your birthday party. 걔가 네 생일파티를 계획하고 있어.
	I **planned** everything really well. 난 모든 일을 매우 잘 계획했어.
plan to+V	…할 작정이다(plan on ~ing)
	I **plan to** stay for a week. 일주일간 머물거야.
	What **are** you **planning to** do on the 31st of December?
	12월 31일에 뭐할 계획이야?

place

plan out	면밀히 계획하다
	I thought you had this all **planned out.** 난 네가 이걸 다 면밀히 계획한 줄 알았어.
as planned	계획대로
	If all goes **as planned,** I will not be here anymore. 모든 게 계획대로 되면 난 더 이상 여기 없을거야.
make a plan	계획을 세우다
	I'**ve already made other plans.** 난 이미 다른 계획이 있어.
	I wish I could, but I'**ve made plans to** walk around. 나도 그러고 싶은데 산책할 계획이라서 말이야.
have a plan	계획이 있다
	Do you **have any plans?** 무슨 계획있어?
	Do you **have any plans** for summer vacation? 여름휴가계획 있어?
	I'**ve got plans.** 약속이 있어.
be against[for] the plan	그 계획에 반대[찬성]하다
	My neighbor **is against the plan to** build a park here. 내 이웃은 여기에 공원짓는 걸 반대해.
~plan is to~	…의 계획은 …하는 거야
	Our plan is to leave in ten minutes. 계획은 10분 안에 떠나는거야.
	Her plan is to hook you up with her sister. 걔의 계획은 걔 누이와 널 엮어줄려는거야.
plan B	차선책
	I have no **plan B.** 예비 계획따윈 없어.
	You need a **plan B.** 예비 계획이 필요해.
	We have to move on to **plan B.** 우린 차선책으로 가야겠어.
(That) Sounds like a plan	좋은 생각이야
	Sounds like a plan. I'll see you at 8:00. 좋은 생각이야. 8시에 보자고.
	That sounds like a plan. Count me in. 좋은 생각이야. 나도 껴줘.

good plan	좋은 계획
	That's a **good plan,** Jill. 훌륭한 생각이었어, 질.
	Good plan, but it'll never work. 좋은 계획이지만 절대로 되지 않을거야.
Here's the plan	이렇게 하자
	Here's the plan. We're not going home today. 이렇게 하자. 우리 오늘 집에 안 가는거야.

202 play

v. 놀다, 운동[연주]하다, …의 역을 하다, 상연하다　**n.** 연극, 놀이

play+운동명	…운동을 하다
	I sprained my ankle while **playing** basketball. 농구하다 발목삐었어.
play the+악기명	…악기를 연주하다
	She is good at **playing the violin.** 걔는 바이올린을 잘 켜.
play a part [role] in	…의 역할을 하다
	Fred's illness **played a part in** his decision to retire. 프레드의 병이 퇴직하는데 큰 역할을 했어.
play it safe	안전하게 하다, 신중을 기하다
	If life is short, it's dumb to **play it safe.** 인생이 짧다면 안전만 추구하는 건 어리석은 짓이야.
play dumb	멍청한 척하다
	Don't **play dumb** with me! 날 바보 취급하지마!
play game	게임을 하다, 수작부리다
	Don't **play games** with me. 날 가지고 놀 생각은 마. I don't **play games.** 수작 부리는거 아니야. I don't **play games** anymore. 난 더 이상 게임 안 해.

plan

play hooky	무단결석하다(play truant)
	I don't feel like going to school so I'll **play hooky.** 학교가기 싫어서 땡땡이 쳤어.

play hard to get	잡기 힘든 척 연기하다, 관심없는 척하다
	Don't start **playing hard to get** again, John. 존 관심없는 척하지마.

play hardball	적극적으로 하다, 악착스럽게 굴다
	He**'s playing hardball.** 걔 아주 적극적으로 임하고 있어. You want to **play hardball?** 세게 나오시겠다?

play it by ear	임기응변하다
	Let's just **play it by ear.** 그때그때 상황에 맞게 행동하자.

make a play for sby	갖은 노력을 하다, 온갖 수단으로 유혹하다
	Mark **made a play for** the manager's position. 마크는 부장자리를 얻으려고 갖은 노력을 했어. You should **make a play for** that cute girl. 넌 저 예쁜 애를 유혹하려면 갖은 방법을 써야 돼.

play	공연하다, (명사) 연극
	What**'s playing** now? 지금 뭐 공연해? Sam is the principal actor in **the play.** 샘은 그 연극에서 주연 배우야.

 203

point

n 요점, 의견 **v** 가리키다, …에 이르게 하다

get[see] the point	이해하다(understand)
	I **get your point.** I'll be more careful with my tongue in the future. 네말 알겠어. 앞으로는 더욱 말 조심할게.

you've got a point (there)	일리있다, 맞는 말이다 = that's a point **You've got a point there,** it would be a tough decision. 그점은 네 말이 맞아. 어려운 결정이 될거야.
strong points	강점 *weak points 약점 One of my **strong points** is that I'm cautious. 내 강점중의 하나는 신중하다는거야.
at this point	현재는, 현시점에서는 **At this point,** no one has canceled the meeting. 현재 누구도 회의를 취소하지 않았어.
to the point	간단명료한, 간결한 *come to the point 요점을 말하다 Please make it neat, short, and **to the point.** 깔끔하고 짤막하면서도 적절하게 해 주세요. I don't have the time. Please **come to the point.** 시간이 없어. 요점만 말해줘.
at some point	어떤 시점에서, 일정 시점에서 **At some point,** you just got to let it go, right? 언젠가는 그냥 잊어야 하는거야, 알겠니?
get to the point	각설하고 본론으로 들어가다 Could you please **get to the point?** 요지를 말씀해 주시겠어요?
make[prove] your point	자신의 주장을 입증하다 **Make your point** and make it fast. 내가 이해하도록 잘 설명해봐 대신 빨리.
on the point of~	…에 임박하여, …하려는 순간에 I am **on the point of** firing Nelly. 난 넬리를 해고하려고 하고 있어.
point out	지적하다 I merely **pointed out** the pros and cons. 난 단지 장단점을 지적했었어.

post

n. 기둥, (군) 주둔지, 근무지, 인터넷 게시글 **v.** 우편물을 발송하다, 배치하다, 발표하다, (웹에) 게시하다

| **post (on the Internet)** | 인터넷에 게시하다, 올리다 |

I'm going to **post** a message on the Internet.
난 인터넷에 메시지를 올릴 생각이야.

The company **posted** an ad for a job on the Internet.
회사는 인터넷에 구인 광고를 올렸어.

| **post (up) ~** | 게시하다 |

Just **post** an ad for the bike you want to sell.
네가 팔고 싶은 자전거 광고를 게시해.

| **keep sb posted** | …에게 최신 정보를 알리다 |

Keep us posted on what happens to her.
걔 근황 계속 알려줘.

| **be posted (on the website)** | (웹 등에) 게시되다 |

It **was posted on** the school social networking site.
그건 학교 소셜네트워킹 사이트에 올라온거야.

| **post a video on YouTube ~ing[of~]** | …내용의 동영상을 유튜브에 올리다 |

My brother **posted a video on YouTube of** his rock band.
내 형은 자신의 락밴드 동영상을 유튜브에 올렸어.

prefer

v. 선호하다, …을 더 좋아하다

| **prefer+명사 [~ing]** | …를 더 좋아하다 |

Thank you very much, but I **prefer** coffee.
정말 고맙지만 커피를 더 좋아해요.

prefer to+V	…하는 걸 더 좋아하다 I **prefer not to** answer that right now. 그 대답은 바로 하지 않을래. I **prefer to** be alone. Please leave. 혼자 있고 싶어. 그만 가줘.
prefer A[명사, ~ing] to B[명사, ~ing]	B보다 A를 좋아하다 I **prefer** eating out in a restaurant **to** sitting around at home. 집에서 쓸데없이 시간보내는 것보다 밖에서 먹고 싶어.
prefer A rather than B	B하는 것보다는 차라리 A하겠다 Most kids **prefer** to enjoy free time **rather than** study. 대부분의 아이들은 공부보다는 자유시간을 즐기는 걸 좋아해.
I would prefer +명사[to+V]	…하면 좋겠다 I'd **prefer** a beer if you have one. 맥주 있으면 한잔 하고 싶은데. I'd really **prefer** a mountain bike. 산악자전거가 있으면 좋겠어.
I'd prefer it if~	…하면 좋겠다 I **would prefer it if** you didn't. 네가 그러지 않으면 좋겠어. I'd **prefer it if** we didn't make an issue out of this at work. 직장에서 이걸 문제 삼지 않았으면 좋겠어.

prepare
v. 준비하다

prepare sth	…을 준비하다 I didn't **prepare** a speech. 연설을 준비못했어. I tried my best to **prepare** this meal for you. 널 위해 이 음식을 준비하는데 최선을 했어.
prepare (sby) for	(…에게) …을 준비하다 I've been **preparing for** that my entire life! 평생 이걸 준비해왔어!

prefer

prepare to~	···할 준비를 하다 They **are preparing to** leave for the wedding. 걔네들은 결혼식장에 갈 준비를 하고 있어.
prepare oneself (for[to])	(···을) 대비하다, 각오하다 I'm trying to **prepare myself for** what I have to do. 내가 해야 할 일을 대비하려고 하고 있어. You need to **prepare yourself for** that. 너 그거 각오하고 있어야 돼.
have[like] sth prepared	···을 준비하게 하다 How would you **like your steak prepared?** 고기를 어떻게 해드릴까요?
be prepared to[for]	···에 준비되다 I **am prepared to** let that go. 그걸 잊어버릴 준비가 됐어.

 207

promise
n. 약속 **v.** 약속하다

keep a[one's] promise	약속을 지키다 = stick by a promise It's important to **stick by your promises.** 약속을 지키는 것은 중요한 일이야.
break a[one's] promise	약속을 지키지 않다 You shouldn't **break your promise** to her. 넌 걔와의 약속을 꼭 지켜야 돼.
make a promise	약속을 하다 = give a promise Once he **makes a promise,** he never goes back on his word. 걔는 약속을 일단하면 절대로 말을 바꾸지 않아.
promise to+V	···하겠다고 약속하다 I **promise to** make you a happy woman. 널 행복한 여자로 만들 것을 약속해.

promise sb that~	…에게 …을 약속하다 **I promise you** I will not forget this. 절대 이거 안 잊을거라 약속할게. **Promise me that** you will make the best of this. 넌 이거에 최선을 다할거라고 약속해.
promise oneself that S+V	…을 다짐하다 **I promised myself that** I will exercise more. 내가 운동을 좀 더 하겠다고 다짐했어.
promise sth to sby	…에게 …을 약속하다(= promise sb sth) Grandma **promised** her wedding ring **to** my sister. 할머니는 자신의 결혼반지를 내 누이에게 주겠다고 하셨어.
as promised	약속한대로 The new television was delivered **as promised.** 새로운 TV가 약속한대로 배달되었어.
I promise (you)	내 약속하지 **I promise you,** we won't give up on you. 정말, 우린 널 포기하지 않을거야.

208

pull

ⓥ 끌다, 잡아당기다, 떼어내다

pull oneself together	기운내다, 똑바로 하다 Let's **pull it together.** 진정하자고. **Pull yourself together!** Have some pride. 기운내고 자부심을 좀 갖어.
pull sby's leg	놀리다 You're **pulling my leg.** 나 놀리는거지, 농담이지.

promise

pull over	차를 도로가에 대고 세우다
	We're here. **Pull over.** 우리 다 왔어. 차 세워.
	Pull over right here, driver! 여기 차 세워요, 기사아저씨!
	Pull over to the side of the road. 길 한쪽에 차를 세워.

pull up	차를 멈추다, (의자를) 당겨앉다, 끌어올리다
	Tim **pulled up** in front of Jane's house. 팀은 제인 집 앞에 차를 세웠어.
	Pull up a chair and take a close look at this. 의자당기고 이걸 자세히 들여다봐.

pull off	성공하다
	The thieves **pulled off** a bank robbery. 도둑들이 은행터는데 성공했어.
	I don't think you will be able to **pull it off.** 네가 성공할 것 같지 않아.

pull out	잡아빼다
	Have you had your wisdom teeth **pulled out?** 사랑니 뽑았어?

pull out all the stops	최선을 다하다
	We're **pulling out all the stops.** 최선을 다하고 있어요.

pull (the) strings	막후[배후] 조정하다, 연줄을 이용하다
	I've had a lot of people trying to **pull strings** behind the scenes. 난 뒤에서 힘을 써줄려고 하는 사람들이 많아.

put

ⓥ …한 상태에 놓다(put~ +부사구), …하게 하다(put~ to~)

put sth in [on]~	…에 놓다, 넣다
	Where did you **put** it? 그걸 어디에 두었어?
	You can just **put it on** the table. 고마워. 그냥 테이블 위에 올려놔.

put ~ in danger	위험에 빠트리다
	You're **putting** our lives **in danger.** 넌 우리 목숨을 위태롭게 하고 있어.
put ~ at risk	…을 위태롭게 하다
	You **put** our relationship **at risk.** 네가 우리 관계를 위태롭게 했어.
put ~ on the line	…을 위태롭게 하다
	You **put** your career **on the line.** 너의 경력을 위태롭게 했어.
put sth on a list	리스트에 …을 올리다
	You can **put** your name **on a list.** 리스트에 이름을 올리세요.
put sth back	원래 자리에 놓다, 늦추다, 연기하다
	You just **put it back** where you found it. 발견한 자리에 도로 갖다놔.
put sby in jail	투옥시키다
	The police **put me in jail** for stealing. 경찰이 절도죄로 나를 잡아 넣었어.
put sby out of one's misery	곤경에서 구해주다
	Just **put me out of my misery.** 날 비참하게 내버려두지 말아요.
put ~ in a good [bad] mood	…을 기분 좋게[나쁘게] 하다
	Her arrival **put** us all **in a good mood.** 걔가 도착하니 우리 모두가 기분이 좋아졌어.
put ~ out of a job	…을 실직시키다
	Too many immigrants **put** people **out of jobs.** 너무 많은 이민자들 때문에 사람들이 일자리를 잃었어.
put ~ in charge	…에게 책임을 주다, 맡기다
	I **put** Bill **in charge** until I return. 빌한테 내가 돌아올 때까지 맡아달라고 했어.
put ~ to work	…을 돌아가게 하다, 일을 시키다
	It's time to **put** you **to work.** 널 일시켜야 될 때야.
put ~ to death	죽게하다, 사형에 처하다
	The state plans to **put** the murderer **to death.** 그 주에서는 그 살인범을 사형에 처할 계획이야.

put

put a stop to	…을 끝내다(= put an end to~) You can **put a stop to** this right now if you want to. 네가 원한다면 이거 끝내도 돼.
put ~ to sleep [bed]	…를 재우다, 자게 하다 When you're ready, he's going to **put** you **to sleep.** 네가 준비되면 잠들게 할게요.
put ~ to (good) use	…을 (잘) 이용하다 I'm just trying to **put** our mistake **to good use.** 우리 실수를 잘 활용하려고 하고 있어.
put it[this]	표현하다(=express) I don't quite know how to **put this.** 이걸 어떻게 말해야 할지 모르겠어. Let's **put it** this way. 이렇게 말해보자고.
put aside	잠시 제쳐놓다, 잊다, 저축하다(put by) You need to **put aside** your differences with her. 걔하고의 차이점은 잠시 잊어야 돼.
put away	치우다, 비축하다, 투옥하다, 많이 먹어치우다, 물리치다 He is dangerous and I want him **put away!** 걘 위험하니 쳐넣어!
put down	내려놓다, 기록하다, 혼내다, 진압하다, 적다 This is police! **Put down** your weapon. 경찰이다! 총 내려놔. He **put** the bag **down** as he put a cigarette in his mouth. 걘 담배를 입에 물면서 가방을 내려놓았어.
put in	설치하다, (시간을) 쏟다, (돈을) 내다, 공식적으로 요청하다 *put in+시간 노력과 힘을 쏟다 They've had plans to **put in** a tennis court for months. 걔네들은 수개월간 테니스장을 설치할 계획을 갖고 있었어. I can't just walk away! I**'ve put in** four hours! 그냥 물러날 수 없다고! 4시간이나 쏟아부었는데!
put in a request[order]	공식적으로 요청하다, 명령하다 I **had put in a request to** have all my mail forwarded. 우편물을 모두 전송해달라고 공식요청했어.
put one's faith[trust, confidence] in	…을 믿다, 신뢰하다 When you **put your faith in** people, they reward you. 네가 사람들을 신뢰하면 그들도 네게 보답하는거야.

put off	연기하다, 미루다, 기다리게 하다 *put sth off …을 미루다, put off ~ing …하는 것을 미루다 Don't **put off** until tomorrow what you can do today. 오늘 할 일을 내일로 미루지 말라. The meeting **has been put off until** further notice. 회의는 다음 고지가 있을 때까지 연기되었어.
put on	(옷을) 입다, (살이) 찌다, …인 척하다 You don't have to **put on** a brave face for me. 나 때문에 용감한 표정 짓을 필요없어.
put on+옷 [무게, 화장품]	…을 입다, 찌다, 바르다 I had to **put on** lotion. 로션을 발라야했어.
put on+ 장비[노래]	…을 켜다, 노래를 틀다 *put on+콘서트[연극] …을 올리다 Turn off the air condition and **put on** the heat. 에어컨 끄고 히터 켜. I'm going to **put on** the most romantic song. 가장 로맨틱한 노래를 틀어줄게.
put sby on **(the phone)**	(전화) …을 바꿔주다 **Put him on/I'll put you on/You're putting me on.** (전화상에서) 연결해줘요 / 연결해드릴게요/연결됐어요.
put pressure **on~**	…에게 압력을 가하다 **Are** your parents **putting pressure on** you to find a good job? 부모들이 좋은 직장을 잡으라고 압력을 주고 있니?
put out+담배 [불, 장비]	…을 끄다 Just **put out** your cigarette. That's all I ask. 담배꺼. 바라는 건 그뿐이야.
put out sth	…을 밖에 내놓다, 꺼내놓다, 제작하다, 출판하다 Yeah, let's **put out** a broadcast. 그래 이제 방송을 내보내자.

Check it Out!

A: You shouldn't **put off** that work for much longer.
B: I'll try and finish it before I go.

  A: 그 일을 너무 오랫동안 미루어 두지 마라.
  B: 열심히 해서 퇴근하기 전에는 끝내 놓을게.

put

put oneself out
…을 드러내다, 노력하여 …하다

Put yourself out there. You'll meet a nice girl.
자신있게 나서봐. 멋진 여자를 만나게 될거야.

put through
…을 전화연결시키다, …을 겪게하다 *put sby through sth …가 …를 겪게 하다

I never wanted to **put** you **through** this.
결코 네가 이걸 겪게 하고 싶지 않았어.

Why do you **put** me **through** this?
왜 이렇게 힘들게 하는거야?

put sby[sth] through (to)
…을 (…에게) 전화를 돌려주다

I'll **put** you **through** right away. 바로 바꿔드릴게요.

put sby through+학교
…의 학비를 대다

His wife worked to **put** him **through** medical school.
걔 엄마는 걔 의대학비를 대려고 일을 했어.

put together
모으다, 구성하다, 정리(종합)하다, 합하다

Maybe I'll just **put together** another party.
또 다른 파티를 준비할까봐.

put up
세우다, 짓다, 걸다, 게시하다, 높이 들다, 올리다

They all **put up** their hand eagerly.
걔네들은 모두 열심히 손을 들었어.

put up+돈
…을 치루다

They've already **put up** the money.
걔네들은 이미 돈을 치뤘어.

put up
(어떤 목적으로) 내놓다, …을 제안하다,

The opposing lawyer just **put up** a proposal.
상대측 변호사는 진술서를 제출했어.

put sby up
…을 재워주다, 숙박시키다 *put sby up to sth 부추겨 나쁜 짓을 하게 하다

Your mom didn't **put** me **up** to this.
네 엄마가 날 부추켜서 이것을 하게 하지 않았어.

put up a fight
선전하다, 잘 싸우다

She didn't **put up a fight**, did she?
걘 선전했어, 그지?

put up with	…을 참다
	You don't have to **put up with** this. 넌 이걸 참을 필요가 없어.
put A before B	B보다 A를 우선하다
	I **put** my work **before** my family. 난 가족보다 일이 우선이야.
put sth behind sby	(안 좋은 일 등) …을 잊다
	I want to help you **put** it **behind** you. 난 네가 그걸 잊는 걸 도와주고 싶어.
put forth	제출하다(submit)
	I mean, the ideas you **put forth** is not that good. 내 말은 네 제안은 그렇지 좋지 않아.
put into practice	실행하다
	Let's **put** those ideas **into practice.** 이제 우리 생각들을 실행에 옮기자.

210 question
n. 질문

ask a question	질문하다
	Can I **ask** you **a question?** 질문 하나 해도 돼?
answer a question	질문에 답하다
	If you're not hiding anything I suggest you **answer their questions.** 숨기는 게 아무것도 없다면 걔네들 질문에 답을 하지 그래
be out of the question	불가능하다, 소용없다
	It's **out of the question.** New computers are much too expensive. 안돼. 새 컴퓨터는 너무 비싸.
without a question	의심의 여지없이(beyond question)
	His genius is **beyond question.** 걔의 천재성은 의심할 여지가 없어.

there is no question about [that~]	…는 의심의 여지가 없다 **There is no question about** her guilt. 걔가 유죄라는데는 의심의 여지가 없어.
there is no question of sth [sby ~ing]	…가 (…할 가능성은) 없다, 그렇게 되지 않을 것이다 **There is no question of** the economy failing. 경제가 무너지지는 않을거야.

read
v. 읽다

read sth	…을 읽다 My father is trying to relax and **read** his newspaper. 아버지는 쉬시면서 신문을 읽으려고 하셔.
read about [of, that]	…에 관해 읽다 I've **read about** it online. 인터넷에서 봤어.
read (sth) to sby	…에게 …을 읽어주다 Why don't you **read it to** her? 걔한테 네가 읽어줘라.
read between the lines	행간을 읽다, 진의를 파악하다 Did you **read between the lines?** 진의를 파악했어?
read sby's mind	…의 마음을 읽다 You know that. You **read my mind.** 너 알잖아. 내 마음을 읽었잖아.
do you read me?	알겠어?, 잘 들려? This is a radio check. **Do you read me?** (무선통신) 레이디오 체크, 잘 들려?

212

remain
v. 남다

The question remains
문제가 남아있다
The question remains, is she going to get married?
문제가 남아있어. 걔가 결혼할까?

remain+형용사
…인 채로 남아있다
Remain where you are.
거기 그대로 있어.
The donor asked to **remain** anonymous.
기부자는 익명으로 해달라고 했어.

remain at [by, behind]
…에 머물다
Bob has chosen to **remain at** home.
밥은 집에 남아있기로 했어.
My wife decided to **remain by** my side.
아내는 내 옆에 남기로 했어.

remains
먹고 남은 나머지, 유적[유해]
Human **remains** were found during the excavation.
발굴탐사중 인간의 유해가 발견되었다.

213

remember
v. 기억하다

remember sby [sth]
…을 기억하다
You **remember** my brother Louis?
내 오빠 루이스 기억나?

remain

remember ~ing
(과거에) …한 것을 기억하다 *앞으로의 일을 기억하는건 remember to+V

Do you remember talking to me yesterday?
어제 내게 얘기했던거 기억나?

remember sby [sth] ~ing
…가 …한 것을 기억하다

I don't remember you doing the laundry.
네가 세탁하는 걸 본 적이 없어.

How can you not remember us kissing?
어떻게 우리가 키스한 걸 기억못해?

remember to +V
…할 것을 기억하다

Did you remember to buy the toothpaste?
치약사는 걸 기억했어?

Remember to e-mail me.
잊지 말고 메일보내.

remember that ~
…을 기억하다

I want you to remember that I'm a good person.
내가 좋은 사람이라는 걸 기억해줘.

remember what[how] ~
…한 것을 기억하다

You remember what that is?
그게 뭔지 기억나?

Don't you remember why you dumped the guy?
네가 왜 걜 찼는지 기억못해?

I don't remember how we ended up in bed together.
우리가 어떻게 침대로 들어가게 되었는지 기억안나.

remember the last time when ~
…한 마지막 때를 기억하다

I can't remember the last time I was out that late.
그렇게 늦게 외출한 마지막 때를 기억 못하겠어.

I remember the first time I asked a girl out.
내가 여자에게 처음으로 데이트 신청한 때를 기억해.

be remembered for[as]~
…로 기억되다

I will be remembered as the one who saved the company.
난 회사를 구한 사람으로 기억될거야.

remember me to sby
…에게 안부 전해줘

Remember me to your brother.
형한테 안부전해줘.

remind

ⓥ 기억나게 하다, 일깨우다 *reminder 생각나게 하는 사람, 메모

remind A of B

A에게 B를 기억나게 하다

You **remind** me **of** my youngest sister.
넌 내 막내여동생 생각나게 해.

remind sby about~

…에게 …을 기억나게 하다

Remind John **about** the birthday party.
존에게 생일파티 상기시켜줘.

remind sby to~

…에게 …하도록 기억나게 해주다

Remind me **to** introduce you to David.
널 데이빗에게 소개하는거 기억나게 해줘.

remind sby that~

…에게 …을 기억나게 하다

Let me **remind you that** I am the boss here.
여기 내가 사장이라는거 기억나게 해주지.

That remind me of~

그러고 보니 …가 생각나

That reminds me.
그러고 보니 생각나네.

They remind me of how desperate I used to be.
걔네들 보니 내가 과거 얼마나 절박했는지 기억나.

reminder

생각나게 하는 거, 메모

Thanks for the **reminder.**
생각나게 해줘서 고마워.

ride

v 이동수단을 타고 가다

ride the bus [the elevator]
버스[엘리베이터]를 타다

You have to learn how to **ride a bike.**
너 자전거 타는 법 배워야 돼.

give[take] (sby) a ride
…을 태워주다   *get a ride 차를 얻어타다

I'll **give you a ride.** 태워다 줄게.

You want me to **give you a ride home?**
집에까지 태워다 줄까?

go for a ride
드라이브하다   *take sb for a ride 드라이브시켜주다

You guys want to **go for a ride?** 너희들 드라이브 하고 싶어?

I **took him for a ride.** 난 걔 드라이브 시켜줬어.

need a ride
차를 얻어타고 가야 된다

If you **need a ride** to school, I'm happy to drive you.
학교까지 태워주길 원하면 태워다 줄게.

be along for the ride
따라가다, 내키지 않지만 함께 하다

He was going to the store and I **went along for the ride.**
걔가 가게에 가길래 난 따라갔어.

They **were along for the ride** when we took the trip.
걔네들은 우리가 여행을 할 때 따라왔어.

train[cab, subway] ride
기차[택시, 전철]타기

It's just **a subway ride away.** 전철탈 거리에 있어.

It's about **ten minutes' ride.** 차로 약 10분 거리야.

hitch a ride
히치하이크하다

It's so dangerous to **hitch a ride** these days.
요즘 히치하이크하는 것은 매우 위험해.

ride out
(어려운 상황을) 잘 참고 견디다, 이겨내다

I can **ride it out.** 이겨낼 수 있어.

right

a. 옳은, 정확한　**adv.** 즉시, 바로, 제대로　**n.** 옳음, 권리　**v.** 바로잡다

do right	옳은 일을 하다　*do right by~ …을 공정하게 대우하다 I hope he will **do right** by his wife. 걔가 자기 아내를 제대로 대우하기를 바래.
go right	잘되다, 우회전하다　*go right on[ahead] 똑바로 가다 The international meeting didn't **go right.** 그 국제회의는 제대로 되지 않았어.
right away	바로 Please get it done **right away.** 지금 당장 이것 좀 해줘.
right now	바로 지금 All I want to do **right now** is go to New York. 지금 내가 하고 싶은 건 뉴욕에 가는거야.
will be right with ~	…가 곧 올거다 Of course, sir. I'**ll be right with** you. 네, 손님. 바로 오겠습니다.
get sth right [straight]	명확하게 이해하다 Let me **get this straight,** you don't love me? 정리해보자, 날 사랑하지 않는다는거야?
be right about sth	…에 대해서 옳다 You may **be right about** that. 그것에 대한 네 말이 맞을 수도 있어.
be right in saying~	…라고 말하는 것은 …가 맞다 You **are right in saying** it will take a long time. 시간이 많이 걸릴거라는 네말은 맞아.
it's right ~ (of sb) to+V	(…가) …하는 것은 옳다 **It's right of** the manager **to** resign his position. 매니저가 자기 자리를 내놓는게 옳아.

right

It's all right to~
…해도 괜찮아

It's all right to ask the teacher questions.
선생님에게 질문을 해도 괜찮아.

right before [after]
직전[후]에

So you dumped her **right before** her birthday?
그래서 걔 생일 전에 바로 걔를 차버렸니?

right and wrong
옳고 그름

I believe in **right and wrong.**
난 선과 악이 있다고 믿어.

have the right to+V
…할 권리가 있다 ↔ have no right to

No one **has the right to** break the law.
아무도 법을 어길 권리는 없어.

You **have no right to** take it.
넌 그걸 가져갈 권리가 없어.

have every right to~
…할 충분한 이유가 있다

He's my son and I **have every right to** see him.
걘 내 아들이고 난 걜 당연히 만날 수 있지.

give sby the right to~
…에게 …할 권한을 주다

What **gives you the right to** do that?
네가 무슨 권리로 그러는거야?

set things right
일을 바로 잡다

Hopefully the staff can **set things right.**
스태프들이 일을 바로 잡을 수 있으면 좋겠어.

right a wrong
잘못된 것[행동]을 바로 잡다

Chris was willing to expose his secret to **right a wrong.**
크리스는 잘못된 것을 바로잡기 위해 자기 비밀을 기꺼이 내놓았어.

raise

v. 올리다, 일으키다, 제기하다, 키우다 *rise **n.** 증가, 인상 **v.** 올라가다, 오르다

---

raise sth

…을 올리다, 모으다

They **raised** a lot of money during the charity party.
걔네들은 자선파티에서 많은 돈을 모았어.

I'm sorry I **raised** my voice.
목소리를 올려서 미안해.

---

raise sby

…을 기르다

How am I going to **raise** a kid? 내가 어떻게 애를 키우지?

---

get[give] a raise

인상받다[해주다]

I'**m getting a big raise.** 나 월급 많이 올랐어.

Do you **want a raise?** 월급 인상을 원해?

---

rise above

극복하다

You should try to **rise above** your problems.
네 문제점들을 극복하는 법을 배워야 돼.

I tried to **rise above** it. 난 그걸 극복하려고 했어.

---

rise to the occasion

임기응변으로 대처하다

I can't seem to **rise to the occasion.**
난 임기응변으로 대처하지 못할 것 같아.

---

get sby a rise out of

…을 약올리다, 화나게 하다

I tried to **get a rise out of** him by telling jokes.
농담으로 걜 화나게 하려고 했어.

---

rise and shine

잠자리에서 일어나다

Rise and shine, because we have a lot of work to do today.
일어나라. 오늘 할 일 엄청나게 많아.

risk

n. 위험　**v.** 위태롭게 하다, 과감히 …하다

risk sth
…을 위태롭게 하다

We can't do that without **risking** our lives.
목숨을 걸지 않고는 그걸 할 수가 없어.

What's the big deal? Let's **risk** it.
뭐가 그리 대수야? 한번 해보는거지.

risk ~ing
감히 …하다

Did you **risk** slapping his face? 감히 걔 뺨을 때린거야?

risk sby ~ing
…가 …하는 위험을 하게 하다

I don't want to **risk** you **running** into Dad.
네가 아버지와 만나게 할 위험을 하게 할 수 없어.

take[run] a risk
위험을 무릅쓰다

She wouldn't be afraid of **taking a little risk.**
걘 조금 위험을 무릅쓰는 건 무서워하지 않을거야.

That's **a risk** I'm willing to **take!** 저건 기꺼이 해보고 싶은 모험이야!

worth the risk
위험을 감수할 가치가 있는

I guess it **was worth the risk.** 위험 감수할 만했어.

at the risk of
…의 위험을 무릅쓰고

At the risk of making her angry, he told the truth.
걔가 화날걸 무릅쓰고 진실을 말했어.

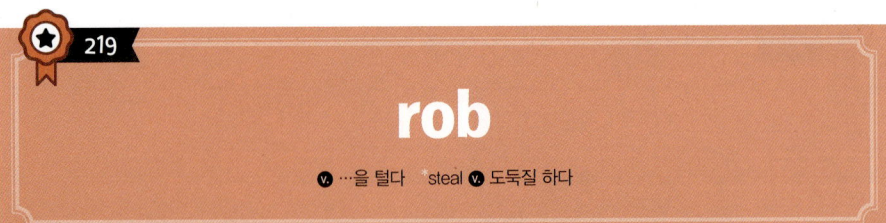

rob

v. …을 털다 *steal **v.** 도둑질 하다

rob sby[sth] of sth	…에서 …을 털다 You just **robbed** me **of** the opportunity to date her. 넌 내가 그녀와 데이트할 기회를 빼앗었어. He **robbed** the bank near my house. 걔는 우리집 근처 은행을 털었어.
steal sth from sby[sth]	…에게서 …을 훔치다 Who would **steal** shoes **from** a party? 누가 파티에서 신발을 훔치겠어? I **have** my notebook **stolen.** 노트북을 도둑맞았어

ruin

v. 망치다, 파산시키다 **n.** 몰락, 파산 *ruins 폐허, 유적

ruin it	그걸 망치다 I can't believe I **ruined this.** 내가 이걸 망치다니 믿을 수가 없어. You've **ruined it!** 네가 망쳤어!
ruin one's ~	…을 망치다 I'm sorry. I completely **ruined your evening.** 미안. 저녁시간을 다 망쳤네. You **ruined the surprise party.** 서프라이즈 파티를 네가 망쳤어. You **ruined everything.** 네가 다 망쳤어. You **ruined my weekend with** Julie. 네가 줄리와의 주말을 망쳤어.

be[get] ruined	망치다
	This **is still ruined,** right? 어차피 망친거잖아, 맞지?
	So nothing **got ruined?** 그래 아무 것도 망치지 않았어?
	Everything**'s ruined.** 모든게 망쳤어.

221 rule
n. 규칙, 통치 **v.** 다스리다

break a rule	규칙을 어기다
	I worked there for years and never **broke a rule.** 난 거기서 오랫동안 일하면서 결코 규칙을 어긴 적이 없어.
follow a rule	규칙을 지키다
	It is very important that everyone **follow this rule.** 모든 사람들이 이 규칙을 따르는게 매우 중요해.
as a rule	일반적으로, 보통
	As a rule, I don't drink much alcohol. 보통, 난 술을 많이 마시지 않아.
make it a rule to+V	…하는 것을 습관으로 하다
	Let's **make it a rule to** turn out the lights every night. 밤에는 언제나 전등을 끄기로 합시다.
rule out	제외하다
	You **rule out** the possibility he was in on it? 걔가 연루되었을 가능성을 배제하는거야?

run

v 달리다, 움직이게 하다, (교통수단)운행되다, 상영되다, 운영하다　**n.** 설사, 상영

run	달리다, 뛰다　*run to[down, toward] …로 달려가다, 뛰어가다, run to+V …하러 급히 가다 I'm going to **run to** the car and get my stuff. 차로 뛰어가서 내 물건 가져올게. I'm going to **run down to** the emergency. 응급실로 뛰어갈게.
come running	기꺼이 달려오다, 도움을 청하다(~to sby) The kids **came running** out of the house. 애들이 집에서 뛰어나왔어.
be running late	늦다　*be late for …에 늦다 I **was running late** for a meeting. 회의에 늦었어. Let's go. We'**re running late.** 가자. 우리 늦었어.
run sth by sby	…에게 …을 상의하다 (You'd better) **Run it by** me. 내게 말해봐, 상의해봐. Just **run it by** Jimmy and tell me what he thinks. 지미한테 가서 물어보고 걔 의견을 내게 알려줘.
be up and running	잘 돌아가다 **Are** the office **up and running?** 사무실은 잘 돌아가?
run errands	심부름하다 = go on an errand, do errand I have to **run an errand.** 심부름해야 돼, 볼 일이 있어.
run a fever	열이 나다 Jane'**s still running a fever.** 제인은 아직도 열이나.
run in the family	…가 집안 내력이다 Good looks **run in the family.** 잘 생긴 것은 집안 내력이야.

run

시간명사+ running	**…연속**
	Our softball team has lost **two years running.** 우리 소프트볼 팀이 2년 연속 졌어.
in the long run	결국
	Well, **in the long run,** it doesn't matter. 어, 결국, 그건 상관없어.
run wild	격해지다
	You let the boys **run wild.** 얘들 신나게 놀게 해.
run after	뒤쫓다, 뒤따라 달려가다
	Michael runs off and Jane **runs after** him. 마이클이 달아나자 제인이 그 뒤를 쫓는다.
run around (with)	뛰어 돌아다니다, 바쁘다 *run around with sby하면 잘못된 만남의 시간을 보내다
	Are you **running around** looking for your earring? 귀걸이 찾느라고 정신없는거야?
	She's **running around** telling that she's going to brake up with Tom. 걘 탐과 헤어질거라고 말하면서 다녀.
run away from	도망치다, 달아나다 *run off 급히 가버리다. 도망치다
	You can't **run away from** that. 넌 그것으로부터 도망칠 수 없어.
	I am going to **run away from** you. 너한테서 도망갈거야.
run down	뛰어내려가다, 차에 치이다, 비난하다, 고장나다, 닳아지다
	I'm going to **run down** to the emergency room and check it out. 응급실로 달려가서 확인해봐야지.
	I've been feeling a little **run down** lately. 최근에 좀 지쳤어.
run into	…로 달려 들어가다, 어려움 만나다, …을 우연히 만나다=run[come] across, bump into
	You **run into** any problems you call me. 무슨 문제 생기면 내게 전화해.
	I **ran into** her. 걔와 우연히 마주쳤어.
run out (of)	부족하다 = run short of, run low *run out on sb …가 어려울 때 도망치다
	My luck **ran out.** 운이 다했어.
	I **ran out of** gas. Where can we fill up? 기름이 다 떨어졌어. 어디서 기름넣어?
	I'**m running out of** time. 시간이 얼마 안 남았어.(I'm running short of time)

run over	…로 달려가다(to), 차로 치다, 훑어보다
	I'm going to have to **run over** there and beg him to love m. 내가 그리로 뛰어가서 걔에게 날 사랑해달라고 간청할거야.
	When I **got run over,** I was on my way to propose to you. 차에 치였을 때 네게 청혼하러 가는 중이었어.
	I'd like to **run over** today's schedule. 오늘 일정을 점검해봤으면 합니다.
run through	…을 가로질러 달려가다, 관통하다, 훑어보다　*run through one's mind는 …가 …의 머리 속을 스치다
	It**'s been running through** me ever since. 그 이후로 그게 내 머리 속에서 잊혀지지 않아.
	Okay, let's **run through** it one more time. 좋아 한번 더 훑어보자.

223 save
ⓥ 절약하다, 구하다

save sth[sby] (from sth)	(…로부터) …을 구하다
	Somebody will come and **save** us. 누군가 와서 우릴 구해줄거야.
	I**'ve saved** your life three times. 네 생명을 3번씩이나 구해줬어.
save (about) +돈	…을 저축하다(save enough to+동사, save for)
	I**'m saving** for a notebook computer. 노트북 살려고 돈을 모으고 있어.
	She wants to **save enough to** buy a car. 걘 차살 돈이 충분하길 바래.
save sby sth (sth for sby)	…에 쓰려고 비축하다, 남겨두다
	Hey, **save** us some pizza. 야, 우리 먹을 피자 좀 남겨놔.
	I'll **save** you parking spot. 네가 주차할 공간 남겨놓을게.
	I'll **save** you a seat. 자리 맡아놓을게.

save

save sby from~	…가 …하지 못하게 하다, …하는 것을 덜어주다 I'm just trying to **save** you **from** wasting your time. 네가 시간 낭비하는 걸 덜어주려는거야.
save (sby) the trouble of ~ing	(…에게) …할 수고를 면하게 하다 Honey, let me **save** you **the trouble.** 자기야, 네 수고 덜어줄게. That would **save** me **the trouble of** hitting him. 그럼 걜 때릴 필요가 없게 돼.
save (sby) time	…의 시간을 아껴주다 I'm going to **save** you **some time.** 너 시간 좀 아껴줄게. I will **save** you **a lot of time** and energy. 많은 시간과 에너지를 네가 아끼도록 해줄게.
save one's life	생명을 구하다 Thank you so much, Kate. You **saved my life.** 정말 고마워, 케이트. 너 때문에 살았어.
save (one's) face	체면을 살리다 There was no way to **save face** after I made the error. 실수한 후에 체면을 살릴 길이 없었어.
save one's breath	잠자코 있다, 쓸데 없는 논쟁을 피하다 **Save your breath.** Nobody? going to hear you. 잠자코 있어. 아무도 네 얘기 안들어줄거야.
save the day	겨우 승리하다, 궁지를 벗어나다 You **saved the day.** I'm a loser. 네가 이겼어. 난 실패자고.
save oneself	자기 몸을 아끼다, 수고를 아끼다 You've got to get out of here! **Save yourself!** 여기서 나가! 몸을 아끼라고!
save up (for)	(…을) 대비해 비축하다 Do you plan to **save up for** your wedding? 결혼식 대비해 저축해?
life-saving	목숨을 구하는 (약), 저축해놓은 전재산 The doctor gave my mom some **life saving** medicine. 의사는 엄마에게 목숨을 구해주는 약을 줬다. That was my **life savings!** 그건 내 전 재산이란말야!

say

v. 말하다, …라고 쓰여져 있다, (삽입구) 이를테면, 예를 들면

say hi
(안녕하세요라고) 인사하다 *say good bye 작별인사하다

I have to go now. I'll have to **say good bye.** 이제 가야 돼. 작별 인사해야 돼.

Say hi to Tony for me. 토니에게 안부 전해 줘.

say no (to)
(…에게) 반대하다, 거절하다 *say so 그렇게 말하다, say more 더 말하다

I'd have to **say no.** 안되겠는데.

I just can't **say no to** my mother. 엄마한테는 반대못해.

Why did you **say yes?** 왜 승낙한거야?

Need I **say more?** 더 말해야 하나요?, 더 말하지 않아도 알겠죠?

Say no more. I know it's your birthday. 알겠어. 네 생일이지.

say something to
…에게 뭔가를 말하다

Can I just **say something to** you as a friend? 친구로서 네게 뭐 좀 얘기할까?

I don't want you to **say anything like that to** her. 걔한데 그런 말 안 했으면 하거든.

say a word
말하다, 누설하다

I promise I won't **say a word.** 한마디로 말하지 않을게.

You can count on my help. Just **say the word.** 내 도움에 의지하라고. 말만해.

have something to say to sb [about sth]
할 말이 있다

I **have something to say.** 할 말이 있어.

I **have nothing to say to** you. 네가 아무 할 말이 없어.

If you **have something to say to** me, just say it. 내게 할 말이 있으면 그냥 말해.

say much [a lot] about
…에게 관해 말을 많이 하다

He doesn't **say much about** it. 걘 그것에 대해 말을 많이 하지 않아.

She didn't **say much to** me. 걘 내게 말을 많이 하지 않았어.

say

say that
…라고 말하다

I said that you had a nice place. 집이 멋있다고 했어.
I thought **you said** it was okay. 난 네가 괜찮다고 말한 줄 알았어.
You said it was going to be fun! 재미있을 거라고 했잖아!

You said you wanted to~
…을 원한다고 말했지

You said you wanted to get involved.
너도 끼고 싶다고 했지.
You said you wanted to say something.
뭔가 얘기하고 싶다고 했지.

I say (that)~
…하라고, 내 말은 …하라는거야 *You say (that)~ 네 말은 …라는 말야

I say you show Jill how much you love her.
질에게 네가 걜 얼마나 사랑하는지 보여주라고.
You say you want to meet men.
네 말은 남자를 만나고 싶다는거지.

You're saying ~
…라는 거지, …라는 말이야? *반대로 I'm saying~하면 자기 말을 정리, 강조할 때 하는 말

You're saying you're attracted to your teacher?
선생님한테 끌린다는 말이야?
You're saying you don't know anything about this?
넌 이거에 대해 아무것도 모른다는 말이야?

I'm saying that~
…라는 말이야

I'm saying that truth is powerful. 진실은 강력하다는 말이야.
I'm saying this as a friend. 친구로서 이거 말하는데.
I'm just saying you never know what could happen.
무슨 일이 일어날지 몰라서 하는 말이야.

Are you saying ~?
…란 말야? *What are you saying?하면 그게 무슨 말이야?라는 말. 또한 You're just saying that하면 그냥 해보는 말이지, 괜한 소리지라는 뜻

Are you saying that you're not going to hire me?
저를 채용 안하겠다는 말씀이죠?
Are you saying this is my fault?
이게 내 잘못이라고 말하는거야?
You're just saying that to make me feel better.
나 기분 좋아지라고 그냥 하는 말이지.
What are you saying? Am I rude?
무슨 말이야? 내가 무례하다는거야?

What I'm saying is that~

내 말은 …라는거야

What I'm trying to say is that she's rich.
내가 하려는 말은 걔가 부자라는거야.

What I'm saying is Allan likes you.
내 말은 앨런이 널 좋아한다는거야.

I have to [must] say ~

…라고 해야 되겠어

I have to say, I'm not surprised.
별로 놀라지 않았다고 말해야겠어.

I must say I'm disappointed in you.
너한테 실망했어.

I want to say~

…라고 말하고 싶어

I want to say thank you.
너한테 고맙다고 말하고 싶어.

I want to say goodbye to my friends.
내 친구들에게 작별인사 해야겠어.

I want to say how sorry I am.
내가 얼마나 미안한지 말하고 싶어.

I can't say ~

…는 아니지, …라곤 말 못하지

I can't say that I'm surprised. 놀란 것은 아니고.

I can't say who did that. 누가 그랬는지 몰라.

I'd say ~

…인 것 같아 *I'd say S+V에서 I'd say는 I would[could] say로 단정적으로 말하지 못하겠지만 …라고 말할 수도 있다라는 표현법으로 의역하면 …인 것 같아라는 말이다.

I would say that you are around 30 years old.
넌 한 30살 쯤으로 보이는데.

I'd say she died when she was about twenty.
걔는 스무살 즈음에 죽은 것 같아.

I guess **you could say** that. 그렇게 말할 수도 있을 걸.

Six feet, **I'd say.** 6피트인 것 같아.

Let's say~

…라고 (가정)해보자, …할까 *그냥 간단히 Say S+V라고 해도 된다

Let's just say he's a married woman.
걔가 유부녀라고 생각해보자.

Let's say we get out of here. I'll show you around.
자 여기서 나갈까. 내가 구경시켜줄게.

Say you never feel like a wife.
네가 아내라는 실감을 전혀 못한다고 하자.

say

What do you say ~ ?

…하는게 어때? *S+V 혹은 to ~ing[명사]의 형태가 이어진다. 또한 What would you say~라 하면 …한다면 어떻게냐고 상대방의 반응을 물어보는 문장

What do you say I take you to dinner tonight?
오늘 밤 저녁먹으러 갈래?

What do you say we get together for a drink?
만나서 술 한잔 하면 어때?

Let's go to China in May. **What do you say?**
5월에 중국가자. 어때?

What would you say if she stayed with us all night?
걔가 우리랑 밤샌다면 어떨까?

How could you say~ ?

어떻게 …말을 할 수 있어?

How can[could] you say that?
어떻게 그렇게 말할 수 있냐?

How can you say that it doesn't matter?
어떻게 그게 중요하지 않다는거야?

How can you say that to me? I'm your boss!
어떻게 그렇게 말하나? 난 네 사장야!

How could you say such a thing?
네가 어떻게 그런 말을 할 수 있어?

Who says S+V?

누가 …라고 해? *Who can say S+V?하면 …을 누가 말할 수 있겠냐, 즉 아무도 알 수 없는 노릇이라는 뜻으로 Who's to say S+V?라고도 한다

Who says I need someone to take care of me?
내가 날 돌볼 사람이 필요하다고 누가 그래?

Who's to say it wasn't you?
네가 아니라는 걸 누가 알 수 있겠어?

Needless to say

말할 필요도 없지만 = to say nothing of

Needless to say, everyone is shocked, including her.
말할 것도 없이 걔 포함해 모두 충격을 받았어.

whatever you say

상대방이 시키는 대로 다 하겠다는 말로 Anything you say라고도 한다.

Whatever you say, boss. 뭐든지 말씀만 하세요, 사장님.

Check it Out!

A: **What do you say to** an offer like that?
B: I would take it if I were you.

> A: 그런 제안은 어떠니?
> B: 내가 너라면 받아들이겠어.

It says here	···라고 되어[쓰여] 있다
	Says here Dr. Smith examined her last week, and everything was fine. 지난주에 스미스 박사가 걜 검사했는데 다 괜찮다고 적혀있어.
They say that ~	···라고들 한다(It is said that~)
	They say times fly. 세월이 유수같다고들 하지.
no matter what I say	내가 뭐라든
	No matter what I say, don't let me do that again. 내가 뭐라든, 내가 그걸 다시 못하게 해.
say ~ in English	···을 영어로 말하다
	I don't know how to **say it in English.** 그걸 영어로 어떻게 하는지 모르겠어.
like I was saying	말했듯이
	Like I was saying, I'm so sorry. 말했듯이 정말 미안해.
say something to one's face	대놓고 뭐라하다, 비난하다
	If you want to say something about me, **say it to my face!** 나한테 할 말 있으면 대놓고 해!
Say when	(술 등을 따르면서) 됐으면 말해 *Say cheese (사진 찍을 때) 치즈라고 해
	Say when, I'll try to get you some help. 됐으면 말해. 도와주도록 할게.
I'll say	정말이야
	I'll say. She seems like a movie star. 정말이야. 걔는 영화배우 같아.
You can say that again	누가 아니래
	You can say that again. I was stuck for over an hour! 내말이 그말야. 한 시간 넘게 꼼짝도 못했어!
You said it	네 말이 맞아 *You said that 네가 그랬잖아
	You said it. And you know what I say? 그러게 말야. 근데 내가 무슨 말하는지 알아?
What she says goes	걔말에 따라야
	What my father says goes in our house. 우리 집에서는 아버지가 왕이셔.

say

What can I say?
난 할 말이 없네, 나더러 어쩌라고?

What can I say? It's just one of those days.
뭐라고 해야 되나? 그냥 그렇고 그런 날야.

You don't say
설마!, 아무려면!, 정말?, 뻔한거 아냐?

You don't say. So Mike, any other little surprises?
설마. 그럼 마이크, 다른 좀 놀라운 소식은 없어?

Never say die!
기운 내!, 약한 소리하지마!

Try again. **Never say die!** 다시 해봐. 약해빠진 소리는 하지말고!

I know what I'm saying
나도 알고 하는 말이야

Don't worry, **I know what I'm saying.**
걱정마. 내가 알아서 말할게.

I know what you're saying
무슨 말인지 알아

I know what you're saying, and you're right.
나도 그렇게 생각해, 네가 맞아.

I don't know what to say
뭐라고 말해야 할지

I'm afraid **I don't know what to say.** 뭐라 말해야 할지 모르겠네요.

What do you want me to say?
무슨 말을 하라는거야?

What do you want me to say? I feel gloomy.
나보고 어쩌라고? 나 우울하다고.

What are you trying to say?
무슨 말을 하려는거야?

What are you trying to say? Do you want to break up with me? 무슨 말 하려는거야? 나랑 헤어지고 싶다는거야?

Is that what you're saying?
이게 당신이 의미하는거야?

You want your bill reduced. **Is that what you're saying?**
청구서금액을 깎아 달라고요? 그 말씀예요?

What did you say?
뭐라고 했는데?, 뭐라고!

I'm sorry. **What did you say?** 미안. 뭐라고 했어?

Stop saying that!
닥치라고!, 그만좀 얘기해!

Stop saying that! I'm trying hard to get a job!
닥치라고! 취직하려고 열심히 하고 있어!

What say? [Say what?]	뭐라고?, 다시 말해줄래?
	You want to break up with me? **Say what?**
	나랑 헤어지고 싶다고? 뭐라고?
See what I'm saying?	무슨 말인지 알지?
	You're just an average worker. **See what I'm saying?**
	넌 평범한 직원이야. 무슨 말인지 알아?
Why do you say that?	왜 그런 말을 하는거야?
	Why do you say that? You hardly know him.
	그게 무슨 말이야? 걔에 대해 잘 모르면서.
Well said	맞아, 바로 그거야, 말 한번 잘했다, 나도 동감이야
	Well said. I totally agree with you.
	맞아. 나도 전적으로 너에게 동의해.
When all is said and done	모든 일이 끝나면, 모든 것을 고려해볼 때
	When all is said and done, you need a new car.
	모든 걸 고려할 때, 넌 새차가 필요해.
I wouldn't say that	그렇지도 않던데
	I wouldn't say that. Some other shoes are better.
	그렇지도 않던데. 다른 구두들 중 더 좋은 것도 있어요.
Don't say it!	듣고 싶지 않아!, 나도 알고 있으니까 말 안해도 돼
	Don't say it! I don't like gossip. 그만해! 소문은 좋아하지 않는다고.
You (really) said a mouthful	의미심장한 말이었어, 아주 적절한 말이었어
	You really said a mouthful. 진짜 적절한 말이야.
Easier said than done	말이야 쉽지
	Easier said than done. I have to wake up early every day.
	말이야 쉽지. 매일 아침 일찍 일어나야 돼.
Don't make me say it[tell you] again!	두 번 말하게 하지마!
	You know the thing. **Don't make me say it.**
	네가 알잖아. 두번 말하게 하지마.
I didn't say that	그렇게 말 안했어
	I didn't say that! That's a lie. 그런 말 안 했어! 그건 거짓말야.

say

scare
v. 겁주다, 놀라게 하다

scare the life out of sby	…을 엄청 놀라게 하다 They **scare the life out of** me. 걔네들이 날 혼비백산하게 만들었어.
scare sby to death	…을 엄청 놀라게 하다 It can literally **scare you to death.** 문자그대로 그건 널 죽도록 무섭게 할거야.
be scared of ~ing	…하는 것을 두려워하다 You're just **scared of** getting hurt again. 넌 단지 다시 다칠까봐 두려워하는거야.
be scared that S+V	…할까 걱정되다 She **was scared that** Terry crashed her car. 걔는 테리가 자기 차를 부셔놓을까봐 걱정됐어.
be scare to+V	…하는데 걱정하다 I **am scared of** flying on airplanes. 난 비행기를 타는 것이 무서워.

schedule
n. 일정, 스케줄 **v.** 일정을 잡다, 예정하다

check one's schedule	일정을 확인하다 Let me **check the schedule.** 일정 좀 보고.
meeting schedule	회의 일정 There's been a change in the **meeting schedule.** 회의 일정이 변경됐어요.

ahead of schedule	일정보다 빨리
	Actually, they will be completed **ahead of schedule**.
	실은 걔네들은 일정보다 빨리 끝낼거야.
behind schedule	일정보다 늦게
	We are **behind schedule** on this work.
	이 작업이 예정보다 뒤쳐져 있어.
on schedule	일정에 맞게
	My father arrived at my house **on schedule**.
	아빠는 예정대로 내 집에 도착했어.
be scheduled to+V	…할 예정이다
	When **is** he **scheduled to** arrive at the airport?
	그 사람이 공항에 언제 도착할 예정이니?

227

search

 n. 찾기, 검색 v. 찾아보다, 수색하다

in search of	…을 찾아서
	I'm still **in search of** a new girlfriend.
	난 아직 새로운 여친을 찾고 있어.
make a search	찾다, 수색하다
	You'll need to **make a search** for it on the Internet.
	넌 그것을 인터넷에서 찾아야 할거야.
search for	해답을 찾기 위해 애쓰다, 찾다
	We **searched for** the keys but didn't find them.
	우리는 열쇠를 찾았지만 발견하지 못했어.
search out	열심히 …을 찾다
	The company will **search out** the best candidate.
	회사는 최고의 후보자들을 찾아낼거야.

schedule

Search me	난 몰라
	Search me. I haven't heard from him. 난 몰라. 걔한테 아무 소식도 못 들었어.
do research on	인터넷에서 찾다 = search the Web 웹을 검색하다
	She **is doing research on** the internet. 걔는 인터넷에서 검색을 하고 있어. Danny **did research on** the Internet for class. 대니는 수업을 위해 인터넷에서 자료를 검색했어.

228

second

ⓐ 두번째의, 둘째로, ⓝ 초, 잠깐 ⓥ 재청[동의]하다

second only to~	…에 버금가는
	It's **second only to** Las Vegas in the number of hotel rooms. 호텔 방수로는 라스베거스에 버금가.
second to none	제일의, 최고의
	This coffee is **second to none.** It is so delicious. 이 커피는 정말 끝내줘. 너무 맛있어.
have second thoughts about	…에 대해 다시 생각해보다
	Not yet. We'**re having second thoughts** about it. 아직. 좀 생각해보는 중야.
not give it a second thought	걱정하지 않다
	Don't give it a second thought. I'm always glad to help. 걱정하지 말아요. 언제나 기꺼이 도와드리죠.
on second thought	다시 생각해보니
	On second thought, I'd love to go. 다시 생각해보니, 나 가고 싶어.

without a second thought	더 생각할 것도 없이 바로 Mark agreed to it **without a second thought.** 마크는 더 생각할 것도 없이 바로 그거에 동의했어.
for a second	잠시 Dad, can I maybe talk to you **for a minute?** 아빠, 잠시 얘기할 수 있어요?
be seconded	재청되다, 동의되다 The motion **has been seconded.** 그 동의는 재청되었습니다.

secret
ⓐ 비밀의, 은밀한 ⓝ 기밀, 비법

keep a secret	비밀을 지키다 Don't worry, he can **keep a secret.** 걱정마, 걘 비밀을 지킬 수 있어.
keep sth secret	…을 비밀로 하다 *keep sth secret (from sby) …을 (…에게) 비밀로 하다 You know, I'm going to **keep** it **secret** for now. 저기, 지금은 비밀로 할거야.
let sb in on a secret	비밀을 누설하다 I'm going to **let you in on a secret** recipe. 내가 비밀레시피를 알려줄게.
tell sb a secret	…에 비밀을 말하다 What I want is to **tell you a secret.** 내가 바라는건 네게 비밀을 말하는 것이야.
in secret	비밀리에, 남몰래 The security staff held the meeting **in secret.** 비서진들은 비밀리에 회의를 가졌어.

see

ⓥ 보다, 이해하다, 만나다, 사귀다

see sby	만나다 I didn't expect to **see** you here. 널 여기서 보리라 예상못했어. **Haven't I seen** you somewhere before? 예전에 어디선가 한번 만난 적이 있던가요?
(It's) Nice[Good] to see you	만나서 반가워 **It's great to see you.** 만나서 정말 반가워.
I'm here to see sby	…을 만나러 왔어 **I'm here to see** some of my relatives. 친척들을 좀 만나러 왔어.
(I'll) See you~	…보자 **See you** in the morning. 내일 아침에 보자. **I'll be seeing you!** 잘 가!, 또 보자!
See you later	나중에 보자 *See you soon 곧 보자 I hope to **see you again.** (sometime) 조만 간에 다시 한번 보자.
See you tomorrow	내일 보자 *See you around 또 보자 I'll **see you around** sometime. 언제 한번 보자.
be seeing sby	사귀다 **Are** you **seeing** someone? 누구 사귀는 사람 있어? **I am seeing** her. 난 그녀하고 사귀고 있어. **I'm not seeing** anybody. 난 지금 사귀는 사람 없어.
see a doctor	진찰받다 = go to a doctor, visit a doctor Maybe you should go and **see a doctor.** 병원가서 진찰 받아 봐.

see a movie	영화보다 We're about to take off and **see a movie.** 바로 나가서 영화보려고
I (can) see your point	무슨 말인지 알겠습니다 **I see your point.** Wait, what's your point? 네 말을 알겠는데 잠깐, 요점이 뭐였지?
see a problem	문제점을 보다 Did you s**ee any problems** with that? 그거에 어떤 문제라도 발견했나요?
see the need of ~	…의 필요성을 이해하다 I don't **see the need of** it. 난 그럴 필요가 없다고 봐.
see sby[sth]+ 동사[~ing]	…가 …하는 것을 보다 I don't **see** that **happening.** 그렇게는 안될걸. I **saw** her **leave** for school this morning. 걔가 오늘 아침에 학교 가는 것 봤어. I never **saw** her **smoke.** 걔가 담배피는 것 전혀 못봤어.
can't see sby [sth]+~ing [전치사구]	…가 …하리라고 상상도 못하다 I **can't see** Angela **selling** her business. 난 안젤라가 자기 사업체를 파는 것을 상상못하겠어.
I (can) see (that) ~	…이구나, …을 알겠어 *I (can) see that 알겠어, I don't see that 난 그렇게 생각 안하는데. **I can see** you're not going to be any help. 넌 도움이 하나도 될 것 같지 않구나. **I see that** beauty runs in the family. 아름다움이 집안 내력이군요.
Don't you see?	모르겠어? This won't help, **don't you see?** 이건 도움이 안될거야, 모르겠어?

> **Check it Out!**
>
> A: Let me see what you've come up with.
> B: It's not much, but it's a start.
>> A: 네가 어떤 안을 내놓았는지 한번 보자.
>> B: 대단하진 않아. 하지만 이건 시작이니까.

see

You'll see	곧 알게 될 거야, 두고 보면 알아
	Give me a chance. **You'll see.** 기회를 한번 줘. 두고 봐.
I (can) see what[why, how] ~	…을 알겠어 *I can't see what[why]~ S+V …을 모르겠어
	I see what this is! You are in love with her! 그게 뭔지 알겠어! 너 걔랑 사랑에 빠졌구나!
	I can see why he likes you. 왜 걔가 널 좋아하는지 알겠어.
	I can't see what I'm doing here. 내가 뭘하고 있는지 모르겠어.
see what sby [sth] can~	…가 뭘 할 수 있는지 보다
	Here is 100 dollars. **See what you can** do. 여기 100 달러. 어떻게 할건지 생각해봐.
I'll see what~	…인지 보다
	I'll see what I can do. 내가 어떻게든 해볼게.
Let me see what~	…인지 보다
	Let's see what you can do. 네 능력을 보여줘, 한번 볼까.
I'll see if S+V	…을 확인해보다
	I'm going to see if I can get a room for the night. 오늘밤 방이 있는지 확인해보려구요.
	We'll see if she wants to come back. 걔가 돌아오고 싶어하는지 알아볼게.
Let me see if S+V	…인지 확인해보다
	Let me see if she's here. 걔가 왔는지 확인해볼게.
I've never seen+명사	…한 거 처음 봐
	I've never seen anything like it. 그런 건 처음 봐요, 대단해요.
	I've never seen him this happy. 이렇게 행복해 하는 것을 본 적이 없어.
be the most+ 형용사+명사 (that) I've ever seen	내가 본 것 중 최고의 …야
	You're the sexiest woman I've ever seen. 내가 본 사람 중에 넌 가장 섹시해.
the way[as] I see it	…내가 보기엔
	So **the way I see it,** you've got two choices. 그래 내가 보기엔 넌 선택이 2가지있어.

be how I see~	내가 …을 생각하는 건 …다 (자기 입장이나 생각을 정리할 때) That's **not the way I see it.** 난 그렇게 안 봐. That's **exactly how I see it.** 바로 그렇게 내가 생각하는거야.
as you can see	아시다시피 **As you can see,** there are many problems here. 알다시피, 여기에는 많은 문제들이 있어.
wait and see what[if] S+V	…을 지켜보다, 두고보다 *You (just) wait and see 두고보라고 Let's **wait a bit and see how** things develop. 상황이 어떻게 되어가는지 좀 지켜보자고. We are going to just **wait and see what** happens. 무슨 일이 일어나는지 지켜보자.
see (to it) that~	…을 주의하다, 확실히 하다 I trust you'll **see that** she gets the message. 걔가 메시지를 확실히 받아보게 할거라 믿어.
see ~ coming	어려움 등이 다가오다 임박하다 I didn't **see it coming.** 그렇게 될 줄 몰랐어.
see ~ as~	…을 …라고 생각하다 He'll **see it as** a sign of relief. 걘 그걸 안도의 사인으로 볼거야.
see about	처리하다, 검토하다(뭔가를 알아보거나 확인해볼 때) Well, we'll **see about** that. (잘 모르면서) 그래, 한번 보자고. Yeah, we'll **see about** that. I am calling her right now. 그래, 한번 보자고. 지금 걔한테 전화할게. Could you **see about** getting my notebook back? 내 노트북 다시 찾을 수 있는지 알아볼래요?
see through	속지 않고 간파하다, 속을 들여다보다, …을 마칠 때까지 계속하다 The jury would **see through** that. 배심원이 눈치챌거야. I started doing something charitable and I'm going to **see it through.** 자선 일을 시작했는데 끝까지 할거야.
see sby through (sth)	(…하는데) 끝까지 도와주다 I'm going to **see you through** this. 네가 이거 하는거 끝까지 도와줄게.

see

see off	배웅하다
	I have been to the airport to **see my mother off.** 어머니 배웅하기 위해 공항에 갔다왔어.

see you to+명사	…까지 같이 가다(go with)
	I'll **see you to** the station. 역까지 배웅해줄게.

see eye to eye (with)	…에 동의하다
	I don't **see eye to eye with** my wife. 아내랑 의견일치가 안돼.

see in sby	…을 좋아하다
	What do you **see in** her? 그 여자 뭐가 좋아?
	I can't imagine what Tom **sees in** her. 탐이 걜 왜 좋아하는지 모르겠어.

seeing as~	…이기 때문에, …이니(seeing that~)
	There isn't going to be no class today, **seeing as** we have no teacher. 선생님이 없으니 오늘 수업이 없겠네.

 231

seem

v. …처럼 보이다

seem+형용사	…처럼 보이다
	You **seem** a little nervous. 너 좀 초조해보여.
	That doesn't **seem** fair. 그건 온당하지 못해.

seem to~	…처럼 보이다, …한 것 같다
	What **seems to** be the problem? 문제가 뭐인 것 같아?
	He **seems to** hate you. 걔는 널 싫어하는 것 같아.

It seems (to me) that~	(내게는) …처럼 보인다
	It seems that I have lost my wallet. 지갑을 잃어버린 것 같아.
	It seems he has left. 걔가 떠난 것 같아.

It seems like that~	…처럼 보인다 **It seems like** it's time to break up with you. 헤어질 때가 된 것 같아. **It seems like** you're smoking a lot these days. 너 요즘 담배 많이 피는 것 같아.
There seems to~	…가 있는 것 같다 **There seems to** be something between us. 우리 사이에 뭔가 있는 것 같아. **There seems to** be a problem for him. 걔한테 무슨 문제가 있는 것 같아.

232 sell
v. 팔다

sell sth	…을 팔다 We'd probably have to **sell** the house. 아마 집을 팔아야 될 지 몰라.
sell sby sth (sth to sby)	…에게 …을 팔다 I'm going to **sell** him a coat. 걔한테 코트를 팔거야.
sell sth for+가격	…의 가격으로 …을 팔다 He's not going to **sell** his car **for** one thousand dollars. 걔 천달러에 자기 차를 팔지 않을거야.
sell sth on[over] the internet	…을 인터넷을 통해 팔다 It's a good idea to **sell** ice **over the Internet**. 얼음을 인터넷을 통해 파는 건 좋은 생각이야. He's trying to **sell** socks **on the Internet**. 걔 인터넷으로 양말을 팔려고 해.
be sold out (of~)	(…가) 매진되다 We're **sold out** for the first time. 우리는 처음으로 매진됐어. Were they **sold out of** winter coats? 겨울코트가 다 팔렸어?

seem

sell sby out

…을 배신하다(sell sby down the river)

You **sold me out!** 너 날 배신했어!

He **sold us out.** 걔가 우릴 팔아넘겼어.

I did not **sell you out.** 난 널 배신하지 않았어.

send
v. 보내다

send sth

…을 보내다

Do you **send** packages overseas?
소포를 해외로 발송했어?

You've got to **send** an ambulance.
앰블런스를 보내야 돼.

send sby sth [sth to sby]

…에게 …을 보내다

I didn't **send** him an invitation. 걔한테 초대장을 보내지 않았어.

I should probably **send** a thank you letter to her.
걔한테 감사카드를 보내야 할 것 같아.

send sby to sth

…로 보내다, …하게 하다(into)

I don't want to **send** him there. 걜 그곳으로 보내기 싫어.

send an email [one's apologies]

이메일[사죄]을 보내다

Did you get **the e-mail I sent** you the other day?
내가 요전날 보낸 이메일 받았어?

send sth back

돌려주다, 되돌려주다

Should we **send** them something **back?**
걔네들에게 그걸 돌려줘야 해?

send away

…을 내쫓다, …을 가지러 보내다, 주문하다(~for)

I **sent away** for it. You want one of your own?
나 그거 주문했는데 너도 하나 필요해?

send for	…을 가지러[데리러] 보내다
	I **sent for** the office manager. 실장 데리러 보냈어.

send out	발송하다, 파견하다
	You want a job? You **send out** a resume! 취직하고 싶다고? 그럼 이력서를 보내!

send in	들여보내다
	Send her **in.** 들어오라고 해. **Send in** the man who was waiting in the lobby. 로비에서 기다리고 있는 사람 들여보내.

send over	파견하다, 전송하다, …보내다
	Can you **send over** some money? 돈 좀 보내줄테야?

send off	발송하다, 전송하다
	It's hard to **send off** your children to school. 네 얘들 학교에 보내기 어려워. I plan to **send off** a letter to a newspaper. 신문사에 편지를 보낼려고.

234

sense

n. 감각, 의미 **v.** 느끼다

sense of direction	방향감각 *sense of humor 유머감각
	We got lost hiking because of his poor **sense of direction**. 개의 형편없는 방향감각 때문에 하이킹하다 길을 잃었어.

bring sb to sby's senses	정신차리게 하다 *senses는 복수로 이성적인 말과 행동
	You'd better talk to your brother and **bring him to his senses**. 넌 네 형에게 얘기해서 정신차리게 하도록 해.

come to one's senses	제정신이 들다
	I'm glad to see you've **come to your senses**. 네가 정신을 차려서 기뻐.

in a sense	어떤 의미에서는
	In a sense she's right. 어떤 의미에서 걔 말이 맞아.

make sense (of)	말이 되다
	I just tried to help her **make sense of** it. 난 걔가 그걸 이해하도록 도와주려고 했어.

I sensed that S+V	…을 알겠어, …을 느꼈어
	I sensed that you didn't want me to do that. 너는 내가 그걸 안하기를 바랬던 것 같아.

 235

serve

v. 봉사하다, 도움되다, 복무하다, 형기를 채우다 *service 봉사, 근무, 복무

serve sth[sby]	…을 준비하다, 시중들다
	What time do you **serve** breakfast? 아침은 몇 시에 먹을 수 있습니까? How can I **serve** you? 뭘 도와 드릴까요?

be served	…가 준비되어 나오다
	Dinner **is served.** 식사가 준비되었습니다.

serve sby right	당연한 취급을 하다
	If (my) memory s**erves me correctly[right].** 내 기억이 맞다면, 내가 기억하는 바로는. It **serves you right!** 넌 그런 일 당해도 싸. 꼴 좋다. 쌤통이다!

serve as	…로 보탬이 되다(be useful[helpful]), …로 근무하다, …로 사용되다
	The office **serves as** a place to sleep when I'm really tired. 사무실은 내가 정말 피곤할 때 잘 수도 있는 곳이야.

serve in (the army)	복무하다
	I **served in the army** about twenty years ago. 난 20년전 군복무했어.

serve time	복역하다 She didn't want to **serve time.** 걘 감방에 들어가길 원치 않았어.
be in the service	복무중이다 When **were** you **in the service?** 언제 복무했어? You were just a kid when I **was in the service.** 내가 복무중일 때 넌 어린애에 불과했어.
It serves sby right (to+V) for ~ing	…하다니 (…해도) 당해싸다 **It serves him right to** fail the class. 그가 낙제를 한 것을 보니 고소하네.

236

set

ⓥ 두다, 놓다, (모범, 예) 세우다, (날짜) 정하다, 설치하다

set a date (for~)	…로 날째[시간]를 정하다 *set the alarm 자명종을 맞춰놓다 Have you **set a date?** Are you really getting married? 날짜 잡았어? 정말 결혼하는거야? They **set the date for** May 11. 5월 11일로 날짜 잡았어.
set the clock (for~)	(몇 시로) 시계를 맞춰놓다 I **set my clock** six minutes fast. 내 시계가 6분 빨리 가도록 맞춰놓았어. I **set the clock for** a quarter to six. 5시 45분에 알람을 맞췄어.
set a goal	목표를 세우다 *set the rules[standard] 규칙[표준]을 세우다 set an example 모범을 보이다 You'd better **set an example** for other people. 다른 사람을 위해 모범을 보이도록 해. I will **set the standard** as a teacher. 교사로서 기준을 세울거야.

serve

set ~ on fire	…에 불을 지르다, 흥분시키다, 열받게하다 I **set** your mother **on fire.** 내가 네 엄마 열받게 했어. She is the woman who **set** my heart **on fire.** 쟤가 내 가슴에 불을 지른 여자야.
set sth in motion	…가 작동하게 하다 It will take a lot of money to **set it in motion.** 그것을 시작하기에는 많은 돈이 들기 시작할거야.
set ~ free	…을 자유롭게 하다, 풀어주다 You enjoy him and then **set him free.** 걜 즐긴 다음 놔줘 버려. She escaped herself or someone **set her free.** 걘 스스로 탈출했거나 아니면 누군가 풀어준거야.
be all set	준비되다 You **all set to** go? 갈 준비 됐어? We're **all set to** leave. 우리 모두 떠날 준비 됐어.
be set to~	…로 해놓다 I'm sorry, but my phone **was set to** vibrate 미안, 휴대폰을 진동으로 해놨거든.
set (sby) to work	일하기 시작하다 How about we **set to work** right now? 이제 일하기 시작하는게 어때?
set one's mind to	…을 무척 얻기 바라다 I'm sure you could accomplish anything you **set your mind to.** 네가 맘먹은 건 뭐든지 얻을 수 있을거라 확신해.
set aside	비축하다, 따로 떼어놓다 He had money **set aside** for this. 걘 이걸 대비해 돈을 따로 비축해두었어. I have a lot of time. I **set aside** my whole weekend. 나 시간 많아. 주말 전체 비워놨어.
set off	출발하다, 작동시키다, 폭발시키다, 알람을 울리게 하다 *set off to+V …하러 출발하다 They **set off to** get the baby back. 걔네들은 아이를 찾으러 출발했어. We **set off to** visit the country. 우린 시골을 방문하러 출발했어.

set on	선동하다, 부추기다 *be set on~ …로 정해지다, …로 마음이 …에 가 있다 You're still set on that? 아직도 그걸로 정한 마음 변함없어? If you're set on divorce, I can help you with that. 이혼을 결심했다면 나도 어쩔 수가 없어.
set eyes on sby	…을 처음보다 I wanted to marry you the first time I set eyes on you. 널 처음 본 순간 너와 결혼하고 싶었어.
have one's heart set on ~	…로 마음을 결정하다 I never really had my heart set on being a novelist. 소설가가 되길 맘속에 결정한 적이 없어.
set out	시작하다, 출발하다 *set out to+V …하기 시작하다 She set out to break some records of her own. 걘 자기 자신의 기록을 깨기 시작했어.
set up	세우다(establish), (일정 등을) 정하다, 속이다 *set a meeting up for~ 회의를 …로 잡다 I'd like to set up an appointment for Thursday. 목요일로 약속을 정하고 싶어. Is everything all set up? 전부 다 준비됐어?
set sby up (for sth)	…을 속여 …하게 하다 You set me up! 네가 날 함정에 빠트렸어!, 네가 날 속였어!
set[fix] sby up (with sby)	(…에게) …를 소개시켜주다 I'm not asking you to set me up. 만남을 주선해달라는 얘기가 아니야. How could you set me up with this creep? 어떻게 그런 이상한 놈을 소개시켜준거야?
set sby up on a date	…을 데이트 시켜주다, 미팅시켜주다 Is it okay with you if I set him up on a date? 걔 미팅시켜줘도 너 괜찮겠어?
set against	반대하게 하다, 반감을 품게 하다 I'm dead set against it. 절대 반대야.

set back
뒤로 물러서게 하다, 방해하다

My boss tried to **set back** my plan for vacation.
사장이 내 휴가계획을 막으려 했어.

set down
내려놓다

Thanks, you can just **set it down** there.
고마워. 그냥 그거 거기에 내려놓아.

set in
시작하다

The shock **set in** 12 hours later. 충격이 12시간 후에 시작됐어.

settle
v. 해결하다, 합의보다, 결정하다, 정착하다

It's settled that~
…하기로 단호히 결정하다

It's settled that they will join us for dinner.
걔네들은 우리와 함께 저녁먹기로 결정했어.

settle sth out of court
당사자간에 합의하다

The case was **to be settled out of the court.**
그 소송은 합의로 해결되게 됐어.

settle the problem
문제를 해결하다

Have you **settled the problem** with your neighbor?
이웃주민과 문제 해결했어?

settle a score with sby
복수하다

Perry still wants to **settle a score with** his brother.
페리는 아직도 형에게 보복을 하고 싶어해.

That settles it
그것으로 결말이 났다

Let's roll the dice and hope **that settles it.**
주사위를 굴려서 해결되기를 바라자.

settle down — 정착하다, 자리잡다

Jane and Dick **settled down** and had some kids.
제인과 딕은 정착해 애들을 몇 낳았어.

238

shame

n. 수치심, 아쉬운 일, 망신   v. 부끄럽게 하다

to one's shame — …가 부끄럽게도, 아쉽게도

Her affair was revealed, **to her shame.**
그녀는 창피하게도 그녀의 부정이 들어났어.

What a shame! — 안됐구나!, 유감이야!

What a shame! How long will it take him to get better?
안됐네! 나아지는데 얼마나 걸릴까?

Shame on you — 안됐네, 창피한줄 알아라

Shame on you! That was bad behavior.
창피한 줄 알아야지! 그건 안 좋은 행동이야.

It's a shame that~ — …은 안따까운 일이다

It's a shame she couldn't be here tonight.
갠 오늘 밤 여기에 올 수 없다니 안됐어.

239

shape

n. 모양, 형태, 체형   v. …의 형태로 만들다

get in shape — 좋은 몸상태를 유지하다   *get back in shape 다시 건강해지다

It's just normal women who want to **get in shape.**
몸매를 유지하려는 정상적인 여자들이야.

settle

out of shape	몸상태가 좋지 않은 So Pam is **out of shape** these days? 그래 팸이 요즘 몸이 엉망이야?
shape up	좋은 방향으로 되어가다, 태도를 개선하다 Things better **shape up** or we're in trouble. 상황이 좋아지거나 아니면 곤경에 처해질거야.
shape up or ship out	제대로 일하지 않으려면 그만두다 You need to **shape up or ship out.** 열심히 하지 않으려면 그만둬.
take shape	형태를 갖추다, 구체화되다 The new committee is beginning to **take shape.** 새로운 위원회가 구체화되기 시작하고 있어.
get all bent out of shape	…에 화나다 What **are** you **getting so bent out of shape** for? Be patient. 그렇게 열 받지마. 조급하게 굴지마.

 240

share

v. 공유하다, 나누다 **n.** 몫, 지분

share sth with sby	…와 …를 공유하다 Do they **share** things **with** you? 걔네들이 물건들을 너와 같이 써?
do one's share of	…의 역할을 다하다, 자기 몫을 하다 You've done more than your share. 넌 네 몫 이상의 일을 해줬어.
have[get] one's share of~	…의 합당한 몫을 받다 I'd still **get my share of** that two million, right? 난 내 몫의 그 2백만 달러를 아직 받을 수 있는거지, 맞아?

shock

n. 충격　**v.** 충격을 주다, 놀래키다

give sby a shock	…을 놀래키다　*get a shock 놀라다 It **gave** us **a shock** to hear our aunt died. 숙모가 돌아가셨다는 말을 듣고 우리는 놀랬어.
come as a shock to sby	…에게 충격으로 다가오다 I know that may **come as a shock.** 그게 충격스러울 수도 있을거라는 것을 알아.
be shocked by~	…로 놀라다 I mean to say that we **were shocked by** the news. 우린 그 소식에 충격먹었다고 말할 생각이었어.

short

a. 짧은, 얼마 안되는, 부족한　**adv.** …이 부족하게

at short notice	촉박하게, 예고없이　*on such short notice 촉박하게 Thank you so much for coming **on such short notice.** 일찍 연락 못했는데 와줘서 고마워.
in the short term	단기간에 The loan of some money will help **in the short term.** 얼마간의 돈을 융자하는 것은 단기적으로 도움이 될거야.
run short of	…이 부족하다, 모자르다 = be short of = run low on = fall short of The stores **are running short of** food. 가게들은 음식이 부족했어.

shock

go short (of)	(음식, 의류 등이) 부족하다
	The baseball **went short of** being a home run. 그 야구공은 홈런까지는 되지 않았어.

have a short temper	쉽게 화를 내다
	I **was a little short tempered** with you. 내가 네게 성질을 좀 부렸었지.

show
v. 보여주다, 상영하다 **n.** 공연, 전시회, TV프로그램

show sby how to~	…에게 …하는 법을 알려주다
	Can you **show** me **how to** go there? 거기 가는 방법 좀 알려줄래요?
	Please **show** me **how to** play the game. 게임 방법 좀 가르쳐 줘.
	Show me **how** it works. 어떻게 작동되는 건지 직접 보여줘.

show sby sth	…에게 …를 보여주다
	Come here, I want to **show** you something! 이리와, 뭐 좀 보여줄게!

show sby the way	…에게 길[방법]을 알려주다
	Let me **show** you **another way.** 다른 길을 알려줄게요.
	Please **show** me **the way.** 길을 안내해줘요.
	I'll **show the way.** 길 안내해드릴게요.

have nothing to show for	(시간, 노력의) 보답으로 보여줄 성과가 없다
	I'll **have nothing to show for** my day! 오늘 내가 일한거 성과가 하나도 없어!

Sth goes to show that~	…임을 증명하다
	It goes to show just how attractive you are. 네가 얼마나 매력적인지 보여주는거야.

show one's (true) colors	본색을 드러내다 Sandy **showed her true colors** when she got angry. 샌디는 화를 낼 때 본색을 드러냈어.
show sby around	구경시켜주다, 관광시켜주다 I'm going to **show him around** town. 내가 걔 시내구경시켜 줄거야. Let me **show you around.** 내가 구경시켜줄게요.
show up	(회의, 모임 등에) 모습을 드러내다 *no show 예약하고 오지 않는 사람 What time do you think you will **show up?** 몇 시에 올 수 있어? She never **showed up** again. 걔 다시는 나타나지 않았어.
show off	자랑하다(boast) He wanted to **show off** his new girlfriend, Alma. 걘 새로운 여친인 앨머를 자랑하고 싶어했어.

244 sick
n. 아픈, 지긋지긋한

make sb sick	…을 엄청 화나게 하다 Stop saying you're sorry when you're not. You **make me sick.** 시도 때도 없이 미안하다고 하지마. 진짜 역겨워.
get[fall, become] sick	아프다 Did Jesse **get sick?** Was there an accident? 제시가 아팠어? 사고가 있었어?
call in sick	아프다고 결근전화를 하다 I'll **call in sick,** and take the day off. 아프다고 전화하고 하루 결근할거야.
be worried sick	매우 걱정하다 Her mother **is worried sick.** 걔 엄마는 속이 다 타들어가.

show

be sick and tired of	…에 지긋지긋해하다
	I'm sick and tired of being lonely! 혼자 있는게 정말 지긋지긋해!

245 side
n. 어느 한쪽, 옆

take sby's side	…의 편을 들다 *take sides 편을 들다
	I'll take her side in the argument. 난 토론할 때 걔 편을 들거야.
Whose side are you on?	너는 누구편이니? *be on one's side …의 편이다
	My husband told me he is on my side. 내 남편은 내 편이라고 했어.
side by side	나란히
	They walked down the beach side by side. 걔네들은 나란히 해변을 걸어내려갔어.
side with sby	…의 편을 들다(agree and support)
	I've got to side with Chris on this party thing. 이 파티건에 대해서는 크리스 편을 들어야겠어.
side effect	부작용
	You're having a side effect! 부작용이 일어나고 있어!

246
sight
n. 시야, 광경

at first sight	첫눈에 *love at first sight 첫눈에 반한 사랑
	It was love **at first sight**. 첫눈에 반했어.
catch sight of	갑자기 …을 보다
	We hoped to **catch sight of** a movie star. 우리는 영화배우 보기를 희망했어.
out of sight	보이지 않는 곳에 *Out of sight, out of mind 안보면 맘도 멀어진다
	The car went down the road until it was **out of sight**. 그 자동차는 시야에서 보이지 않을 때까지 길을 따라 내려갔어.

247
skip
v. 거르다, 빼먹다

skip breakfast [dinner]	아침[저녁]을 거르다
	Because I wasn't hungry, I **skipped breakfast**. 배고프지 않아서, 아침을 걸렀어.
skip work	결근하다 *skip lesson 수업을 빠지다
	Cindy **skipped work** because she was tired. 신디는 피곤했기 때문에 결근했어.
skip sth and go on to~	…을 건너뛰고 …로 가다
	Let's **skip** this exhibit and **go on to** the rest of the museum. 이 전시품은 건너뛰고 박물관의 다른 곳으로 가자.
Let's skip to~	…로 넘어가자
	Why don't we **skip to** the end of the story? 이야기 끝으로 건너뛰자.

sight

Skip it!
그냥 넘어가!

Skip it. I don't want to think about it now.
그건 넘어가자. 지금 그거 생각하고 싶지 않아.

248 sleep
n. 잠 v. 자다

sleep on[in]
…에서 자다

You go **sleep in** the next room. 옆방에 가서 자.

Can I **sleep on** your couch? 소파에서 자도 돼?

sleep well
잘 자다

So did you **sleep well** last night? 그래서 어젯밤은 잘 잤어?

Sleep tight, Sarah. 새러야, 잘 자라.

You're **sleeping** a lot these days. 너 요즘 잠을 많이 자.

sleep on it
곰곰히 생각하다

Let me **sleep on it.** 곰곰이 생각해봐야겠어.

Think about it. **Sleep on it.** 생각해봐. 하룻밤 더 생각해봐.

sleep around
여러 사람과 바람피다

Maybe I've been **sleeping around.** But I love only my wife.
내가 헤프지만 아내만을 사랑해.

sleep together [with sby]
…와 자다

We can be friends who **sleep together.**
우리는 함께 섹스하는 친구가 될 수 있어.

I had to **sleep with** the ugliest guy to get that job.
그 일을 얻기 위해 가장 못생긴 사람하고 자야했어.

get much sleep
잠을 많이 자다

I **got no sleep** last night! 어젯밤에 한숨도 못잤어!

I didn't **get enough sleep.** 난 잠이 충분하지 않았어.

You need to **get some sleep.** 넌 좀 자야 돼.

go to sleep	자다(get back to sleep 다시 자다)
	I'm getting ready to **go to sleep**.
	난 자러 갈 준비됐어.
	Did you **get her back to sleep**?
	걔 다시 재웠어?

249 slip
v. 미끄러지다, 살짝 가다[오다]   n. 작은 실수

let (it) slip (sth)	실수로 비밀을 말하다 *slip out 무심결에 말하다, 몰래 빠져나오다
	Peter **let it slip** that I didn't get the job.
	피터는 무심결에 내가 일을 못 맡았다고 말했어.
slip one's mind	깜박잊다
	I'm so sorry. It **slipped my mind**.
	정말 미안해. 내가 깜박 잊었어.
slip through your fingers	기회 등을 놓치다, 도망치다
	The opportunity to save the marriage **slipped through my fingers**. 결혼의 파국을 피할 기회를 놓치고 말았어.
let sth slip through one's fingers	기회 등을 놓치다
	He's frustrated that he **let another sale slip through his fingers**. 걔 또다른 영업건수를 놓쳐서 좌절했어.
slip up	실수를 하다
	She**'s never slipped up** like this before.
	걔는 전에 이와 같은 실수를 절대로 저지른 적이 없어.

sneak

v. 몰래 가다

sneak into~	몰래 들어가다	
	Those kids tried to **sneak into** the movie.	
	그 아이들은 영화관에 몰래 들어가려고 했어.	
sneak sth into ~	몰래 …을 갖고 들어가다	
	We **snuck** some alcohol **into** the concert.	
	우리는 몰래 술을 갖고 콘서트장에 들어갔어.	
sneak off to +V	몰래 가서 …하다	
	I had to **sneak off to** use the toilet.	
	난 몰래 빠져 나가서 화장실에 가야 했어.	
sneak sb sth	몰래 …에게 …을 주다	
	They **snuck** her a box of chocolates.	
	걔네들은 그녀에게 몰래 초콜릿 한상자를 줬어.	
sneak a look [glance]	흘깃보다	
	Could you **sneak a look** at the people behind us?	
	우리 뒤에 있는 사람들을 흘깃 쳐다볼래?	
sneak up to~	…에게 몰래 다가가다	
	We plan to **sneak up to** the old palace tonight.	
	우리는 오늘밤에 옛궁전에 몰래 가볼 계획이야.	

solve

v. (문제, 곤경) 해결하다

solve[fix] a problem
문제를 풀다

I have to **fix a problem** with this computer.
난 이 컴퓨터 문제를 해결해야만 해.

Problem solved
문제 해결

Perfect. **Problem solved.** Welcome aboard.
완벽해. 문제 해결됐어. 함께 일하게 된 걸 환영해.

sound

n. 소리 **v.** …인 것 같다, …처럼 들리다 **a.** 건실한, 건강한

not make a sound
소리를 내지 않다

He was awake for hours but **didn't make a sound.**
걔는 수시간째 자지 않고 있지만 소리를 내지 않았어.

it sounds like~
…같이 들린다

Sounds like a fun party. 재미있는 파티같아.

Oh, **that sounds like** so much fun. 오, 무척 재미있는 것 같아.

it sounds as if [though]
마치 …인 것 같아

It sounds as if you have a serious problem.
마치 넌 심각한 문제가 있는 것처럼 보여.

sounds good [great]
좋다

Sounds good to me. 저는 괜찮아요.

That **sounds good** too. Could I try a bite of it?
좋은 생각이야. 좀 먹어봐도 될까?

solve

 253

speak

v. 말하다, 연설하다

speak to

…에게 이야기하다, 말하다 = speak with

Could I **speak to** Mr. Smith?
스미스 씨 좀 바꿔줄래요?

I thought I told you not to speak to him anymore.
걔하고 더 이상 얘기하지 말라고 한 것 같은데.

speak English

영어를 말하다 *not speak a word of …을 한마디도 못하다

Does anyone here **speak Korean?**
여기 누구 한국말 하는 사람 있어요?

I am sorry but I can't **speak English** very well.
미안하지만 영어를 잘 못해요.

speak as

…의 자격으로 말하다 *speak as a parent는 부모의 자격으로 말하다

May I **speak as** a girlfriend for a second?
잠시 애인의 자격으로 말할 수 있어?

Now I'm speaking as a doctor.
지금 난 의사로서 말하는거야.

speak up

좀 더 크게 말하다, 의견을 말하다 *speak up for sby …을 지지하는 말을 하다

I can't hear you. You'll have to **speak up.**
잘 안 들려요. 큰 소리로 말하세요.

Could you speak up, please? 좀 더 크게 말해줄래요?

speak for sby

…의 감정, 입장을 표현하다, 대변하다 *Sth speak itself[themselves] 자명하다, 명백하다

I need you to **speak for** someone who can't **speak for** herself. 스스로를 대변하지 못하는 사람을 대변하도록 해.

Speak for yourself

너한테나 맞는 이야기이지

Speak for yourself. I really hate to jog.
너나 그렇지. 난 정말 조깅하는 게 싫어.

Speaking of~	…얘기가 나와서 말인데	
	Speaking of winter, did you go skiing this year? 겨울 얘기가 나와서 그런데, 금년에 스키탔어?	
Speaking of which	말이 나와서 말인데	
	Speaking of which, are you ready to go to lunch? 말이 나왔으니 말인데, 점심 먹으러 갈 준비됐어?	
Roughly speaking	대강 말해서 *Frankly speaking 솔직히 말해서, Strictly speaking 엄격히 말해서	
	Strictly speaking, you don't deserve this. 엄격히 말해서 너 이런 자격없어.	
	Frankly speaking, you're not invited to the party. 솔직히 말해서 넌 파티에 초대받지 못했어.	
so to speak	말하자면	
	So to speak, she's a maniac. 말하자면 걘 매니아야.	
	I'd like go back to the days when I was young, **so to speak.** 어린 시절로 가고 싶어, 말하자면.	
speak the same language	의견이 일치하다	
	We **are not speaking the same language.** 우리는 뜻이 전혀 맞지가 않아.	
speak ill[well] of	…을 비난[칭찬]하다	
	I'm not good at **speaking well of** other. 난 다른 사람 칭찬하는데 어눌해.	
	Don't **speak ill of** him. 그 사람 욕하지마.	
speak out of turn	말이 잘못 나오다	
	I didn't mean it. I **spoke out of turn.** 내 말뜻은 그게 아냐. 말이 잘못 나왔어.	
speak one's mind	까놓고 말하다	
	She has nerve to **speak her mind** even in front of the boss. 걘 사장 앞에서도 다 얘기할 강단이 있어.	

speak

spend

v. 소비하다, 쓰다, (시간) 보내다

---

spend sth

…을 소비하다, 쓰다

You shouldn't **spend** so much money.
그렇게 돈을 많이 쓰면 안돼.

How did you **spend** so much money?
어떻게 그렇게 많은 돈을 썼어?

---

spend (much) time with [together]

…와[함께] 시간을 보내다

I want to **spend more time with** my family.
가족과 함께 시간을 보내고 싶어.

---

spend the day [night] with [together]

…와[함께] 하루[밤]을 보내다

He's going to **spend the whole day with** you!
걘 너랑 하루 종일 같이 있을거야!

I want to **spend the night with** Becky.
난 베키와 하루밤을 보내고 싶어.

---

spend Christmas with[together]

…와[함께] 크리스마스를 보내다

Why don't you **spend Christmas with** me?
크리스마스 함께 보내자

I can **spend this Thanksgiving with** my family.
이번 추수감사절은 가족과 함께 보낼 수 있어.

---

spend my life with[together]

…와[함께] 일생을 보내다

We agreed we'd **spend the rest of our lives** together.
우린 앞으로의 인생을 함께 보내기로 했어.

I want to **spend my life with** you.
난 너와 인생을 함께 하고 싶어.

---

spend sth on~

…에 …을 쓰다

I'm not going to **spend** all of the money **on** one party.
한 파티에 돈을 몽땅 쓰지는 않을거야.

I can't believe you're going to **spend** 250 dollars **on** the lottery! 로또에 250 달러를 쓰다니!

spend sth (in) ~ing	…하는데 …을 쓰다
	I had to **spend** all day **clearing** out stuff. 하루 종일 물건 치우는데 소비해야 했어.

255

split

v 분열되다, 나뉘다, 나누다, 쪼개지다, 헤어지다 **n** 불화, 분할

split the bill	비용을 함께 내다
	It's expensive, so let's **split the bill**. 비싸다, 그래 우리 나누어 내자.
split with sby	…와 헤어지다
	Have you **split with** your wife? 부인과 헤어졌어?
split up	결별하다, 이혼하다
	I **split up with** a bitch who broke my heart. 내 맘을 찢어 놓은 년과 헤어졌어.

256

stand

v 서다, 일어서다, 참다, 견디다 **n** 받침대, 노점, 매점

stand at[in, on]~	…에 서 있다
	Tom **is standing at** the window waving at her. 탐은 창가에 서서 걔한테 손을 흔들고 있어.
stand next to~	…옆에 서 있다
	Ben **is standing next to** her. 벤은 걔 옆에 서있어.

spend

stand (장소) ~ing	**(…에) …하면서 서 있다** I **stood** there trying to remember why she left me. 난 거기 서서 왜 걔가 날 떠났는지 기억해내려 했어.
stand+형용사	**…한 상태로 있다** They **stood** close to each other. 걔네들은 서로 가까이 서 있었어. She took a few steps around the desk, to **stand** closer. 걘 책상으로 몇 발짝 다가와 더 가까이 섰다.
stand still	**정지하다, 멈추다** *stand firm 단호하다, 뒤로 물러서지 않다 It's like time **has stood still** in this room. 이 방에선 시간이 멈춘 것 같아.
can't stand~	**…을 참지 못하다** I **can't stand** this[you]. 이걸[널] 못 참겠어. Oh, God. I **can't stand** it any longer. 어휴, 맙소사. 더 이상 못 참겠어. I **can't stand** the boss. She sucks! 더 이상 사장을 못 참겠어. 아주 재수없어! I **can't stand** the smell of hot dogs. They make me sick. 핫도그 냄새 못 참겠어. 구역질 나.
can't stand ~ing	**…하는 것을 못참다** My parents **can't stand** being in the same room together. 우리 부모님은 같은 방에 함께 계시는 걸 싫어하셔.
can't stand sby ~ing	**…가 …하는 것을 싫어하다, 못 참다** I **can't stand** you **being** here. 난 네가 여기 있는게 싫어. I just **can't stand** you two **fighting** over me! 난 니네들이 날놓고 싸우는 걸 더 이상 못 보겠어. You **can't stand** me **getting** closer to her. 넌 내가 걔하고 친해지는 걸 못 참는구나.
can't stand to +V	**…하는 것을 못 참다** I **can't stand to** lose. 난 지는 걸 못 참아.
can't stand the thought of~	**…라는 생각을 받아들이지 못하다** I **can't stand the thought of** you with another woman! 난 네가 다른 여자와 있다는 생각을 참을 수 없어!

can't stand that S+V	…을 참지 못하다
	I **can't stand that** I hurt you.
	내가 네게 상처를 입혔다는 걸 참을 수가 없어.

stand in the (sby's) way	방해하다 *stand 대신에 be, get을 써도 된다.
	Ok then. I won't **stand in your way.**
	좋아 그럼. 방해하지 않을게.
	I'm not going to **stand in your way of** doing it.
	네가 그걸 하는데 방해가 되지 않을게.

stand one one's own (two) feet	자립하다
	I can **stand on my own two feet** now. 난 자립할 수 있어.
	I am trying my hardest to **stand on my own two feet.**
	자립하기 위해 최선을 다하고 있어.

It stands to reason that S+V	…은 사리에 맞다, 당연하다
	It stands to reason. 그건 이치에 맞아.

stand a chance(of)	(…할) 기회가 있다, 유망하다 *stand no chance (of) (…할) 가망이 없다
	You think we even **stand a chance?**
	우리에게 기회조차 없을거라 생각해?
	She **stands no chance of** marrying Peter.
	걘 피터랑 결혼할 가능성이 없어.

I stand corrected	내가 잘못했다는 거 인정해요
	I stand corrected. I always get that wrong.
	내가 틀렸다는 거 인정해. 항상 그걸 오해해.

not have a leg to stand on	증명할 수가 없다
	You **don't have a leg to stand on.**
	넌 그런 주장을 할 수 있는 근거가 없어.

take the stand	증언대에 서다
	You may **take the stand.**
	증언대에 서주세요.

stand by (sby)	대기하다, …을 지지하다 *stand behind 지지하다
	I'll **stand by** you. 네게 힘이 되어줄게.
	She's the only one who **stood by** me in all this.
	걘 이 모든 일에 날 지지해준 유일한 사람이야.

stand

stand for
나타내다, 지지하다

What exactly does that **stand for?**
그게 뜻하는 게 정확히 뭐야?

You said that you **stood for** the poor.
가난한 사람들의 편을 들겠다고 말했잖아.

stand out
눈에 잘 띄다, 두드러지다 *stand out in a crowd 사람들 속에 두드러져 보이다

She **stands out** in the rain.
걘 비가 오는데 밖에 서 있어.

He **stands out** in a crowd because he's so tall.
걘 키가 커서 군중 속에서 두드러져 보여.

stand sby up
바람맞히다 *get[be] stood up 바람맞다

I don't like **being stood up!**
바람맞는 것 싫어해!

How could she just **stood me up** for a date?
어떻게 걔가 날 바람맞힐 수 있어?

stand up for
지지하다, 옹호하다 *stand up for oneself 자립하다, 남에게 좌지우지되지 않다

Could you **stand up for** me, please?
내 편 좀 되어줄래요?

Don't be afraid to **stand up for** what is right.
옳은 일을 지지하는 걸 두려워하지마.

stand up to
…에 맞서다 *stand up to+V …하기 위해 일어서다

You **stood up to** the boss, nobody does that.
넌 사장님한테 맞섰어, 아무도 안그러는데.

She **stands up to** follow him to the door.
걘 일어서서 걔를 문까지 따라가고 있어.

stand back
뒤로 물러서다

Just **stand back.** Give me some room.
뒤로 물러서. 내게 공간을 달라고.

start

v. 시작하다, 출발하다　**n.** 시작, 출발, 개시

| **start to~** | …하기 시작하다　*start to+V[~ing] …하기 시작하다 |

What time do you **start to** board? 몇 시부터 탈 수 있나요?

We should **start** working on the report.
우린 보고서 작업을 하기 시작해야 돼.

I just **started** driving this month.
이번 달에 운전을 시작했어.

| **start a family** | 가정을 꾸리다 |

She wants to **start a family.** 걘 가정을 꾸미고 싶어해.

| **start the car** | 자동차를 출발시키다 |

I can't **start the car.** 차가 시동이 걸리지 않아.

| **start a company [business]** | 회사[사업]를 시작하다 |

Joan applied for a loan to **start a business.**
조앤은 사업을 시작하려고 사업자금 대출을 신청했어.

| **start school [college]** | 학교를 다니기 시작하다 |

Students will **start school** at the end of August.
학생들은 8월말에 학교를 다니기 시작할거야.

| **start a fight [fire]** | 싸움을 시작하다, 불을 지르다 |

Did you **start a fight** in the bar yesterday?
네가 어제 바에서 싸움을 시작했어?

| **start it** | 그걸 시작하다 |

I **started it** but, now it's scary me. 내가 시작한거지만 이제 무서워.

She's the one that **started it.** 걔가 시작한 얘야.

You **started it.** 네가 시작했어.

| **get started on** | 시작하다 |

Let's **get started on** the wedding plans!
결혼식 계획 실행합시다!

start

start from scratch
처음부터

I'd like to have lunch again. **Start from scratch.**
점심을 다시 먹고 싶어. 처음부터.

from the start
처음부터

As I said **from the start,** they don't support us here.
처음부터 말했듯이, 걔네들은 우리 편이 아냐.

start off
시작하다

I always like to **start off** with a hug.
난 항상 껴안는 것으로 시작하길 좋아해.

She **started off** toward the church.
걘 교회로 출발했다.

start on
…을 시작하다, 사용하다

You can **start on** your essay now.
수필을 쓰기 시작해도 좋아.

start in on
…을 비난하다

I told her I was going to leave her. And then she **started in on** me. 걔한테 떠날거라고 했더니 날 비난하기 시작했어.

start out
시작하다, (직업 등) 시작하다　*start out as …로 시작하다, start out on[with] …을[로] 시작하다

It **started out** this way. Nothing caused it to happen.
처음부터 이랬던거야. 원인은 따로 없어.

I actually **started out** as a playwright, and then I went into law. 실은 난 극작가로 시작했지만 지금은 법조계에 있어.

start out (of)
…에서 나오다

He **started out of** the bathroom to the door. She followed him. 걘 화장실에서 나와 문으로 가는데 걔가 따라갔어.

start (all) over
처음부터 다시 시작하다

Can we just **start all over?**
처음부터 다시 시작하면 안될까?

We're going to have to **start all over** again.
우리는 처음부터 다시 시작해야 할거야.

start up

시작하다, (회사 등) 세우다, (엔진 등) 작동하게 하다 *start up (sth) with sby …와 (…을) 시작하다

I am not starting up with him again.
난 걔랑 다시 시작하지 않을거야.

His heart's too weak to **start up** again.
걔의 심장은 너무 약해 다시 움직일 수가 없어.

The police car **starts up** and begins to drive away.
경찰차가 시동을 걸고 움직이기 시작해.

start with

…부터 시작하다

Which one would you like me to **start with?**
뭐부터 시작하고 싶어?

Let's speak in turn, **starting with** you.
너부터 시작해서 돌아가며 이야기하자.

starting~

…부터 시작해서 *starting+시간명사 …부터 시작해서 *starting now[next week] 지금[다음 주]부터

I'll be on vacation **starting** next week.
난 다음 주부터 휴가야.

Would it be all right if I took a week off **starting** tomorrow?
내일부터 일주일 휴가가도 돼요?

Starting next month, I'm going to pay you to live here.
다음달부터 숙박비 낼게.

be where sby started

…가 시작한 곳이다

Isn't that **where you started?**
네가 시작한 곳 아냐?

This **is where he started.**
이게 걔가 시작한 곳이야.

be back where sby started

원점으로 돌아오다

I'm right back where I started!
다시 원점으로 돌아왔어!

stay

v. 머무르다, 거주하다, …한 상태로 있다 **n.** 머무름, 체류기간

stay and+V
남아서 …하다 *stay to+V 남아서 …하다

Would you just **stay and** help me get dressed?
좀 남아서 나 옷입는 것 좀 도와줄래?

He **stayed to** see if it's done. 걘 남아서 그게 마무리 되었는지 확인했어.

let sby stay
…을 남게 하다

Will you please **let her stay** for me?
걔가 날 위해 남게 해줄래요?

stay the same
그대로다, 변함이 없다 *stay (as)+명사 …로 남다

Everything is great! Everything **stays the same!**
모든 게 다 좋아! 모든 게 다 변함없어!

Promise me that you and I will always **stay the same.**
너와 내가 항상 변치않을거라 약속해줘.

stay the course
어려움 속에서도 완수하다, 끝까지 버티다

Why shouldn't I **stay the course?** 왜 난 계속 난관을 헤쳐 나갈 수가 없을까?

stay+형용사
…한 상태로 있다

Stay cool, Cindy. 잘 지내라, 신디.

I'm just trying to **stay** awake. 졸지 않으려고 애쓰고 있어.

Can we please **stay** focused on my problem here?
여기 내 문제에 집중해줄래요?

stay put
가만히 있다, 움직이지 않다 =stay still

All right, you two **stay put** right there.
좋아, 너희 둘 거기 그대로 있어.

Look, shut up and **stay still.** 이봐, 입다물고 가만히 있어.

stay home
집에 머물다 *stay home from work[school] 출근[등교]하지 않다

Do you mind if we **stay home** tonight?
오늘밤 집에 머물러도 돼?

stay here	여기에 남다 *Sby stays here ···가 여기에 남다 *Sth stays here ···은 비밀이다
	I'll just **stay here** with you. 너와 함께 여기 있을게.
	I'm going to **stay there** for a while. 잠시 거기에 머물게.
	What is said here, **stays here.** 여기서 한 말은 모두 비밀을 지켜야 돼.
stay+(for)	···동안 머물다 *stay longer 더 머물다 *stay another day 하루 더 머물다
	I need to **stay another day.** 하루 더 묵으려고 하는데.
	Maybe we should **stay longer.** 우리가 좀 더 남아있어야 될지 몰라.
stay the night	밤새 머물다(stay overnight)
	Are you planning on **staying the night?** 밤을 샐 계획이야?
stay as long as sby want	···가 원하는 만큼 머물다
	You can **stay as long as you want.** 원하는 만큼 있어도 돼.
stay for+기간명사	···동안 머물다 *stay for sby[sth] ···때문에 남다
	Can you **stay for** dinner? 남아서 저녁먹을 수 있어?
	Can you **stay for** some tea? 남아서 커피 좀 마실 수 있어?
stay tuned	(TV나 라디오) 채널을 고정하다
	Don't go away and **stay tuned.** 어디 가시지 마시고 채널을 고정하세요.
stay at	···에서 머물다 *stay at +사람이름's ···의 집에 머물다
	I'm **staying at** the Intercontinental Hotel. 난 인터콘티넨탈 호텔에 투숙하고 있어.
	I **stayed at** Julie's last night. 간밤에 줄리 집에 있었어.
stay at one's place	···의 집에 머물다 *stay at some place ···에 머물다
	Tonight I will **stay at my place.** 오늘 밤 난 집에 있을거야.
stay away from	···에서 떨어지다, ···을 멀리하다
	Stay away from me! 꺼져!
	Don't **stay away** so long. 자주 좀 와.
	She is so mean. I think you should **stay away from** her. 걔 무척 야비하니까 멀리하는게 나아.
	Stay away from the traffic accident. 그 교통사고얘긴 꺼내지마.

stay

stay back
뒤로 물러서다

You have to stay back. I got a bad flu.
뒤로 물러서야 돼. 난 독감걸렸어.

Stay back! Bulldozer! I'm married.
뒤로 물러나! 이 불도저 같은 놈아! 난 유부남이라고.

stay in
⋯에 머물다 *stay in there 거기에 있어, 참고 견디다

Well **stay in** the car. 그럼 차에 계세요.

It's best you **stay in** there. 네가 거기에 머무는게 최선야.

Let's **stay outside** a while. 잠시 밖에 머물자.

stay in touch with
⋯와 연락이 되다

How did you **stay in touch with** your classmates?
넌 어떻게 네 친구들과 연락을 주고 받았어?

stay out of
⋯에 가까이 가지 않다, 참견하지 않다 *stay out of one's way[face] ⋯에서 사라지다

If you **stay out of** the way and stay quiet, you stay alive.
끼어들지 말고 조용히 있으면 넌 살아.

That's fine too. Just **stay out of my face.**
그것까지도 괜찮아. 그냥 내 눈에 띄지마.

(You) Stay out of this[it]!
좀 비켜라!, 넌 이것에 끼어 들지마!

I asked you to **stay out of this.** 이거 끼어들지 말라고 했을 텐데.

Just **stay out of this.** 그만 두라고.

Tim, could you just **stay out of** it? 팀. 그만 좀 둘래?

stay out of trouble
문제없이 잘 지내다

You keep your noses up. You **stay out of trouble.**
앞 똑바로 보고 문제 일으키지마.

Well, good luck to everyone. **Stay out of trouble.**
자, 다들 행운을 빌어. 문제없이 잘 지내고.

(You) Stay out of here!
비켜 주라!

Stay out of here! You have been stealing things!
비켜! 넌 물건들을 훔친 적이 있잖아!

stay up
자지 않고 있다 *stay up late 밤늦게까지 자지 않다 stay up until sth ⋯할 때까지 자지 않다

If you don't mind, I could **stay up** late.
괜찮다면 밤늦게까지 자지 않을 수 있어.

stay up all night (~ing)	(…하면서) 밤을 꼬박 새다
	We just **stayed up all night** talking on the internet. 우린 밤을 꼬박 새며 인터넷으로 대화했어.

stay with	…와 머물다, …에 계속 있다(with sth)
	If you want, you can **stay with** me tonight. 네가 괜찮다면, 오늘밤 나랑 같이 지내자.
	When we get to Chicago, can I **stay with** you? 우리가 시카고가면 너랑 같이 있어도 돼?

Stay with me!	내 말 계속 들어!, (죽어가는 사람에게) 정신차려!
	Can you hear me? **Stay with me.** 내 말 들려요? 내 말 들어요.

step
n. 걸음, 조치, 단계

take[move] a step	조치를 취하다, 한걸음을 걷다
	Helen was afraid to **take a step** closer to the snake. 헬렌은 뱀에 한걸음 더 가까이 가는 것을 겁내했어.

step by step	차근차근, 단계적으로
	Step by step, your business will get bigger. 단계적으로 커질거야.

watch[mind] your step	발밑을 조심하다
	I'm onto you. **Watch your step.** 난 네 속셈을 알아. 조심하라고.

step back	한걸음 물러서다
	You go for it. I'll **step back.** 네가 한번 해봐. 나는 물러서 있을 테니.

Step on it	세게 밟아라
	I haven't got all day. **Step on it!** 시간없어. 서둘러!

stay

step forward	도움을 제의하다, 앞으로 나오다
	Anyone wanting to volunteer please **step forward.** 자원하기 원하는 사람은 누구든지 앞으로 나와주세요.

step up	증가하다, 공식석상에 나아가다
	You'll need to **step up** and complete the job. 너는 더 속력을 내서 일을 마치도록 해.

260 stick
ⓥ 찌르다, …에 끼여 꼼짝못하다

be stuck	꼼짝도 못하다
	I **was stuck at** home. 난 집에 콕 박혀 있었어.

be stuck in traffic	교통체증에 갇히다
	I **was stuck in** traffic. 차가 막혀서 꼼짝달싹 못했어.

stick out for	옹호하다, 대변하다
	I always **stick up for** people who are bullied. 난 항상 괴롭힘을 당하는 사람들을 옹호하고 있어.

stick to	계속 …하다, …을 지키다 *stick to the rules 규칙에 따르다
	You have to **stick to** your diet. 넌 다이어트를 계속해야 돼.

stick together	뭉치다, 단결하다
	They **stuck together** even during difficult times. 걔네들은 어려운 시기에 단결했어.

stick with	…의 곁에 머물다, …와 함께 있다
	Then why **am** I **stuck with** her? 그럼 내가 왜 걔와 같이 있어야 하는데?

stock 261

n. 재고품, 주식 **v.** 상품을 갖추고 있다, 채우다

in stock	재고가 있는 I'll check to see if we have any **in stock.** 재고가 있는지 찾아 보겠습니다.
out of stock	재고가 떨어진 Unfortunately, the computer was **out of stock** at the store. 아쉽게도, 컴퓨터는 가게에 재고가 없습니다.
stock sth with sth	…에 …을 채우다 They **stocked** the shelves **with** various fruits. 걔네들은 선반에 다양한 과일들로 채워넣었어.
play the (stock) market	주식을 하다 They lost their money **playing the market.** 걔들은 주식 투자에서 돈을 잃었어.

stop 262

v. 멈추다, 정지하다, 그만두다 **n.** 멈춤, 중지, 정거(장)

stop sth[sby]	…을 멈추게 하다 *Stop it[that]! 멈춰!, 그만둬! *stop what sby's doing …가 하던 일을 멈추다 Please **stop** the fighting! 제발 싸움 좀 멈춰! We couldn't **stop** the bleeding. 우린 출혈을 막을 수가 없었어. **Stop it,** I'm serious! 그만둬! 나 장난아니야!

stock

stop for sth	…하기 위해 멈추다, 멈춰서 …하다 *stop for a moment 잠시 멈추다	

You can go to the toilet when we stop for gas.
기름넣을 때 화장실에 가.

We stopped for a cocktail after work.
퇴근 후에 잠시 칵테일 마시러 들렀어.

Can we stop for a moment please?
잠깐만 멈출래요?

stop to~	멈춰서…하다, …하기 위해 들르다 *stop and+V 멈춰서 …하다 *stop to think 곰곰이 생각하다

I just stopped to see if I could help.
내가 도움이 될 수 있나 알아보기 위해 들렀어.

Why don't you stop and ask for directions?
잠시 멈춰서 길을 물어보지 그래.

stop ~ing	…하기를 그만두다

I always stop eating before I feel full.
난 배가 부르기 전까지만 먹어.

Stop acting like my mother. 내 엄마처럼 행동하지마.

Will you stop doing that? 그만 좀 할래?

(Please) Stop ~ing!	…를 그만둬! *Don't stop ~ing …을 계속해라

Please stop bugging me. 나 좀 귀찮게 하지마.

Stop doing that! 그러지마!

Stop lying to me! 거짓말마!

Stop looking at me like tha. 그렇게 쳐다보지마.

Stop saying that! Will you say something else?
그런 말마! 다른 얘기할래?

stop sby from ~ing	…가 …하는 것을 막다, 못하게 하다

I couldn't stop you from doing this.
네가 이걸 하는 걸 막을 수가 없었어.

Why did she stop me from dating Adam?
왜 걘 내가 아담과 데이트를 못하게 하는거야?

You will do anything to stop me from having sex with him.
무슨 수를 써서라도 내가 걔랑 섹스하는거 말려.

There's nothing to stop sby (from) ~ing	…는 반드시 …할거야

There's nothing to stop me from divorcing her.
난 걔랑 기필코 이혼할거야.

| **stop oneself from ~ing** | …하는 걸 참다 *stop oneself 자제하다, 참다

I can't **stop myself from** loving you. 너에 대한 사랑을 멈출 수가 없어.

She **stopped herself from** laughing. 걘 웃음을 참을 수가 없었어. |
|---|---|
| **can't stop +~ing** | 계속 …할 수밖에 없다

I **can't stop** crying. 계속 울 수밖에 없어.

I'm sure you **can't stop** loving me.
넌 날 계속 사랑할 수밖에 없다는 걸 알아.

I **couldn't stop** laughing at your story.
하지만 네 얘기에 웃음을 멈출 수가 없었어. |
| **stop at** | …에 멈추다

How about we **stop at** the store and get something to eat?
가게에 들려 먹을거 좀 사자?

Why don't you **stop at** a bar for a couple of drinks?
바에 가서 술 좀 하자. |
| **stop by[in]** | 방문하다 *stop by and see (how~) …을 보려고(…인지) 잠시 들르다 *swing by 잠시 들르다

Stop by any time after Friday.
금요일 이후엔 아무 때나 와.

We just wanted to **stop by** and say good night.
잘 자라고 말하려고 잠깐 들렸어.

I just **stopped by** to see how you're doing.
네가 어떻게 지내는지 보려고 들렸어.

I'll **stop by** the drugstore.
약국에 들를거야. |
| **stop off** | 잠시 들르다 *stop off for sth …하러 잠시 들르다 *stop off at someplace …에 잠시 들르다

I **stopped off** at the Korean deli to get some crackers.
한국 델리에 들러 크래커를 좀 샀어.

Let's **stop off** for a drink. 술마시러 잠시 들르자. |
| **stop over** | 여행지에서 잠시 머물다, 도중하차하다 *stopover 단기 기착지

Why don't you just **stop over** for coffee sometime?
커피마시러 잠시 들러.

We had to **stop over** one night in Los Angeles.
LA에서 하룻밤 머물러야 했어. |

stop short of	(위험한 짓) …까지는 하지 않다
	She **stopped short of** hurting herself. 걘 자해까지는 하지 않았어.
pull out all the stop	…하기 위해 최선을 다하다, 갖가지 수를 하다
	We'**re pulling out all the stops.** 최선을 다하고 있어요.
bring[come] to a stop	멈추다
	The car **came to a stop** on the side of the road. 차는 길 건너편에 멈추었다.

straight

adv. 똑바로, 곧장 **a.** 곧은, 똑바른

come straight to the point	말하고 싶은 바를 직설적으로 말하다
	He doesn't waste time, he **comes straight to the point.** 걘 시간을 낭비하지 않고 바로 직설적으로 말했어.
tell sb straight	솔직히 말하다
	Tell me **straight** up. 내게 솔직히 말해줘.
give it to me straight	사실대로 말하다
	Just **give it to me straight,** it'll save us a lot of time. 그냥 사실대로 말해줘. 그럼 시간이 많이 절약될거야.
cannot think straight	분명히 생각하지 못하다
	He may not have been in any shape to **think straight.** 걘 생각을 제대로 할 상태가 전혀 아니었는지도 몰라.
go straight	똑바로 가다
	We're supposed to **go straight** home. 우린 곧장 집으로 가야 돼.

get[make] ~ straight	바로 잡다 Let's just **get** one thing **straight.** I don't want to date you. 한가지 분명히 해두자고. 너랑 데이트하기 싫어.
keep a straight face	농담을 해도 웃지 않고 정색을 하다 Jack is having a very difficult time **keeping a straight face.** 잭은 아무일 없는 듯한 표정을 짓고 있는데 힘들었어.

264 strike

v. 치다, 공격하다, 발생하다, 갑자기 떠오르다, …라는 인상을 주다, 파업하다

be struck by	…에 감명받다, …에 물리적으로 맞다, 차에 치이다 I **was struck by** your honesty and devotion to Kevin. 난 너의 정직함과 케빈에 대한 헌신에 놀랬어.
it strikes me that ~	내게는 …라는 생각이 든다 **It strikes me that** you didn't ever pay me back. 네가 내게 돈을 갚은 적이 없었던 것 같아.
strike a deal [bargain] (with~)	(…와) 유리한 타협을 하다 It was impossible to **strike a deal with** our competitor. 우리 경쟁자와 타협을 하는 것은 불가능했어.
strike sby as sth[~ing]	…에게는 …으로[…하는 것으로] 보이다 That actress **strikes** me **as** annoying. 저 여배우는 난 짜증나.
strike sby as funny[odd]	…가 이상하게 보이다 And that didn't **strike** you **as odd?** 그리고 그게 이상하게 느껴지지 않았어?
be on strike	파업중이다 Well, they're always **on strike.** 그래, 걔네들은 항상 파업중이야.

suck
v. 빨아대다, 엉망이다

suck it up
어쩔 수 없이 참다
You need to **suck it up** if you want to lose weight.
살을 빼고 싶으면 참고 열심히 해야 돼.

suck up to sby
아부하다
You're going to have to **suck up to** Jim.
맞아. 넌 짐에게 잘 보여야 돼.

S+sucks
…는 정말 형편없다
This place **sucks.** I hate everything about it.
여기 별로야. 난 다 맘에 안들어.

suggest
v. 제안하다, 추천하다, 암시하다

I suggest S+V
…라고 생각하는데
I suggest we grab a bite to eat. 간단히 먹을 것 좀 먹도록 하자.

I suggest ~ing
…을 생각해봐
I suggest taking some time off. 좀 쉬는 것을 생각해봐.

I'd suggest~
…을 한번 해봐라
I'd suggest you find an online dating site.
온라인 데이트 사이트를 찾아보는게 어때.

I'd like to suggest~
…을 제안하고 싶어
I'd like to suggest a movie for tonight. 오늘밤에 영화를 보자.

I'm not suggesting~	…라고 말하는 것은 아냐
	I'm not suggesting that you quit your job.
	너보고 직장을 그만두라고 하는 것은 아냐.

have a suggestion	제안사항이 있다
	Bob **has a suggestion** we should listen to.
	우리가 귀를 기울여야 한다는게 밥의 제안이야.

My suggestion is that~	내가 제안하는 것은 …야
	My suggestion is that we vacation at the beach this year.
	나의 제안은 금년에 해변에서 휴가를 보내자는거야.

267 suit

n. 정장 **v.** 어울리다, 적당하다

suit~	…에게 어울리다, 괜찮다
	Do you think this color **suits** me?
	이 색깔이 내게 맞는 것 같아?

suit sth to~	…에게 …을 맞추다, …가 …해도 괜찮아
	It **suits** the council **to** ignore this matter.
	위원회가 이 문제를 무시해도 좋아.

It suits me to +V	…해도 난 괜찮아
	It suits me to stay home on weekends.
	주말마다 집에 있어도 난 괜찮아.

It suits me fine	난 괜찮아, 좋아
	The agreement **suits me fine.** 이 협정은 내 생각에 괜찮아.

follow suit	선례를 따르다
	I decided to leave, and everyone **followed suit.**
	난 떠나기로 결정했고 다들 따랐어.

suggest

Suit yourself

마음대로 해

Suit yourself, but you'll be sorry later.
네 좋을 대로 해, 그런데 나중에 후회할 걸.

I decorated the apartment to **suit myself.**
난 아파트를 나 좋을 대로 장식했어.

suppose
ⓥ 생각하다, 추정하다, 가정하다, …인 것 같다

I suppose so

그런 것 같아

I suppose so. I could use the time to study more.
그렇긴 해. 그럼 공부할 시간이 더 많을거야.

be supposed to+V

…하기로 되어 있다

I**'m supposed to** finish this report by tomorrow.
이 보고서 내일까지 끝내야 해.

be not supposed to+V

…하기로 되어 있지 않다

You**'re not supposed to** do that. 너 그러면 안돼.

I suppose that ~

…라고 생각해

I suppose that doesn't matter to you, does it?
너한테 상관없잖아, 그지?

Suppose [Supposing]~

만약 …라면

Suppose we say yes? 만약에 우리가 예라고 긍정하면?

Why do you suppose S+V?

왜 …한 것 같아?

Why do you suppose she never called me?
왜 걔가 내게 전화 한통 하지 않았다고 생각해?

What do you suppose S+V?

뭘 …하고 있는 것 같아?

What do you suppose they're doing out there?
걔네들이 거기서 뭘하고 있다고 생각해?

sure

a. 확신하는　**adv.** 그래요, 정말, 뭘요

be sure that~　…을 확신하다
I'm sure that you hurt his feelings. 네가 걔 감정을 아프게 한 게 맞아.

not be sure that ~　…을 확신하지 못하다
I'm not sure that was the best method.
그게 최선의 방법이었는지는 잘 모르겠어.

be sure to~　반드시 …하다
I'll be sure to give you a call. 내가 꼭 네게 전화를 할게.

Sure thing　응, 확실히
Sure thing, she is coming over now. 확실해, 걔가 이제 올거야.

for sure　확실히, 틀림없이
I think she might be a little late but I don't know **for sure.**
걔가 좀 늦을 수도 있는데 확실히 몰라.

make sure of [that~]　…을 확실히 하다
Make sure that you log off when you're through.
끝나면 접속을 끊는거 잊지마

to be sure　틀림없이
Let's go over it again, just **to be sure.**
다시 한번 검토하자, 확실히 하기 위해.

Sure,　물론, 응
Sure, I received your e-mail. 그래, 네 이메일을 받았어

It sure is~　그건 정말 …야
It sure is. It's five minutes from here. 그럼요, 여기서 5분 걸려요.

sure enough　물론
Sure enough, we'll be over tomorrow afternoon.
물론, 우리는 내일 오후에 끝날거야.

take

v. 이동하다, 데리고가다, 선택하다, 먹다, 받아들이다, 참다

take a taxi	택시를 타다 The easiest way is to **take a taxi.** 가장 빠른 방법은 택시를 타는거야.
take a look (at)	쳐다보다 Would you **take a look** at this paper? 이 서류 좀 한번 봐주실래요?
take a shower	샤워하다 *take a bath 목욕하다 I'm going to go **take a shower.** 가서 샤워할거야.
take a walk	산보하다 *take a vacation 휴가가다 I want to **take a walk** around the park. 공원 근처에 산책하러 가려고.
take a rest	쉬다 *take a seat 자리에 앉다 You can **take a rest** in our spare bedroom. 넌 빈 침실에서 좀 쉬어.
take a picture	사진찍다 Can you **take a picture of** us? 우리 사진 좀 찍어줘요?
take a breath	숨을 쉬다 All right. Just **take a breath.** Calm down. 좋아, 심호흡을 하고. 진정해.
take a break	잠시 쉬다 *take ten-minute break 10분간 쉬다 Let's **take a ten-minute break.** 10분 간 쉽시다.
take a lesson	수업을 받다 *take dancing lessons Why don't **take a yoga class?** 요가 수업을 받아봐.
take a rain check	다음으로 미루다 You mind if I **take a rain check?** 다음으로 미루어도 돼?

take the lead	앞장서다
	Chris is gonna **take the lead.** 크리스가 선두에 설거야.
take a bite	한 입 먹다
	He tries to **take a bite** out of my cookie.
	갠 내 과자를 조금 먹으려고 해.
take a hint	눈치채다
	Chris doesn't understand, and could never **take a hint.**
	크리스는 이해를 못했고, 결코 눈치챌 수가 없었어.
take a message	메시지를 받다 *leave a message 메시지를 남기다
	She didn't answer her phone. I **left a message.**
	갠 전화를 받지 않아 메시지를 남겼어.
take a test	시험을 보다
	I don't need to **take a test.** 난 시험볼 필요가 없어.
take an interest	관심을 갖다
	He **took an interest** in books at an early age.
	갠 어린 나이에 책에 관심을 가졌어.
take it	(그걸로) 선택하다, 결정하다
	If this food item is available, I'll **take it.**
	이 식품을 가져갈 수 있다고 이걸로 할게요.
take it personally	개인적으로[감정이 있는 것으로] 받아들이다
	I didn't think she'd **take it personally.**
	난 걔가 기분 나쁘게 받아들이지 않을거라 생각했어.
take it anymore	더이상 참지 못하다
	I can't **take it anymore.** I am out of here!
	더 이상 못 참겠어. 나 간다!
take it slow	천천히 하다
	You're going to want to **take it slow.**
	넌 천천히 하기를 원하게 될거야.
take the job	직장을 잡다
	You bet your ass I'll **take the job.** 내가 그 직업을 갖는거 물론이지.

take

take it from sby	…의 말을 믿다 **Take it from me,** Mom loves you. 내 말을 믿어. 엄만 널 사랑하셔.
take one's word (for it)	…의 말을 믿다 We'll have to **take your word for it.** 우리는 네 말을 믿어야 돼.
take one's time	서두르지 않다(take it easy) Please **take your time.** It's an important decision. 시간을 갖고 해. 중요한 결정이니까.
take the blame (for~)	책임을 지다　*take the responsibility 책임을 지다 You might **take the blame for** something you didn't. 하지도 않은 일에 대한 비난을 뒤집어 쓸 수도 있다.
take the opportunity to	기회를 잡다 I'd like to **take this opportunity to** say I'm getting married next month. 이번 기회를 빌어 담달에 결혼한다는 사실을 말하겠습니다.
take credit for	…에 대한 공을 인정받다 I can't **take credit for** this. We both know that this wasn't me. 내가 이 공을 가로챌 수는 없어. 우리 둘 다 내가 아니라는 걸 알잖아. You **took credit for** my work, Peter! 피터, 넌 내 공을 가로챘어!
take chances	위험을 무릅쓰다, 운에 맡기고 해보다(take a chance) I want you to **take a chance** and trust me. 운에 맡기고 날 믿었으면 해.
take one's chances	운에 맡기고 해보다(take a risk) Sometimes you have to **take chances.** 때론 위험을 감수해야 돼.
take medicine	약을 먹다 I**'m not taking any medicine.** 아무런 약도 먹지 않아요. He **took some tablets** with a drink of water. 갠 물로 약을 몇 알 먹었어.
take care of	돌보다, 처리하다 Can you **take care of** my work until I'm away? 내가 없는 동안 내 일 좀 처리해줄래?

take call	전화받다 (take this call, take one's calls) He won't **take my calls** anymore. 더 이상 내 전화를 안 받으려고 해.
take actions	조치를 취하다 We **took action** to prevent the problem from getting worse. 우리는 문제가 더 악화되는 것을 막기 위해 조치를 취했어.
take advantage of	이용하다 We're not going to **take advantage of** the situation. 우린 이 상황을 이용하지 않을거야.
take place	생기다, 발생하다 Most exchanges **take place** by email or text message. 대부분 교환은 이메일이나, 문자 메시지를 통해 이루어진다.
take notes	받아적다, 기록하다 That's okay. I'll **take notes** for you. 걱정마. 내가 대신 노트해줄게.
take pity on	동정하다 Does she often **take pity on** you? 걔가 가끔 널 동정하니?
take sby to~	…을 …로 데리고 가다 You told me you were going to **take me to** lunch. 나 점심 사준다고 했잖아. I'd like to **take her out for** dinner on the weekend. 걔 주말에 저녁사주러 데리고 나가고 싶어.
Take me to~	…로 데려다줘 Please **take me to** the airport. 공항까지 가주세요.
take+시간+to~	…의 시간이 걸리다 It[This] will just **take** a second. 잠깐이면 된다.
It takes sby+ 시간+to~	…의 시간이 걸리다 **It takes me** five minutes **to** get ready. 내가 준비하는데 5분 걸려.
It takes+시간+ for sby to~	…의 시간이 걸리다 **It takes** a few days **for me to** finish a job like this. 내가 이런 일을 마치는데 며칠 걸려.

take

How long does it take to~?
…하는데 시간이 얼마나 걸려?

How long does it take to get to the airport?
공항까지 가는데 얼마나 걸려요?

take a minute [second] (to)
잠깐 걸리다

I have to **take a minute to** check it out.
잠깐 시간내서 그걸 확인해봐야겠어.

what it takes
성공하는데 필요한 자질, 소질

I didn't have **what it takes** to be a doctor.
난 의사가 되기엔 갖춰야 할 게 부족해.

take A for B
A를 B로 생각하다, 착각하다

Do you **take me for** an idiot? 날 바보로 아는거니?

take away
없애다, 줄이다, 뺏었다 *take sby's breath away …을 놀라게 하다

I thought your dad **took away** your credit card.
네 아빠가 신용카드 뺏어간 줄 알았어.

She **took it away** and gave it to somebody else.
걘 그걸 뺏어서 다른 사람에게 줬어.

take back
돌려받다, 반품하다, 취소하다

I just **took back** what was mine. 내 것이던 걸 가져왔을 뿐이야.

Take back what you said! 네가 한 말 취소해!

take down
혼내주다

I'm gonna **take her down.** 걔 콧대를 꺾어놓을거야.

take up
(일,취미생활) 시작하다, 주제로 선택하다, (시간공간) 차지하다

Being a lawyer must **take up** a lot of time.
변호사가 되려면 많은 시간이 걸려.

take sby up on~
(제안) 받아들이다

I'll **take you up on** that. 네 제안을 받아들일게.

Check it Out !

A: **How long does it take to** cook a turkey?
B: That depends on how heavy the bird is.

　A: 칠면조 요리하는데 시간이 얼마나 걸려?
　B: 칠면조 크기에 따라 다르지.

take from	빼앗다, 빼다
	I **took** a few books **from** your shelves. 난 책장에서 책 몇권을 뺐어.
take over	일을 떠맡다, 양도받다 *take over for sby는 …을 대신해서(…을 위해서) 맡다
	Why're you trying to **take over** my company? 왜 내 회사를 인수할려고 하는거야?
take A over to	…에게 …을 가져다주다, 데려다주다
	Can you **take** Grandma **over to** the clinic? 할머니를 병원으로 모셔다줄 수 있어?
take after	닮다
	She **takes after** her mother. 걘 엄마를 닮았어.
take out	데리고 나가다, 인출하다, 음식포장하다
	So who's going to **take me out to** dinner? 그래 누가 날 데리고 나가 저녁먹을거야?
	Eat here or **take it out?** 여기 드시겠어요 아니면 포장이예요?
take it out on~	…에게 분풀이하다
	Just because you got mad, don't **take it out on** me. 화났다고 내게 분풀이하지마.
take on	떠맡다, 맞서다
	I'm really ready to **take on** more responsibility around here. 난 여기서 더 많은 책임을 질 준비가 정말 되었어요.
take off	옷을 벗다, 쉬다, 가다(leave)
	Would it be all right if I **took a week off** starting tomorrow? 내일부터 일주일간 휴가내도 괜찮겠어요?
	I'm going to **take off.** 그만 일어서야겠어.
take one's eyes off	눈을 떼지 못하다
	I couldn't **take my eyes off** you. 눈을 뗄 수가 없어.
be taken ill	병에 걸리다
	My grandpa **has taken ill.** 할아버지가 병에 걸리셨어.

be taken with [by]	깜짝 놀라다 Absolutely not. He **was taken by** surprise. 전혀 몰랐어. 걘 깜짝 놀랐어.
be taken aback	당황하다 He **was taken aback** by what was on display. 걘 전시된 것 보고 놀랐어.
Point well-taken	무슨 말인지 잘 알았어 **Point well taken.** I'll have to discuss it with them. 무슨 말인지 잘 알겠어. 가족과 상의해봐야겠어.

271 talk
ⓥ 대화하다, 설득하다

talk to~	…에게 이야기하다 It's been good **talking to** you. 만나서 반가웠어. Who do you think you're **talking to**? 내가 그렇게 바보처럼 보이냐? Can I **talk to** you for a second? 잠깐 얘기 좀 할 수 있어요?
talk with	…와 이야기하다 *have a talk with sby …와 이야기하다 Nice **talking with** you. 만나서 즐거웠어. I'm going to have to **have a talk with** Julie. 줄리와 이야기해야 될거야.
talk about	…에 대해 이야기하다 *talk about+명사[what/how]~ …에 대해[…을] 이야기하다 I don't want to **talk about** it[this]. 이 얘기하기 싫어. I can't **talk about** it. 이 얘기할 수 없어. Can we **talk about** this later? 이 얘기는 나중에 하자. I can't **talk about** it here. It's complicated. 여기서 그거 말 못해. 복잡해서. How about we **talk about** this over dinner? 점심하면서 이 문제 얘기해보면 어때?

talk about ~ behind one's back	…을 뒤에서 험담하다 She's very good at **talking about me behind my back.** 걘 뒤에서 험담하는데 일가견이 있어.
talk over	논의하다, 토의하다 *talk out 어떤 문제를 풀기 위해 끝까지 철저히 논의하다 I have to **talk it over** with the boss. 사장님하고 논의해야겠어. **Talk it over.** You have 2 days. 의논해봐. 이틀을 주지.
talk sby into+ 명사[~ing]	…에게 얘기해서 …하게 하다 How did she **talk me into** doing that? 어떻게 걔가 날 이거 하게 할 수 있어? You **talked me into** it. 네가 날 이거 하게 했어.
talk sby out of +명사[~ing]	…에게 얘기해서 …못하게 하다 I **talked him out of** it. 걔에게 말해서 일을 중단시켰어.
talk to oneself	혼잣말하다 I'm a bad liar, can't even lie about **talking to myself.** 난 거짓말쟁이야. 혼잣말할 때 조차 거짓말 해.
talk like that	그렇게[그런 식으로] 말하다 Jack, you don't **talk like that** to anyone. 잭, 누구한테도 그런 식으로 말하지마. Don't **talk like that.** Everything is going to be fine. 그런 식으로 말마. 다 좋아질거야.
talk back	말대꾸하다 Don't **talk back to** your teacher. 선생님한테 말대답하지 마라.
talk dirty to~	…에게 야한 말을 하다 I love when you **talk dirty to** me. 네가 야한 말할 때가 좋더라.
Let's talk~	…에 대해 이야기하다 *Let's talk (about)~ …에 관해 이야기하자 **Let's talk about** that. 그 얘기 하자. So **let's talk about** what you can do for me. 네가 날 위해 뭘 할 수 있는지 얘기해보자. **Let's not talk about** the past. 과거 얘기는 하지 말자.

talk

I'm[We're] ~ talking
…을 말하고 있어, …와 말하는 중이야

I'm talking about chicks, not gambling.
노름이 아니라 여자애들 말하는거야.

You're talking~
넌 …을 말하고 있어, …을 말하는거야

You're talking to the wrong man. 딴데가서 얘기해.

Are you talking~?
…을 말하는거야?

Are you talking about getting married?
결혼하는거 말하는거야?

~what you're talking about
네가 말하는 것

I know **what you're talking about**. 그럴 만도 해.

This is exactly **what I'm talking about**.
이게 바로 내가 얘기하는거야.

I have no idea **what you're talking about**.
네가 무슨 얘기하는지 모르겠어.

talk one's way out of
어려운 상황에서 빠져나오다

You're not going to **talk your way out of** this.
넌 여기서 빠져나오지 못할거야.

talk the same language
말이 통하다

We're **talking the same language**. 이제 얘기가 된다.

You're **talking my language**. 넌 나하고 말이 통해.

talk sby through sth
…에게 잘 설명해서 이해시키다

You want to **talk me through** this? 이거 내게 이해시켜줄래?

talk some sense into sby
분별있게 행동하도록 …을 설득하다

I'd try one more time to **talk some sense into** her.
걔가 분별있게 행동하도록 한번 더 노력할게.

Talk about~
…에 관한 최고다

Talk about selfish! 이기적인거 따라 갈 사람이 없어!

Talk about feeling like a failure! 낙오자로 느끼는 것은 알아줘야 돼!

teach

v 가르치다

---

teach sby sth

…에게 …을 가르쳐주다

Let me **teach** you a new game.
새로운 게임 알려줄게.

Did your teacher **teach** you that in your class?
선생님이 수업시간에 그걸 알려주셨어?

teach sby about~

…에게 …관해 가르쳐주다

It's my job to **teach** you **about** responsibility.
책임에 대해 네게 가르쳐주는게 나의 의무야.

teach sby a lesson

본 때를 보여주다

I'll **teach him a lesson.** 걔 버르장머리를 고쳐놓을거야.

I'm going to go down there and **teach that guy a lesson.**
거기 내려 가서 그 자식 본 때를 보여줄거야.

teach sby how to~

…에게 …(하는 법) 을 가르치다

I'm just going to **teach** him **how to** make pizza.
걔한테 피자 만드는 법을 알려줄거야.

I'm trying to **teach** her **how to** drive.
걔한테 운전하는 법을 가르쳐 줄려고 하고 있어.

That'll teach sby ~

…에게 …을 깨닫게 하다

That'll teach her[him]!
그래도 싸지!, 당연한 대가야!, 좋은 공부가 될거야!

I got a speeding ticket. **That'll teach** me to drive fast.
속도위반 딱지 끊겼어. 빨리 달리면 어떻게 되는지 깨달았어.

I was taught that~

…을 배웠어

I was taught that it's important to be polite.
예의바르게 중요하단 걸 배웠어.

tear
v. 찢다, 빼내다 **n.** 눈물

tear apart — 갈가리 찢어놓다, 가슴을 미어지게 하다, 마구 뒤적이다

The cops **tore apart** the house searching for him.
경찰은 그를 찾기 위해 집안 구석구석을 마구 뒤적였어.

tear down — 허물다

If we **tear down** that plant, hundreds of people will be laid off. 그 공장을 허물면 많은 직원들이 해고당할텐데요.

tear into — 심하게 비난하다

My father **tore into** me for getting low grades.
아버지는 내가 성적이 좋지 않다고 혼내셨어.

wear and tear — 마모

My notebook computer has suffered a lot of **wear and tear.**
내 노트북이 많이 닳았어.

burst into tears — 벌컥 눈물을 터트리다

She **burst into tears.** She was very upset.
걘 울음을 터트렸지. 무척이나 당황했어.

tell
v. 이야기하다, 말하다, 충고하다, 구분하다

tell sby sth — …에게 …를 말하다

Do you want me **tell** you the rumor people spread?
사람들이 내는 소문을 말하라고?

tell sby the way to	…로 가는 길을 말해주다 Can you **tell me the way to** the station? 역으로 가는 길 좀 알려주세요?
tell sby this [that]	…에게 이걸[그걸] 말하다 I'm sorry I didn't **tell you this** before[sooner]. 이걸 미리[더 빨리] 말해주지 못해 미안. She didn't **tell you that.** 걔는 너한테 그걸 말하지 않았어.
tell sby about	…에게 …대해 이야기하다 What did Mike **tell you about** her? 마이크가 걔에 대해 뭐라고 했어?
Tell me about sth	…에 대해 말해봐 **Tell me about** your new girlfriend. 새로 사귄 애인에 대해 얘기해봐.
I didn't tell sby about~	…에게 …에 대해 말하지 않았어 **I didn't tell him about** you. 걔에게 너에 대해서 이야기 안했어.
tell a lie	거짓말하다 *tell the truth 진실[사실]을 말하다 You better **tell him the truth.** 걔한테 사실대로 말하는게 좋을거야. He **told me a white lie.** 그 사람이 나에게 선의의 거짓말을 했어.
tell a story	이야기하다 *tell a joke 농담하다 The presenter will **tell a story** to the audience. 연사가 청중에게 이야기를 하게 될 것입니다.
tell sby to~	…에게 …을 시키다 He **told me to** save my money for our honeymoon. 걘 나보고 신혼여행 대비해 돈을 저축하라고 했어.
Don't tell me to+V	…하라고 하지마 **Don't tell me to** calm down! 나보고 조용히 하라고 하지마!
I told sby to+V	…에게 …하라고 했어 **I told you to** prevent this from happening 이런 일 일어나지 않도록 하라고 했잖아 **I told him to** drop by for a drink 난 걔보고 잠깐 들러 술 한잔 하자고 했어

tell

tell sby that ~	…에게 …을 말하다

Tell him his brother misses him.
걔한테 걔 형이 보고 싶어한다고 해.

Would you **tell him that** James Smith called?
제임스 스미스가 전화했다고 걔한테 전해줄래요?

Can you tell me what S+V?	…을 말해줄래?

Can you tell me where you're going to stay?
어디 묵으실건가요?

I will tell him [her] that S+V	…에게 …을 말해줄게

I'll tell him that you called.
걔한테 네가 전화했다고 말해줄게.

I told you that S+V	내가 …라고 했잖아

I told you he didn't do it. 걔가 그러지 않았다고 했잖아.

You told me that S+V	네가 나한테 …라고 했잖아

You told me that you didn't like Chris.
크리스를 싫어한다고 내게 말했잖아.

tell sby what~	…에게 …을 말하다

You're going to **tell me what** I want to know.
내가 알고 싶은 걸 말해줄거지.

I need you to **tell me who** did it.
누가 그랬는지 내게 말해줘.

Can you tell me what[when, who~] S+V?	…을 말해줄래?

Can you tell me what's going on in there?
거기 무슨 일인지 말해줄래?

Can you tell me where you're going to stay?
어디에 머물건지 말해줄래?

I will tell him what[when, who~] S+V	…에게 …을 말해줄게

I'll tell you what they were fighting over.
걔네들이 뭐 때문에 싸웠는지 말해줄게.

Tell me what [when, who~]	…을 말해봐

Tell me what you're thinking.
네 생각이 뭔지 말해봐.

tell sby how~	…에게 …을 말하다
	Did I **tell you how** beautiful you look in that dress? 네가 그 옷입으면 얼마나 예쁜지 내가 말했었나?
Can you tell me how[why, if~] S+V?	…을 말해줄래?
	Can you tell me how this happened? 어떻게 이런 일이 일어났는지 말해줄래?
	Can you tell me why? 이유를 말해주겠어?
	Could you tell me when to get off? 어디서 내려야 하는지 알려주세요.
I will tell him how [why, if~] S+V	…에게 …을 말해줄게
	I'll tell you how bad it is. 이거 얼마나 안 좋은지 말해줄게.
Tell me how [why, if~] S+V	…을 말해봐
	Tell me if you're still upset about this. 네가 이 때문에 아직도 화나있는지 말해줘.
	Tell me why we're going to this again? 우리가 왜 이걸 다시 해야 하는지 말해줘
tell sby how to~	…에게 …하는 방법을 말하다
	Can you **tell me how to** do it? 그걸 어떻게 하는지 좀 가르쳐줄래?
	You're going to **tell me how to** do it? 그거 어떻게 하는지 알려줄거지?
Can you tell me how to get to +장소?	…로 가는 방법을 알려주시겠어요?
	Could you tell me how to get to gate 3? 3번 게이트 어떻게 가는지 알려줄래요?
I will tell you how to+V	…하는 법을 알려줄게
	I will tell you how to make money. 돈 어떻게 버는지 알려줄게.
I told you to +V	…라고 했잖아
	I told you to give him whatever he wants. 쟤가 원하는 건 다 주라고 했잖아.
	I told you not to do that! 그러지 말라고 했잖아!

tell

I told you (that) S+V

…라고 했잖아

See? **I told you** it was impossible.
거봐? 할 수 없다고 했잖아.

I told you that I didn't know exactly where she lived.
걔가 어디 사는지 모른다고 했잖아.

I thought I told you~

…라고 말한 것 같은데

I thought I told you not to come. 오지 말라고 한 것 같은데.

I told you (so)

내가 그랬잖아

See? **I told you so.** 거봐? 내가 그랬잖아.

I told you that

내가 그랬잖아

We don't have sex. **I told you that.**
우리는 섹스 안해. 내가 말했잖아.

I told you before

전에 내가 말했잖아 *as I told you before 전에 내가 말했듯이

As I told you before, I have no time for that.
전에 말했듯이 난 그럴 시간이 없어.

You told me to~

…라고 했잖아

You told me to be nice. 친절하게 굴라고 했잖아.

You told me to call you a cab at 10:00.
10시에 택시 불러달라고 했잖아.

You told me (that) S+V

…라고 했잖아

You told me that you didn't like Jack.
잭을 싫어한다고 내게 말했잖아.

You told me you were going to take me for lunch.
나 점심 사준다고 했잖아.

Let me tell you (about)+명사~

너에게 …를 말해줄게

Let me tell you my story. 내 이야기해줄게.

Let me tell you about my sister. 내 누이에 대해 말해줄게.

Check it Out!

A: **I thought I told you to** get out of here.
B: You did, but I'm not finished my report yet.

A: 나가라고 말했던 것 같은데.
B: 예 그러셨어요. 그런데 아직 과제물을 끝내지 못했거든요.

Let me tell you something [one thing]

말할게 있는데

Let me tell you something. Your girlfriend isn't cute.
말할게 있는데. 네 애인 안 귀여워.

I have to tell you something. It's about your ex-wife.
말할게 있는데 네 전 부인이야기야.

Let me tell you what [how~]

…을 말해줄게

Let me tell you what I mean. 내가 무슨 말을 하는 건지 말해줄게.

Don't tell me that ~

…라고 말하지마, 설마 …라는 얘기는 아니겠지? *Don't tell me what~ …라고 하지마
*Don't tell me 설마!

Don't tell me what to do! 나에게 이래라 저래라 하지마!

Don't tell me what's in it. 그 안에 뭐가 들어있는지 말하지마.

Don't tell me you don't remember. 기억 안 난다고 하지마.

There's no telling [knowing] what [how~] S+V

…을 알 수가 없어

There's no telling what their date will be like.
걔들 데이트가 어떻게 될지 알 수가 없어.

There's no way to tell what [who] S+V

…을 알 방법이 없어

There's no way to tell what the future will bring.
미래가 어떻게 될지 알 길이 없어.

You're telling me(that) S+V?

…라고 말하는거야? *You're telling me! 누가 아니래!, 정말 그래!

You're telling me you didn't try to hit him?
넌 걔를 치려고 하지 않았다는 말야?

You're telling me there's a million dollars in here?
여기에 백만 달러가 있다는 말야?

I can tell you ~

…하기는 해, …라고 말할 수 있어

I can tell you that the prices of cars are a bit high.
자동차 가격이 좀 높기는 해.

I can tell you what he's going to find.
걘 무엇을 찾을 지는 말할 수 있어.

I can('t) tell you that S+V

…하기는 해, …라고 말할 수 없어

I can tell you it's a nightmare.
그거 악몽이라고 할 수 있겠네.

tell

I can('t) tell you what[how~] S+V
…을 말할 수 있어(없어)

I can tell you why I did. 내가 왜 그랬는지 말해줄 수 있어.

I can tell you that
그렇긴 해 *I can't tell you that 그렇게는 못 말해

I was popular with the people then, **I can tell you that.**
그 당시 사람들에게 난 인기있었어, 그렇긴 했어.

I was [I've been] told (that) S+V
…라고 들었어, 내가 듣기론…

I was told that the doors close at nine.
내가 듣기로 문은 9시에 닫힌대.

I was told you had a question for me.
너 내게 질문있다며.

I was told that
(누군가 나에게) 그것을 말해 줬어, 그렇게 들었어

The bank is going out of business. **I was told that.**
그 은행은 파산할거라고 들었어.

tell A from B
A와 B를 구분하다

Can you **tell** Cindy **from** Betty? They're a lot alike.
신디와 베티 구분돼? 넘 비슷해.

I can **tell the difference** between them.
난 걔들간 구분을 못하겠어.

tell the difference
차이점을 구분하다

It was hard to **tell the difference between** them.
그것들의 차이점을 구분하는 것은 어려웠어.

tell on
고자질하다

I didn't **tell on** you before. 전에 널 고자질한 적 없어.

Don't **tell on** me, okay? 날 고자질하지마, 알았어?

all told
다 합해서

All told, the damage will cost millions of dollars.
다 합해서, 피해는 수백만 달러에 이를거야.

(Do) You mean to tell me ~?
…라는 말 진심이니?

Do you mean to tell me I got fired? 내가 잘린 게 사실야?

tell a soul
…에게 말하다

I won't **tell a soul.** 누구에게도 말하지 않을게, 입 꼭 다물고 있을게.

Don't **tell a soul.** 이 소문에 대해 발설하지마.

thank

v. 고마워하다　**n.** 감사

---

thank sby

…에게 감사하다

I can't **thank** you enough. 뭐라고 감사의 말을 드려야 할지.

I don't know how to **thank** you. 뭐라 감사해야 할지 모르겠어요.

Thank you for +명사[~ing]

…에 감사해

Thank you for calling. 전화줘서 고마워.

Thank you for inviting us. 우릴 초대해줘서 고마워.

Thanks for+ 명사[~ing]

…에 고마워

Thanks for being so nice to us. 우리에게 잘해줘서 고마워.

Thanks a lot. 정말 고마워.

---

have sby to thank for

…은 …의 덕택이다

I believe I **have** you **to thank for** this, John. 존 이건 네 덕택이야.

I **have** you **to thank for** that video. 저 비디오 네 덕택이야.

---

say thank you (to sby)

(…에게) 감사하다고 말하다

I just wanted to **say thank you.** 감사하다고 말하고 싶었어.

I just stopped by to **say thank you.** 감사하다고 말하려고 들렸어.

---

thanks to~

…의 덕택으로

I've been relaxing, **thanks to** you. 네 덕에 편히 잘 쉬고 있어.

Thanks to you I'm not single anymore. 네 덕에 난 더 이상 혼자가 아냐.

---

thank sb for

…에게 …로 감사하다

You'll **thank** me **for** this one day. 언젠가 내게 감사할거야.

Don't take it personally. You'll **thank** me **for** this one day. 화내지마. 언젠가 감사할거야.

thank God [heavens] (for~)	(…가) 고마워라, 다행이다, 고맙게도
	Oh, **thank God.** I've been looking for you all night. 오, 다행이다. 밤새 널 찾아다녔어.
	Thank God. I was so worried. 고맙게도, 걱정 많이 했어.

No, thank you	고맙지만 됐어
	No, thank you. I have to run. 고맙지만 됐어. 빨리 가야 돼.
	Nothing for me, **thanks.** 고맙지만 전 됐어요.
	Not right now, **thanks.** 지금은 됐어요.

276

thing

n. 일, 물건, 상황

do the right thing	올바른 일을 하다
	Give her a minute to **do the right thing.** 걔가 일을 올바로 하도록 시간을 줘.

it's a bad thing that~	…하는 것은 안좋은 일이다
	It's a bad thing to kick people when they are down. 사람들이 어려울 때 비난하는 것은 나쁜 일이야.

all things considered	모든 것을 고려해볼 때
	All things considered, you had fun tonight. 모든 걸 고려할 때 넌 오늘밤 즐긴거야.

have things on one's mind	생각하는게 있어
	No time to talk now, I **have things on my mind.** 지금 말할 시간은 안되지만, 내가 생각하는게 있어.

things like	…와 같은 것들
	Why do you tell her **things like** that? 왜 걔한테 그런 것들을 말해주는거야?

among other things	다른 무엇보다도
	Among other things, I thought it appropriate. 무엇보다도, 난 그게 적절하다고 생각했어.

do your own thing	자기 하고 싶은 일을 하다
	I'm happy just **doing my own thing.** 난 내 자신의 일을 해서 기뻐.

have a thing for[about]	좋아하다, 관심이 있다
	Do you **have a thing for** little women? 조그만 여자들을 좋아해?

The thing is~	중요한 것은 …이다
	The thing is I need to find a date. 중요한 건 데이트 상대를 찾아야 된다는거야.

~ is a thing	…가 유행하다
	Having a blog **is a thing** these days. 블로그를 하는게 요즘 유행이야.

for one thing	우선 한가지 이유는
	For one thing, they're pretty cute. 우선 첫째로, 걔네들은 무척 귀여워.

make a big thing out of sth	침소봉대하다
	Just please don't **make a big thing out of** this. 이걸로 제발 야단법석 떨지마라.

277

think

v. 생각하다, …할 생각이다, 간주하다

think (that) ~	…라고 생각하다 *I don't think (that) S+V …가 아니라고 생각하다
	I think you have a problem. 너 불만 있나본데. **I don't think** we've met before. 초면인 것 같은데요.

thing

Do you think (that)~?	**…라고 생각해?**
	Do you think we should go there? 우리가 거기 가야 된다고 생각해?
	Do you think there's a chance to do it? 그걸 할 기회가 있을 것 같아?

Don't you think S+V?	**…한 것 같지 않아?**
	Don't you think it's time you went home? 벌써 집에 늦을 것 같지 않아?
	Don't you think it's a little too early? 좀 이르다고 생각되지 않나?

I thought (that)~	**…했어, …한지 알았어**
	I thought last night was great. 지난밤은 정말 좋았어.
	I thought that it isn't important to you. 네게 중요하지 않다고 생각했어.

I thought I could+V	**…할 수 있을거라 생각했어**
	You let me down. **I thought I could** trust you. 실망했어. 널 믿을 수 있다고 생각했는데.

I thought we had+명사	**…한 줄 알았어**
	I thought we had plans for tonight. 오늘 저녁 계획이 있는 줄 알았어.
	I thought we had an understanding. 우린 약속된 거 아니었어.

I think I will~	**…을 할까 봐**
	I think I will stay here with her. 걔랑 여기 남아 있을까 봐.
	I think I'll have a martini. 마티니로 할게요.
	I think I'll pass. 통과할래.

I'm thinking of [about] ~ing	**…할까 생각하다**
	I'm thinking of retiring soon. 곧 퇴직할까 생각해.
	I'm thinking about moving this chair. 이 의자를 이동하려고 해.

think so	**그렇게 생각하다**
	I don't **think so.** 그렇지 않을 걸.
	I'm glad you **think so.** 그렇게 생각해주니 기분 좋은데.
	I **thought so** (too). (나도) 그렇게 생각했어. 그럴 것 같았어.
	Don't you **think so?** 그렇게 생각되지 않아?

391

You would think (that) S+V?	…라 생각하고 싶지? **You would think!** 그렇게 생각하고 싶은거지! Yeah, **you would think** that. 넌 그렇게 생각할 줄 알았다.
I would think (that) S+V	…라고 생각했는데 **I would think** you'd be happy. 네가 행복할 거라고 생각했는데. **I would think that** they would be looking for me. 걔네들이 날 찾을거라 생각했는데.
Who would have thought (that) S+V?	(놀람) 누가 …라고 생각이나 했겠어? **Who could[would] have thought?** 누가 생각이나 했겠어?, 상상도 못했네. **Who would have thought** an earthquake would have killed so many people? 지진이 그렇게 많은 인명을 해칠 줄 누가 상상이나 했겠어?
think twice (before~)	(…하기에 앞서) 재고하다, 신중히 생각하다 You should **think twice** before having kids. 애를 갖기 전에 신중히 생각해. Why don't you **think twice** before you start a family. 가정을 꾸리기 전에 숙고해.
think hard	깊이 오래 생각하다 *think big 넓게 생각하다 *think positive(ly) 적극적[긍정적]으로 생각하다 There's always something bugging you. **Think hard.** 항상 널 힘들게 하는게 있어. 깊이 생각해봐. I suggest you **think long.** 아주 진지하게 고민을 해봐.
think over	오래 신중히 생각하다 I'd like to **think it over.** 좀 더 생각해보고. Let me have time to **think over it.** 생각해볼 시간을 줘.
~ don't you think?	그렇지 않아? It's a little excessive, **don't you think?** 그건 좀 지나치네, 그렇지 않아? It's a little soon for that, **don't you think?** 그러기에는 좀 일러, 그렇지 않아?
I hate to think ~	…라고 생각하기는 싫어 **I hate to think that** you have been cheating on me. 네가 바람펴왔다는 걸 생각하기도 싫어.

think

be thought to be ~ing[명사]	…로 여겨지다 (= be believed to) **The president is thought to be** staying in this hotel. 대통령은 이 호텔에 머무는 것으로 여겨져.
What do you think of[about] +명사[~ing]?	…가 어때? **What do you think (of that)?** (그거) 어떻게 생각해?, 네 생각은 어때?, 그걸 말이라고 해? **What do you think of** this weather? 날씨 어때?
What do you think of[about] sby ~ing?	…가 …하는거 어때? **What do you think about** me **staying** the night? 내가 밤새 머물러는거 어때?
What do you think~ ?	…가 …한다고 생각해? **What do you think** I am? 날 뭘로 보는거야? **What do you think** you are? 네가 도대체 뭐가 그리 잘났어? **What do you think** you're doing? 이게 무슨 짓이야?
~what I[you] think	내가(네가) 생각하는거 You know **what I think?** 저 말이야(의견을 말하기 전에 하는 말). Here's **what I think.** 내 생각은 이래. That's **what I think.** 그게 바로 내 생각이야. That's[It's] **what you think.** 그건 네 생각이고. Is that **what you think?** 네가 생각하는 게 이거야? That's **what I thought.** 나도 그렇게 생각했어.
~what I[you] think (S)+V	내[네] 생각에 (…가) …하는 것 Is that **what I think** it is? 그게 내가 생각하는 그거 맞아? Let me tell you **what I think** happened. 어떻게 된건지 내 생각을 말해줄게. You know **what I think** you should do? 네가 뭘 해야 된다고 내가 생각하는지 알아?
I think,	내가 생각하기에는 Since you saw mine, **I think,** you have to show yours. 네가 내 꺼 봤으니 너도 네 꺼 보여줘야 돼 I look at you and **I think,** this is what I want. 난 바라봤고, 난 생각했어. 이게 바로 내가 원하는거라고

think less[little, nothing] of~	···을 하찮게 여기다, 무시하다, 개의치 않다 (Please) **Think nothing of** it. 마음쓰지마. No, I don't **think less of** you. 아니, 난 널 신경 많이 써.
think much of~	···을 중히 여기다(think a lot of) She's not a big talker so I didn't **think much of** it. 걘 떠벌이가 아니어서 개의치않기로 했어.
think of [about]~	···을 생각하다 I **haven't thought about** marriage yet. 아직 결혼 생각 안해봤어. What **were you thinking about?** 정신을 어디다 놓고 다녀? Don't even **think about** (doing) it. 꿈도 꾸지마.
think about what S+V	···을 생각해보다 You should **think about what** movie we'll see. 무슨 영화를 우리가 볼지 생각해봐.
think of ~ as ~	···를 ···라고 여기다　*think of oneself as~ 스스로를 ···라고 생각하다 People **think of me as** a hard worker. 사람들은 내가 열심히 일한다고 생각해.
think it best (for sby) to~	(···에게) ···하는 게 최선이라 생각하다 I **thought it best to** work with Tony. 토니랑 일하는게 최선이라 생각했어. I **thought it best for us to** keep this quiet. 우리가 이걸 비밀로 하는게 최선이라 생각했어.
I think the best thing to do~	최선의 행동은 ···이라고 생각해 **I think the best thing to do** is just smile. 최선의 행동은 그냥 웃는거라 생각해.
come to think of it	생각해보니까 말야, 말이 나왔으니 말인데 **Come to think of it,** why don't you come to the movies with us? 그러고 보니, 너도 우리랑 영화보러 가는게 어때?
have second thoughts	재고하다 Don't **give it a second thought.** 걱정하지마. I'm **having second thoughts** about the wedding. 결혼 다시 생각하고 있어.

think

On second thought 다시 생각해보니

You know, **on second thought,** gum would be perfection.
다시 생각해 보니까, 껌 하나 주시면 더할 나위가 없겠군요..

278

throw
v. 던지다, (파티) 벌이다

throw sth to sby [at sth, sby] …을 …에게 던지다

She **threw** a glass bottle **at** her rival.
걔는 경쟁자에게 유리병을 던졌어.

throw up 토하다, 급조하다

Why do I feel like **throwing up?** 왜 토하고 싶을까?

throw a party 파티를 벌이다

I'm going to **throw a party** this Friday.
이번 주 금요일에 파티를 열거야.

throw a fit 발작하다, 화를 내다

Next time look more carefully before you **throw a fit.**
다음부터는 화를 내기 전에 신중히 둘러봐.

throw out 쫓겨나다 *throw away 버리다

Anybody who fails this course will **be thrown out.**
이 과정에서 낙제하는 사람은 누구든 쫓겨날거야.

time

n. 시간 v. 시간을 맞추다, 타이밍을 맞추다

next time	다음번에
	I will go with you **next time.** 다음 번에 너와 함께 갈게.
at that[this] time	제[이]번에
	There are a lot of sales going on **at this time** of year. 이맘 때쯤이면 세일하는 데가 많거든.
at the time of~	…할 때에
	There was no more information **at the time of** the report. 레포트를 쓸 때 어떤 레포트를 써야 되는지에 대한 추가적인 정보가 없었어.
ahead of time	예정보다 빨리
	We bought our tickets **ahead of time.** 우린 사전에 표를 샀었지.
all the time	항상
	We used to play together **all the time.** 우린 항상 함께 놀곤 했어.
at all times	언제나, 늘
	This door should be closed **at all times.** 이 문은 항상 닫혀져 있어야 한다.
at a time	한 때
	What the hell? Let's take it one step **at a time.** 도대체 뭐야? 천천히 해나가자고.
in no time (at all)	즉시
	The flight arrived **in no time.** 비행편이 금세 도착할거야.
at one time	한꺼번에, 동시에
	It's not possible to be in two places **at one time.** 동시에 두 장소에 있을 수는 없어.

time

by the time S+V	…할 때, …즈음에	
	By the time I get home, he'll be asleep. 내가 집에 올 때 쯤에, 걔는 자고 있을거야.	
do time	복역하다	
	You're willing to **do time** for that? 그거 때문에 감방 살고 싶어?	
for some time	한동안 *for a time 당분간, 잠시	
	I'm really sorry I've been distant **for some time**. 한동안 신경 못 써서 정말 미안해.	
from time to time	때때로	
	From time to time the battery goes dead. 이따금 배터리가 죽어버려.	
have no time for	…할 시간이 없다	
	I work 24/7. I **have no time for** my family. 난 온종일 일해. 난 가족에게 낼 시간이 없어.	
make time	시간을 내다	
	We need to **make time** to interview some of these candidates. 지원자들 좀 면접할 시간을 내야겠어요.	
in time	시간에 맞춰 *on time 정시에	
	You'll never get to the interview **in time**. 넌 절대로 제 시간에 면접장소에 도착할 수 없을거야.	
there's no time to~	…할 시간이 없다	
	There's no time to repair the broken phone. 망가진 핸드폰을 수리할 시간이 없어.	
It's only a matter [question] ~ of time	…는 시간문제이다	
	You know **it's only a matter of time** before she spills. 걔가 폭로하는건 시간문제일 뿐이야.	
when the time comes	때가 되면	
	There will be an announcement **when the time comes**. 때가 되면 발표가 있을거야.	
time will tell	시간이 지나면 알게 될 것이다 *Time flies 세월이 빠르다	
	I'm not sure. **Time will tell.** 몰라. 시간이 지나면 알겠지.	

280 tip
n. 팁, 정보 **v.** 기울어지다

give[leave] a tip	팁을 주다, 정보를 주다 *get a tip 팁을 받다, 정보를 얻다
	I **got a tip** from a concerned citizen. 관심있는 시민으로부터 정보를 하나 얻었어.

the tip of the iceberg	빙산의 일각
	And that's just **the tip of the iceberg.** 그리고 저건 빙산의 일각에 불과해.

on the tip of one's tongue	말이 혀끝에서 뱅뱅 도는데 생각이 안나는
	The phrase was **on the tip of Teresa's tongue.** 그 문구가 테레사의 혀끝에서 뱅뱅 돌았어.

tip over	넘어지다
	The statue **tipped over** during the storm. 그 조각상은 폭풍이 불 때 넘어졌어.

281 top
n. 정상 **a.** 맨위의 **v.** 능가하다, 최고이다

over the top	지나치게
	Jack's behavior around the office is a bit **over the top**, don't you think? 잭은 회사에서 좀 오버하는 것 같지 않아?

on top of	…의 위에
	He's **on top of** things. 걘 매사를 잘 관리하고 있어.

off the top of one's head	생각없이, 즉석에서 **Off the top of your head,** how d'you feel about Jim? 금방 생각이 나서 그러는데, 짐을 어떻게 생각해?
at the top of	…의 위에 How about **at the top of** the mountain? 산 정상에서는 어때?
top sth	…보다 뛰어나다 *can't top that …보다 낫다 She got a perfect score and you can't **top** that. 걔 거의 만점을 받았고 넌 상대가 안돼.

282 touch

 만지다, 접촉하다, 감동시키다   만지기, 접촉

be touched by	…에 감명받다 I **was really touched by** your call. It was so big of you. 전화해줘서 감동했어. 정말 고마웠어.
get in touch with	…와 연락하다 We're still trying to **get in touch with** him. 걔한테 연락을 시도하고 있어.
keep[stay] in touch with	…와 연락을 주고 받다 You still **keep in touch with** her? 걔하고 아직 연락해?
lose touch with~	…와 연락이 끊기다 They **had lost touch with** her and they needed to find her. 걔네들은 걔와 연락이 끊겨서 걜 찾아야 돼.
be in touch with sth	이해하다, 파악하다 I've just never been so **in touch with** my body. 난 내 몸을 그렇게 잘 이해했던 적이 없어.
lose one's touch	기량이 떨어지다 The cook here **has lost his touch.** 주방장이 감을 잃었나 봐.

 283

track

n. 길, 자국 **v.** 추적하다

keep track of	…에 대해 잘 파악하고 있다, 기록하다
	We just wanted to **keep track of** each other.
	우리는 단지 서로를 잊지 않고 있기를 원했어.
lose track of~	…을 놓치다 *lose track of time 시간가는 줄 모르다
	I'm sorry, I **lost track of** time.
	미안, 내가 시간가는 줄 몰랐네.
on the right [wrong] track	올바른[잘못된] 방향으로 가는
	We're obviously **on the right track.**
	우리는 분명 제대로 된 길을 가고 있어.
be (right) on track to+V	성공할 길에 들어서다
	David **is on track to** graduate from law school.
	데이빗은 계획대로 법대를 졸업할거야.
track down	…을 찾아내다
	We're trying to **track down** the ex.
	우리는 전 남편을 추적하려고 하고 있어.
be on the fast track	성공가도를 달리다
	It seems he'**s on the fast track** to become president.
	그는 사장으로 가는 성공가도를 가고 있어.

treat

v. 다루다, 대접하다, 논하다 **n.** 한턱, 대접

treat sby well [badly]
…을 잘(못) 대하다

I think you're **treating** me **unfairly**.
네가 날 공평하게 대하는 것 같지 않아.

I haven't always **treated** you **well**.
난 항상 널 잘 대해주지 못했어.

She **was treated badly** in the last time.
걘 지난번에 안 좋게 대했줬어.

treat sby that way
…을 그런 식을 대하다

You can't **treat me that way.**
넌 날 그런 식으로 대하면 안돼.

How dare you **treat Sam that way!**
어떻게 네가 샘을 그런 식을 대하니!

How's sth treating you?
…가 어때?

So, Kate, **how's** married life **treating you?**
그래, 케이트야 네 결혼 생활이 어때?

How's the stock market **treating you?**
주식시장에서 어때?

How's life[the world] **treating you?**
사는 건 어때?

treat sby like
…처럼 대하다

No one **treats** my friends **like that.**
아무도 내 친구들을 그렇게 안 대해.

How could you **treat** him **like that?**
어떻게 걜 그런 식으로 대접할 수 있어?

treat sby with respect
…을 존경심을 갖고 대하다

I **treated** you **with respect** and understanding.
난 널 존경심과 이해하는 마음으로 대했어.

treat sby to sth
…에게 …을 대접하다

I'll **treat** you **to** dinner tonight. 오늘 저녁 대접할게.

treat oneself to	(큰마음 먹고) …을 즐기다, 대접하다
	After your hard work, **treat yourself** a vacation. 열심히 일했으니, 휴가를 즐겨라.
	I'm going to **treat myself to** a big breakfast. 아침을 거나하게 먹어볼려고.
be my treat	…는 내가 낼게
	This **is my treat.** 내가 낼게.
	I'll **treat** you. 내가 한턱 쏠게.
	Let me **treat** you. 내가 낼게.
~'s treat	…가 내는거야
	David's treat! Where do you want to eat? 데이빗이 쏜대! 너 뭐 먹을래?
	I'll take you to dinner. **My treat.** 저녁 먹으러 가자. 내가 낼게.

trouble

n. 문제, 곤란, 병　**v.** 괴롭히다, 애먹이다

have trouble with	…에 애를 먹다 *have trouble ~ing …하는데 애를 먹다
	I **have some trouble with** sleeping. 나 수면에 좀 문제가 있어.
	I **have trouble** keeping up with her. 걔를 따라잡는데 어려워.
make trouble for ~	…를 애먹이다, 괴롭히다
	Don't **make trouble for** me. 내게 장난치지마, 내게 문제 일으키지마.
cause[give] sb a lot of trouble	…를 곤경에 빠트리다
	He always **caused a lot of trouble.** 걘 항상 많은 문제를 일으켰지.
	It can **get you in a lot of trouble.** 그 때문에 네가 큰 어려움에 처할 수 있어.

treat

back trouble	등통증
	I'm in constant pain because of **back trouble.** 등통증 때문에 계속해서 고통속에 지내고 있어.

be in trouble	곤경에 처하다
	We are really going to **be in trouble** now. 이제 우린 정말 난처하게 되겠어.

get into trouble	곤경에 빠지다
	You will **get in trouble** if you do that. 그렇게 하면 곤란해질거야.

get sb into trouble	···을 곤경에 빠트리다
	Your behavior will **get you in trouble** this time. 이번엔 네 행동때문에 곤경에 빠질거야.

be asking for trouble	화를 자초하다
	Driving without a license **is asking for trouble.** 면허증없이 운전을 하면 화를 자초하게 돼.

if it's no trouble	폐가 되지 않는다면
	If it's no trouble, could we switch seats? 괜찮으면, 자리를 바꿀 수 있을까?

I hate to trouble you	폐를 끼쳐 죄송합니다만
	I hate to trouble you, but do you have a cigarette? 폐를 끼쳐 죄송합니다만, 담배 있으세요?

286

trust

n 신뢰 **v** 신뢰하다, 믿다

earn one's trust	신뢰를 얻다
	How do you expect to **earn anyone's trust** if you don't keep your word? 약속도 못지키면서 어떻게 남의 신뢰를 받기를 바래?

put one's trust in sb	신뢰하다
	Jill **put her trust in** her mom's advice. 질은 엄마의 충고를 믿었어.

betray one's trust	배신하다
	He would never **betray my trust.** 걘 절대로 나의 신뢰를 배신하지 않을거야.

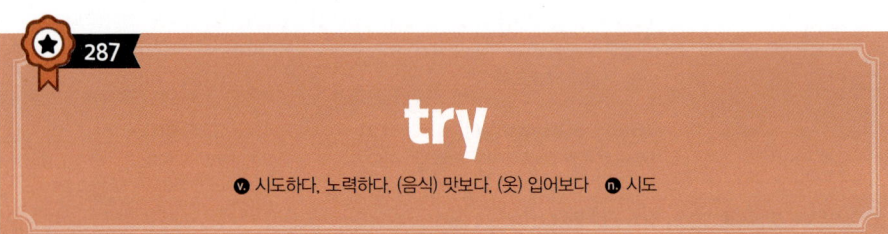

287 try

v. 시도하다, 노력하다, (음식) 맛보다, (옷) 입어보다 n. 시도

try something (else, new)	뭔가 (다른 것, 새로운 것)을 해보다
	Let's **try something else.** 뭔가 다른 것을 해보자.
	I've **tried everything.** I give up. 갖가지 다 해봤어. 나 포기할래.

try everything (to+V)	(…하기 위해) 모든 것을 다하다
	I **tried everything to** make myself feel better. 내가 기분 좋아지도록 안해본 게 없어.

try+음식명사	…을 먹어보다 *try some (of)+음식 …을 좀 먹어보다, I'd like try+음식명사 …을 먹고 싶다
	I'd like to take you to **try** some Indian food. 널 데리고 식당가서 인도음식 맛보자.
	Do you want to **try** some of my pie? 내 파이 좀 먹어볼래?
	Go ahead. **Try** a piece. 한 조각 먹어봐.
	I **tried** eating Korean food. 나는 한국 음식을 먹어보았어.

try it	그걸 해보다
	Why don't you **try it?** 한번 해봐, 이거 한번 먹어볼래?
	We've already **tried it** twice. 우리 이미 그거 두 번 했어.
	Andy, you must[have got to] **try this.** 앤디, 너 이거 해봐야 돼.

trust

try again	다시 시도하다 *try hard 열심히 하다, try next time 다음 번에 하다
	Don't give up. Let's try it again. 포기하지마, 다시 한번 하자.
	You want to try it again? 한 번 더 해볼래?
	You've got to try harder next time. 다음 번에 더 열심히 하라고.
try to+V	…하려고 시도하다, 애쓰다(try and+동사)
	I tried to help her. 나는 걔를 도와주려고 했어.
	What are you trying to say? 무슨 말을 하려는거야?
try hard to+V	…하려고 무척 애쓰다
	I'm trying hard to get a job! 취직하려고 열심히 노력하고 있어!
I'll try to+V	…해볼게
	I'll try to forget it. 잊으려고 노력할게.
	I'll try to get back as soon as I can. 가능한 빨리 돌아오도록 할게.
	I'll try to catch you later. 나중에 다시 이야기하자.
I'm trying to +V	…하는 중이야, …하려고 하고 있어
	I'm trying to ease up and enjoy life more. 천천히 하면서 인생을 좀 더 즐기려고.
Are you trying to+V?	너 …하려는 거야?
	Are you trying to threaten me? 날 협박하려는거야?
	What are you doing? Are you trying to hurt me? 뭐 하는거야? 날 아프게 하려고?
	Are you trying to say that this is wrong? 이게 틀렸다고 말하려는거야?
Are you trying to say[tell me] that S+V?	너 지금 …라고 말하려는 거야?
	Are you trying to tell me that you're not going? 넌 안가겠다고 말하는거야?
What are you trying to~ ?	뭘 …하려는거야?
	What are you trying to say? 무슨 말 하는거야?
	What are you trying to do, hit me? 어쩔려고, 날 칠려고?
	Why are you trying to get away from me? 왜 내게서 멀어지려는거야?

What I'm trying to say is (that)~

내가 말하려는 것은 …이다 *All I'm saying is (that)~

What I'm trying to say is that she's not rich.
내가 말하려는 건 걘 부자가 아니라는거야.

What I'm trying to say is I want you to leave.
내가 말하고자 하는 건 네가 떠나길 바란다는거야.

Don't try to~

…하려고 하지마 *Try not to+V

Don't try to apologize right now. 지금 당장 사죄하지마

Please try not to think about it. 그거 생각하려고 하지마

try for~

…을 얻으려고 차지하려고 애쓰다

So you think you will **try for** another adoption?
그래서 넌 또 입양을 하겠다는거야?

You want to **try for** it again? 그거 다시 한번 해볼테야?

let me try~

내가 …해볼게

I believe I can do it. **Let me try.**
내가 할 수 있으니 내가 해볼게.

Does it not taste good? **Let me try it.**
맛없어? 내가 먹어볼게.

Let me try to explain it to you.
네게 내가 설명해볼게.

try one's best

최선을 다하다 *try one's luck 운을 시험해보다 *try one's patience 인내심을 테스트해보다

I'**m trying my best.** 최선을 다하고 있어.

I will **try my luck.** (되든 안되든) 한번 해봐야겠어.

You'**re trying my patience.** 너 정말 짜증난다.

try on

…을 한번 입어보다

Would you like to **try it on?** 입어 볼래요?

Is it okay to **try on** anything I want?
뭐든지 신어봐도 돼요?

try out

(제대로 작동되는지) 테스트해보다 *try out for~ 오디션에 참가하다

She **is trying out** different cookie recipes.
걘 다른 과자만드는 법을 테스트해보고 있어.

She **tried out for** the movie.
걘 영화배우 선발대회에 나갔었어.

give ~ a try	…에게 기회를 주다　*give it a try 시도하다
	I'll **give them a try.** 걔들에게 기회를 줘볼거야.
	Maybe I'll **give him a try.** 기회나 한번 줘보지.
	I guess it**'s worth a try.** 한번 해 봄직도 한데.
Nice try	목적달성에는 실패했지만 그래도 좋은 시도였어
	It's too bad you lost the contest. **Nice try.** 네가 지다니 안됐네. 하지만 잘했어

turn

v. 돌리다, 바꾸다, 변화하다, (나이, 시간) …이 되다

turn and[to] +V	돌아서 …하다
	He **turns to** leave, then turns back quickly. 걘 돌아서 가려다가 잽싸게 돌아선다.
	She **turns to** her side to turn off her cell phone. 걘 몸을 옆으로 돌려 핸드폰을 껐다.
turn to~	몸을 돌려 …하다, 도움을 얻다, 의지하다
	Can we **turn to** the case? 사건에 집중할래요?
	You shouldn't **turn to** drugs to avoid the troubles. 어려움을 피할 목적으로 약물에 의지하면 안돼.
turn a blind eye to	외면하다, …을 못본 척하다　*turn a deaf ear to 외면하다, …을 못들은 척하다
	I tried to talk to him, but he **turned a deaf ear to** me. 걔하고 얘기하려 했는데 걘 날 외면했어.
turn left [right]	좌(우)회전하다
	Go east for two blocks and then **turn right.** 동쪽으로 2블록 간 다음 우회전해요.
	Take this road until it ends and then **turn right.** 이 길이 끝날 때까지 가서 우회전해요.

turn one's back on sby [sth]	…에서 눈을 떼다, 외면하다, 거절하다 Why did you **turn your back?** I told you to take care of him! 왜 자리를 비운거야? 잘 보살피라고 했잖아! Now I only **turned my back** for a second and she was gone. 잠시 눈을 뗐는데 걔가 사라졌어. Don't **turn your back on** him. 걔를 외면하지마.
take turns ~ing	교대로 …하다 They **took turns** looking at each other. 걔네들은 교대로 서로를 쳐다봤어.
be one's turn (to+V)	(…할) …의 차례이다 Maybe it'**s my turn to** watch out for you. 이제 내가 널 지켜봐야 할 순서인 것 같아.
in turn	교대로 Let's speak **in turn.** 교대로 말하자.
wait one's turn	차례를 기다리다 **Whose turn** is it next? 다음은 누구 차례죠?
turn a profit	수익을 내다(make a profit) We'**ve barely turned a profit.** 우린 거의 수익을 내지 못하고 있어.
turn one's attention to~	…에 관심을 기울이다 Please **turn your attention to** the big screen. 대형화면에 관심을 기울여주세요.
turn the corner	모퉁이를 돌다, 고비를 넘기다 I **turned the corner** of the house and entered the backyard. 난 코너를 돌아 뒷마당으로 들어갔어. We'**ve finally turned the corner.** 우리 마침내 고비를 넘겼어.
turn the tables on	역전시키다, 보복하다 I'm going to **turn the tables on** them. 걔네들에게 보복할거야.
turn sth inside out	속을 뒤집다 It's kind of like **turning a sock inside out.** 그건 양말을 뒤집는 것과 같아.

turn

turn sth upside down
…을 샅샅이 뒤지다

They will **turn** this whole place **upside down** till they find it.
걔네들은 그걸 발견할 때까지 이곳을 샅샅이 뒤질거야.

turn around
방향을 바꾸다, 상황이 호전되다, 호전시키다   *turn around and[to]+동사 몸을 돌려 …하다

I **turned around** to see where it was coming from.
그게 어디서 왔는지 보기 위해 돌아섰어.

He **turned around** and said "Again, I'm sorry."
걔 돌아서서 "다시 한번 미안해"라고 말했어.

turn away
고개를 돌리다, 외면하다   *turn away from sby …을 피하다, 거절하다

She kept trying to kiss me on the mouth, and I kept **turning away.** 걔가 자꾸 입에 키스하려고 해서 난 계속 얼굴을 돌렸어.

Don't you **turn away from** me. Look at me!
날 외면하지 말고, 날 봐!

turn back (to)
뒤돌아서다, 돌아오다   *turn sby[sth] back …을 돌아오게 하다

They both **turned back to** look at the building.
걔네들은 돌아서서 그 빌딩을 바라보았어.

You have a right to **turn back** if you're scared.
겁나면 돌아갈 권리가 있어.

turn down
거절하다, 약하게 하다, 줄이다   *turn up 세게 하다, 키우다, 모습을 드러내다

I just had to **turn down** a job in Indonesia.
인도네시아에서의 일자리를 거절했어.

Tell the kids to **turn down** the TV. 애들보고 TV 소리 줄이라고 해.

I'm sure they'll **turn up.** 걔네들이 모습을 드러낼게 확실해.

turn in
제출하다, 돌려주다, 잠자리에 들다, 밀고하다   *turn into …로 바꾸다, …로 변하다

Please **turn in** your papers by tomorrow.
내일까지는 서류를 제출하도록 해요.

She went to the police to **turn in** a client.
걘 손님을 밀고하기 위해 경찰서에 갔어.

I had this room **turned into** a nursery.
난 이 방을 놀이방으로 바꾸었어.

Look at you! You **turned into** such a beautiful girl!
얘봐라! 너 정말 예쁘게 바뀌었어!

turn on
켜다, …가 흥미를 갖게 하다, 흥분시키다

You turn me on. 넌 내 맘에 쏙 들어. 넌 날 흥분시켜.

Whatever turns you on. 뭐든 좋을 대로.

I got very turned on by you. 너한테 나 많이 흥분했어.

turn off
끄다, 흥미를 못 느끼게 하다, 흥분을 가라앉히다

I forgot to **turn off** the bathroom light.
화장실 불 끄는 걸 깜박했어.

Turn off the lights before you come to bed.
자기 전에 불을 꺼라.

Do you want me to **turn off TV?** TV 끌까?

turn out
…으로 판명되다(prove) *turn out to be+명사 …로 판명되다

In the end it **turned out for** the best.
결국 그게 최선인 것으로 판명됐어.

Let's **turn out** all the lights and we'll just watch the movie!
불 다 끄고 영화보자!

She was engaged to a guy who **turned out to** be gay!
걘 약혼을 했는데 상대가 게이였대!

It turns out (that) S+V
…로 판명되다 *as it turns out 밝혀진 바와 같이

It turns out it was a mistake. 그건 실수였다고 판명됐어.

It turns out that he lied to us. 걔가 우리에게 거짓말 한 것으로 밝혀졌어.

turn out well [fine, bad]
잘되다, 잘못되다

I thought the turkey **turned out well,** although it is a little salty.
칠면조 요리가 좀 짜지만 잘됐어.

I just have a feeling that everything's going to **turn out fine.**
만사가 잘 될거라는 느낌이 들어.

turn over
(몸을) 뒤집다, 양도하다, 넘기다 *turn over to …에게 (…를) 넘기다

We **turned over** and faced each other. 우린 몸을 뒤집고 서로를 쳐다봤어.

When did you **turn it over?** 그걸 언제 넘겨준거야?

turn

understand

ⓥ 이해하다

---

understand — 이해하다

You don't **understand**. Get away from me. 넌 날 이해못해. 꺼져.
I don't think you **understand**. 너 이해못했을걸.
Do you **understand**? 알겠어?
Now I **understand**. 이제 알겠어.

---

understand sth[that] — …을 이해하다

I **understand** your frustration. 너의 좌절을 이해해.
You **understood** that? 이해했어?
I don't **understand** it. 왜 그런지 모르겠어.
You have to **understand** that. 넌 그걸 이해해야 돼.

---

understand sby — …을 이해하다

She **understood** you clearly? 걔가 널 분명히 이해한거야?
We **understand** each other. 우린 서로 이해해.

---

make oneself understood — 자기의 말을 남에게 이해시키다

I couldn't **make myself understood** in China.
난 중국에서 의사소통을 할 수가 없었어.

Be clear and **make yourself understood.**
명확하게 네 의사를 전달해봐.

---

understand (that)~ — …을 이해하다, …을 알고 있다

I **understand** you had a little talk with Sam.
네가 샘하고 얘기 좀 나눈 걸 알고 있어.

---

understand what[why, where~] — …을 이해하다

He **understood why** you did it.
걘 네가 왜 그랬는지 이해했어.

You can't possibly **understand how** I feel.
내 기분이 어떤지 넌 전혀 이해못해.

understand sby ~ing	…가 …하는 걸 이해하다
	I **understand** her not **going** to school. 걔가 학교가지 않는 걸 이해해.

be understood	이해되다
	Is that **understood?** 아시겠나요?
	I thought that **was understood.** 그거 이해된다고 생각했어.

do you understand?	알겠어?
	You have to clear the room, **do you understand?** 네 방을 치워야 돼, 알겠어?

misunderstand	오해하다
	I think that you just **misunderstood** her. 네가 걜 오해한 것 같아.
	I think you **misunderstood** what I was saying. 내가 한 말을 네가 오해한 것 같아.

understanding	이해, 오해(misunderstanding)
	There's been a **misunderstanding.** 오해가 있었어.
	There's got to be some **misunderstanding.** 뭔가 오해가 있었어.
	I thought we **had an understanding.** 우린 약속된 걸로 알았는데.

290 upset

ⓥ 속상하게 하다　ⓐ 속상한, 마음이 상한

be upset about~	…에 속상하다, 화나다
	I don't understand why you're **so upset about** this. 네가 이 문제로 왜 그렇게 속상해하는지 이해가 안돼.

I'm so upset that~	…에 너무 속상해
	I'm so upset that you forgot our anniversary. 당신이 결혼 기념일을 잊어버려서 너무 속상해.

understand

get upset	속상하다, 화나다
	She's likely to **get upset** about this.
	걔는 이거에 화를 낼 것 같아.
upset ~	…을 걱정하게 하다, 화나게 하다, (계획 등을) 망치다
	Do yourself a favor. Don't let him **upset** you.
	네 자신을 생각해야지. 걔 신경 건드리지마.
upset sb's stomach	배탈나게 하다
	The Indian curry **upset Lana's stomach.**
	인도 카레라이스를 먹고 레이나는 배탈이 났어.

291 use

v 사용하다, 이용하다, 소비하다   **n** 사용, 이용, 효과

use one's head [brain]	머리를 쓰다, 생각을 해보다
	Use your head! How come you fell for it twice?
	머리를 써! 어떻게 두 번이나 넘어가?
	I expect you to **use your brain** this time.
	이번에는 머리쓰길 바래.
get[be] used to~	…에 익숙하다
	I**'m getting used to** driving at night. 밤에 운전하는데 적응하고 있어.
	You have to **get used to** it. 적응해야지.
	You'll **get used to** it. 곧 익숙해 질거야.
be used to+V	…하는데 사용되다
	A lawn mower **is used to** cut grass. 잔디깎는 기계는 풀을 베는데 사용돼.
used to~	…하곤 했어
	We **used to** work together. 우리 함께 일했었어.
	I **used to** be just like you. 나도 전엔 너 같았어.

use up	다 써버리다
	The budget's **almost used up**. 예산이 거의 소진됐어.
	My wife **used up** all my money. 아내가 돈을 다 써버렸어.
can[could] use~	…이 필요하다
	I **can use** a Coke. 콜라 좀 마셔야겠어.
	I **could use** a little help here. 여기 누가 도와주었으면 해.
make (good or bad) use of	…을 이용하다
	They **made a good use of** extra money. 걔네들은 여분의 돈을 잘 활용했어.
	The children **made good use of** the toys they got. 얘들은 받은 장난감을 갖고 잘 이용했어.
put ~ to (good) use	이용하다
	I think it'd be better if we **put** it all **to good use.** 그걸 잘 이용한다면 더 좋을 것 같아.
be of use	유용하다
	I have some information that will **be of use** to you. 네게 유용할 정보가 좀 있어.
It's no use ~ing	해봤자 소용없다
	It's no use! 아무 소용없어!
	Come on, **it's no use** fighting. 이봐, 싸워봤자 소용없어.
What's the use of ~ing?	…해봤자 무슨 소용이 있어?
	What's the use of asking your boss for a raise? 네 사장한테 급여올려달라고 해봤자 무슨 소용이 있어?

visit

v. 방문하다 **n.** 방문, 구경

visit

방문하다

I'd love to ask you in, but my sister**'s visiting.**
들어오라고 하고 싶지만 누이가 방문해서요.

Hi! We**'re visiting!** 안녕! 우리 왔어!

visit sby

…을 방문하다

I**'m just visiting** my good friend Mike.
친한 친구 마이크를 방문하는 중야.

We have to go **visit** John in the hospital.
병원에 존 병문안하러 가야 돼

visit somewhere

…을 방문하다

Excuse me, I have to **visit** the ladies' room.
미안하지만 화장실에 가야 돼요.

Have you ever **visited** New York?
뉴욕에 가본 적 있어?

come (and or to) visit

방문하러 오다

You should **come visit.** 놀러 와.

You're going to **come and visit** me? 놀러 올거지?

Can you **come and visit** us for dinner tonight?
오늘밤 와서 저녁 먹을래?

pay[make, give] a visit to

…을 방문하다

We **paid a visit to** the gallery. 우린 화랑을 방문했어.

You're going to **return our visit** soon? 곧 우리 집에도 들릴거죠?

be on a visit

방문중이다

My mother**'s here on a visit.** She's leaving tomorrow.
어머니가 방문중이셔. 내일 가실거야.

Have you **been on a visit to** Japan yet?
일본 방문해봤어?

have a visitor
방문객이 있다

You **had some visitors.** 방문객이 있었어요.

You **have a visitor** at the front desk. 안내데스크에 손님 오셨어요.

293 wait
v 기다리다, 봉사하다 n 기다림, 대기

wait for
…을 기다리다 *wait for sby[sth] …을 기다리다

Everyone**'s waiting for** us. 다들 우릴 기다리고 있어.

I**'ve been waiting for** this a long time. 이거 오랫동안 기다렸어.

I**'m waiting for** a call from her. 걔 전화 기다리고 있어.

wait for sby to +V
…가 …하는 것을 기다리다 *wait to+동사 …하는 것을 기다리다

We**'re all still waiting for** someone **to** come.
우리 모두 다른 누가 오기를 기다리고 있어.

wait until[till]
…(할) 때까지 기다리다 *뒤에는 시간명사나 S+V가 이어진다.

We'll **wait until** next weekend. 우린 다음주까지 기다릴거야.

We can't **wait until** Tuesday. We're having a party tonight.
화요일까지 못 기다려, 오늘밤에 파티가 있어.

wait a week
일주일간 기다리다

Why did you **wait 2 hours** out there?
왜 거기서 2시간이나 기다렸어?

I just don't **wait too long.** Okay?
더 오래는 못 기다려, 알았어?

I can wait+시간
…동안 기다릴 수 있어

I **can wait** a bit longer. 좀 더 기다릴 수 있어.

I've been waiting+시간
…동안 기다렸어

I**'ve been waiting** four hours for you to show up.
네가 오기까지 4시간이나 기다렸어.

visit

wait outside [inside]	밖[안]에서 기다리다 *wait here[there] 여기서[거기서] 기다리다	
	Wait out here. I'll be right back. 여기서 기다려. 곧 돌아올게.	
	Okay, **wait there,** I'll be over in a second. 좋아, 거기서 기다려. 곧 그리로 갈게.	
Wait a minute	잠깐만	
	Wait a minute. Hold still. 잠깐 그대로 있어.	
	Wait a minute. What are you talking about? 잠깐만. 너 무슨 말 하는거야?	
	Wait a minute. I forgot something in the car. 잠깐. 차에다 뭘 놓고 내렸어.	
can't wait to +V	몹시 …하고 싶어하다(=I'm dying to+V)	
	I can't wait to do it. 지금 당장이라고 하고 싶어.	
	I can't wait to tell you this. 네게 이걸 빨리 말하고 싶어.	
	I cannot wait to get to New York. 어서 뉴욕에 가고 싶어.	
I can't wait for sby to+동사	…가 …하기를 몹시 바라다	
	I can't wait for you **to** meet my grandma. 네가 빨리 내 할머니를 만나기를 바래.	
~ can[can't] wait	급해[급하지 않아]	
	This **can wait.** 그건 나중에 해도 돼.	
	That **can't wait.** 이건 급해.	
	The rest **can wait.** 나머지는 천천히 해도 돼.	
	Can't that **wait?** 뒤로 미룰 수 없어요?	
	Can't this **wait** until morning? 내일 아침까지 미룰 수 없어?	
wait one's turn	…의 차례를 기다리다	
	Well, you'll have to **wait your turn.** 글쎄, 차례를 기다려야 돼요.	
	Okay, we'll **wait our turn.** 좋아, 우리 차례를 기다리지.	
keep sby waiting	…을 기다리게 하다	
	Sorry to have **kept you waiting** so long. 그렇게 오래 기다리게 해서 미안.	
	I'm so sorry to **keep you waiting.** 기다리게 해서 정말 미안해.	
	Come on now, don't **keep me waiting.** 이봐, 나 오래 기다리게 하지마.	

wait and see	관망하다
	Let's **wait and see** how things go. 일이 어떻게 돼가는지 지켜보자.

wait on	도착하기를 기다리다, 시중들다
	We **were waiting on** you to check the desk. 우린 너희들이 와서 책상을 확인해보기를 기다렸어.

wait up	자지 않고 기다리다
	Don't **wait up.** 자지 않고 기다려.

294 wake
v. 깨우다, 일어나다

wake sby (up)	…을 깨우다
	Did I **wake** you? 내가 널 깨웠어? Did the TV **wake you up?** TV 때문에 일어난거야? I hope I didn't **wake you up.** 내가 잠을 깨게 하지 않기를 바래.

wake up	일어나다
	I don't want to **wake up** early. 일찍 일어나기 싫어. She doesn't want to **wake up** alone. 걘 혼자서 일어나는 걸 싫어해.

wake up for	대비하다
	Just a sec, give me a minute to **wake up for** this. 잠깐만, 이거 대비할 시간 조금만 줘.

wake-up call	모닝콜
	She just got her usual **wake-up call.** 걘 모닝콜을 방금 받았어. I'd like to request a **wake-up call.** 모닝콜을 부탁해요.

walk

v. 걷다, 산보하다

walk

걷다

She likes to **walk** in the street.
걔는 거리를 걷는 걸 좋아해.

Is it safe to **walk** the street at night?
밤에 거리를 걷는 게 안전해?

walk sby to~

…와 …까지 함께 걸어가다, (개 등을) 산보시키다

You don't have to **walk me home.**
집까지 안 데려다 줘도 되는데.

He **walked me to** the subway.
걘 지하철까지 걸어서 데려다 줬어.

walk (up, over) to

…로 걸어가다

Ron **walked up to** the door and knocked.
론은 문으로 다가가서 노크를 했어.

I **walked to** her and kissed her.
난 걔한테 걸어가서 키스를 했어.

walk around

돌아다니다

Did you enjoy **walking around** today?
오늘 둘러보는 거 좋았어?

I'm out **walking around** the neighborhood.
난 나가서 집 주변을 돌아다니고 있어.

walk away (from)

(…에서) 가버리다

Don't **walk away from** me. 내게서 떠나지마.

You just **walked away?** What's wrong with you?
그냥 가버렸다고? 너 왜그래?

walk away [off] with

…을 가지고 가버리다

Someone **walked off with** my new cellular phone.
누가 내 새로운 휴대폰을 가져가 버렸어

walk in(to)
걸어 들어오다

I was so upset. I **walked into** my office.
난 화가 나서 내 사무실로 들어갔어.

walk down
…을 걸어내려가다

I usually **walk up and down** the stairs instead of taking elevators.
난 보통 엘리베이터 대신 계단을 오르내려.

walk along
…을 따라 걷다

We **walked along** the hallway without saying a word.
우린 한 마디도 하지 않고 복도를 따라 걸어갔어.

walk out (of)
(…에서) 걸어나가다

I'll **walk out with** you. 너랑 같이 나갈거야.

I was sweating when I **walked out of** the police station.
경찰서에서 나올 때 진땀을 흘렸어.

walk out on
…을 떠나 버리다, …을 버리다

She **walked out on** her husband.
걘 남편을 떠나 버렸어.

You'd better find one who won't **walk out on** you.
널 떠나 버리지 않을 사람을 찾아라.

walk (all) over
맘대로 좌지우지하다

He's **walking all over** me. 걘 날 무시해.

She'll do whatever you want. You can just **walk all over** her.
걘 네가 원하는거 다 할거야. 맘대로 해도 돼.

walk with
…와 함께 걷다

Oh, wait. I'll **walk with** you. 잠깐 기다려. 너와 함께 걸을게.

Why don't you let me **walk with** you? 너랑 같이 걸어 갈게.

walk sby through
…을 안내해주다, 단계적으로 알려주다

I'll **walk you through** it. 자세히 안내해 드리겠습니다.

You guys just **walk through** the door. 너희들은 문으로 걸어가라.

walk on air
무척 기뻐하다

I'm **walking on air.** 날 듯이 기뻐.

Steve loves me. I **am walking on air.** 스티브가 날 사랑해. 너무 기뻐.

walking distance	걸어서 갈 수 있는 거리
	Is it within **walking distance**? 걸어서 가도 돼나요?
	That's three miles from here. That's **walking distance**. 여기서 3마일 거리야. 걸어서 갈만한 거리야.

want

v. 원하다, 필요하다, …을 하고 싶다

want sby[sth]	…을 원하다 *(Do you) Want+명사~? …가 필요해?
	The boss **wants** you in his office now. 사장님이 사무실로 지금 오래.
	Do you **want** some more? 더 들래?
	Do you **want** a mirror? 거울줄까?
want to+V	…을 하고 싶어
	I **want to** go to a movie tonight. 오늘 밤에 영화를 보러 가고 싶어.
	I **want to** talk to you (about that). 얘기 좀 하자고.
	I **don't want to** buy trouble. 말썽 일으키긴 싫어.
want sby to~	…가 …하기를 바래
	I **want** you **to** tell me the truth. 난 네가 내게 진실을 말해주기 원해.
	Do you **want** me **to** stay with you? 내가 함께 있을까?
I want you to know (that)~	…하니 그리 알아, 알아주길 바래
	I just want you to know I love you. 내가 널 사랑한다는 걸 알아주길 바래.
	I want you to know I didn't used to be like this. 난 예전에 지금과 같지 않았다는 걸 알아줘.
	I want you to know how sorry I am. 내가 얼마나 미안한 지 알아줬으면 해.
I just wanted to~	단지 …을 하고 싶었을 뿐이야
	I just wanted to be with you. 난 단지 너와 함께 있고 싶었어.

I just wanted to say~

단지 …라고 말하고 싶었을 뿐이야

I just wanted to say thank you. 단지 네가 고맙다고 하고 싶었을 뿐이야.

Well **I just wanted to say** I'm sorry. 미안하다고 말하고 싶었어.

I just wanted to make sure S+V

단지 …을 확인하고 싶었을 뿐이야

I just wanted to make sure that you were doing OK.
단지 네가 괜찮은지 확인하고 싶을 뿐이었어.

I just wanted to ask you if S+V

단지 …인지 물어보고 싶었을 뿐이야

I just wanted to ask you if you'd go out with me.
나와 데이트를 할건지 물어보고 싶었어.

want sby[sth]+형용사[pp, 부사]

…을 …한 상태로 되기를 원하다

I **want** you right here. 당장 이리로 와.

I **want** it on my desk. 그거 내 책상에 올려놔.

When I ask you to do something, I **want** it done!
내가 뭐를 하라고 했을 때는 다 마치라는 얘기야!

want sby[sth] back

되찾기를 바라다, 돌려받기를 원하다

I **want** this **back**. 이거 돌려줘.

I miss my wife. I **want** her **back**. 아내가 그리워. 돌아오길 바래.

don't want anything~

전혀 …하고 싶지 않다

I **don't want anything from** you.
너한테 바라는게 아무 것도 없어.

I **don't want anything to** upset Betty tonight.
오늘 밤 절대로 베티를 속상하게 하고 싶지 않아.

I **don't want anything to** do with you!
너랑은 절대로 아무 것도 하고 싶지 않아. 난 너하고 손뗐어!

make sby want to~

…가 …하고 싶어지게 만들다

He **makes me want to** be a better man.
걘 내가 더 좋은 사람이 되고 싶게 만들어.

Just watching you **makes me want to** have sex with you.
널 바라만 봐도 너랑 섹스하고 싶어져.

Thinking of you **makes me want to** puke.
널 생각만 해도 토하고 싶어.

may[might] want to~

…하는 게 좋을거야

Well, you **might want to** get used to it.
저기, 그거에 익숙하는 게 좋을거야.

want

wouldn't want to	…하는 게 좋은 생각 같지 않아 **I wouldn't want to** spend tonight with you. 너랑 저녁을 같이 보내는 건 좋은 생각같지 않아. **You wouldn't want to** see me lose my job, would you? 내가 실직하는 걸 보고 싶지 않지, 그지?
You don't want to~	…하지 않는 게 나아 **You don't want to** know. 모르는게 나아.
All I want is +명사	내가 바라는 것은 …가 다야 **All I want is** my freedom. 내가 바라는 건 내 자유뿐이야.
All I wanted was (for sby) to+V	내가 원했던 건 (…가) …하는 것이었어 **All I wanted was to** meet a nice girl. 내가 바랬던 건 멋진 여자를 만나는거였어. **All I wanted was** for you **to** like me. 내가 바랬던 건 네가 날 좋아하는거였어. **All I want to do is** help her. 내가 하고 싶은 건 걜 도와주는거야.
All I want to know is what [when~] S+V	내가 꼭 알고 싶은 건 …야 **All I want to know is** how fast you run. 내가 알고 싶은 건 네가 얼마나 빨리 달리냐는거야.
What I want to know is what [when~] S+V	내가 알고 싶은 건 …야 **What I want to know is,** did you play computer games? 내가 알고 싶은 건 네가 어제 컴퓨터 게임을 했냐는거야?
The last thing I want to do is+V	내가 가장 하기 싫은 일은 …이다 **The last thing I want to do is to** make you feel uncomfortable. 내가 가장 하기 싫은 건 널 불편하게 만드는거야.
be what I wanted~	내가 바라던 것이다 This[That] **is what I want(ed).** 내가 원하는[던] 거야. This[That] **is what I want(ed).** 내가 원하는[던] 게 아냐. I'll tell you **what I want.** 내가 원하는 걸 말해줄게. Here**'s what I want** you to do. 네가 했으면 바라는 건 이거야. That**'s what I wanted** to hear! 그게 바로 내가 듣고 싶었던거야!

What do you want (me) to~?

뭐하고 싶어?, 내가 뭘 하길 바래?

What do you want to eat for lunch today?
오늘 점심으로 뭘 먹고 싶어?

What do you want me to say? 무슨 말을 하라는거야?

What do you want from me? 나보고 어쩌라는거야?

Where do you want (me) to+V?

어디에서 …할래?, 어디에서 내가 …할까?

Where do you want to go? 어디에 갈건데?

When do you want (me) to+V?

언제 …할래?, 언제 내가 …할까?

When do you want me to start? 내가 언제 시작할까?

Why do you want (me) to~?

왜 …하고 싶어?, 왜 내가 …하길 바래?

Why do you want to work for me?
왜 내 밑에서 일하려고 해?

Why do you want me to have a date with other men?
왜 내가 다른 남자랑 데이트하길 바래?

How do you want (me) to+V?

어떻게 …하길 바래?

How do you want to pay me? 어떻게 지불할거야?

Who do you want (me) to+V?

누구를 …하고 싶어?, 내가 누구를 …하길 바래?

Who do you want me to follow? 내가 누굴 따라가라고?

Who wants to +V?

누가 …하고 싶어?

Who wants to go first? 누가 가장 먼저 가고 싶어?

If you want to~, do~

…을 원한다면 …해라

If you want to know about girl stuff, ask Allan.
여자 얘기라면 앨런에게 물어봐.

If you want to~ you've got to [you have to]~

…을 원한다면 …해야 한다

You better get out of town **if you want to** stay safe.
안전하고 싶으면 꺼지는게 좋아.

If you want to~ I will~

…을 원한다면 내가 …할게

If you want to stay, **I'm not going to** stop you.
더 있겠다면 막지 않을게.

424

want

if you want (to)	원한다면
	You can come with us, **if you want to.** 원한다면 우리랑 같이 가.
	I could even help you study **if you want.** 원한다면 공부도 도와줄 수 있어.
want in	들어가고 싶다, 가입하고 싶다
	You **want in?** 들어올래?
want out	나가고 싶다, 빠지고 싶다
	You **want out?** 나가고 싶어?
	I just **wanted out.** 난 그냥 빠지고(끼고) 싶었어.
be wanted on the telephone	…에게 전화가 오다
	You **are wanted on the telephone.** 너한테 전화왔어.

 297

warn

v 경고하다 **n** 경고

I should[have to] warn you	내 말해두지만
	All right, but **I should warn you,** I'm not going. 좋아, 하지만 내 말해두는데 난 안가.
	I have to warn you. This might hurt a little bit. 내 말해두는데 이거 좀 아플지 몰라.
I('ve) warned you	난 경고했어
	I warn you, it'll be totally boring. 미리 말해두는데 정말 지겨울거야.
	I've warned you. If anything happens to her, you're responsible. 난 경고했어. 걔한테 무슨 일 생기면 네 책임이야.
warn sby	…에게 경고[주의]하다
	I'm not going to **warn** you again. 네게 다시 경고하지 않을거야.
	Fine! Thank you for **warning** me. 좋아! 네가 경고해줘서 고마워.

warn sby about[of] sth

…에게 …을 경고하다

Didn't I **warn** you **about** calling me names?
날 욕하지말라고 경고하지 않했던가?

I **warned** her **about** those guys.
저 놈들 조심하라고 걔한테 경고했어.

warn sby that~

…에게 …을 경고하다

The workers all **warned** me you were picky, boss.
직원들이 모두 사장님이 까다롭다고 하던대요.

My lawyer **warned** me **that** you were going to try this.
내 변호사가 네가 이걸 시도할거라고 내게 경고했어.

give sby a warning

…에게 경고하다

I just can't believe that Mike didn't **give me any warning.**
마이크가 내게 아무런 경고도 하지 않다니 믿을 수 없어.

298 wash

v. 씻다 n. 씻기, 세탁

wash (sth)

(…을) 씻다

I'm going to **wash** the dishes that are still in the sink.
싱크대에 있는거 설거지 할게.

Did you **wash** your hands? 손 씻었어?

wash away

깨끗이 씻다

The storm will **wash away** the dirt on your car.
폭풍은 네 차의 먼지들을 다 쓸어갈거야.

wash off

씻어내다

Uh, most of the ink **is washed off.**
어, 대부분의 잉크는 씻어졌어.

Wash off our hands before coming to dinner.
손씻고 저녁먹으러 와라.

wash out	지치게 하다
	I am all washed out. 난 완전히 기운이 소진됐어.

wash up	씻다, 화장실을 사용하다, 실패하다
	Where can I **wash up**? 화장실이 어디죠?
	It's lunchtime. You go **wash up.** 점심 시간야. 가서 손 씻어라.
	The plans **were all washed up!** 그 계획들은 다 실패했어!

watch
v 지켜보다, 주시하다

watch ~+V	…가 …하는 것을 보다 *watch A ~ing
	I want to **watch** Heather act in the play.
	헤더가 연극에서 연기하는 걸 보고 싶어서.

watch one's back	조심하다 *watch one's mouth 말조심하다
	I'm just telling you to **watch your back.**
	난 단지 조심하라고 말하는거야.

Watch yourself!	조심해! *Watch it! 조심해!
	I'm going down. **Watch yourself.** 내가 내려가니까 조심해.

watch out	조심하다
	Watch out! There's ice on the ground.
	조심해! 바닥에 얼음있어

watch out for	(무슨 일이 일어날지) 조심하다, 돌보다 = watch for
	Watch out for my wife. She's on a tear.
	네 아내를 잘 지켜봐. 흥청거리고 있어.

way

n. 길, 방식, 방법 **ad.** 훨씬

get[have] one's way	자기 식대로 하다 You always **get your way.** 넌 늘 네 멋대로야.
have a way of ~ing	짜증나게 하는 특별한 재주가 있다 You **have a way of** asking questions that beg more questions. 넌 더 많은 질문을 하게 되는 질문들을 해.
have a way with~	…을 잘 다루다 You sure **have a way with** words. 넌 정말 말솜씨가 좋아.
know one's way around~	어떤 장소나 행동을 잘 알다 I **know my way around** New York City. 난 뉴욕시를 잘 알고 있어.
There's no way~	…할리가 없다 **There's no way** you're going to talk me into this. 날 설득해 그걸 하게 할 수는 없어.
be out of the [one's] way	방해하지 않다 You will have the sense to **stay out of my way** this time. 이번에는 날 방해하지 않을 양식은 있겠지.
be on the [one's] way	가는 중이다 I**'m on my way** now. 지금 가고 있는 중이야. I**'m just on my way** out to meet a client. 고객과 만나러 막 나가려는 참 이거든요.
on the way to~	…하는 길에 This morning my car broke down **on the way to** work. 오늘 아침에 출근 길에 차가 고장났어.

way

by the way
그건 그렇고 *by the way S+V …하는 방식에

She's annoyed **by the way that** Nick is acting.
걘 닉의 행동방식에 짜증이 났어.

Love it. You look awesome, **by the way.**
좋아. 어쨌든 너 굉장히 멋져 보여.

all the way
내내 *go all the way 갈데까지 가다

We're behind you **all the way.** 우리는 너를 끝까지 지지할거야.

in a way
어떤 면에서는, 어느 정도는

Well, I guess that's a relief **in a way.**
저기, 어떤식으로든 다행인 것 같아.

one way or another
어떻게 해서든

One way or another, you got to pay what you owe.
어떻게 해서든 빚진 건 갚아야 돼.

way~
아주(very)

I was partying **way** too much last week.
난 지난주에 너무 즐기고 놀았어.

 301

wear

v. 옷을 입고 있다, 닳다, 낡다 **n.** 착용, 사용, 닳음

wear+옷,안경 등
입다, 쓰다

That shirt you**'re wearing** has gone out of style.
네가 입고 있는 옷은 한물간거야.

wear+화장품
바르다, 칠하다 *wear make-up 화장하다

She'**s wearing** a lot of makeup.
걔는 화장을 떡칠해.

wear out one's welcome
너무 오래있어 폐를 끼치다

I wouldn't want to **wear out my welcome.**
넘 오래 머물러 미움받기 싫은데.

be worn out	지치다, 뻗다
	The poor man, he **was all worn out.** 그 불쌍한 사람은 완전히 뻗어버렸어.

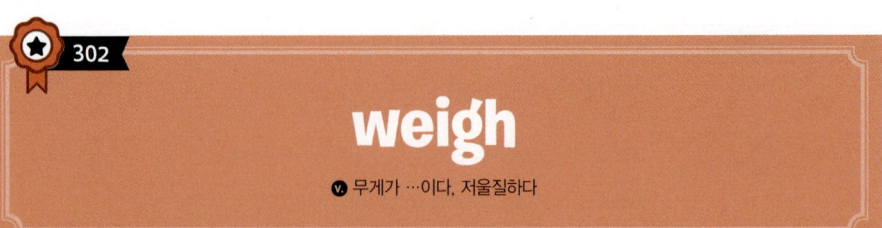

302 weigh
v. 무게가 …이다, 저울질하다

weigh+숫자	무게가 …이다
	Oh, please, you **weigh** 90 pounds. 제발 그러지마, 너 몸무게가 90파운드잖아. I **weigh** 74 kilograms now. 지금 74킬로 나가.
weigh+물품	무게를 재다
	Let's **weigh** the diamond to see how heavy it is. 얼마나 무거운지 다이아몬드의 무게를 재보자.
weigh sth	고려하다
	Henry needs some time to **weigh** his options. 헨리는 자기의 선택권을 고려할 시간이 필요해.
gain weight	살이 찌다(= put on)
	This is why she couldn't **gain weight.** 이것이 걔가 살이 찔 수가 없는 이유이야.
lose weight	살이 빠지다
	Tim doesn't want you to **lose weight,** does he? 팀은 네가 살이 빠지는 걸 원하지 않지, 그지?

welcome

v. 환영하다 **a.** …해도 좋은 **n.** 환영

Welcome home
집에 온걸 환영해 *Welcome back 돌아와서 환영해

Welcome home. We've really missed you.
어서 와. 정말 보고 싶었다고.

Welcome to~
…에 온걸 환영해

Welcome to our Christmas party. May I take your coat?
크리스마스 파티에 온걸 환영해. 코트받아줄까?

You're welcome
천만에 *You're more than welcome 천만에 말씀

You're welcome. I mean it, thank you for everything.
천만의 말씀. 정말야. 모든게 다 고마워.

be welcome to +V
마음대로 …해

I have some work to do, but you**'re welcome to** stay.
할 일이 좀 있지만 편히 있어도 돼.

give ~ welcome to~
…을 환영하다 *get ~ welcome 환영을 받다

The audience **gave** a warm **welcome to** the speaker.
청중은 연사를 따뜻하게 환영했어.

overstay one's welcome
너무 오래 머물다

He **overstayed his welcome** and upset his hosts.
걘 너무 오래 머물러 초대한 사람을 불편하게 했어.

well
adv. 잘, 좋게, 철저히　**a.** 건강한, 상태가 좋은

as well
…도
We have been pretty busy **as well.** 우리도 그동안 꽤 바빴는 걸 뭐.

as well as
…뿐만 아니라
She speaks English **as well as** you.
걘 너만큼 영어를 잘 해.

be doing well
잘하고 있다
I know the feeling. My team **isn't doing well** either.
그 심정 알겠어. 내가 좋아하는 팀도 역시 잘 못해.

Well done
잘했다
Well done. It tasted great. 잘했어. 아주 맛이 좋아.

get well (soon)
(곧) 건강해지다
I hope you **get well** soon. 곧 낫기를 바래.

may[might] as well+V
…하는게 낫다
We **might as well** just go to sleep.
우린 자러가는 편이 나아.

whole
a. 전체의, 모든　**n.** 전부

the whole story
자초지종, 전모
Can't wait to hear **the whole story.**
이야기 전말을 몹시 듣고 싶어.

well

the whole thing	모든 것
	She was too serious about **the whole thing.** 걘 모든 일에 전부 진지했었어.

as a whole	일반적으로, 전반적으로
	This artwork looks good, **as a whole.** 이 예술품은 전반적으로 좋아 보여.

on the whole	대체로, 전반적으로
	You would say that **on the whole** she's a good employee. 전반적으로 볼 때 그 여자가 유능한 직원이라는 말을 하고 싶은 거죠.

306
win
v. 이기다, 따다

Who won~ ?	누가 …에서 이겼어?
	Who won the game last night? 지난밤에 누가 이겼어?

win+경기, 전쟁	…에서 이기다, 승리하다
	Do you really think he'll **win** the race? 정말 그 사람이 경주에서 이길 거라고 보니?
	You can't **win** them all. 항상 이길 수는 없지.

win+메달, 상금, 복권	…을 얻다, 당첨되다
	How was your weekend? You **win** the lottery? 주말 어땠어? 로또 당첨됐어?

You win!	네가 이겼어!, 내가 졌어!, 그래 그렇게 하자!
	It's over. **You win.** 다 끝났어. 내가 졌어.

307 wind

n. 바람 **v.** 감다

get wind of sth — …를 소문으로 듣다
I think so. I just **got wind of** it. 그럴 걸. 풍문으로 들었어.

break wind — 방귀뀌다(fart)
She **broke wind** and really embarrassed herself.
그녀는 방귀를 뀌고 정말 창피해했어.

wind up — 어떤 상황에 처하게 되다, 마무리짓다
Who knows? Maybe we'll **wind up** getting married someday.
누가 알겠어? 언젠가 우리가 결혼하게 될지 몰라.

308 wish

v. …이면 좋겠다, 기원하다, 바라다 **n.** 바람, 의도, 소망

wish to~ — …하고 싶다
We **wish to** apologize for the late arrival of this train.
기차연착을 사죄드립니다.
Do you **wish to** say anything, John? 존, 뭐 할 말 있습니까?

wish sby sth — …에게 …을 빌다
I **wish** you a Merry Christmas! 성탄절 즐겁게 보내!
I have to go. **Wish** me luck! 나 가야 돼. 행운을 빌어줘!
I just stopped by to **wish** you good luck. 행운을 빌어줄려고 들렸어.

I wish I was~ — 내가 …라면 좋겠어
I **wish you were** here. 같이 왔더라면 정말 좋았을텐데.

wind

I wish I had +명사

내게 …가 있으면 좋겠어

I wish I had a lot of money. 돈이 많았으면 좋을텐데.

I wish I could +V

내가 …을 할 수 있다면 좋겠어

I wish I could stay longer. 더 남아 있으면 좋을텐데.

I wish I had +pp

…했더라면 좋았을텐데 *wish I hadn't+pp …하지 않았다면 좋았을텐데

I wish I had been married to you. 너와 결혼했더라면 좋았을텐데.

I wish I had told you before. 너한테 전에 얘기했더라면 좋았을텐데.

I wish I could but I can't ~

그러고 싶지만 안돼

I wish I could but I can't. I have much work to do.
그러고 싶지만 안돼. 할 일이 너무 많아.

I wish I could +동사, but ~

…하고 싶지만 …해

I wish I could come, but I'm busy on Friday.
가고 싶지만, 금요일날 바빠.

I wish I could help you, but I can't.
도와주고 싶지만 그럴 수가 없어.

I wish sby would

…가 …했으면 해 *I wish you would 네가 그러길 바래

I wish you wouldn't say like that.
네가 그런 식으로 말 안했으면 해.

Honey, **I wish you would** get over her.
자기야, 네가 걜 잊었으면 해.

I wish he would just tell me the truth.
걔가 내게 사실을 말해주었으면 해.

if you wish

원한다면(as you wish)

We can leave now, **if you wish.**
네가 원하면 우린 지금 떠날 수 있어.

Best wishes on

…을 축하해

Best wishes on the birth of your first son.
첫아들을 낳은 것을 축하해.

make a wish

소원을 빌다

Make a wish when you blow out the birthday candles.
생일촛불을 끌 때 소원을 빌어.

wonder

v. 궁금해하다, …인가 생각하다, 놀라다 **n.** 경이

wonder about	…을 궁금해하다 That is how it's done. **I was wondering about** that. 저렇게 하는거구나. 궁금했었어. There's something I**'ve always wondered about**. 내가 항상 궁금해하는게 있어.
I wonder what [how, if] S+V	…일까, …할까 **I wonder why** she called. 왜 걔가 전화했는지 모르겠어. **I wonder why** she broke up with me. 걔가 왜 나랑 헤어졌는지 모르겠어.
I was wondering if I[you] could +V	좀 …할 수 있을까요[해주시겠어요] **I was wondering if I could** take tomorrow off? 내일 쉬어도 돼요? **I was wondering if I could** ask you something? 혹 뭐 좀 물어봐도 될까요?
It's a wonder (that)~	…은 이상한 일이다 **It's a wonder** he didn't go to work yesterday. 걔가 어제 출근하지 않은 건 이상한 일이야.
(It's) No wonder (that)~	…은 당연하다 **No wonder.** 당연하지. **No wonder** they're getting so fat. 걔네들이 그렇게 살찔 만도 하군.
I'm just wondering	그냥 물어봤어 What's your job? **I was just wondering.** 직업이 뭐야? 그냥 궁금해서. **I was just wondering.** I'm sorry, forget it. 그냥 물어봤어. 미안, 잊어버려.

word

n. 단어, 말, 약속, 소문

have a word with sby	…와 얘기를 나누다 *want a word with sb …와 얘기하기를 원하다	
	I need to **have a word with** the manager. 매니저와 얘기를 나누어야겠어.	
give sby one's word	약속하다	
	I **give you my word.** I will always be here. 내 약속하지만 항상 여기 옆에 있을게.	
keep one's word	약속을 지키다	
	I'm going to do my best to **keep my word.** 내 약속을 지키려고 최선을 다할거야.	
have one's word	약속을 지키다	
	I won't bother you again. **You have my word.** 널 다시는 괴롭히지 않을게. 내 약속할게.	
have words with sby	언쟁하다	
	The drunken man **had words with** the cop. 만취한 사람이 경찰과 말다툼했어.	
in a word	한마디로 말해서	
	In a word, yes. 한마디로 말해서 그렇지.	
in other words	다시 말해서	
	In other words, you'll be making more money? 달리 말해서 넌 돈을 더 벌게 될거라고?	
put in a good word for sby	좋은 말을 해주다	
	I **put in a good word for** you. 난 널 위해 좋게 말해줬어.	
Take my word for it	내 말을 믿어줘	
	You just have to **take my word for it.** Do not trust her. 너 그거 내 말을 믿어야 돼. 걔 믿지말고.	

Word is that~	…라는 소문이 있어
	Word is that you have separated from your wife. 네가 아내와 별거했다는 소문이 있어.

mum's the word	비밀이야
	Mum's the word until we announce the results. 우리가 그 결과를 발표할 때까지는 비밀이야.

311 work

ⓥ 일하다, 근무하다, 제대로 움직이다, 잘 진행되다, 효과있다

work for	…에서 일하다 *I work for[at, in] …에서 일해
	Who do you **work for**? 어디서 일해?
	I **work for** a government agency. 정부기관에서 일해.
	I **work for** Mr. James. 제임스 씨 회사에서 일해.

have a lot of work to do	할 일이 많다 *have (got) a lot of[much] work to do 해야 할 일이 많다
	Can I go? I've got a **lot of work to do**. 가도 돼? 할 일이 많아서.
	I **have so much work to do** on the case. 그 건으로 해야 할 일이 많아.
	I **have some work to do** in my office. 사무실에서 할 일이 좀 있어.

have a lot of work left	할 일이 많이 남아있다
	I've got three or four hours more **work left**. 한 세네 시간 일 더 해야 돼.
	How much **work** do you **have left** now? 얼마나 일이 남았지?

word

work hard
열심히 일하다 *work hard (to+V) (…하려고) 열심히 일하다

It's been a long day. We've worked hard today.
오늘 참 힘들었어. 오늘 열심히 일했어.

You'd better work harder. 너 좀 더 열심히 해라.

I'm working hard to become a better man.
좋은 사람이 되려고 열심히 하고 있어.

work around the clock
무척 열심히 일하다

We're working around the clock.
최선을 다하고 있어요.

work overtime
야근하다

I have to work overtime today.
오늘 야근해야 돼.

Are you working overtime tonight?
오늘 야근해야 돼?

work late
야근하다

I don't work late tomorrow night.
내일 밤에는 늦게까지 일 안해.

work+시간
…동안 일해 *be on a five-day work 주 5일제 근무이다

I get to work 60 hours a week for the same salary.
같은 월급받고 주 60시간을 일해야 돼.

work nights [days]
주간[야간] 근무이다

I'm a waitress. Work nights. 난 웨이트리스야. 저녁근무해.

after work
퇴근 후

I'll be home right after work. 퇴근 후에 바로 집으로 갈거야.

Hey, what are you doing after work? 야, 퇴근 후에 뭐해?

at work
직장에서 *be at work 근무중이다

I'm supposed to be at work all night.
난 밤새 근무해야 돼.

work
제대로 돌아가다

It works! 제대로 되네!, 효과가 있네!

It doesn't work. 제대로 안돼, 그렇겐 안돼.

That's not how it works. 그렇게는 안돼.

make sth work
…을 돌아가게 하다 (get sth to work)

There are ways to **make this work.** 이걸 작동하게 할 방법이 있을거야.

~ works for me [you]
내게[너에게] …이 괜찮다, 좋다

It **works for** me. 난 괜찮아, 찬성이야.

Does it[that] **work for** you? 네 생각은 어때?, 너도 좋아?

Does this afternoon **work for** you? 오후 괜찮으세요?

work one's way to[through]
뼈빠지게 …하다

He's **working his head off.** 그는 뼈빠지게 일해.

I **worked my way through** med school. 내가 학비를 벌면서 의대를 다녔어.

I've **been working my way through** your checkbook. 네 수표책을 꼼꼼히 뒤져봤어.

work one's way[butt, ass] to[through]~
…하는데 뼈빠지게 일하다

It's possible to **work your way to** the top. 일을 열심히 해서 최고가 되는 것은 가능해.

work one's way through+학교
학비를 벌어서 학교를 다니다

It took five years to **work my way through** school. 고학하며 대학졸업하는데 5년 걸렸어.

work at+장소
…에서 일하다 (work for sby)

They think I **work at** Starbuck's. 내가 스타벅스에서 일한다고들 생각해.

How long did you **work at** the store? 그 가게에서 일한 지 얼마나 됐어?

work at sth [~ing]
…에 열심히 하다

I **worked at** getting this job done. 이 일을 끝내는데 열심히 했어.

I tried my best to **work at** this marriage. 이 결혼을 성사시키려고 최선을 다했어.

work on sth
…일을 하다

I **am working on** it. 지금 하고 있어.

I'll get to **work on** it right now. 지금 이 일을 시작할거야.

I'm going to **work on** this stuff at home tonight. 오늘 밤 집에서 이 일을 할거야.

work

work on sby
…을 설득하다, 영향을 주다

It would **work on** me when I was young.
내가 어렸을 때라면 그게 내게 통할지도 모르겠군.

Sth works out
나아지다(get better) *Sby works out 잘 고안해내다, 좋은 계획을 짜다, 운동하다

I hope it **works out with** you and Mike.
너하고 마이크하고 잘 되기를 바래.

How did everything **work out?**
어떻게 일은 잘 풀렸나요?

How**'s** that **working out for** you?
그러니까 어때요?

It never **would have worked out.**
애초에 가망이 없었어.

Sth works out well[badly]
좋게(나쁘게) 되다(turn out)

Things will **work out all right.** 잘 해결될거야.

Things didn't **work out** and he broke up with her.
사정이 잘 풀리지 않아 걔랑 헤어졌어.

work out for the best
결국은 잘 되다

Everything will **work out for the best.** 다 잘될거야.

work things out (with sby)
(…와) 일을 잘 풀어가다, 문제를 해결하다

Things **work out.** 일이 잘 풀리다.

I really think it's great they **work things out.**
걔네들이 일을 잘 풀어가가 정말 좋은 것 같아.

I wanted to **work things out** with my husband.
남편과 일을 잘 풀어가기를 원했어.

work up+명사 (interest, appetite)
주어가 …(관심, 식욕)을 갖게 하다

That'll really **work up your appetite** for lunch.
그렇게 하면 점심 먹고 싶은 생각이 들거야.

Go **work up some new ideas** and then we'll go over it during lunch. 가서 좋은 생각을 만들어내봐 그럼 점심때 검토해볼게.

work sby up
…을 열받게 하다 *work oneself up 화를 내다 =get worked up

I just think you**'re getting worked up** over nothing.
난 네가 아무것도 아닌 일에 화내는 것 같아.

What **are** you **so worked up** about? 뭐 때문에 화났어?

He **got worked up.** 걔 열 받았어.

work on one's own	혼자 처리하다 I can't **handle all this work on my own.** 이 모든 일을 혼자 처리 못해.
work through	(어려운 문제를) 다루다, 풀어나가다 I have some issues I need to **work through.** 내가 풀어야 하는 문제가 몇 개 있어. Every family has problems you have to **work through.** 모든 가정은 풀어나가야 할 문제들이 있어.

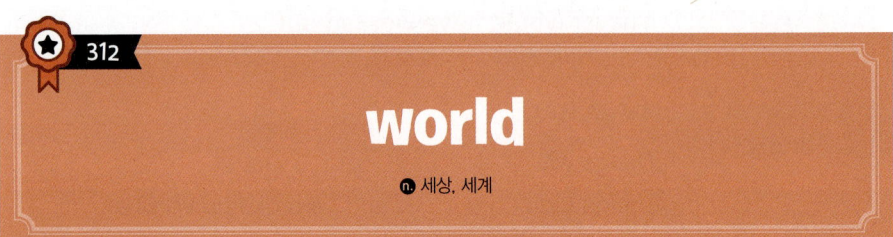

312 world
n. 세상, 세계

all over the world	세계 도처에 She and I have traveled **all over the world.** 그녀와 난 세계일주를 했어.
throughout the world	전세계에 걸쳐 This fashion is popular **throughout the world.** 이 패션은 전세계에 걸쳐 유행하고 있어.
mean the world to sb	…에게는 무엇과도 바꿀 수 없다 Your gift **means the world to** me. 네 선물은 내게는 너무너무 소중해.
for the world	강조어구 *in the world What **in the world** is Neil doing? 도대체 닐이 뭘하고 있는거야?
world-class	세계적인 They say BMW is a **world-class** automobile. BMW는 세계적인 자동차라고들 해.
would give the world to+V	…하기 위해서 뭐든지 할거야 She **would give the world to** get famous. 걘 유명해지려면 뭐든지 할거야.

work

worry

v 걱정하다 **n** 걱정, 근심거리

worry about
…을 걱정하다

You **worry about** me too much. 넌 내 걱정을 너무 많이 해.

You don't have to **worry about** a thing. 걱정 할 필요 전혀 없어.

You don't have to **worry.** 걱정할 필요가 없어.

be worried about[that~]
…에 대해 걱정하다

You're **so worried about** me. 넌 날 무척 걱정해.

Are you **worried about** me? 넌 내 걱정해?

We're **worried about** getting sued. 소송당할까봐 걱정야.

I'm **so worried that** I might fail the exam.
시험에 떨어질까 걱정야.

Don't worry (about)
(…을) 걱정마

Don't worry, you can count on me. 걱정마. 나만 믿어.

Don't worry about a thing. 걱정하지 마세요.

Don't worry. It's our treat. 걱정마. 우리가 낼게.

Not to worry
걱정 안해도 돼

Not to worry. 걱정 안해도 돼.

Not to worry, she's fine. 걱정마, 걘 괜찮을거야.

worse

a. 더 나쁜, 더 심한 **ad.** 더 나쁘게

---

get worse | 나빠지다, 악화되다
The problem **got worse** when it wasn't fixed.
문제가 해결되지 않아 더 악화되었어.

get worse and worse | 점점 더 나빠지다
It just keeps **getting worse and worse**.
점점 더 나빠지고 있어.

Could be worse | 그나마 다행이다 *↪ Could be better 별로야
Come on, Jack, things **could be worse**.
이봐, 잭, 상황이 더 나빴을 수도 있잖아.
I **could be better.** I'm still sick. 별로야. 여전히 아파.

make matters [things] worse | 문제나 상황을 악화시키다
It's only going to **make matters worse** for us.
그건 우리 상황을 더 악화시킬 뿐이야.

there's nothing worse than +N [~ing] | …보다 더 끔찍한 것은 없어
There's nothing worse than losing a child.
아이를 잃는 것보다 더 최악인 것은 없어.

for the worse | 악화되어
Things at ballet class have taken a turn **for the worse**.
발레수업에서의 상황이 더 악화되었어.

see the worst of it | 최악의 상황을 보다
The storm is still occurring, but we**'ve seen the worst of it**.
폭풍이 아직 계속되고 있지만 벌써 최악의 상황을 봤어.

at worst | 최악의 경우에 *at one's worst 최악의 상태에
At worst, you'll just lose a little money.
최악의 경우라도, 넌 돈을 조금 잃을거야.

worse

worst of all	무엇보다 나쁜 것은
	Worst of all, she refused to speak to me again.
	최악은, 걔는 다시는 내게 말을 걸지않겠다고 했어.

315 worth

ⓐ …의 가치가 있는, …해볼 만한 ⓝ 가치, 값어치

sth worth+가격	…가치가 되다
	That painting is **worth** twelve million pounds.
	이 그림은 120만 파운드의 가치가 있어.
be worth ~ing	…을 해볼 가치가 있다
	I want to see if it's **worth** fighting for.
	그게 싸울 만한 가치가 있는지 확인해보고 싶어.
be worth a try	시도해볼 만하다
	I guess it's **worth a try.** 한번 해 봄직도 한데.
be worth the effort[time, trouble]	노력[시간, 수고]할 가치가 있다
	It **isn't worth the trouble.**
	괜히 번거롭기만 할거야.
be worth a lot [a great deal] to~	…에게 큰 의미가 되다
	Some antiques **are worth a great deal to** collectors.
	어떤 골동품들은 수집가들에게 엄청난 의미가 되기도 해.
make it worth sb's while	…의 노고에 답하다
	I'll **make it worth your while.** 네 노력을 헛되이 하지 않게 할게.
be worthy of +N	…의 가치가 있다
	Her boss decided Jenna **was worthy of** confidence.
	사장은 제나를 믿을 만하다고 했어.

write

v. 쓰다, 작성하다

write sth
…을 쓰다
I think I want to **write** a song about all this.
이 모든 것에 관한 노래를 쓰고 싶어.

write about
…에 관해 쓰다
You should **write about** me sometime.
언젠가 나에 대해 글을 써봐.

write (to) sby
…에게 편지쓰다(write a letter)
I was up all night **writing** this letter **to** her.
걔한테 이 편지를 쓰느라 밤샜어.

be written on
…에 적혀있다
Your phone number **was written on** her hand.
네 전화번호는 걔 손에 적혀있어.

write a check
수표를 쓰다
You can **write a check** to pay for dinner.
저녁값으로 수표로 내도 됩니다.

have sth[be written] all over your face
…가 …의 얼굴에 온통 적혀있다
Surprise and horror **were written all over her face.**
놀람과 두려움이 걔의 얼굴에 온통 적혀있어.

write down
기록하다, 적다
Be ready to **write down** whatever she says.
걔가 뭐라든 다 적을 준비됐어.

wrong

a. 틀린, 잘못된, 부적절한, 잘못된 **ad.** 틀리게 **n.** 나쁜 짓

Don't get me wrong
나를 오해하지마

Don't get me wrong. I think they are OK.
오해하지마. 괜찮은 것 같아.

What's wrong with~?
…가 뭐가 문제야?

What's wrong with my computer? 내 컴퓨터 뭐가 잘못된거야?

get on the wrong side of sb
…을 화나게 하다

I **am on the wrong side of** the law.
난 법을 어겼어.

Make trouble and you'll **get on the wrong side of** our boss.
사고치면 넌 사장의 노여움을 살거야.

get sth wrong
실수하다 *get ~ all wrong about …에 대해 완전히 틀리다

I **got it all wrong** about your family. 너희 가족에 대해 내가 틀렸어.

go wrong
잘못되다

In short, everything **went wrong.** 요약하면 모든 것이 잘못 되었어

You can't go wrong with~
…에는 전혀 문제가 없을거야

You can't go wrong with a new suit. 너 새로운 정장은 전혀 문제없어.

do sb wrong
잘못대하다 *do sth wrong 일을 그르치다

I think I **did it wrong.** 내가 일을 그르친 것 같아.

do wrong
잘못을 저지르다

What did I **do wrong?** 내가 무슨 잘못을 했는데?